App

Prof. Idel's Letter of Recommendation to Oxford:

February 3, 2005

Dear Prof. van Lint,   Jerusalem

I am writing in my capacity as thesis advisor (together with Dr. Norman Solomon) to Marc Gafni. I am pleased to be able to formally report that I found the thesis to be an excellent work of original scholarship. Gafni demonstrates a high level of proficiency in close textual reading as well as in the proper use of previous scholarship and scholarly apparatus.

Gafni, in his thesis, challenges the accepted scholarly reading of Mordechai Lainer of Izbica's thought. He does this by a careful reading of the primary source material bringing a large body of texts to bear heretofore not addressed by scholarship. He then subjects those texts to close scholarly reading in developing his persuasive reading of Lainer's theology. He coins a new scholarly term to capture Lainer's thought, namely, acosmic humanism.

He then proceeds to trace the intellectual history of Lainer's acosmic humanism within Jewish intellectual history as well as in the final chapters locating him within the European zeitgeist of his time. He also shows the influence of this thinker on later stages of Jewish mystical thought, notably that of R. Kook. In doing so he makes extensive use of the previous scholarship in the field, as well bringing to bear a large number of new sources, which he adduces may have not been previously discussed in scholarship.

All of this together introduces an important, fascinating and original new reading of a major Jewish thinker. Gafni's work may well become the definitive work on this thinker, a thinker I might add who may become highly relevant in the next stages of Jewish theology and is already an important theologian in the contemporary Neo-Hassidic movement.

Sincerely,
Prof. Moshe Idel
Max Cooper Chair of Philosophy at the Hebrew University

This is a great work of inspired and audacious scholarship. Professor Moshe Idel's letter of recommendation to Oxford University, and Professor Richard Mann's words (comparing Marc's work on Kabbalah to Elaine Pagels' work on the Gnostic gospels), which introduce these volumes, speak for themselves. Similarly, the statements by Michael Zimmerman from the perspective of a chief justice of an American supreme court and by Sally Kempton, Dr. Gabriel Cousens, and Rabbi Winkler as scholars and teachers of enlightenment show something of the broad relevance of the volumes, as do the remarks by Sean Esbjörn-Hargens and Zachary Stein.

I read Dr. Gafni's masterwork on *Radical Kabbalah* in its first drafts almost seven years ago. It was then over a thousand pages long, and I read it over two or three days with great excitement. I sent Marc a series delighted emails, after reading every few chapters. The breadth, depth and the sheer importance of the work moved me. I immediately recognized it as a seminal work, identifying a critical lineage of enlightenment from the tradition of Kabbalah, which needed to be incorporated into the Integral model.

We have done this work of integration in a special issue of the Journal of Integral Theory and Practice, under the leadership of Sean Esbjörn-Hargens, dedicated to this new chapter in Integral Theory, Unique Self. (JITP 6:1) This issue was guest edited by Dr. Gafni. Marc has further elaborated on this work in his book entitled, *Your Unique Self: The Radical Path to Personal Enlightenment*, published by Integral Publishers.

All this writing and discussion on Unique Self, including our first Integral Spiritual Experience Retreat on the same topic, was to a significant extent informed and catalyzed by Marc's scholarly work, teaching and leadership. This is the kind of work that the Center for World Spirituality, of which I am an active member, exists to bring forth, drawing on every great tradition, pre-modern, modern and post-modern. All this will inform the emergence of a genuine framework for a world spirituality based on Integral principles, which is one of the critical needs of this moment in time.

Ken Wilber
Integral Philosopher and Author

Marc Gafni has written a magisterial work. For a student of Kabala, a scholar of religion, or a practitioner of any integral approach to spirituality, this book contains treasures. Like Gafni himself, it combines depth of intellect with integrity of heart, and has much to teach us both from a scholarly perspective and as a contemporary transmission of what Gafni calls Evolutionary Kabbalah, in this case wisdom of Mordechai Lainer's Izbica school of Kabala.

As a reader from outside the tradition, I was struck by Gafni's exposition of how Mordechai Lainer subtly balances the wisdom of conventional ethics with a recognition of the absolute freedom that comes to an aspirant who longs for full union with the divine. As in some other devotional traditions, such as the Vaishnava Bhakti movements in Hinduism, the intimacy of yearning for divine union is seen to take the practitioner outside the bounds of convention. Yet this is never a casual flouting of convention. Rather it is the expression of an evolutionary urge towards the merging of the individual with the divine, which is always beyond social bounds. This, in Lainer and Gafni's teaching, can lead the individual simultaneously to a nondual realization of identity with God, and to a recognition of his or her essential uniqueness as a human expression of divine creativity.

In short, the book provides an spiritual, intellectual and existential matrix for Gafni's teaching on Unique Self as an enlightened individual expression of the divine. This is one of Lainer's most important and radical ideas, and it has, as Gafni describes it here, profound implications for the understanding of enlightenment in the post-traditional American spiritual community.

In some sense this work can also be seen as Gafni's spiritual autobiography. The dialectic between Jewish law and its transcendence in nondual incarnation of the divine will is a profound tension in Gafni's own life. A commitment to what Lainer calls *Berur*—the clarification of inner motivation and desire—is a similarly strong motif in Gafni's teaching and life. Gafni's people-centered, communal approach to spirituality finds expression in what he terms Lainer's democratization of enlightenment. His refusal to allow for intermediaries between himself and the divine, and his iconoclastic style all find expression in the school of Izbica.

I was also struck by an idea, which Gafni subtly unpacks from Izbica, regarding the relationship between the divine feminine and interpersonal ethics. In Gafni's reading of Izbica, the passionate, erotic quality—which Izbica associates with the Goddess—is expressed through the details of interpersonal ethics, love for human beings and their welfare. Thus, in the Izbica school, the legalistic 'masculine' structure of law and obligation is infused with the erotic 'feminine' concern with relationship, joy and individual well-being. This is part of its profoundly integral message, and part of what makes this book such a seminal contribution to the next stage of spirit's unfoldment.

Sally Kempton
Sally Kempton has been a leading second wave feminist and is a prominent and beloved teacher/practitioner of meditation Kashmir Shaivism

This magisterial work by Dr. Marc Gafni, *Radical Kabbalah*, makes a seminal contribution to a number of fields, particularly the fields of transpersonal psychology, theology and integral studies and are here offered a crucial building block as they attempt to fashion a model of consciousness that is grounded in traditional wisdom, but still open to the next creative synthesis that is now emerging.

As each ancient wisdom tradition is revealed to contain within it the seeds of such radical formulations as nondualism, a sensed balance, ideally between the male and female energies, and an antinomian response to the conventional role and rule of law, the convergence between the mystical traditions is clearer and clearer. I am reminded in reading Dr. Gafni's work of the legitimate excitement that was generated by Elaine Pagels and others as they opened the parallel tradition of the Gnostic Gospels that had been expunged from the Church's teachings.

These volumes promise just such a burst of excitement as scholars and the vast community of seekers discover key parallels and points of divergence with the traditional, mystical teachings of Christianity, Islam, Hinduism, and Buddhism that these understandings of Jewish sensibilities turn out to be. What they all share in common, nondualism, appreciation of the feminine, and antinomianism are all part of the contemporary synthesis that is still in evolutionary flux. This well-grounded subtle and creative contribution of high scholarship will set a marker for many years to come and will be a great benefit to many within and beyond the academic domains.

Kabbalah is not my academic field, but the letter of recommendation by one of the foremost scholars in Kabbalah in the world today, Moshe Idel, as well as by a leading rabbinic thinker, Rabbi Gershon Winkler, I believe answers the question of scholarship. Prof. Idel was the co-supervisor of the thesis and Prof. Admiel Kosman, also a world-class Jewish studies scholar, was on the dissertation committee. The excellent reception it received at Oxford by an eminent scholar suggests to me that Gafni's critique of previous scholarship constructed on a scholarly framework that will stand the tests that will make a significant contribution to the field of Kabbalah as well as to the evolution of spiritual studies across narrow religious lines.

The organization is masterful. It is beautifully structured and the result is that each new and deeper probe into this complex teacher's position builds on the prior analysis.

Scholarship of this caliber is never a quick read. This reader had to return to some passages for greater comprehension, but the best measure of whether a manuscript is readable is whether one can sustain the sense of eagerness to read on, and that was how I experienced the long but fascinating read of this lengthy tome.

The strengths of the book are many. It is timely. It is a missing link in the chain of great teachings that turn out to have a great deal in common, far more than it seemed from comparing the exoteric, dogma-laden formulations that the various traditions also manifest.

But it is really more than all that. This is, at its core, far more than a scholar shining a spotlight on a single teacher; it is a scholar who is on fire with the beauty and life-altering moment of a great teacher's many subtle offerings. Gafni is that rare combination of evolutionary activist, public intellectual, academic scholar and spiritual teacher. Having established himself by mastering the authentic sources of a still developing tradition, it can be expected that this author is now in a position to carry the dialog further, as indeed Gafni does in his emergent teachings on Unique Self, Eros and the Enlightenment of Fullness, all which will be fully articulated in forthcoming volumes.

But without this masterful explication, it is doubtful that many would be able to realize just how much this author knows whereof he speaks. Particularly I expect Gafni to gradually emerge as one of the significant intellectual figures of our time and to make a significant contribution to the evolution of consciousness.

Richard Mann
Editor, Transpersonal Series, Suny Press; Professor, University of Michigan; Founding Member Integral Institute.

As I wrote in my forward to the Journal of Integral Theory and Practice, 6:1, Dr. Marc Gafni has played a foundational role in emergence and development of Integral Spirituality. Marc is a lineage holder in his native tradition of Hebrew mysticism, as well as an accomplished academic scholar in the same field. He is unfolding some of the critical intellectual and spiritual scaffolding for Integral Spirituality. His formulation of "Second person spirituality" was catalytic in the emergence of the "three faces of God" construct that Ken Wilber articulated in his 2006 book, *Integral Spirituality*. Gafni is involved in an ongoing process of ecstatic teaching and scholarship. That his work is birthing new forms of evolutionary spirituality is evidenced in his emergent articulations of World Spirituality and Unique Self.

Unique Self, a term coined and a concept and realization developed by Marc over the last fifteen years, represents a truly world-centric, planet-centric and kosmocentric evolutionary mysticism. It changes the way we think about enlightenment by integrating the enlightenment traditions of the pre-modern east and modern west in a higher integral embrace.

In the book before you, Radical Kabbalah, Gafni anchors an emergent creative embodied concept, (i.e. the Unique Self) in a living tradition of awakening. This creates a wonderful dialectical tension between creative emergence and the karmic lineage teachings. Moreover, he challenges Orthodoxy by arguing against established interpretations of Lainer's corpus. This demonstrates how the development of a meta-principle of Integral Spirituality will at times have to go against convention. Marc's engagement of Lainer's texts is a form of what he terms "ecstatic scholarship," (see Gabriel Cousens' and

Gershon Winkler's introductions to this volume) and what Jeffrey Kripal has termed "mystical hermeneutics."

In mystical hermeneutics, according to Kripal, the reading of mystical texts is engaged with such devotion and transcendental openness that the very act of reading becomes an injunction of mystical practice and revelation. Such is the nature of the work before you.

Sean Esbjörn-Hargens
Meta Integral

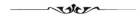

RADICAL KABBALAH

Other works by Dr. Rabbi Marc (Mordechai) Gafni:

Your Unique Self: The Radical Path to Personal Enlightenment
Soul Prints
The Mystery of Love
The Erotic and the Holy (audio)
Soul Print Workshop (audio)

Published in Hebrew:
Reclaiming Uncertainty as a Spiritual Value
Re-defining Certainty from "It Is True" to "I Am True"
Lillith: Re-Reading Feminine Shadow
First Steps in Judaism

Forthcoming:
World Spirituality Based on Integral Principles with Ken Wilber
The Dance of Tears and Rosh Hashanah: First Steps Toward
        an Integrally Informed Judaism
On Eros

RADICAL KABBALAH

The Enlightenment Teaching of Unique Self,
Nondual Humanism and the Wisdom of Solomon–
The Great Teaching of Ethics and Eros
from Mordechai Lainer of Izbica

Book 1

by Dr. Rabbi Marc (Mordechai) Gafni

FIRST EDITION

Revised

Designed by Kathryn Lloyd
Crafty Coyote Book Design

Radical Kabbalah Two Book Set ISBN: 978-1-4675-2274-8

Radical Kabbalah Book One ISBN: 978-1-4675-2275-5

Radical Kabbalah Book Two ISBN: 978-1-4675-2276-2

Radical Kabbalah Book One Paperback ISBN: 978-1-4951-5912-1

Radical Kabbalah Book Two Paperback 978-1-4951-5913-8

Printed by Lightning Source. Lightning Source is
♦ Sustainable Forestry Initiative® (SFI®) certified and their certificate is active.

♦ Programme for the Endorsement of Forest Certification™ (PEFC™) certified
and their certificate is active.

♦ Forest Stewardship Council™ (FSC®) certified
and their certificate is active. FSC® C084699

To Dalit Arnon, Metuka Benjamin,
Sally Kempton and Diane Hamilton

Incarnations of the Goddess who held me as
this work on the Eros and Ethos was being completed

You never change things by fighting the existing reality. To change something, build a new model that makes the existing model obsolete.

~ R. Buckminster Fuller

Table of Contents Book 1

VOLUME 1

Mordechai Lainer of Izbica's Theology of Unique Self and Nondual
Acosmic Humanism

Table of Contents Book 2

PREFACE

by Michael D. Zimmerman

It is a pleasure to write these brief prefatory remarks. As the chairman of the Board of Idra, the charitable foundation that has supported the work of Dr. Marc Gafni in bringing this book to fruition, it is a pleasure to be asked to help launch this remarkable piece of scholarly and religious analysis.

As far back as I can remember I have always been drawn to the question of how we are to find moral guidance in our personal and communal lives. This question has made me a life-long student of ethics, drew me to be a lawyer and a judge, and has begun to be answered through my practice of Zen.[1] How are we to determine what is "fair" to all concerned as we wield power daily over each other and over the world? By what standards should we judge our own conduct and that of others? Do we rely entirely on established convention, whether it is represented by secular law or by explicitly religious injunction, or do we place our trust in our personal judgment? Convention is inevitably expressed in general rules which, no matter how subtle, can produce injustice in specific application if mechanically followed. Yet reliance on one's individual judgment, while capable of the most nuanced adaptation to events, raises the specter of action seriously biased by self-interest, by self-deception. It is between these two poles that we navigate as sensitive moral agents. Under what conditions is it appropriate for the individual to look inward, rather than to the judgment of the group, to determine what is appropriate? Can the individual develop the capacity to reliably act without crippling egoistic bias? This is a concern shared equally by, among others, moral and legal philosophers, Zen masters, and Mordechai Lainer of Izbica.

In Dr. Gafni's fascinating exploration of the teachings and personal path of Mordechai Lainer of Izbica, there is an affirmation of the individual as a reliable moral agent, albeit an individual who has been through a mystical unity with the divine and has been purged of self-orientation. The parallels with the ethical teachings of Eihei Dogen Zenji, the founder of the Soto school of Zen, are intriguing.[2] While Rebbe Lainer's theism contrasts with Dogen Zenji's non-theism, and their cultural contexts give their teachings radically differing flavors, beneath the differences is a strikingly similar evocation of the potential for each of us to rely on our ability to make sound ethical choices in our daily lives without wooden adherence to convention. Each teaches that if we engage in the practices they advocate, we can find within us a nondual awareness empty of self, yet simultaneously fully present to all that is manifest in each moment. From this place, reliably ethical action springs.

Being skeptical by nature and by training, it has taken me years of practice and study to embrace the view that only from this intimate interior place can we take a perspective that is fully alert to the exquisite subtlety of the constantly shifting matrix within which the individual is embedded, and respond in each moment in a way that is reliably appropriate. This is the place of fine ethical judgment, and this is the place of total responsibility. The lodestone for Mordechai Lainer of Izbica, as for Dogen Zenji, is complete assurance that one's insights are free of ego. Given the human capacity for self-deception, actually being in this place is certainly more rare than believing one is in this place, and the real world consequences of acting from this place in the face of conventional standards exposes the individual to peril, as the life of the Sage of Izbica suggests. Yet singular reliance on external sources for guidance in ethical matters is, I have come to believe, even more perilous, as the fate of the world in which Mordechai Lainer of Izbica lived bears testament.

Dr. Gafni's provocative study of Mordechai Lainer of Izbica, and his dialogue with various of Lainer's analysts, will leave the reader enriched, both from the scholarly discourse, and from an internal dialogue first with the Sage of Izbica, then with Dr. Gafni and the others who have written on the subject, and finally with the self, the one who is called upon to make decisions and take action.

Michael D. Zimmerman
Salt Lake City, Utah

Michael Zimmerman is the former Chief Justice of the Utah Supreme Court, a highly respected legal scholar and practitioner as well as a transmitted Zen teacher from the lineage of Maezumi Roshi.

---

1 I note my deep gratitude to my Zen teacher, Dennis Genpo Merzel, Roshi.
2 See the discussion of the "steelyard" metaphor in Dogen Zenji's Shobogenzo, "Muchu setsumu", in Hee-Jin Kim, Dogen on meditation and thinking: a reflection on his view of Zen, p. 42 et seq. (2007).

FOREWORD

by Gabriel Cousens

Author's note: Rabbi Dr. Gabriel Cousens was asked to read and comment on this work from the perspective of a teacher of liberation. He did so with depth and generosity. His foreword is written in non-academic style, using the lexicon and conceptual framework often employed in the context of liberation teaching. His comments, in their unique genre, will feel alien to academic readers, and are intended for those living in the discourse of spiritual liberation. Gabriel's comments are greatly appreciated and honored. Often Gabriel will suggest a reading of Lainer in which he feels Lainer to be saying something with which the author agrees with in principle as expressing a sacred pathway of liberation but which may not be -from a scholarly perspective consonant with Lainer's reading of Liberation. The author like Gabriel moves between worlds which include both scholarship and teaching the way of Liberation. These are distinctive roles each with its own demands of integrity. As our sages have already written; "All paths lead to the one" and "these and these and these are the words of the living God".

In this brilliant and spiritually expansive book, Rabbi Mordechai Gafni has transcended previous interpretations of Lainer's work through his intense study and interaction with this material, which led him to imbibe the material at the level of *ruah ha-kodesh,* the holy Spirit. It is Rabbi Gafni's insights on this level—meaning the level of divine inspiration rather than prophetic revelation, which ended at the fall of the First Temple—that let us understand this work as a detailed map of the process of liberation in the Jewish path.

In a historical context, though these teachings appear to be novel, they are consistent with the pre-Temple understandings and ways of liberation and revelation. This understanding is part of an ancient Jewish continuum of liberation teachings, which became contracted and, to a great extent lost, after the fall of the second Temple, under the harsh repression of the Romans. For survival reasons, people began to focus on the law as a way of maintaining a portion of the tradition during the diaspora, while *Am Israel,* the Jewish people, was dispersed and under severe attack throughout generations in many of the countries where we lived.

This focus on the Torah and its law was a brilliant move by the rabbis to preserve Judaism. However, it is only with the *Zohar* that we begin to deduce the mystical tradition of great liberated beings such as Shimon bar Yochai and Rabbi Akiva. The mystical tradition was reactivated during the twelfth century by Moshe de Leon, and a number of great teachers who followed him, such as the Arizal, Moshe Haim Luzzatto, the Bal Shem Tov, Rabbi Dov Ber, Rav Elimelech, Rav Zusha, Rav Premislaner, and Rabbi Nachman of Breslov. Later in the 1800's, Mordechai Lainer of Izbica appeared. His was perhaps the most sophisticated articulation of the Jewish way of liberation since the time of the *Sefer Yetzirah*, attributed to Avraham.

Lainer's revelatory work deserves to be celebrated, but it is often seen as dangerous, for a variety of reasons. First, the idea of transcending the *mitzvot* to become an expression of the Divine has not been a part of the collective consciousness or culture in the diaspora. We are only now recovering from the spiritual contraction that lost familiarity with the liberation teachings of the Jewish tradition. Even the great Baal Shem Tov, as a liberated being, was attacked for breaking with tradition by living in the world of *deveikut*, God-merging through the *Shekhinah*. In this merging, called *herut* freedom or *he'arah* enlightenment, the Baal Shem Tov was blazing a path far ahead of the people. The Hasidic movement created by the Baal Shem Tov was the spiritual seed of Rabbi Simha Bunim, who was the teacher of Rabbi Mordechai Joseph of Izbica.

Another aspect of resistance to Rabbi Mordechai Lainer's work has to do with a lack of understanding of the process of liberation. Resistance to liberation exists in all traditions; it is not exclusively a Jewish trait. Liberated beings are an implicit threat to the general mundane culture. So it is normal that there would be resistance to this great work or to any powerful articulation of the Jewish way as a path to liberation, of *deveikut*, or *herut*. Moshe Haim Luzzatto, another great liberated being, was exiled from Italy for his deep teaching of liberation.

Of course, a major reason for resistance to Lainer's work is the fact that most people have no understanding of which of the four worlds, the four levels of being, he was speaking from. The story of Rabbi Akiva taking three rabbis into *Pardes* expresses this difficulty. Only Rabbi Akiva left the Garden as an integrated multi-dimensional being who experienced the continuity of all four worlds, while the other three were tragically harmed by their encounter with the Divine.

Without understanding this continuity or continuum of being, even hearing teachings of liberation can be confusing or harmful. For example, one must realize that Mordechai Lainer is speaking from an enlightened place, from the world of *Atzilut*, the world of transcendent Love, which in the Jewish tradition often results in radical activism. Yet how can radical activism appear within the world of *Atzilut*, beyond time and space, where nothing ever 'happens'? The key is that a multi-dimensional being can exist in total peace, love, and joy, while his or her actions appear to manifest as radical activism on the physical plane. When we lack clarity as to the plane on which a particular discussion is happening, confusion and resistance ensue. In short, without a context, Mordechai Lainer's work is hard to fully appreciate.

Lainer's work was radically new within the context of the 1800's. In the broader historical Jewish context, however, as well as in the context of all liberation paths, we begin to see that there is nothing new here. Though not well-acknowledged, the concept of liberation has always been a part of this tradition, and it has always been democratic. But in the Middle Ages, and well into the 19th century, only scholars were regarded as capable of liberation (*herut, he'arah, or deveikut*). While the democratization of liberation was always present throughout history, in the context of Lainer's times it was a radical concept.

To be a valid path to liberation, a liberation teaching must ultimately be congruent with the liberation teachings of all paths. In all traditions, aligning with the Divine includes both *bitul ha-yesh* and *berur*—the annihilation of the ego, and the recognition that our belief in the separate ego-self is a case of mistaken identity. Yet we also need to understand that the Jewish way of liberation, while not so different from the Eastern mystical traditions, offers a more individual and communal emphasis. In the book of *Genesis*, the entire path of creation is outlined for us. The steps of *herut* are somewhat the reverse of this creation process. In the context of liberation, the Torah is a masterful guidebook, not a rulebook, to *herut/deveikut*.

The concept of 'God-evolving', however, creates confusion regardless of the historical context. Lainer's work could be misunderstood as teaching that God in the absolute sense evolves, but a full understanding of the Divine must include the Talmudic teaching of *ani lo shaniti*, 'I never change' (Malachi 3:6). This absolute level of God is a *noun*. In contrast, in the evolving of God-consciousness within the human mind, God is a *verb*. This evolution is the expression of the Divine on the plane of *'Asiyah* that is inspired by *Atzilut*. This is why we see in Isaiah 55:8-9, 'My way is not your way, and my thoughts are not your thoughts.' We see this in Job also when God challenges Job. This message is present in a variety of ways. We exist on two separate levels, but at the same time we are 'one' as an expression of the Divine.

Though it appears awkward, the writer of this introduction, Rabbi Gabriel Cousens, will speak from here on in the third person. Gabriel began speaking in this manner after a revelation that occurred at the end of a twenty-one day water fast in 1995. At that time it became clear that the truth needed to be articulated in this way; this is the way of the Judah archetype. It is also the way of Rabbi Gabriel's particular rabbinical lineage, which began with the Baal Shem Tov, and which includes both Rav Zusha and Rav Premislaner (who both spoke in the third person). Although we are not aware of it, speaking in the third person is also a part of our liberation tradition.

Gabriel's context for writing this introduction is not academic, but arises from direct awareness. He has been acknowledged as being in *herut/ he'arah/deveikut* (i.e., liberation) by his two spiritual teachers. Liberation is different from the temporary inspiration of *ruah ha-kodesh*, or an inspired moment. *Herut* is a steady state of awareness, which can be experienced more or less deeply, but which never leaves. In 1983, at the end of a forty-day water fast, he was in a state of full and extended God-merging. For three days, a *hashmal* (or whisper) instructed him to return to his body and understand the roots of his people and learn how to support them. Over the last twenty-six years, Gabriel has searched for a way to bring this *herut* understanding into the stream of Jewish thought. Rabbi Mordechai Gafni's wonderful illuminating book is an extraordinary opportunity to do this.

The beginning level of self-realization is to understand that we are not the 'body–mind–I-am complex'. Then we live as 'I am One with God', which dissolves into the emptiness of the void. Through the emptiness (*bitul ha-yesh*) we can access the Divine light within us. In *bitul ha-yesh* the predominant inner experience is uncaused joy, peace, love, and the pleasure of the ecstasy of the Divine Eros. Within this continuum is the first stage of liberation. It is an ongoing process, but marks what Mordechai Lainer speaks of in his work as the merging with the *Shekhinah* energy, or the sacred feminine. We are one with *That*, because in the emptiness we are filled with *That*. Then the Eros of the Divine (the *Shekhinah*) becomes our direct inner experience at all times. One of the great insights in Rabbi Mordechai's illumination of Mordechai Lainer's teaching is the understanding that the uniqueness is not lost upon liberation. *Hashem* expressing as the unique one is expressed as the unique self which is not disconnected from the divine, but an articulated expression of the Divine through the uniqueness of the individual body-mind-complex of the individual. The unique self, as everything else in creation is not separate from the divine. By definition, the beginning stages of liberation is knowing ones essential oneness. The unique expression then emerges out of this and is not separate from this.

This is different from the short, time-limited revelations of *ruah ha-kodesh* in which Uniqueness may disappear. In yoga this steady non-causal awareness of peace, love, joy, and contentment is called *sahaja samadhi*, which means on-going *samadhi* while living in the mundane world. It seems all paths to liberation include this steady state of *sahaja samadhi*. It comes from *swarupa*, or the natural way of awakening. Liberation, *herut*, is an act of grace that is very natural. As we move through *bitul ha-yesh* and *berur*, our every word and action becomes a unique expression of God. Liberation is essentially erotic. Eros is not separate from God; it is the expression and experience of God in the moment to moment everyday experience.

It took Gabriel ten years to understand and experience *Keter*, the will of God, playing through the expression of his 'body-mind-I-am complex'. When we reach this point, we recognize that the personality is a case of mistaken identity. We begin to experience that our name and the name of God are One. This is the key understanding of acosmic (nondual) humanism, which Lainer discusses. He emphasizes a very sophisticated level of this, namely that each personality is a personal expression of the Divine for the evolution of consciousness on the planet. This is simultaneously awesome and humbling. Rabbi Mordechai Lainer shares a most evolved understanding of *herut/he'arah*. It is the Unique Self, as the expression of Divine will, the next evolving after *bitul ha-yesh*.

Rabbi Gafni's brilliant interpretation of Mordechai Lainer's liberated work is outlined in a deeply inspired, articulate, and complex manner. The groundbreaking significance of this book is that Rabbi Gafni has been able to create a new context for understanding the traditional Jewish liberation teachings. Most Jews are unaware of the depth of their own tradition. This book marks the restoration of a deep tradition. It is a tradition that has lost context. Before the 1700's there were no Orthodox, Conservative, or Reform denominations. We were Mosaic. We are being called back to a pre-denominational understanding of our great liberated teachers: Avraham, Yitzhak, Yaakov, Moshe, Aharon, Miriam, Yehudah Hanasi, Rabbi Akiva, Honi the Circle-drawer, Aba Helkia (Honi's grandson), Moshe Chaim Luzzatto, Hillel the Elder, Baal Shem Tov, Rav Zusha, Rav Premislaner, and others.

Rabbi Gafni, reflecting Lainer, speaks of the archetypes of Joseph and Judah, contrasting them as models for Jewish liberation. In practice and in my personal experience, there may be a continuum between the archetype of Joseph and the archetype of Judah. This is seen also in other liberation traditions. Joseph might naturally will evolve into Judah as he moves towards liberation. Along the way, Joseph focuses on the *mitzvot* and the ten 'Speakings' or commandments. He might perform austerities, such as the fasting that Moshe and the Baal Shem Tov did. The way of the archetype of Joseph is to follow the law, developing *midot* (character), using *berur*, *bitul ha-yesh*, austerities, charity, *kedushah* (holiness), before awakening to the potential beyond the law and into the Judah archetype. This does not mean disregarding the law; rather, the Judah archetype *has already incorporated the law into his very being*, and then goes beyond the consciousness of following the law as a separate person, to being the One, who is naturally living as the expression of the law in every moment. This is Gabriel's experience, living as a modern observant Jew.

A second path offered by Lainer and the dominant motif in his thought in Rabbi Mordechai's exposition, is to view Judah and Joseph as being paths available to different types of people or to people at different stages in their lives.

As another example of this seeming paradox is the great scholar and mystic Rav Kook. Rav Kook was beyond the law and yet chose to follow it, as he was free to move in any direction. As Lainer articulates so beautifully, in this state, the human being becomes the Torah. The human being is the revelation of the Divine.

As the Kabbalah makes clear, the 'big bang', or *hitpashtut*, is that moment when boundaries are transcended. And this is happening in every moment. *Keter*, as God's will, is always expressing itself anew in each moment. That is the consciousness in which the Judah archetype as a liberated being lives.

We must understand, as we learn in *Ki Tavo*, that humanity is the *bikurim*, the first fruits of God's work. In every moment, the Judah archetype is living as the very first offering. In every moment, *hitpashtut* is happening.

Rabbi Gershon Winkler, in *The Way of the Boundary Crosser*, cites a teaching of Rabbi Simlai about the evolution from the 613 *mitzvot* into the essence of *mitzvot*, which is the One, in *bMakot* 23b-24a:

> Six hundred thirteen *mitzvot* were given to Moses at Sinai…
> Then King David came and narrowed them down to eleven.
> As it is written, 'Oh God, who shall merit living in your tent?
> Who shall merit to dwell on your holy mountain? The One
> who walks the path in simplicity and performs acts of benevo-
> lence. And whose heart resonates with truthfulness. Whose
> speech knows no deceit and who does not wrong fellow
> creatures or shame those who are kin. Who despises those
> who are sinister and honors those who appreciate the gifts of
> the creator. Who keeps promises to others and will not renege
> even at personal hardship: who does not exact interest for
> money loaned, nor accept bribes at the expense of the inno-
> cent' (Psalms 15). Then came Isaiah and narrowed it down
> to six, as it is written, 'The one who walks with the deeds of
> benevolence and resonates with righteousness; who despises
> offers of profits gained from oppression; whose hands recoil
> at the offer of bribes; whose ears are muffled from the hearing
> of destructive schemes; whose eyes are shut from gazing upon
> evil' (Isa. 33:15). Then came Micah and narrowed it down to
> three, as it is written, 'Perform justice, love benevolence, and
> humble your walking with your creator' (Micah 6:8). Then
> came Isaiah again and narrowed them down to two, as it is
> written, 'Be ever so cautious to do justice, and do charity.'
> (Isa. 56:1) Then came Amos and narrowed them down to
> one, as it is written, 'Seek God and live' (Amos 5:4). Then
> came Habakkuk and narrowed them down to one in another
> way, as it is written, 'The just person shall live by their trust in
> God' (Habak. 2:4).

Living the *mitzvot* based on this teaching is the outlook of the Judah archetype, who understands that the *mitzvot* are not a goal in themselves, but a way of living a fully human life. Moshe, as the messenger of the Judah archetype, walked up the mountain into the unknown, the essence of the mystery of God, and rejected the consciousness symbolized by the golden calf, the desire to 'put-God-in-a-box', which gives safety but not liberation. That is why the liberated way of Judaism rejects idol worship—because it traps people into a boxed-in relationship and limited understanding of God. Moshe's journey takes us beyond the delusion that we can find God solely through observances. On the path of liberation, we are asked to be the one walking up the mountain into the unknown.

Liberation is beyond the mind. We cannot 'technique' our way to God, or eat our way to God, or think our way to God, or even meditate our way to God. We even cannot 'berur' our way to God, and we cannot 'mitzvot' our way to God. The Izhbitzer speaks about a liberated being in whom this character development has already occurred. It was not an approach for beginners. The mitzvot were meant to wake people up and develop character as part of the pre-conditions to deveikut (becoming God-merged). The Joseph archetype represents the beginning of the path. The Izbica work describes the other end of the path, and thus offers the Joseph archetype a fuller perspective of the path, so he can see the full greatness of the Judaic way to deveikut.

In this context, the Torah of Moshe is a very clear statement, 'Make Hashem your context. Make Hashem your way of life.' This is different than, 'Here is a list of rules for you to follow.' As the prophet Habakkuk said, 'I will rejoice in God.' This means, 'I will make God my frame of reference.' In the liberation process, the natural emotions of non-causal joy, peace, contentment, love, and bliss—all part of the ongoing eros of the merging with the Divine as the Shekhinah—come to us. The Talmud makes the point that the presence of God as the Shekhinah does not enter us unless we are in the right relationship. Only when we are in the expression of God, at whatever level, does the Shekhinah begin to radiate out as the expression of the Divine through us. Here we become our Unique Self.

The Psalmist tells us that the human being is born a wild ass, and the Torah teaches us that our natural inclination is to have a Divine purpose. Our task on the planet is to transform these wild drives into the highest octave of human expression. This way we can live consciously on God's mountain. This is what it means to merit living in the divine tent, and this is what it means to be a mensch. A mensch is a fully authentic human being who is honest with himself or herself, sensitive to others, just, loving, spiritual, and ethical in relationships. This is the result of living the *mitzvot*. When this happens, then through grace we become lived by love, lived by liberation, and lived by holiness. Mordechai Lainer is speaking in this context. In the Talmud it says, 'Whether you do a lot or a little bit, what matters is that your heart is directed to the heavens.' It is not merely our actions that establish us in God's tent. The path of the Torah is about changing our character so that we can live on the planet in God's tent at the highest level.

This is the teaching Mordechai Lainer was expressing, although the people of his day may not have been ready for it. He makes the point that the liberated human being is a text of revelation, an expression of the unmediated divine will. This is supported by the Baal Shem Tov in *Tzava'at Harivash* when he says that meditation is seven times more important than studying the Torah. He never said to cease Torah study, but, as in the case of Lainer, that is how the statement was sometimes misinterpreted by those who either could not understand his teaching or who thought people were not ready for it.

The focus is not on overriding the law of Mt. Sinai, but on becoming a fuller conscious expression of the law of Sinai. From Mordechai Lainer's perspective, the truth is that this is what we must become for the sake of all humanity.

In short, from the point of view of the liberation process, there is no ultimate duality between the archetypes of Joseph and Judah. In the end these two archetypes will come to understand and respect each other for their perspectives because they will see that they are part of a Divine continuum. To try to begin the spiritual path at the level of the Judah archetype is like refusing to work for a living because you think you are going to win the lottery. It is a rare and unusual person who can do this. Gabriel's spiritual teacher's teacher, at the age of twelve, was discovered at the bottom of a pool by his uncle. He had been there for four hours and came out laughing. He was recognized at an early age as a special being who was already born liberated. Unless you are that 1 in 100,000,000 who can stay under water for four hours, it is best that you do not delude yourself. Choose to start with the basics of the Joseph archetype. It is important for spiritual aspirants not to fall into the egocentric trap of believing that they have prematurely reached a higher level of awareness and can skip the Joseph archetype on the evolutionary continuum.

A part of the resistance to the Izbica teachings is the fact that it is hard for the unawakened to appreciate the awakened. This has been true throughout all history, as is exemplified by the Cassandra story in Greek mythology. Many of the prophets were also killed. There is a natural resistance to awake or inspired people, because an awakened person reminds others of their unawake shadow, which is uncomfortable for them. It is time for us as a Jewish and world community to go beyond this, and pull aside the veil of ignorance.

In this context, *berur* (clarification of the real self) and *bitul ha-yesh* (nullification of the illusory self) are part of a process. *Berur* both precedes and follows *bitul ha-yesh*. It is analogous to the Eastern tradition of self-inquiry. In this process we become a witness to ourselves. The ultimate eros of the *Shekhinah* is the ongoing unlimited pleasurable experience of the Divine. This experience is 'non-causal', meaning it is unrelated to anything we do or to anything that happens to us. It is a direct inner experience, and our true natural state. The Divine pleasure we experience in this state is the motivation that powers *teshukat deveikut*.

Historically the divine merging is called *zivug*. Hanokh awoke to the unmediated access to the Divine. He was taken up alive. 'He walked with God, and was no more *(bitul)* for God took him.' (Gen. 5:25). Hanokh's merging with Metatron is symbolic of the merging with *Shekhinah*. Metatron is identified with the *sefirah Binah* and the energy of the Judah archetype. Each awake being is a living text, and able to share their understanding of the truth in that overall truth. This gives us a deeper appreciation of Mordechai Lainer's work.

When the first Temple was destroyed in 586 BCE and eros was exiled, it was externally textualized in Torah study, but ultimately eros becomes internally experienced, as exemplified in the lives of the Baal Shem Tov and Moshe Haim Luzzatto, as it was before in the lives of King David, and King Solomon.

This brings us to the concept of *unio mystico*, where the ego-self is annihilated in the process of the Unique Self emerging. The process does not stop with the *unio mystico*. The Unique Self is a post-liberation integration. Gabriel personally experienced this ten years after his two spiritual teachers declared his liberation. It takes time, especially because there is very little teaching which shows the path of liberation. This is different than the *ruah ha-kodesh* that temporarily inspires a musician, an artist, or an inspired interpreter of Torah.

Berur generates the conditions for becoming the Unique Self. It points to the deeper truth of subtle bliss, which is the baseline, internal perspective of liberation that can blossom into wild bliss at any time. It is different than a transitory prophetic bliss, which is an amplified ecstasy for a limited time to bring in revelation.

This subtler bliss leaves one in a constant state of being *lema'alah mida'ato*, in 'no-boundary consciousness'. We are consciously and consistently in *hitpashtut*, which leads us to and establishes us in *'olam ha-ba*—direct knowledge of God. '*Olam ha-ba* is a constant awareness once we have stabilized in *cherut/he'arah*. Our individual name and the divine name are one. Our hands and the hand of God are one.

In this process, there is something beyond us, initiated by the Divine kiss (*neshikah Elohit*). This is the divine urge or *teshukat deveikut*. *Teshukat deveikut* is a driving force within us. In a certain way spiritual life really begins with the Divine kiss (*neshikah Elohit*). The following are excerpts from three of Rabbi Gabriel's poems that help to clarify this experience.

> *The subtle kiss of liberation/ Has no lips,/ But you taste it in every cell;/ An ecstatic wild pulsing of every DNA oscillation/…*
> *And there is nothing else worth living for/ Except to be the ecstatic naked wild dance of Yah./ Hashem's kiss is the Cosmic Death,/ And the Cosmic Rebirth into immortality./ Once kissed you become the breath of Yah/ As the play of the world.*

Once Divinely kissed we become driven by *teshukat deveikut*, the Divine Urge:

> *The seed of truth eternally planted/ Within the body—mind—I-am complex/ Is awakened by your touch./ The seed of cosmic fire/ Ignites the eternal divine urge/ Into a roaring flame./ This one is like a bull in heat/ Seeking to mate with the One,/ Crashing through the illusion of all barriers,/…Berur,/ Slamming this one into the emptiness of divine stillness./ A wild love-crazed moth/ Irreversibly pulled toward the divine fire…*

This takes us into the subtle initial experience of liberation as that which is beyond the mind. **This is my personal experience. This experiences however does not erase Uniqueness but rather is the ground from and in which Unique Self lives and emerges. This is not reducible to conceptual academic categories but is rather, in Gabriel's lived understanding of the actual experiences of liberation.**

> *One day the windy Grace of Yah/ Blew so hard/ The glass table of the mind/ Turned over and shattered/ Into thousands of useless fragments/ It happened so suddenly,/…After so many years and lifetimes/ Of thinning this glass ceiling of illusion,/ So suddenly/…The scintillating sublime Absolute/ Burst through/ Uninterrupted/…The illusion of 'I' was not even there to claim it as mine./ There was no place to stand/ And no one to be standing./ The Great Way/ Which has no gate/ Opened/ And there was no 'me' there to walk through.*

These poems capture the process of Bitul as outlined in Chassidic texts a way that gives some insight into the overall picture of what we would call the divine urge. This is the motivation activated by the divine kiss, an erotic metaphor that is key to understanding the path of King Solomon and King David and ultimately of Moshe, who walked up the mountain into the unknown. The inner eros is the direct experience of God within. King Solomon sought to activate the outer eros with his thousand wives and kingdom. While he did this in his own authentic way, in the end he taught that all was vanity, and all that has meaning is to know God. Solomon tried what is known in the Eastern tradition as the left-handed tantric path. He spiritually survived it, although perhaps only barely. Most have not. What Lainer adds to this story is that after the me disappears in the kiss of liberation, the divine essence of the human being re-appears as the Unique Self. Lainer, in Rabbi Mordechai's exposition of his teaching in other works, understands the great teaching of Mahyana Buddhism that there is no emptiness without form and no form without emptiness. An evolved understanding of this teaching teaches us that Enlightenment has a perspective. There is no emptiness without form and form is always Unique. True self in authentic liberation always gives way to the Liberation of Unique Self.

Lainer's nondual humanism is rooted in the human being reconnecting to this inner experience of the endless *Shekhinah* energy. The true root is inside our personal temple (*mikdash me'at*), which was externalized in the first Temple. Another way of understanding this concept is the five levels of the soul. The five levels of the soul are *nefesh, ruah, neshamah, hayah* (the Oversoul), and *yehidah*. The fifth level of *yehidah* is the unique soul expression of God. At that level, the dialogue ends between witness and self; there is only *Hashem* expressing itself as the Unique One. *Hashem*, literally the name is as Rabbi Mordechai points out in this volume, refers both to the name of God and the name of the human being manifesting at the liberated level of Unique Self. This liberation is the emphasis of the great Jewish path of *herut/he'arah* (enlightenment).

Again, context is key to understanding Mordechai Lainer's liberated teaching of the Unique Self. Three levels of consciousness are outlined in Mordechai Lainer's teaching. Firstly, there is the level at which most people live, in which the personality is seen as one's true identity. There is the delusion of an ego separate from God. Everything is in the hands of heaven, except that there is fear (awe) of God.

At the second level, there is a sense that all is in the hands of heaven, that human choice is an illusion, and that even the fear is in the hands of heaven, and the personality is seen as a case of mistaken identity.

At the third level, after enlightenment, the hands of humans and the hands of heaven are one. God's eminence is in the world. God's hands are the hands of the righteous and human deeds are God's actions. It is in this context that those rare Judah archetypes uphold a deeper Torah, although they may appear to temporarily violate a particular *mitzvah* for a higher purpose. Lainer's work is not an invitation for the unawake, naïve ego-ics to use the Judah archetype to justify their ego-motivated action. For the true Judah archetypes, such as Rav Kook, the way to do such actions was extremely thoughtfully, yet spontaneously. The Joseph and Judah perspectives appear to be in contradiction only if we do not recognize the possibility that may appear as different states of consciousness along the spiritual evolutionary continuum.

In the context of Lainer, the word fear is actually better translated as awe. As it is written in *Masekhet Atzilut*, an ancient kabbalistic text, 'And the one who (truly) fears heaven pursues the concealed and *Ma'aseh Merkavah*, the essence of wisdom and knowledge, as it is written, 'The beginning of wisdom is fear (awe) of God (Psalm 102)…This is the meaning of 'The secret of *Hashem* is for those who fear him', and it is written, 'The fear of *Hashem* is wisdom, and turning from wisdom to understanding' (Job 21). The fear, or awe, is at this level deeper than the concept of fear based on the dualistic consciousness of separation from God and/or the degeneration into superstition that can be typical of the Joseph archetype, or the rote performance of the *mitzvot*. *Masekhet Atzilut* clearly states that without possessing the sincere quality of *yirat shamayim*, the fear and awe of Heaven, any and all study of Torah—the greatest *mitzvah* of them all—is considered null and void. Without *yirat shamayim*, all religious observances are hypocritical (see *Sefer Baal Shem Tov* Shemot 1).

The implication of this is that what is expected of one who is *yirat shamayim* is to be actively exploring and living the secrets of the Torah through both intellectual understanding and meditative practices associated with the expansion of consciousness, also known as *Ma'aseh Merkavah*. The teaching of the ancients are clear—without these two levels of intellectual (*Binah*) and mystical-intuitive (*Hokhmah*) study of the secrets of the Torah, one is not considered to be in *yirat shamayim*. It must be an active way of life, because it is only in the consciousness of the wakeful states of the Judah archetype that one can gaze into the Torah and perceive deep intuitive secrets.

At this level of intuitive apperception, which is the world of *Hokhmah* (the dimension of *Atzilut*), there is truly the beginning of intuitive understanding of knowing the Divine. Those who have combined understanding (*Binah*) and wisdom (*Hokhmah*) and have the wisdom to hear (*ta shema'*) and the inner eye to see (*ta hazi*) are in *yirat shamayim*. This is the true Torah. In other words, true *yirat shamayim* is not motivated by superstition, anxiety, and fears. Therefore, when Mordechai Lainer is saying the Judah archetype does not have the 'fear' of God, it means that Judah does not have superstition and fears, but rather lives in the wisdom, awe, and wonderment of the living Torah. In essence, that which is alive as the living Torah is what keeps us alive as spiritual beings. As it says *Pirkei Avot*, a Voice cries out from Sinai every day, 'Woe to the world for the disgrace shown to the Torah.' In this way Torah is uplifted and shines for the world.

All of God's holy ones—those who act from love—are in the Divine hands, and God is present within them. There is an unmediated presence in all those who act from a God-merged Judah experience of love. This is the key to understanding the teaching of unmediated encounter with the Divine.

In the larger context, the apparent paradox of acosmic (nondual) humanism disappears, because we understand that God and the liberated soul are one, and we act accordingly. The word 'Amen' expresses this paradox through its *gematria*: *Adonai* (65), the illusion of separation between human and *Elohim*, and *YHVH* (26), as grace and unmediated presence, combine to create *Amen* (91). The Judah archetype teaches us that each moment is a new speaking that cannot be captured by the general purpose of the law and the *mitzvot*. The awakened person is naturally open to being the expression of God in every moment. As we said, this is the meaning of *hitpashtut*.

As part of his work, Lainer talks about healing the shadow (*hisaron*). Healing one's *hisaron* is part of the pathway to the Divine in all traditions, but it is especially emphasized in the Jewish path of liberation. This is the way we develop our character, by addressing and healing our unique shadows. In this process of spiritual evolution, our name and the divine name become one.

Rav Kook, the great mystic and *halakhah* scholar, is an example of someone who may well have transcended the contradiction between the Joseph and Judah archetypes. To say there is no need for law, he explained, is not to say that we do not follow the law as a unique expression of the Divine. We walk in the world knowing all concepts are illusions, but also understanding that they keep order in the world. As we said earlier, the subtle teaching is that the Judah archetype is not against the law, but is the unbroken expression of the Divine Law.

Here we are on the cutting edge of evolution. One cannot be in the way of Judah unless one has been purified, and has already lived within the conventional ethics of the law. Only upon this foundation can we talk about having the awareness to go beyond the limited understanding of the *mitzvot* as an expression of the Torah. The *mitzvot* are our foundation. When we understand this, the paradox is resolved.

The Judah archetype is about action out of love and choicelessness. Judah is free to move in any direction with a heart connected to the will of God. We live in 'omek (spiritual depth), which is a nondual understanding of reality, as we walk in the dual world, between *belimah*—the void, and *mah*—the 'real'.

Lainer points out that when one's heart is one with the will of God, one may do whatever the heart desires. How does one know when the heart is aligned? The ego can misunderstand and use this natural truth in an unprincipled way. In the awareness of *herut*, there is no work; there is no striving, effort or responsibility—at least not in the limited sense of the egoic responsibility of the separate self. That is why Rav Zusha is such a great example of the Judah archetype. He taught while in the awareness that Eastern traditions call 'crazy wisdom', yet lived very traditionally, following both the *mitzvot* and also the essence of the *mitzvot*.

Teshukat deveikut is an act of grace activated by the Divine kiss. The Divine urge drives us. The Judah archetype is one who has realized unity with the will of God through their love of God. For the Judah archetype there is only the unique action of the Divine happening effortlessly, even under the most apparently difficult circumstances. This is the third, *mikdash* level of consciousness beyond *shabbat*-consciousness, which is linked to time.

Once we are beyond time, and we understand that from an ultimate perspective there is no transformation because all is part of the Eternal. When one is in the consciousness of the Judah archetype, *yirah*, *berur*, and *mitzvot* are no longer necessary, but one may choose to use them. One is simply the outflowing expression of the Divine, beyond approaches and techniques. We embody the rabbinical statement, 'Greater is serving Torah *(shimushah)* than learning her *(limudah)*.' Service is driven by *teshukah*. At another level of paradox, however, for the liberated there can be no service in the world because there is no other. Rather, service furthers our spiritual evolution, whether done as the Judah or Joseph archetype.

One who is not living in all four worlds as a multi-dimensional person may choose to interpret Mordechai Lainer as a radically theocentric determinist, or as affirming radical human autonomy, but his nondual humanism truly includes both poles in all four worlds, as the Divine is expressed through people.

Similarly, Mordechai Lainer, because of his liberated context, was able to incorporate *mitzido* (the divine perspective) and *mitzideinu* (the human perspective) beautifully, because of his understanding that we are multi-dimensional beings. Rabbi Gafni's book will be an indispensable text for those who want to get to the deep essence of Judaism in its original meaning, at its deepest level, as taught by Mordechai Lainer. This incredible book is a sophisticated discussion of enlightenment and its many levels are on a par with anything found in the East, elevated by the *ruah ha-kodesh* and intellectual brilliance of Rabbi Mordechai Gafni. It gives us a context and a starting point from which to understand liberation in the Jewish tradition, and it establishes Judaism as a historical path of liberation with an emphasis on each liberated being as a unique expression of the Divine.

Rabbi Gabriel congratulates Rabbi Gafni for his ability to draw out the essence of the mystical teachings of Lainer in a way that goes beyond academic interpretations. Rabbi Gabriel's feeling is that Mordechai Lainer had the direct apperception of the truth of self-realization, and that his teachings initially developed through following of the Joseph archetypal path before he evolved/woke up into the Judah archetypal path of liberation. Rabbi Gafni's holy understanding of this great teacher is absolutely vital and compelling for our times, and it can open us up to the Divine urge. These teachings bring us back to Avraham sitting in his tent in the heat—the spiritual passion—of the day. This inspired interpretation of Lainer by Rabbi Gafni reading of Lainer offered in this volume is a pioneering work transmitting Judaism as it was originally intended—as an inspired path to full liberation.

May we all be blessed to be as passionate for the love of God as was Avraham. May we all sip of the divine wine of he'arah, of revelation and liberation. May we all live as the first fruit offering to God. AMEN

ACKNOWLEDGEMENTS

It is my pleasure to thank a number of people who were critical to the fruition of this project. First I want to thank my good friend Claudia Kleefeld and the board of the Foundation that has supported this work. At various stages of the Foundation's unfolding, the board has included Michael Zimmerman, Diane Hamilton, John Kesler, Gabriel Cousens, Rabbi Gershon Winkler, Suzy Rogovin, Derek Evans and other distinguished communal leaders. Michael Zimmerman provided guidance and leadership to the foundation. I have enjoyed many conversations with Michael, Gabriel, Sally, Diane and John about the core content of the enlightenment teachings in the Izbica lineage. It is my pleasure as well to thank Ken Wilber for his very careful reading of an early version of this manuscript, and for his provocative and insightful comments and inquiries. Thanks are pleasantly due as well to Prof. Elliot Wolfson for his scholarship and personal integrity both of which serve as a model for me. I have benefited from my all my contacts with him and his work.

The board of the foundation also included as the initiating creative force a close friend for many years who supported the vision of the foundation. I hold her in my heart and express my friendship and gratitude. I also owe much gratitude to a group of friends, colleagues and supporters which include Metuka Benjamin, Arthur Kurzweil, Rabbi Avram Davis, Dr. Joseph Berke, Miriam Maron, Sara Hendelman, Shanti Cousens, and Sue Morningstar and Prof. Admiel Kosman, and many others from the Jewish community whose public and private support has held my heart in these years.

I owe a great debt to Professor Moshe Idel, whose wisdom, scholarship and integrity made my dissertation—the first volume of this book—possible. Prof. Idel's unwavering support of this work through no small travail reminded me that integrity lives in our world. His work on Metatron, a one-letter tradition in Kaballah directly informed two key sections of this book. His incisive, magisterial scholarship, and the many illuminating models he has drawn, have been of extraordinary value. Prof. Idel, together with Dr. Norman Solomon, served as advisors to my doctoral thesis at Oxford University, where the core of this material was written.

The Foundation has been transcended by and included in the Center for World Spirituality. The Center is a think tank, training institute and international community which is both my intellectual and spiritual home. I am delighted to thank the board of the Center for World Spirituality for their work in supporting the emergence of the Unique Self and World Spirituality teachings. They include John Mackey and Lori Galperin as board chairs, Sally Kempton, Mariana Caplan, Wyatt Woodsmall, Eben Pagan, Warren Farrell, Terry Nelson, Victoria Myer, Shawn Ramer, Heather Fester, Lesley Freeman, Joe Perez, Chahat Corten, Leon Gras, Mauk Peiper, Tom Goddard, Elizabeth Helen Bullock, Liza Braude, Marty Cooper, Heather Ussery Knight, Mike Ginn, Kathy Brownback, Bill Little, Kristen Ulmer, Babs Yohai, Vidyadeva, Peter Britton, Claudia Kleeselz, and Jane Eigner Mintz.

Thanks also are due with delight to Sean Esbjörn-Hargens who together with Zachary Stein and Clint Fuhs are the academic co-chairs of the Center for World Spirituality and are important interlocutors for me in the world of Integral theory, as well as good friends. Sean particularly published and introduced a portion of this work in the Integral academic journal, (JITP 6:1 Suny Press 2011).

I give special thanks to Avraham Leader who is effectively the co-author of the third volume of this work. Avraham and I spent some of the most delightful times of my life in study and profound brotherhood. This will always remain. I am hopeful that life will allow us to study the sacred texts again. The section of the work that Avraham was involved in was not part of my doctorate at Oxford, but it is a critical and foundational part of this work.

Without Rabbi Dr. David Seidenberg's masterful editing, over nearly five years, this book could not exist. David was a vital force in turning a long and sprawling dissertation manuscript into a finely-honed work of academic style and precision. David's long contact with this manuscript also gave him a thorough knowledge of both my voice and of the subject, which enabled him to take the second two volumes and turn them into fully realized parts of the whole. His challenges and queries which emerged from his own profound depth of scholarship and realization have made this work more precise, and more accessible to readers and seekers. And of course, whatever errors or omissions remain are my own. For much of the final period of this work, I was in great pain. It is clear to me that without

David's wisdom and integrity and ethical core, I would not have found the resources to complete this work.

Izbica at its heart is a work about Eros, the divine feminine, the *Shekhinah*. It is for this reason that this work is dedicated to incarnations of the divine feminine who have each in very different, special, and singular ways, challenged me, supported me, and provoked my own evolution during the final years of this work's preparation when I was living first in Salt Lake City and then in Marin County. Their support held my heart in the most difficult of times. They are, in alphabetical order, Dalit Arnon, Metuka Benjamin, Mariana Caplan, Diane Hamilton, Sally Kempton and, finally, Lori Galperin.

~ Carmel Ca. 2012

INTRODUCTION

Mordechai Lainer of Izbica is my chosen lineage master. My prayer is that I have honored him with a correct and proper understanding of his transmission and teaching. I believe that I have. Though this personal introduction is not meant to fully outline his teachings, a few remarks may orient the general reader and guide the initiate.

An Esoteric Transmission

First of all, this book is both an academic study and a transmission of an esoteric doctrine. Part of the disguise of this work is its presentation as a piece of academic scholarship.

Of course, on one level it *is* precisely that, for which I have to thank Professor Moshe Idel. At some point in 2001 or so, Professor Idel told me off-handedly that I needed to do an academic doctorate at a good university in order to insure that my non-academic writing and teaching be taken seriously. He very kindly accepted my request that he act as my co-advisor at Oxford University. I am in his debt for his gracious, insightful and often penetratingly brilliant remarks, which guided the unfolding of this work in an academic context.

Having said that, the academic framework is just that, a framework—and something of a fig leaf—for the deeper teaching of Lainer, which I have humbly and perhaps audaciously tried to unfold in this volume.

When I was thirty-one, living in Israel near Tel Aviv, Prof. Moshe Halamish suggested that I study and write about this great master. I had barely heard of Mordechai Joseph Lainer, and was wholly unfamiliar with his writings collected in two volumes under the title *Mei Hashiloah (MH)*. Halamish's prompt was the beginning of my relationship with Lainer, which deepened and shifted again many times over the years. At the time, thanks to Rabbi Shlomo Carlebach, who was deeply connected to Lainer's teaching, the Torah of Izbica was just beginning to gain currency in certain neo-Hasidic circles in Israel and the United States. At some point,

I realized that I felt a soul root connection with his teaching, and began to teach his Torah to my own circles of students.

This period of teaching *Mei Hashiloah* lasted about ten years. Some five years into this teaching period, I spent one year of 16 hour days in the library at Oxford in an intense, in-depth encounter with Mordechai Lainer.

In approaching the master and his text during that year, I followed the three-stage path of textual reading taught by the Baal Shem Tov. First, in a state of what the Baal Shem calls *hahna'ah*, reverential submission to what one is learning, I read every passage again and again, praying that I might realize Lainer's deeper intention and receive his transmission. Second, I moved from submission to what the Baal Shem calls *havdalah*, separation. In this stage of *havdalah*, I deployed a method of analysis which involved two basic steps. As I read, I made a list of key topics, words and texts in Lainer. I subsequently gathered every reference to that text, theme or image, searching for the underlying pattern. At the same time I learned, together with my friend Avraham Leader, many of the original Zoharic sources that would have influenced *Mei Hashiloah*, to get a sense of how he was reading the tradition, what he changed in his interpretation, and why.

Eventually, stage two yielded to stage three, which the Baal Shem Tov calls *hamtakah*, sweetening. *Hamtakah* involves an erotic 'nondual' merger with the text, which occurs when the reader and that which is read become one. It is at this stage that the deeper intention of the Lainer's Torah became startlingly lucid, delightful, and beautiful, and the entire teaching opened up with radical clarity and joy.

As I continued my teaching in the world, I sought, as every authentic student does, to both teach and evolve this Torah. One expression of this process was the book *Soul Prints* (Simon and Schuster 2001) and the *Soul Prints Workshop,* (Sounds True 2004) which I published during the years 2001–2003. Another is the book you have before you. This academic work of mystical hermeneutics is complimented by the Journal of Integral Theory and Practice 6:1 (Suny Press 2011) and *Your Unique Self: The Radical Path to Personal Enlightenment,* (Integral Publishing 2012).

1

Love and Teaching

I am in love with these teachings, awed by their subtlety and profundity, moved by their commitment and depth and enchanted by their possibility. In the book before you, however, I have remained faithful to the academy in deploying the tools of scholarship, seeking to uncover Lainer's teaching exclusively, without entangling it, explicitly or subtly, with my own. Nonetheless, the initiated reader must remember that this is an esoteric work, one which, in understated tones, intends to lay down a revolutionary and evolutionary set of spiritual principles which will be recognized as such by those with a pure heart and a clarified self.

The implications of Lainer's Torah are radical, dramatic and stunningly beautiful, especially in the marriage of a profound ethos and an equally profound eros. This teaching demands intense work, practice, and radical dedication. Such intense, consistent and dedicated engagement may well yield the fierce grace of a fully enlightened and liberated human being who lives as one with the Source, whose every casual word is Torah, spoken from the mouth of the living God, and whose every action is tied to liberation.

How the Book is Ordered

Some of the most important esoteric content found in this book does not emerge until volume 2, entitled *The Wisdom of Solomon*, and volume 3, in which texts of the *Zohar*, Luria, and other kabbalists and Hasidic masters are adduced and explained.

The main part of this book, volume 1, begins in Part One by discussing four key ideas: unique self, unique shadow, unique Torah, and unique *tikun*. Every person has a unique self that creates his unique obligation. Every person has a unique shadow that arises when they do not access and live their unique self. The unique shadow is, paradoxically, the door to one's unique self.

In Part Two, I delve into the intellectual history of the lineage teaching about unique self. In this section, some critical esoteric teachings on prophecy are laid down, and the line of transmission between Lainer and Isaac Luria, the 'Lion of Safed', is made clear.

Part Three begins to unfold the core essence of it all, what I call nondual or acosmic humanism. In Part Four, particularly in the sections on God, Torah and Israel, on *Shekhinah*, on the unification of names, and elsewhere, the full power of Lainer's teaching begins to appear. Then, in volumes 2 and 3, everything moves to a different level of consciousness, so to speak, as we unpack the hidden trope of the Wisdom of Solomon in Lainer and in his line of transmission.

All of these teachings, in Lainer's understanding, form the core of the esoteric wisdom known as the Wisdom of Solomon. Lainer's intention is to transmit nothing less than the teachings of King Solomon that lead to liberation and enlightenment. These teachings evolved through generations of great esoteric masters of the Kabbalah, and were ultimately received and transmitted by Lainer.

Paradoxically, as Lainer teaches, if one is not at the level of consciousness required to realize these teachings, then one will feel compelled to vociferously oppose them as dangerous. Indeed, it is true that they are dangerous—and the student must listen 'dangerously'.

Nondual Humanism and the Democratization of Enlightenment

The goal of Lainer's teaching is no less than the full democratization of enlightenment. He implicitly identifies and distinguishes between two forms of enlightened consciousness. The first is what we might call the instrumental level. At this stage of realization, the person is an instrument, like a flute or shofar, played by the divine. Images describing this stage of illumination were replete in the Hasidic teachings and writings which constituted Lainer's intellectual framework. This is the level of utter surrender to the divine.

As one internalizes this level and transcends it, one comes to another level, which Lainer associates with Temple energy and the Judah archetype. At this level, God does not move through the person as an external force animating and filling the person's voice, but rather God is incarnate within the person, who achieves a radical identity with the divine. Lainer makes clear that this enlightenment is a possibility for every member of the community. Every human being has the potential of Moses.

The Voice of Moses:

Individuation beyond ego

It is in this sense that we can begin to understand Lainer's provocative idea that the Torah was given by a Moses who is merged with God—not in the voice of God, but in the voice of Moses. Because this idea exemplifies so much of Lainer's spiritual project, we will explore it briefly here.

Lainer uses the Zoharic phrase 'The *Shekhinah* speaks through the voice of Moses' as a foundation for his position. This Zoharic phrase, describing the authorship of Deuteronomy, was understood in two very different ways. The theocentric understanding, reflected in most Hasidic works, is that Moses was so completely effaced that he became a kind of channel for the divine voice. For Lainer this is only the first instrumental level of enlightenment. The second possible understanding of the phrase 'the *Shekhinah* speaks through the voice of Moses', corresponding to the higher level of enlightenment in Lainer's teaching, is almost the opposite: Moses is not effaced, but is rather so completely present that his voice and the voice of the *Shekhinah* become one. Moses' unique persona, his unique perspective, his voice and personality, incarnate the *Shekhinah*; through radical uniqueness, he participates in ontic unity with God. We will explore the history of this phrase in the body of this book, but a cursory synopsis drawn from volume 1 may illuminate what exactly was Lainer's spiritual project.

> In the first stage of Hasidic thought, Moses' 'saying' the book of Deuteronomy was generalized to include the *tzadik's* (righteous master's) 'saying Torah'. Then in the second stage, the *tzadik* saying Torah was expanded to include all the words of the *tzadik*. Finally, in *Mei Hashiloah*, the concept of 'the *Shekhinah* speaks through his throat' was expanded from the *tzadik* to include the Judah archetype, which in theory could be accessed by any person. This last expansion by Lainer is radically different: in *Mei Hashiloah*, the *Shekhinah* speaking comes through the *intensification of individuality*, rather than through its effacement.

Because the human is a part of God, the principle of acosmism does not negate but rather empowers the individual. The divine voice finds expression in the voice of the unique soul, modeled by the prophet who manifests

liii

God's voice through the clear prism of his unique individuality. This is the core of Lainer's nondual humanism.

As we will return to again and again throughout the book, Lainer argues, both explicitly and implicitly, that the unique individual is the portal through which comes the revelation of the unmediated divine will, the new Torah that can override the law of Sinai. In effect every person incarnates the individualized mind of God. In various writings I have called this pivot in Lainer's thought 'sacred autobiography', 'soul print' or 'unique self'. In later writing I distinguished *Soul Print* from *Unique Self*. Soul print is understood to be the eternal unique quality of the individual soul which is in some sense part of God, and unique self is understood to be an enlightened quality of being in which the separate self is entirely transcended as one realizes true self. True Self then realizes that it sees through a unique perspective, a unique set of eyes. It is this level of consciousness which is the fullest flowering of what I term Unique Self realization. In Lainer's corpus however the distinction between soul print and unique self is blurred, often within the same passage. I will use the terms interchangeably in this work in the same manner as Lainer.

Levels of Consciousness

The consciousness which comes with realizing the potential of one's soul print is the goal of Lainer's theology. In contrast with this, the classical Hasidic model of enlightenment as effacement of self, or *bitul*, is only a first stage of consciousness on the path of enlightenment in *Mei Hashiloah*. The recognition that there are different stages of developmental consciousness being alluded to in *Mei Hashiloah* is the hermeneutic key I deployed to unlock many of the contradictions in Lainer's teaching. While levels of consciousness are almost never referred to explicitly as such, they form a core underlying matrix of Lainer's spiritual teaching. The levels nearly always come in threes.

In one trinity, for example, there is the pre-personal level, where one is not able to exercise genuine free choice. "Then there is the level of the personal, where one is able to make real individual choices. Finally, one attains the enlightened transpersonal level, where there is the choicelessness of one who is merged in the divine will.

In another trinity, operating on a different axis, there is the first level, in which human action appears to be real and necessary, and the illusion of the separate self reigns. Through committed spiritual work and dedicated practice which is both nomian and anominan—that is, through *mitzvot*, prayer and the different forms of contemplative clarification and introspection which Lainer calls *berur*—one ascends to the second level, which Lainer associates with *shabbat* and which I therefore call 'shabbat-consciousness'. At this level, one realizes that all human action is meaningless because there is no choice. Finally, one ascends to 'Temple-consciousness', the third level, which transcends and includes the previous two. At this level, human action is lionized as ontologically identical with divine action. Man realizes his full splendor as the language of the divine, becoming God's verb, noun and adjective.

Lainer's nondual humanism is profoundly activist. Human action is essential to the evolving Godhead. Lainer sets up human freedom and evolutionary human activism as the central defining characteristic of his religious anthropology.

The Hands of Heaven and the Humanist Agenda

One text which defines Lainer's approach to human activism is the well-known rabbinic dictum, 'All is in the hands of heaven except for the fear of heaven'. Lainer stands this saying on its head so that it means, 'All is in the hands of heaven, *even* the fear of heaven'. This would appear to conform to an extremely theocentric understanding, in which the human individual has no capacity for action on even the most internal level. However, Lainer's true position is that 'the hands of heaven' are identical with 'the hands of the human', that is, the human is an expression of the evolving Godhead.

These three interpretations of 'All is in the hands of heaven' correspond to the three levels of consciousness above. The first level is the illusion of a sphere of human independence beyond the reach of 'the hands of heaven', even if this sphere is limited to the fear of heaven. The second level of consciousness is the theocentric level where a person understands that human choice and autonomy are illusions because 'all is the in hands of heaven'. At the third level of consciousness, nondual acosmic humanism, 'the hands of heaven' and 'the hands of man' are realized as sharing one identity.

In the midst of this very realization, the human-divine being exerts fierce, courageous evolutionary effort to heal and repair the world. This is the realized stage where a person recognizes and acts as 'God's verb'.

The Judah Archetype

This core esoteric teaching in *MHs* is characterized by the Judah archetype, which is embodied not only by Judah but also by Moses, as I mentioned above, and by other figures like David, and most importantly, by Solomon, as we will see in volume 2.

Judah is original, powerful, divine, sensuous, profound and ethical in small as well as large ways. It is Judah—who acts with *tekufot*, boldness or holy *chutzpah*—who holds the nondual realization of genuine enlightenment, and it is Judah who will ultimately usher in a new order in which eros and ethics are manifestly one, an era in which the original unique face of every human being will be recognized, honored and exalted. This is the messianic era, in which all human beings will realize that they were always, and are forever, nothing less than perfect expressions of divine consciousness, and that exile (whether from Eden or from Jerusalem) is an illusion. The key for Lainer is that this level of consciousness—'Judah-consciousness'—is already available when we are fully inside the present moment and have evolved our consciousness to be able to recognize the interior face of the cosmos living in us, as us and through us.

Judah and Joseph: Conventional and Post-Conventional

Lainer's Torah is grounded throughout in the classical opposition between Judah and Joseph, between messianic consciousness and normative consciousness. The latter 'Joseph-consciousness' is conventional, classical, dedicated to the social order and the rules which support it, committed to both the law and to the ethics it represents, in all of their beauty. The Joseph level approximates what developmental theorist Clare Graves calls the Blue meme or conventional level of consciousness. The Joseph people never understand the Judah people. They think them heretical and dangerous at best, and do everything in their power to oppose them.

Judah-consciousness, on the other hand, is post-conventional, ecstatic, spontaneous, seeking to give birth to the unmediated divine revelation pregnant in every evolved moment of time. The Judah personae is also often lonely, isolated from a community which distorts his actions, interpreting them through a conventional prism even as they mock his suggestion that it might be otherwise. The Judah level corresponds to what Graves terms Second Tier consciousness. In Spiral Dynamics developmental theory, these levels begin at what is called Yellow and are more fully crystallized at Turquoise, in Integral theory at Teal and Indigo and in other developmental theories (Suzanne Cook-Greuter), as construct aware and then unitive consciousness.

While the Joseph persona speaks to God and even feels God animating his interior, the Judah persona acts *as* God. Joseph loves and Judah lives *as* love. While the Joseph persona is in communion with the divine, the Judah persona achieves a radical *transformation of identity* in which he realizes his ontological identity with the divine. In this identity, his will becomes identical with God's will, which then becomes the locus of his power, ethics and spiritual audacity.

The advent of Judah-consciousness, however, does not exhaust the value of Joseph-consciousness. Rather, the Joseph moment lives in creative dialectical tension with the Judah moment. It is this which creates the tension that runs through Lainer's teaching. One cannot resolve this tension simply by taking sides, by locating oneself in either camp, for the dialectic of Judah and Joseph lives in heart and soul of every authentic servant of God.

Berur and the Pre/Trans Fallacy

What allows one to move from the conventional to the post-conventional is *berur*. *Berur* is the rigorous clarification of desire, motive and inner psychology which enables one to move beyond the ego-ic level of separate self—which, of necessity, must be governed and regulated by Joseph-consciousness—to the enlightened stage animated by Judah-consciousness, Unique Self. In *berur*, according to Lainer, one deconstructs the false self, learning to distinguish between motivations that well up from the emptiness of the false self and motivations that arise from the fullness of the unique self which is identical to the divine. One achieves *berur* by delving deeply into one's unique shadow, *hisaron*, the lack or deficiency that both defines one's uniqueness and becomes the portal to the divine. At that point, one can begin to live and act in the world from the place of enlightened Judah-consciousness.

This process of *berur* is meant to avoid the self-deception that mistakes a pre-rational or pre-moral state for a transpersonal state that confuses the ethically questionable actions and attitudes of pre-*berur* consciousness for the spontaneity of post-*berur* enlightenment. This confusion between levels of consciousness is what I called in Mystery of Love (2002) a level

lvii

one/level three confusion and what Integral philosopher Ken Wilber has termed the pre/trans fallacy, in this case pre-*berur* and post-*berur*.

Embracing, Merging with the *Shekhinah*

For Lainer, one who has become fully clarified becomes both the source of revelation and the incarnation of the *Shekhinah*. *Shekhinah* is identified with the name of God, while in a post-*berur* state, all action, and even the *Shekhinah* herself, become identified with the name of man. Name is one of the core symbols in Lainer's mystical teaching; when something is 'called by the name of man', this indicates that its meaning is real and everlasting. The unification of the names of God and man means that the human being merges with and incarnates *Shekhinah*. The highest expression of personal name in Lainer's writing is virtually synonymous with Unique Self.

In this light, we understand that Lainer's idea of the *Shekhinah* speaking through the human differs from conceptions that preceded him. In *Mei Hashiloah (MH)*, the *divrei hulin*, the casual words, of the Judah archetype are 'the words of the living God'. Unlike most of the earlier sources, the kabbalist is not an empty vessel channeling the divine. Rather, the unique consciousness of the purified person, and even their unique unconscious, is divine. This implies that the *Shekhinah* that is one's essence speaks *naturally* from within the enlightened individual. For Lainer, the self of the mystic becomes so conscious as to become transparent to his divine self. Erotic merger with the *Shekhinah* yields not only the hermeneutics of sacred text, but the hermeneutics of sacred autobiography. In this way, Lainer extends the erotic motif beyond traditional hermeneutics and applies it to reading the 'text' of the person's soul print.

This allows the individual to recover the personal revelation of divine will which is addressed uniquely to him. This revelation comes through the un-mediated embrace of the *Shekhinah*, which is antinomian in a way in that is clearly different than any previous sources. Lainer's incarnational *Shekhinah* theology is both empowering and limned with humanistic undertones.

The Human Being as Revelation's Source

In all of this, Lainer makes a crucial leap beyond previous Kabbalists and Hasidic masters. In the pre-Lainer sources, no matter how bold the reach of human creativity, engagement with the sacred text was always the locus of creativity, and the text always mediated between the human being and God. Lainer's momentous leap is to remove the sacred text of revelation and law from standing between human and God. The human being becomes the source of revelation. More than this, the human being *is* a text of revelation. Lainer argues that the human Torah of the unmediated divine will is capable of overriding—*and at times must override*—the old revelation. This is because God's will is always revealing itself originally and freshly in the present moment, and the old Torah is yesterday's revelation, not today's.

Eros and the Wisdom of Solomon

The hidden framework or matrix underlying Lainer's religious theology of nondual humanism is *hokhmat Shelomoh* 'The Wisdom of Solomon'. Volume 2 uncovers this teaching in *Mei Hashiloah*, while volume 3 reveals a distinctive Zoharic genre on the Wisdom of Solomon, which served as the direct source for Lainer. In fact, the term *hokhmat Shelomoh* is one of the *Zohar's* expressions for *Shekhinah*.

Lainer understands his own thought to be a continuation and an unfolding of the Wisdom of Solomon, which includes all the principles that fall under the rubric of nondual acosmic humanism. As we have touched on above and will see in the main volume of this book, these principles include the ability to gain unmediated access to the divine will, and to access, on occasion, a truth higher than the law, as well as the expansion of consciousness, called *hitpashtut*, that allows this transcendence to take place; the idea that every person has a unique personal pathology, their *hisaron* or shadow, which is the paradoxical gate to the spiritual journey that makes a person whole; the radical individualism embodied in the Judah archetype, which is found in potential in everyone; the theological significance of *teshukah* desire and the essentially erotic quality of merging with the *Shekhinah*; and the ontic identity of the human and divine names. All of these principles are tied in to the primary focus of Solomon's wisdom, which is the drive to embrace the *Shekhinah*, the erotic feminine manifestation of the divine, in a direct and unmediated fashion. For Lainer the Wisdom of Solomon is the human incarnation of eros in the form of the irreducible Unique Self.

Dionysian Ecstasy in Service of the Law:

Erotic motifs appear throughout the Wisdom of Solomon passages in *Mei Hashiloah—teshukah* 'passion', *tei'uvta denukva* 'the desire of the feminine', moon, and various pagan motifs all appear here limned with eros. One might well characterize Lainer's entire Wisdom of Solomon project as an impassioned desire for full erotic abandon in the lap of the Goddess. One desires to be overpowered, *menutzah*, by the Goddess, and in that experience to realize the fullness of *teshukah*, the realization of sacred desire. This, however, is not for Lainer an erotic impulse that expresses itself in sexual engagement, except on the extremely rare occasions where the post-*berur*, post-conventional context creates a vessel to hold such explosive light. Rather the erotic passion for the Goddess that so defines Solomon is directed in a gorgeous manner towards the ethics of the law.

This passion is transmuted by Lainer into the passion for justice and for deep integrity in resolving disputes between conflicting parties, which Lainer terms the desire for *emet le'amito*, the deepest truth. This truth which is beyond legal precedent and evidentiary rules, discloses the essence of a situation beyond the level of the letter of the law and the discernment that the courts can reach. In truth, the word transmutes is not quite accurate. Ethical sensitivity to justice and to meta-justice is for Lainer the heart of the sensual goddess herself. The ethical sensitivity and the raw ethical beauty of Lainer in these texts has more than once moved me to tears.

Lainer thus imbues this struggle with and for the law with all of the erotic energy of paganism, the Goddess, and the moon. Even if for Lainer the value of the law is sometimes found in its transcendence, engagement with the law is primary. Lainer's quest is to break out of the idolatries of law and to touch *retzon Hashem*, God's immediate will, which is the same as touching the Goddess, the *Shekhinah*, without her *levushim*, her clothing. The methods are various, whether sacred individuality, or ecstasy, or the higher intuition of *rei'ah* that can allow one to judge *emet le'amito*. All, however, are realized through embracing one's unique self story, the primary gate through which one accesses *retzon Hashem*, the unmediated *Shekhinah*.

One More Word about the Goddess:

There are two primary source lineages for the living mystical goddess energies of the divine feminine incarnate in the world today. One is Hindu, expressed in part in the yoga traditions, and the other is kabbalistic, expressed in part in the Hasidic traditions. A particularly radical form of the Hebrew goddess tradition is expressed in the words and between the lines of the radical Kabbalah of Mordechai Lainer. For Lainer, it is precisely in this transcending and including of the conventional within post-conventional contexts that the eros of the goddess, the *Shekhinah*, is incarnate. For Lainer, the entire eros of the goddess is poured into assuring the correct verdict in what appears to be a petty case in small claims court. It is in the precision and caring of justice—in the details of justice—that the eros of the goddess lives. Certainly when issues of even greater import are at hand, with crucial implications for the lives of individuals and entire communities, the genuine eros of *Shekhinah* demands careful fact checking; revealing of complex motivations at play; appropriate deliberation; and appropriate mechanisms to assure fairness, decency, and healing. In the Hebrew goddess, eros and ethos merge as one in the great Yichud, Unification. The failure to put such mechanisms of fairness and integrity in place, because of fear and the seduction of the pseudo-goddesses of political correctness and community acceptance, is exactly the kind of violation of the goddess for which many post-conventional contexts, whether of the developmental or new age variety, are culpable.

Lainer's teaching on *berur*, the need to clarify the post-conventional, stems from his knowing that high states and stages of spiritual realization all too often do not result in the good, the true, or the beautiful. The attention to justice and kindness for Lainer—and the goddess-drunk kabbalists from which he emerges—must always take center stage. There is great danger to the goddess in both the New Age idolization of state experiences and the excessive premium that much of the developmental community places on complex levels of cognition. By "developmental community," we mean many people who understand that spiritual development unfolds along developmental lines and who position their own level of consciousness somewhere near the top of the spiral. As I have pointed out many times, higher levels of cognitive complexity do not a better human being make. It is not by accident that we rarely see posts in the blogs of higher development about kindness. Developmental theorists can talk for hours about people at blue, green, or yellow; first-tier and second-tier; Diplomat, Achiever, Individualist. But where is the Developmental love behind it all? Kindness is a value that all too often is relegated to the lower levels of amber or blue consciousness in the Developmental and Spiral Dynamics models of development. It rarely appears as a value in many developmental books, conferences, and websites. Or worse still, it is given lip service even as it is ignored in practice when the real gods of cognition and power are worshipped.

In New Age contexts, love is a post-conventional slogan which often means very little. The more practical and actionable forms of day-to-day kindness get very little play. The most powerful mechanism to assure day-to-day sustainable kindness is fairness, a conventional value of law and integrity. For the goddess, however, fairness applied conventionally is not sufficiently fair or just. For Lainer, the eros of the goddess seeks to amplify fairness and justice in the most prosaic and banal contexts as well as in the larger meta contexts. The goddess is incarnate by boundary breaking, seeking after radical justice and fairness. The erotic goddess is for Lainer, not only antinomian, but as Kabbalah scholar Eliot Wolfson might say, hypernomian. All this is to say that Lainer is not satisfied by the law. He wants to transcend the law, antinomian, and he wants to enact more law, hypernomian. Lainer's sense of the law is obviously Hebraic and not Pauline in nature. For him, law is the pouring out of the infinite into the finite. He wants to either break through the law of yesterday—yesterday's revelation symbolized as garments—and kiss the naked *Shekhinah*, or to enact more and more just law, which is, from Lainer's perspective, but another way of enacting more and more *Shekhinah*. This, for Lainer, is the highest and most erotic expression of the post-conventional. It is post-conventional in that it will not be contained by the more general parameters of the law. Principles and precedent, the core of conventional law, is insufficient to feed or incarnate the goddess of radical situational justice, which is subjective, not in the sense of being relative, but in the sense of being always an ultimate subject, not subject to objectification. Her eros is specific and precise and presents itself afresh in every new moment. The eros of the goddess is revealed in the specific and personal interstices of the unique self and the unique moment.

Unique Self/Soul Print Realization

What I have termed, inspired by Lainer, sacred autobiography, when purified of the superficial through the process of *berur*, is itself a sacred text. It is the book of life. This is Lainer's implicit reading of the old Kabbalistic teaching from Safed that every person has their own 'letter in the Torah'. Sacred autobiography both interacts with and, occasionally, even trumps sacred text, superseding one's obligation to the written canon. The initiate will understand that, far from giving easy license to one's desires, this post-conventional path requires extraordinary discipline.

According to Lainer, one can only access this revelation through the identification and embrace of one's uniqueness. Lainer makes a strong distinction between the sense of specialness or uniqueness at an ego-ic level, which needs to be purified, and uniqueness at the enlightened level of Judah-consciousness, which is both the expression of and the path to full realization. This level of enlightenment may be achieved consistently or even just for a time in an individual's life.

It is through the depths of one's unique individuality, one's soul print, rather than in the transcendence of individuality, that one hears the voice of the infinite God in the *lehishah*, the whisper of personal revelation. It is, however, commitment to the canon of law and to rigorous practice that allows one to discern those moments accurately and to respond to the call of one's soul print, and thus to achieve the liberation of the Judah archetype.

For Lainer, in contrast with many other enlightenment teachings, uniqueness or specialness is not something to be jettisoned or transcended. Rather, it may be compared to the puzzle piece that fits uniquely into the whole. The unique shape of the individual puzzle piece is what connects one seamlessly to the 'uni-verse', the great text of divine names that is reality.

Soul print is the prism of unmediated revelation of the divine. The portal to enlightenment and its highest expression is the unique self. The path and the destination are the same.

From Soul Print to Unique Self

I have been privileged to teach the Torah of soul prints for the last twenty years. The term 'soul print' first came down to me in a talk given to some five hundred senior citizens at Kol Emet Synagogue in Del Ray Beach, Florida in 1989. Soul print meant for me then, as it still does now in part, the unique expression of divinity manifest in every human being. That expression of uniqueness is the source of human dignity, meaning, joy and obligation.

A key passage in the book, *Soul Prints*, which I wrote some ten years later, introduces the term 'unique self': 'The address of the divine commands us each to realize our highest Unique Self.' In my written communications with Ken Wilber in 2003 (republished in the footnotes to *The Evolutionary Emergent of Unique Self, A New Chapter in Integral Theory*, JITP 6:1

2011, Suny Press) I articulated Unique Self as the unique perspective of the God-realized person—who has achieved the supreme identity with the godhead—on the text. This emergent consciousness wells from the esoteric texts of the Kabbalah in which I live. When the human being transcends separate self into true self he or she becomes a unique letter in the Torah. New Torah, which from the kabbalistic perspective means New God, is literally created. The human being effects a *Tikkun*, best translated as an evolutionary unfolding of God. The essential task of Unique Self is thus according to Lainer to participate in the evolution of God. Which for Lainer is no less then the evolution of love. And love is in the details. Hence for Lainer the eros of the *Shekhinah* expresses itself in the intimate details of caring and justice that emerge from a proper judgement, beyond the letter of the law, even in the narrowest legal arena, as he characterizes for example in a teaching about small claims court. Like any great lover, true eros lives in the particulars.

One's unique letter in the Torah is the Unique Self rooted in the unique ontological perspective of the individual. This backdrop gave birth to the post metaphysical formula of Unique Self in Integral theory: True Self + Perspective = Unique Self.

In 2005, I gave a presentation on soul prints at the Integral Spiritual Center, a gathering of lineage holders brought together from several major traditions by philosopher Ken Wilber. Later, as the idea of soul print began to move from the Jewish teaching world into a wider community in the evolved form of Unique Self—as a direct result of this gathering—Wilber wisely suggested using my term 'unique self' instead of 'soul print'. This, he correctly asserted, would make the teaching equally available to all lineages, whether theistic and non-theistic. Unique Self evolved the soul print insight by soaking itself in the developmental insights of post modernity. As a result of all of these conversations, Diane Musho Hamilton and Genpo Roshi began, in the Zen-based Big Mind Process, to use the realization of unique self to characterize an emergent voice arising from the ground of Big Mind. Genpo Roshi also included a section on unique self in his book *Big Mind, Big Heart*, which he was kind to attribute to the Unique Self teaching he received (personal communication). At that time, my discussions with Ken, and later with Diane, Genpo Roshi, Sally Kempton and others, enriched the nuances of the unique self teaching. Inspired by this teaching, Terry Patten, Marco Morelli and Adam Leonard added a final chapter on unique self to their *Integral Life Practice* book, written under the supervision and guidance of Ken Wilber. I initiated with Diane Hamilton, Ken Wilber and Robb Smith, the Integral Spiritual Experience which in 2009 devoted five days with five hundred people to an exploration and transmission of the Unique Self teaching. Many who were present or who listened to the recordings adopted some version of Unique Self or Unique Gift teaching, implicitly or explicitly, into their consciousness and transmission, always enriched and mediated through their own rich lineages and unique selves. Joanne Hunt and her masterful school, Integral Coaching Canada ran a weekend for their coaches on Unique Self teaching. Sally Kempton integrated the teaching as a way of re-understanding a core teaching in her lineage, "God appears in you as you". Another teacher who has opposed Unique Self teaching on principled grounds, began to talk about his teaching being emergent from his "Unique Perspective". Articles were written comparing Unique Self and Authentic Self teaching (Zak Stein and Chris Dierkes). Important public dialogues took place with Andrew Cohen on the implications of Unique Self vs. Authentic Self. Dialogues were held with Don Beck and Suzanne Cook Greuter on the developmental arc of Unique Self. Discussion of Unique We, (which is based on Unique Self, see Volume 1 and see Dustin Diperna on Unique Self and Unique We, 2011) in relation to Unique Self began to emerge. Leading Yoga teachers began to understand Asana, yogic poses and dharma in light of Unique Self. One leading Yoga master, John Friend, wrote that Unique Self was the clearest articulation of Tantric teaching he had encountered and Michael Murphy of Esalen wrote that this teaching of Unique Self "changes the game". There are many other examples. All of this is testament neither to my ability to teach nor to the depth of my realization, but to the power of the Unique Self recognition itself which clearly wanted to emerge at this time.

In my conversations with Ken, we clarified that the notion of unique self could only find its penultimate expression after one has evolved beyond exclusive identification with separate self-ego. This is a crucial discernment, since without it, the idea of soul print can all too easily be hijacked and understood as another reification of the ego. Here again, I would like to reiterate this important truth: First, one must nullify the *ani*, the 'I', to *ayin*, nothingness (as in the Buddhist concept of *sunyatta* 'emptiness'). Only from the ground of *ayin* does the *ani* re-emerge as the unique self, the Judah archetype of Lainer.

Your Unique Self

As the soul print idea has grown in me over the last two decades, I have understood it more and more not so much as a conceptual frame but as an urgent, desperate, passionate realization. It is the realization that every human being is endowed with infinite adequacy and worth, and therefore dignity, that every human being has a story worth living, worth sharing and worth being received. Fully living our stories and having them received is the fundamental right of every person. Having one's authentic Unique Self story taken seriously is the essential dignity of a human being.

In fact, it is not only a right, it is an obligation. To realize that you have a soul print, expressed in the unique perspective of your unique self, creates radical obligation, meaning that you have something to do for yourself, for your community, and for God, that no other being that was, is, or will be, can do except you. There is a gift to be given by you alone, a healing which can be effected by you alone, a way of living, laughing, loving, being and becoming in the world that is yours alone to live. In this gift one finds radical meaning and radical joy.

Your uniqueness creates the obligation of the part which is uniquely you towards the larger whole. Your uniqueness is also the portal for you to move from your separate self into the larger Whole.

All of these teaching are implicit or explicit in the radical kabbalah of my teacher Mordechai Lainer of Izbica. The purpose of this work is not to present these teachings in popular form. Rather the intention is to, in a highly rigorous act of ecstatic scholarship, transmit to you dear reader, the lineage teaching and transmission of the sacred texts themselves, that serves as part of the basis for the Unique Self teaching and the Enlightenment of Fullness teachings (see *Essays on the Enlightenment of Fullness,* forthcoming ed. Dr. Heather Fester) that lay at the heart of World Spirituality. (see *World Spirituality Based on Integral Principles,* Ken Wilber and Marc Gafni, forthcoming). The core of this work was written in 2001 and 2002 before meeting Ken Wilber and Integral theory. Other then an occasional change and David's excellent editing I have left the formulations as they were originally written and have not re-written them to formally incorporate integral developmental theory. I prefer to let the original writing stand in the original integrity of the lineage.

May the blessing and grace of liberation, transmitted by a liberated being, Mordechai Lainer, animate your heart, mind and body as you study his text and incarnate its truth in the holy and humble audacity of your unique self.

Notes on Transliteration, Style and Citation

The edition of *Mei Hashiloah (MH)* cited herein is the most recent edition, which has become the standard. It differs from a commonly available edition cited in some scholarly articles in several significant ways. It includes an index compiled by Lainer's descendants, as well as several new sections of comments at the end of the second volume, including a second section of Likutim, which we have noted herein as 'vol. 2 Likutim 2'. In addition, the first volume adds additional headings for comments that appear at the very end, in particular separating Likutim that are not connected to particular Biblical or rabbinic texts from the preceding sections of Likutei Hashas; comments from that section are noted herein as 'vol. 1 Likutim'.

The method of transliteration for Hebrew terms and passages this work follows is a modified version of the rules for general (as opposed to scientific) transliteration found in the *Encyclopedia Judaica*. A forward or reverse apostrophe respectively indicates the letters א (') or ע ('), while the *tserei* vowel is indicated by either 'e' or the combination 'ei'. The indicator for א is omitted from the beginning and end of words (e.g., *eilav* and *vayikra*). For book and article titles and for names, indications of the letters ע ('), א ('), and of היריעה 'ה (*ha-*) have been left out. An apostrophe has also sometimes been used to separate vowels where its lack might create confusion for the English-speaking reader.

Quotation style follows British conventions, reflecting the fact that the main volume of this work was originally written as a dissertation at Oxford University. Concerning extended quotations from *Mei Hashiloah*, I have frequently included a larger portion of the Hebrew text than what has been translated in the English. The purpose of this is twofold: the English is kept more succinct in order to focus the reader on the most salient points, while the Hebrew provides a slightly more in-depth picture for the reader who can master the texts in the original language.

VOLUME 1

Mordechai Lainer of Izbica's Theology
of Unique Self and Nondual
Acosmic Humanism

INTRODUCTION TO VOLUME 1

The Paradox of Mordechai Lainer's Thought

Mordechai Joseph Lainer, the founder of the Izbica (or Izhbitzer) Chasidic dynasty, is known for the radical nature of his teachings, collected in the book *Mei Hashiloah*, and for the tremendous challenge to normative religious consciousness that he represents. Yet the nature of his thought is such that there are two schools of interpretation among scholars that are diametrically opposed to each other.

One school, originating with Joseph Weiss and continued by Morris Faierstein and most other scholars, holds that Lainer completely denies the existence of any human autonomy or will, and that therefore all human action is meaningless.[1] The other, originating with Rivka Schatz-Uffenheimer, holds that Lainer affirms radical human autonomy, even to the extent of allowing that an individual's will can override the laws of the Torah. Clearly these two views are not easily reconciled. Moreover, it is unusual that a text should yield seemingly diametrically opposed understandings. One aspect of this problem is that the term 'autonomy', with its secular implications, is anachronistic when applied to Lainer—this problem is addressed in the afterword to this volume. A more essential aspect of this problem, however, is that when Lainer says apparently contradictory things, he is actually delineating different levels of consciousness.

Levels of Consciousness

The key to understanding *Mei Hashiloah* (*MHs* below) is this understanding that different passages in the text refer to different levels of consciousness.[2] The first level of consciousness described by Lainer is the illusion of human independence. As we shall see, this illusion is an expression of divine will and plays an important role in spiritual development. However, the illusion of human freedom is shattered when a person reaches the second level of consciousness, where the human being attains a deeper understanding of the true nature of reality. The second level of consciousness, which Lainer often archetypically identifies with שבת shabbat and which we therefore term 'shabbat-consciousness', involves the complete nullification of human freedom as well as the realization of the total insignificance of human activism. The defining characteristic of the second level of consciousness is its radical theocentric axis.

Weiss, and in his wake much of Izbica scholarship, focuses on this second level of consciousness in interpreting *MHs*. However, close reading of *MHs* reveals that there is a third and higher level of consciousness whose achievement is the essential goal of Lainer's theology. The defining characteristics of this level of consciousness, which Lainer virtually always identifies with מקדש *mikdash*, the Jerusalem Temple, are radical human freedom, the ultimate ontological significance of human action, and what we term 'acosmic humanism'. Acosmic humanism is Lainer's uniquely anthropocentric reading of the classic acosmic understanding that dominates Hasidic discourse. This acosmic humanism is in fact the primary goal of Lainer's religious anthropology and thus the centerpiece of his theology. On this highest level of consciousness, all distinctions, such as theocentric versus anthropocentric, or autonomous versus heteronomous, collapse. Indeed, according to Lainer, this collapse demarcates the highest level of spiritual consciousness.

As mentioned, Weiss's reading of *MHs* focuses on Lainer's second level of consciousness. This reading is correct insofar as it describes a limited aspect of Lainer's theology. Schatz-Uffenheimer actually does focus on some material referring elliptically to the third level of consciousness. However, basing herself on narrow selection of texts, Schatz-Uffenheimer seems to confuse third-level acosmic humanism with first-level autonomy.

In this work we will show that neither Weiss's nor Schatz-Uffenheimer's view accurately reflects the fullness or depth of Lainer's theology. Instead, we will suggest that Lainer's ideal religious type is rooted in a far more nuanced and provocative theology: nondual acosmic humanism.

The Acosmic Dimension

Acosmism, the belief that there is no existence independent of divinity, is virtually an axiom for almost every Hasidic master who shaped Lainer's worldview.[3] However, it is critical to realize that acosmism can yield two different positions. The first position is theocentric, involving the effacing of man. At times the theocentric position expresses itself in a kind of quietist orientation. After all, if אלץ איז גאט *altz iz Got*, 'all is God', then there is little room for human initiative. Theocentric acosmic positions can be found in various forms in the writings of the Magid of Mezerich and many of his students, including Schneur Zalman of Liadi.[4] Theocentric acosmism can also be found at the shabbat stage of religious consciousness as outlined in *MHs*.

The second position yielded by acosmism is almost diametrically opposed to the theocentric position. According to the second, anthropocentric, position, if all is God, then humans, in some sense, are God as well. This 'incarnational theology'[5] is, as we will demonstrate, the foundation of the third and highest level of religious consciousness, whose attainment by the devotee is the goal of Lainer's religious system. A highly humanist religious anthropology lies at the heart of Lainer's thought.

The Scope and Plan of This Work

Lainer's acosmic humanism is defined by several major characteristics that will unfold over the course of this work. In Part One, I will begin by showing that individuality lies at the center of Lainer's humanism, and begin to demonstrate that Lainer's highly unique notion of individuality is not rooted in distance from the divine, but rather in the acosmic matrix that underlies his theology.

In Part Two, I trace three strands of prior Jewish rabbinic and kabbalistic thought which were woven together by Lainer to form the fabric of his notion of individuality.

In Part Three, I turn to Lainer's acosmic humanism itself. This framework includes the core features of unity consciousness, the experience of interconnectivity, participation mystique and the relational context of love, all of which demarcate the ways in which Lainer's acosmism expresses itself in a humanistic framework. It also includes the empowering nature of the acosmic realization (referred to as תקופות *tekufot* in Lainer's thought), the radical uniqueness of the individual, and the affirmation of human activism, as well as the ontic identity of human and divine, the dignity of desire, and the affirmation of the suprarational, and, finally, the explicit democratization of enlightenment. For each feature, I adduce some of the major texts in *MHs* and subject them to close readings in order to unfold the textual and ideational core of Lainer's thought.

In Part Four, I turn to the intellectual history of Lainer's acosmic humanism within prior kabbalistic thought. My goal here is not to provide an exhaustive intellectual history but to identify the elements of that history implicit in *MHs* itself. Lainer's acosmic humanism, I will argue, is a unique combination of five distinct models drawn from earlier kabbalistic traditions.

In Part Five, I reflect on possible parallels to Lainer's thought in the European Zeitgeist of his time.

In the final section, Part Six, I make some general remarks about the impact of Lainer on contemporary Jewish thought. The specific emphasis of Part Six is on Abraham Kook; there is also some discussion of Heschel and initial observations on Lainer's impact on neo-Hasidism within Orthodoxy and beyond.

Two shorter volumes are appended to this one. In volume 2, we return to our fifth model, delineated in Part Four, the 'Wisdom of Solomon'. In this volume, the sources that deal specifically with this genre and set of motifs are grouped according to theme and interpreted with respect to the overarching notion that the entirety of Lainer's theology can be found in this one multifaceted focal point of his work. In *volume 3*, passages from the *Zohar*, Luria, and the Hasidic masters are brought to show that Lainer's radical formulations were well-grounded in earlier texts. With this backdrop, we will see very clearly how Lainer elevated the Wisdom of Solomon genre beyond any of its past expressions. I also briefly adduce and analyze the Wisdom of Solomon genre in the work of Lainer's student Tzadok Hakohen towards the end of that volume.

One last methodological point, which I will return to in the afterword to this volume: I suggest throughout that the mistakes in reading Lainer's thought are often a function of working from too narrow a selection of texts. The method I have adopted to counter this problem is to demonstrate our core points by reading not merely individual texts, but rather by identifying heretofore unnoticed 'textual clusters'—large groups of passages, drawn from all over *MHs*—which all militate toward a similar understanding. This methodology will become especially clear in *volume 2*.

Precedents for Lainer's Thought

The five models mentioned above as precedents for Lainer's thought are all alluded to in *MHs*, yet they have not been discussed in prior scholarship. The first model is the ontic identity between the name of God and the name of humanity. The second model, which really is an expression of an earlier tradition, is the theory of the צדיק *tzadik*, who is often viewed as a semi-divine being, and sometimes even as actually divine. This tradition of the *tzadik*, a later expression of the old rabbinic and later kabbalistic tradition of apotheosis, expresses itself in a democratized form in Lainer's work as the Judah archetype. The third model is connected to the identification of humans as a primary source of revelation. The fourth model is the notion of the erotic merger of the human being with the שכינה *Shekhinah*, the immanent Divine, classically referred to in kabbalistic material as זיווג עם השכינה *zivug 'im ha-Shekhinah*. The fifth model is the concept of the Wisdom of Solomon and its identification with messianic fulfillment and transcendence of the law within history and within the present.

These models are the core matrices of *MHs*. The sources for these models are much older rabbinic and especially kabbalistic traditions. While Lainer does not dwell on these texts, it is possible to gather the relevant passages and reconstruct the intellectual history that undergirds Lainer's thought. This book aims to begin that project.

In making this claim, I hope to contend with the claim implicit in most Izbica scholarship and explicit in Faierstein, who wrote the only published work devoted solely to Izbica. Faierstein wrote:

> Unfortunately there are no Jewish sources or thinkers cited in *MHs* that can even remotely be considered possible forerunners of Mordechai Joseph's thought. Mordechai Joseph remains a unique thinker with a highly personal vision of Judaism.[6]

While the latter point is true, it is not for the reasons that Faierstein claims. Rather, Lainer's uniqueness lies in his original combination and extension of a series of earlier sources and ideational structures.[7]

Weiss, who preceded Faierstein, refers to Lainer's 'audacious heresy' that engenders 'radical conclusions in regards to the traditional faith of Israel'.[8]

Weiss's thesis is expressed again in his second article on Izbica, in which he writes: '…according to Mordechai Joseph, divine revelation bestowed upon a whole people, as understood in transmitted Jewish theology by the collective revelation at the Mount, has in the final analysis no real function'.[9] Actually, as will become clear, the revelation of Sinai plays a very real ontological function in Lainer's thought, even if it can at times be overridden by the personal revelation of the enlightened individual.

The project of situating Lainer in relation to previous Jewish thought also has theological ramifications that are perhaps more significant than its scholarly ramifications. In regard to theology, I believe that the more we can show affinity between Lainer and older strains of kabbalistic thought, the more significant Lainer's impact may be on contemporary Jewish theology.

Intellectual Biography

This book is devoted to analyzing the radical theology of one of the key figures in what is known as Polish Hasidism, Mordechai Lainer, who spent most of his career as a master in Izbica (also called 'Ishbitz'), a small hamlet in the Radom province of central Poland.[10] The core biographical issues of Lainer's career have been treated in other works;[11] here we will outline a limited biographical sketch that focuses specifically on several issues of particular relevance to Mordechai Lainer's theology as unfolded in this volume. Our aim is simply to note the striking interface of biography and theology in Mordechai Lainer's life.

What is referred to as the 'Polish Hasidism' school emerges in central Poland in the early nineteenth century as a result of the activity of its founding figure, Jacob Isaac Halevi, the Seer of Lublin.[12] Two distinct lines emerge from the school of the Seer. The first line is the Hasidism of Zidachov which later continues in the Komarno dynasty.[13] The second line, which gives birth to the master whose thought is the subject of this book, is the Przysucha line founded by Jacob Isaac of Przysucha, known as 'the Holy Jew', who was succeeded by his student, Simcha Bunim of Przysucha.[14] From this line emerged the Kotzk, Izbica, Gur, and Alexander Hasidic courts, all of which generated what would become central Hasidic texts and, with the notable exception of Kotzk, produced major Hasidic dynasties.

A demarcating characteristic of the Izbica Hasidic line is its emphasis on individuality.[15] This emphasis is highly developed in Mordechai Lainer's writings as a messianic and antinomian doctrine. This doctrine is reflected in the dramatic history of this Hasidic line. The Holy Jew (Jacob Isaac of Przysucha) left the court of the Seer, his master, while the latter was still living, apparently over sharp disagreements on theological issues.[16] When the Holy Jew died, although his son Yerahmiel succeeded him, most of his followers instead followed his disciple Simcha Bunim. Among his leading disciples was Menahem Mendel Halperin (aka Morgenstern), later to succeed him and become known as the Rebbe of Kotzk. He initiated the young Mordechai Lainer into the inner circle of Simcha Bunim.[17] When Simcha Bunim died unexpectedly in 1827, a number of smaller Hasidic courts emerged. However, the major successor was Menahem Mendel.[18] For thirteen years, Mordechai Lainer was a close confidante of Menahem Mendel and a leading figure in his Hasidic court. In 1839-40, for reasons that have been subject of much controversy within the Hasidic world and which have been analyzed by scholars, Mordechai Joseph, like the Holy Jew before him, broke with his teacher, and founded his own dynasty.[19]

While in Izbica the break tends to be minimized, with some versions even having the son of Menahem Mendel escort Mordechai Joseph on his way,[20] the Kotzk version of the story portrays a traumatic split which may well have contributed to the strange and terrible self-imposed isolation of Menahem Mendel during the last twenty years of his life.[21] What I want to point out for the moment is simply that both the Holy Jew and Mordechai Lainer engaged in bitter disputes with their teachers, ultimately rebelling against them and asserting their own independence. The implicit theological construct which finds expression in this historical moment is that a person can access a unique understanding of the divine will, unmediated by teacher or tradition, which may even override the authority of both teacher and tradition. This is, as we shall see, a key dimension of Lainer's theology.

Secular Influences

Part Five of this volume will outline nine striking parallels between the religious thought of Mordechai Lainer and the guiding spirit and principles of the Romantic movement. It is possible that there was no direct contact between Lainer and Romantic literature and that the striking parallels are the result of participating in the same Zeitgeist. However, it is also quite possible that some direct exposure to secular knowledge was part of the spiritual patrimony inherited by Mordechai Lainer through the Przysucha-Kotzk line. Lainer's teacher, Simcha Bunim, had a rather atypical background for a Hasidic rebbe.[22] In his initial career, he was a traveling lumber merchant who did business in Danzig and other large cities. Later he qualified as a pharmacist and earned his livelihood in this way for many years. He was known to have attended the theatre and played cards. Simcha Bunim's detractors argued that he had been contaminated by the secular world. Even his supporters did not deny his deep involvement in the secular world. They merely claimed that he had not been tainted; his body had participated in the secular world but not his soul.

Simcha Bunim might have had some real exposure to the Romantic and Idealist Movements. Indeed, Hasidim of the Przysucha school were actually accused of the study of 'dangerous' literature.[23] This even resulted in an attempt to excommunicate the Przysucha group. Lainer's friend and teacher Menahem Mendel of Kotzk, who was very involved in this controversy, is credited with convincing Simcha Bunim not to answer his accusers directly but only through a group of emissaries. Indeed, Menahem Mendel is also reported to have maintained several correspondences with the express purpose of keeping 'himself informed on developments in the wider world'.[24] Although the attempt at excommunication failed, suspicion of the secular influence within Przysucha and Kotzk was not wholly dissipated.[25] It is not impossible that Lainer's exposure to Romanticism and Idealism was not merely cultural osmosis or based on his own study but was actually part of his spiritual patrimony from his teachers Menahem Mendel and Simcha Bunim.[26] However, it is more likely that the influence was not direct but more of an osmosis of the zeitgeist in which different schools of spiritual practice accessed similar realizations of spirit.

Historical Context

The 'wider world', Poland of Lainer's time, was undergoing significant changes. The Polish revolt against Russia in 1830 brought in its wake 'a new era of qualified tolerance to Jews'.[27] This, coupled with a new Pope in 1846, Pius IX, contributed to the rapid modernization of Poland with all of the attendant enlightenment influences upon the Jewish and general community within Mordechai Lainer's lifetime. The process was accelerated even more after his death with the coronation of Alexander II as Czar of Russia in 1855 and partial emancipation of both Polish peasant farmers and Jews as a result of the Polish Farmers rebellion of 1863. This revolt, in which Jews participated, ushered in an era of tolerance, the likes of which had been previously unknown in Poland.[28] These circumstances make it all the more relevant to consider the Zeitgeist which produced Mordechai Joseph.

The Direct Influence of Kotzk

When discussing possible enlightenment influences on Lainer, it is perhaps also worthy of notice that the notion of 'sinning for the sake of God',[29] an important dimension of Mordechai Joseph's teaching, seems to have antecedents in Kotzk as well. This category in his thought is a particularly important basis for his antinomian doctrine. For Izbica (unlike his student Tzadok Hakohen), sinning for the sake of God involves no actual sin but rather only the appearance of sin.[30] In reality, the person is fulfilling the will of God, which at times transcends the narrow bounds of the law. An allusion to the complex relation of Kotzk to the standard categories of sin and mitzvah is alluded to in the following popular saying:

> What is the difference between the Hasidim of Kotzk and other Hasidim? The latter perform the commandments openly but commit transgressions in secret, while the Hasidim of Kotzk commit transgressions openly and perform the commandments secretly.[31]

Indeed, the well-known dictum of Menahem Mendel, 'Where is God? Wherever you let Him in,'[32] seems to be suggesting that God is not necessarily found in the law. This is a core principle of *MHs*. It is not superfluous to add that the most famous biographical incident in the Kotzk dynasty involves what might be seen as an act of sinning for the sake of God. Whether the incident is history or legend is for our purposes besides the point.[33] Even if it is legend, what is significant is that this specific legend became the most widespread tale about Menahem Mendel.

One version of the tale, sometimes referred to as the 'Friday Night Incident', goes as follows: Menahem Mendel is reported to have said, 'My son, do what your heart desires, for there is no law and there is no judge!' The gathering was astounded. Menahem Mendel continued, 'You don't believe me? Here is a sign: It is the Sabbath. See what I do!' With these words he grabbed the lit candles and, at least according to some versions of the story, he extinguished them, an explicit violation of Sabbath law.[34]

While one could interpret this act as a denial of God's existence, overt atheism seems a farfetched possibility for Menahem Mendel of Kotzk. It certainly does not fit with everything else we know about his teaching and life.[35] More likely, the act described in the story could be understood as a rejection of the absolute binding character of the law. One might understand in similar fashion the popular accounts in post-World War I Poland depicting a court of Kotzk which was a 'hotbed of antinomianism'[36] as well as reports like that of Jiri Langer about rumors that Menahem Mendel was seen smoking on the Sabbath.[37]

A core idea of *MHs*, which is discussed in detail below, is that the enlightened individual can access the unmediated will of God, which may even contradict the law. A careful study of Kotzk and Przysucha to determine the precise extent to which this idea has roots in Lainer's spiritual patrimony is beyond the scope of this work. However, it seems that we can safely say that on the face of it, the biographical data support such a direction.

Personal Revelation

A last biographical incident, which I am mentioning only briefly because it has been adequately addressed in previous scholarship, is the departure of Mordechai Joseph from Kotzk not long after the 'Friday Night Incident' described above. We will examine this incident in order to note its significant theological implications for Lainer's theology and self-understanding. In the description of the motivation for his departure offered by his grandson, Gershom Henokh, it is clear that he was moved by a personal divine revelation. 'After the passing of Simcha Bunim, he suffered the pain of being hidden in the cave of Adulam, for the time had not come for him to teach in public…until the word of God came and the time came and the spirit of God began to move within him'.[38] Gershom Henokh goes on to explain that the time was the year 5600, in which, according to the *Zohar*, 'the gates of supernal wisdom will be opened…and this will be close to the time of the Messiah…and at this time God sent him from the heavens to redeem him, sending him his love and truth….'.

Gershom Henokh describes a personal revelation occasioned by a specific time which, he explains, overrode the prohibition to reveal the secrets of the Torah. Although in this description, as in virtually all of those which emerge from the Izbica dynasty, the split with Kotzk is not mentioned, it is implicit. The thirteen years spent hiding in the 'cave of Adulam' is a clear reference to Lainer's thirteen years in the court of Kotzk. According to the internal tradition of Izbica, a direct personal revelation, addressed to Mordechai Joseph alone, moved him to reject both the spiritual authority and religious path of his teacher and friend Menahem Mendel.[39] The story is reported in a similar way by Isaac of Varka, a disciple, later a master himself, who remained loyal to Kotzk. When Isaac asked Mordechai Joseph about the reason for the break, Mordechai is reported to have said that he heard a heavenly voice commanding him to lead a community of Hasidim. Isaac is supposed to have replied by comparing this voice to the voice heard by the young Samuel in the house of Eli the high priest. Samuel hears the divine voice and goes to Eli to ask its meaning. The clear implication is that Mordechai Joseph should have gone to Menahem Mendel to find out the nature of the voice.[40] This of course is the crux of the argument between Mordechai Joseph and virtually the whole Hasidic movement. According to Mordechai Joseph, one is able to and must interpret the divine voice individually. One cannot rely on any outsider to interpret[41] one's own unique personal revelation.

Messianic Self-Understanding

The other theological issue that is alluded to in the story of Mordechai Joseph's departure from Kotzk is Lainer's own messianic self-understanding. His departure in the fall of 1839, and his establishment of a new court in Izbica in 1840 after a short stay in Tomashov, tapped into the messianic excitement felt by all sectors of the religious community in Eastern Europe. This excitement, as noted above, was based in large part on the Zoharic forecast that in 1840 the gates of supernal wisdom would be opened, so that 'when the days of the Messiah are near even children will discover secrets of wisdom'.[42] Gershom Henokh's description of his grandfather's departure is replete with messianic allusions. Faierstein adduces the sources in which Gershom Henokh paints his grandfather in messianic colors. However, he rejects those sources as inauthentic, conjecturing that they represent Gershom Henokh's own messianic self-perception inappropriately retrojected onto Mordechai Joseph. Faierstein states:

> Messianism is not a meaningful category in Mordechai Joseph's thought. In some respects Mordechai Joseph's approach is comparable to the 'neutralization' of messianism characteristic of the Magid of Mezirech and his school. The process is different but the final result is similar.[43]

Faierstein is referring to Scholem's well-known thesis that argues for the neutralization of the messianic element in Hasidic texts.[44] Both Scholem and Faierstein's characterizations of messianism appear to be a form of what Walter Kaufmann termed 'religious gerrymandering'.[45] Moshe Idel points out that while Scholem, Buber, and Tishby all disagree in their evaluation of the nature of Hasidic texts with regard to messianism, they agree on a particular and highly limited definition of what messianism means.[46] For all of them, messianism is a temporal and public category, which must be manifested on the stage of history. Idel goes on to point out that Scholem, who assumes necessary linkage between history and messianism, is in effect imposing a 'quasi-Zionist' category on the texts. The texts themselves, however, admit many varieties of messianism, including ones that are highly private and personal.[47]

A close reading of relevant passages in *MHs* that have heretofore been overlooked by Izbica scholarship—what I term the Wisdom of Solomon genre[48]—fully supports Idel's contention about messianism in Hasidic texts. It is clear in these passages, and in the Zoharic passages upon which Lainer is consciously drawing, that messianism is not neutralized in Lainer's thought; rather, it is an active and conscious motif. Faierstein's major point—that redemption and messianism, because they are closely bound up with the process of בירור *berur* 'clarification', are fundamentally individualistic in character and not 'publicly implemented'—does not stand in the way of this conclusion.[49] To use Schatz-Uffenheimer's phrase, Mordechai Lainer's self-understanding is that he is 'revealing a new Torah for the messianic age and a new understanding of Judaism'.[50] Given all of these arguments, Gershom Henokh must be seen as accurately portraying the messianic character of his grandfather's teaching.

All of this is critical for another reason as well. The major focus of *MHs* is personified in what I have referred to above as Lainer's Judah archetype. The Judah archetype is a messianic figure who achieves enlightened consciousness in a pre-eschaton reality. A close reading of internal sources in *MHs* along with Gershom Henokh's description of his grandfather is that Mordechai Lainer views himself as a manifestation of this archetype. Gershom Henokh, in his reference to the years his grandfather 'spent hidden in the cave of Adulam', is identifying Mordechai Joseph with King David and with Shimon bar Yohai. David sought refuge from the murderous rage of Saul in the cave of Adulam; thirteen years is also the amount of time according to the Talmud and the *Zohar* that Shimon bar Yohai and his son spent hidden in a cave as they studied.[51] Moreover, Gershom Henokh traces Mordechai Joseph's lineage back to David.[52] The new Torah revealed in *MHs*, is, according to Gershom Henokh, vitally necessary in response to the crisis of modernity due to which every person can, without consequence, reject their Jewish identity. It is in response to this crisis that the new Torah must be revealed by Mordechai Joseph. Clearly, Mordechai Joseph is perceived both by himself and his family as a Judah-David-Messianic figure whose role it is to reveal a new Torah. Thus, *MHs*, whose central figure is the Judah archetype, must in some sense be understood as Lainer's spiritual autobiography. This work is dedicated to an analysis of the core conceptions of his new Torah.

After leaving Kotzk and setting up his own Hasidic center in Izbica, Lainer taught his theology of acosmic humanism to his Hasidim until his death in 1854. It was during these years that his grandson and redactor, the young Gershom Henokh, studied with him and ostensibly absorbed his core teachings.[53]

Textual Issues

A final issue that needs to be addressed before turning to theology of Mordechai Lainer is the nature of the book *MHs* itself. The book that we know as *MHs* is made up of two distinct volumes. The first volume was published in Vienna in 1860,[54] six years after Mordechai Joseph's death, and the second volume was published in 1922 in Lublin. Neither volume was written by Mordechai Joseph, nor did he see either volume. The process of their writing, however, may be inferred from the biographical information provided for us in three distinct sources. These are (a) the introduction to the first volume, written by Mordechai Joseph's grandson Gershom Henokh; (b) the introduction to the second volume, written after Gershom Henokh's death by his brother, named Mordechai Joseph after his grandfather; and (c) an essay on the family history written by Gershom Henokh and published in the introduction to the first volume of Beit Yaakov, his father Jacob Lainer's commentary on the Torah. Drawing on these sources, we will briefly reconstruct the history of the publication of *MHs* in terms of its ramifications for studying *MHs*.[55]

In the introduction to the first volume of *MHs*, Gershom Henokh writes, 'The words of this book were not yet written'[56] in the lifetime of Mordechai Joseph. His brother Mordechai Joseph the grandson writes in the introduction to the second volume, 'Although he had thousands of students…among them great scholars and righteous men…nonetheless there was not one of them who wrote down the Torah of our master'.[57] The reasons for this strange phenomenon, as explained by Mordechai Joseph the grandson, are rather weak. He writes that the students either did not have enough time to write, or they felt no need for the written word as the master's Oral Torah was sufficient to guide them, or they did not want to dishonor the ideas by constricting the oral discourses in a written medium. To us it seems more likely that the hesitancy to record and publish Mordechai Joseph's ideas might have to do with their controversial nature. Indeed, Gershom Henokh warns of their radical nature: 'I am aware that in several places [in *MHs*] the words will be difficult for the ear (i.e., the classically religious), which has never heard or become accustomed to these kinds of things. However I collected them only for our community, who know their true value…'.[58]

Gershom Henokh and his brother Mordechai Joseph both describe the impetus to write down Mordechai Lainer's 'Torah' as coming from Mordechai Joseph's Hasidim, who turned to Jacob Lainer in the years following Mordechai Lainer's death, urging him to record in writing his father's Torah.

Mordechai Joseph's Torah is drawn from years of oral teaching. His grandson Mordechai Joseph writes in the introduction to the second volume of *MHs* that his grandfather 'gave a daily class in Talmud according to the way of truth, and on Sabbaths and holidays he presented several hour-long discourses on matters relating to the day…and taught wisdom to his students who gathered around him…seeking guidance in…how to serve God'.[59]

It would appear then that this material comes from the period beginning when Mordechai Joseph begins his court in Izbica and ending with his death, a period of thirteen years. However, it is also possible that some of the material comes from an earlier period. Mordechai Joseph is reported to have said after the break with Menahem Mendel that he had been a disciple in Kotzk for seven years. Since he spent a total of thirteen years in Kotzk, the implication is that for the last six years he did not consider himself a disciple of Menahem Mendel.[60] It is possible that some of the material recorded in *MHs* comes from this period as well.

Gershom Henokh writes regarding the first volume of *MHs*: 'Five years after his death…I gathered [the Torah] from that which was remembered by the members of our community'. He also shares with us some of the process he used. 'As I was very young when I gathered the material…I wrote the words as I heard them'.[61] Moreover, he writes that what was gathered after his grandfather's death was only 'a fraction of a fraction of what those who learned his Torah remembered'. Thus, the material gathered in *Volume One* is from oral testimony gathered by his grandson within five years after Lainer's death, and the first volume was published six years after his death. In preface to the second volume, Mordechai Joseph the grandson writes:

> After the publication of *Volume One*, a great deal more written material was gathered by my brother, who intended to publish it. The material had already been turned over for arrangement, copying, and printing. However, before the copying work was completed, he was taken from us…and it was my merit…to publish these holy words…'[62]

He adds later in the introduction:

> Since the words were written with wondrous precision and brevity, they are 'a little that holds a lot' of great quality. Since the editing of even one letter could change the intention, I was afraid to edit [the material gathered and recorded by my brother Gershom Henokh]. I edited therefore only in places where necessity forced me.

It would appear therefore that the second volume of the oral discourses underwent some level of minor editing. Since Mordechai Joseph notes that his brother had already given the material to the printer before he died, such that the material was already complete at that time, it would seem that necessity here was not just stylistic. It is fair to conjecture that Mordechai Joseph the grandson's 'necessity' was doctrinal, referring to a softening of the most radical passages in *MHs*.[63]

One can surmise that the time lapse between a disciple hearing a homily from Mordechai Joseph and his sharing that homily with Gershom Henokh was between one and thirty-three years. Regarding the material collected by Gershom Henokh and published in the second volume of *MHs*, the time lapse is even greater. Gershom Henokh died in 1891. If we conjecture that Gershom Henokh collected the last homilies in 1880, that would mean that a minimum of 36 years.

Two other factors are worthy of note in this regard. First, we need to keep in mind the role of Gershom Henokh. It was he who selected what Torah to include and what Torah to exclude. Second, although Gershom Henokh claims to have written the homilies as he heard them, we cannot be sure that he did not change their internal structure. Specifically, there is a series of homilies in *MHs* whose full radicalism and power is muted by the order of presentation of the ideas. These homilies start by rejecting a particular radical reading, only to subtly adopt that same reading at a later point in the homily.[64] Often the reader may not notice that what was initially rejected has been reincorporated into the text. Leo Strauss wrote of literary strategies which obfuscate the truly radical ideas without excising them entirely, allowing a text to be read in two very different ways.[65] It is possible that Strauss' strategy is employed in *MHs*, whether this was Mordechai Joseph's strategy or whether this strategy was introduced by Gershom Henokh.

Four methodological observations can be derived from the nature of *MHs'* compilation. First, it was not written as a systematic work. Thus, there is the possibility of internal contradiction. Second, since the homilies were delivered over a relatively long period of time, it is also possible that evolution in Mordechai Joseph's thought is reflected in the work. Third, given the nature of its composition, one might have expected *MHs* to be a relatively fragmented and haphazard work. Perusal of *MHs*, however, yields a very different picture. It becomes immediately clear that Mordechai Joseph was presenting a coherent system with a clear set of radical core conceptions. At the same time, given the nature of the composition, the most one can expect is that while a primary conception appears in most of the texts, often a text or two does not quite fit that conception. This is the implicit assumption of all scholars who have written on Izbica, with which I concur.

The fourth and final observation is the most relevant to our thesis. Given the nature of the book's composition, it seems problematic at best to draw far-reaching conclusions based on too narrow a selection of texts. Weiss to some extent and Schatz-Uffenheimer to a much larger extent can be criticized on this basis. The method I have adopted is to draw conclusions only after identifying what I call a textual cluster, a substantial series of texts that present a particular issue in the same manner.

Notes for Introduction

1 For citations to the scholarly literature referred to in this section, please see the Afterword to this volume, where discussion and citations from the various scholars of both schools can be found.

2 Extensive scholarship exists concerning levels of consciousness as a hermeneutic key in resolving apparently contradictory sets of data, including contradictory texts. The most effective proponent of this idea in modern thought is probably philosopher Ken Wilber ('A Developmental'). Also see Keegan, 'The Evolving' and Loevinger, *Ego*.

3 See the discussion of acomism in Chapter Five. On acosmism as a central feature of Hasidic thought, see Ross, 'Shenei' 153–154. See also Elior, *Hasidic Thought* 99–115.

4 On this idea in the thought of various Hasidic masters, see Weiss, 'Via Passiva'.

5 We borrow this term from Arthur Green, who noted the appearance of this notion in certain strands of Hasidic thought (personal communication, 2004). For discussion by Green of this train of thought in Hasidism, see 'Hasidism: Discovery' 104–131.

6 Faierstein, *Hands* 110. Even Elior who, writing later than Faierstein, does seek to root Lainer's thought in the Torah of the Seer of Lublin, reads Lainer as a rupture with traditional faith, the only difference being that she suggests that the source of Lainer's starkly original thought is the Seer of Lublin ('Temurot' 408–430). For a similar view, also see Lever, *Principles* 141 n. 100. Idel (preface to Faierstein *Hands* ix–xii) notes that new religious modalities arose in Polish Hasidism. One intention of this work is to explore the continuity between some of these modalities.

7 In volume 3 we will extensively explore some of these sources related specifically to 'the Wisdom of Solomon'.

8 'Determinism' 448. The Hebrew term translated as 'radical', *hamurot*, also has the connotation of 'radically negative'.

9 'A Late Jewish Utopia', 212.

10 See Idel's brief but highly relevant discussion of Polish Hasidism in the preface to Faierstein's *Hands*.

11 See Faierstein, *Hands* 3–26.

12 For a general picture of the Seer—which is, however, somewhat of a mix of scholarship and hagiography—see Alfasi, *Hahozeh*. See also Elior, 'Bein' 393–445, and Elior, 'Temurot' 382–402, which addresses the conceptual underpinnings of both Mordechai Lainer's and the Seer of Lublin's theological systems. For a partial critique of Elior's understanding of the Seer's theology, and in particular the dialectical quality of *yesh* and *'ayin*, see Idel, *Hasidism* 112, 123, 310.

13 See Idel's brief description of the nature of this dynasty in the preface to Faierstein, *Hands* xi.

14 On Simcha Bunim, see the hagiographies by Rabinowicz (Rabbi) and Yohanan Levi Eybeschutz (*Simcha Bunim of Przysucha*). For a brief scholarly view of one

dimension of Simcha Bumin's thought, see Brill, 'Grandeur'.

15 See Faierstein, *Hands* 6; Idel, Preface to *Hands* xii.

16 Faierstein, *Hands* 4.

17 Alfasi, *Hahozeh* 91; Faierstein, *Hands* 16.

18 Magid, *Hasidism* xix.

19 Faierstein, *Hands* 17–23 and 89–93.

20 Faierstein, *Hands* 23. Magid, *Hasidism* 261 nn. 14–17, even cites written records of the Lainer family that portray Menahem Mendel himself escorting Mordechai Lainer.

21 See Faierstein, *Hands* 19–25 for a detailed discussion of the break and how it was viewed respectively in Kotzk and Izbica over the course of generations. See also Shragai, *Benetivei vol. 1* 72.

22 Faierstein *Hands* 5.

23 *Hands* 7.

24 Faierstein, *Hands* 19.

25 For further discussion of this incident, see Rabinowicz, *Rabbi* 29–31. See also Berl, *Rabi Avraham Yehoshua Heschel* 46–50.

26 It must be noted that in the internal Lainer tradition (*Dor Yesharim* 83), Mordechai Joseph is viewed as a student of Simcha Bunim and as a colleague— but not student—of Menahem Mendel.

27 Magid, *Hasidism* xvii.

28 In addition to Magid, several important studies are relevant here: Mahler, *Hasidism* 171–243; Ruerup, 'The European'; and Blejwas, 'Polish'. Of particular relevance to Mordechai Lainer, since it deals with the province of Radom in which he lived, are Penkella, 'The Socio-Cultural' and Hundert, 'An Advantage'. Also cf. Magid, *Hasidism* 259.

29 See Gellman, 'Sinning for God'.

30 This distinction between Lainer and Tzadok is the main topic of Gellman's chapter. We will have occasion to use Tzadok to explicate Lainer below in areas where they concur. However, a fuller comparison between Tzadok and Lainer is beyond the scope of this work.

31 Mahler, *Hasidism* 292, cited in Faierstein, *Hands* 6.

32 Cited in Buber, 'Tales' 277. On Kotzk epigrams, see, however, Levinger, 'Imrot'; 'Torat'.

33 For an analysis of the 'incident', which may have caused Mordecai Lainer's split with Kotzk, see Faierstein, *Hands* 11–124. On the historicity of the story, see *Hands* 123–124 and relevant footnotes there.

34 Faierstein, *Hands* 111.

35 On Menachem Mendel's teachings, see Levinger, 'Imrot'; 'Torat'.

36 Faierstein, *Hands* 118.

37 Langer, *Nine Gates* 256–261, cited in Faierstein, *Hands* 121.

38 G. H. Lainer, Introduction 10b.

39 Faierstein, *Hands* 17, 20; see also *Hands* 25.

40 Rakatz, *Siah* 4:68–69; cited in Faierstein, *Hands* 24–25.

41 Faierstein, *Hands* 78.

42 *Zohar* 1:119a, cited in G. H. Lainer, Introduction 10b. For a more detailed exposition of the messianism in Gershom Henokh's writings, particularly in regard to his understanding of his grandfather's life, see Faierstein, *Hands* 98–105.

43 *Hands* 97.

44 On Scholem's view, see *Major Trends* 329, and 'The Neutralization'; also see 'Gilgul' 244–250. See also Scholem's student Schatz-Uffenheimer, 'Hayesod'.

45 Kaufmann, *Critique* 157.

46 Idel, *Messianic* 401 nn. 1–3. For Scholem, see *The Messianic Idea*, esp. 14–37 and 212–247, 'Gilgul' 250. For Tishby, see *Hikrei* vol. 2 475–519. For a discussion of Buber's position, see Shapira, 'Shetei' 426–429. See further discussion in endnotes 379–381.

47 Idel, *Messianic* 30–35, 212, 218. For a detailed bibliography of a spiritualized understanding of redemption in Hasidic thought, see Idel, *Messianic* 235–241 and relevant footnotes there.

48 See *volume 2* for a detailed analysis of these Wisdom of Solomon texts. The messianic nature of Lainer's theology is reflected especially in *MHs* vol. 1 Likutim s.v. *ule'atid*; vol. 2 Behaalotekha s.v. *im yihyeh* (Source 5 in *volume 2*); Proverbs s.v. *ki va'ar* (Source 11 in *volume 2*). Note that in the previous edition of *MHs*, Likutim s.v. *ule'atid* is listed under the heading of Uktzin.

49 *Hands* 96.

50 See Schatz-Uffenheimer, 'Autonomiah' 555. See also Morgenstern, 'Tzipiyot'. Morgenstern provides the Kotzk background to Lainer's messianism.

51 *bShab.* 33b. See Faierstein, *Hands* 102–103.

52 G. H. Lainer, Introduction 10b.

53 See Magid, *Hasidism* xx.

54 There is some controversy among scholars as to whether it was published in Vienna or Jostefow. See Faierstein, *Hands* 9.

55 These issues are addressed by scholarship in a number of places, including Faierstein, *Hands* 9–11, and, more thoroughly, Ben Dor, *Normative* 5–10.

56 G. H. Lainer, Introduction 10b.

57 *MHs vol. 2* Introduction 5.

58 G. H. Lainer, *MHs vol. 1* Introduction 7.

59 *MHs vol. 2* Introduction 5.

60 Rakatz, *Siah* 3:15, cited in Faierstein, *Hands* 19.

61 G. H. Lainer, *Beit Yaakov*, Introduction 17.

62 *MHs vol. 2* Introduction 6.

63 See Ben Dor, *Normative* 11–12.

64 See e.g. *vol. 1* Kedoshim s.v. *beha-sidrah*; *vol. 2* 2 Samuel s.v. *vayosef.* Further examples can be found below, p. 139 and p. 215.

65 *Persecution.*

PART ONE

Uniqueness and Individuality as a Theme
in *Mei Hashiloah*

Chapter One
Individualism in Context

In this chapter, we will investigate the radical notion of individualism that defines the thought of Mordechai Lainer. I use the term 'radical' because, as I shall outline below, Lainer believes—against the weight of virtually the entire classical Jewish tradition—that the individual has the ability to access an unmediated revelation of divinity that overrides the binding normative character of the national revelation at Sinai. Moreover, the portal for this revelatory experience, according to Lainer, is not the effacement of the self but rather the identification and intensification of the person's unique individuality.

The focus in this chapter will be on primary texts within the *MHs* corpus, irrespective of the European Zeitgeist within which Lainer developed his ideas. It is worth noting here, however, that Lainer's individualism was primarily of the Romantic variety and not of the rational enlightenment variety.[1] The entire intellectual project of the Enlightenment was to assert that the individual per se was a sufficient locus of authority and dignity and therefore not inexorably bound to the larger organizing systems of religion or state. By contrast, the Romantic notion of individuality suggested that it was, paradoxically, in the revelation of the unique individual that the cosmic spirit of the divine—the God within, the natural divine—was also revealed.

Lainer's concept of individualism has largely been ignored or glossed over by scholars as not integral to his system. This, in my view, is a fundamental misreading of *MHs*. The reason for this mistake lies primarily in the claim first put forth by Joseph Weiss as to the radically theocentric nature of *MHs*. In Weiss's reading of Lainer, the human being is but a 'passive instrument'[2] of the divine. Weiss further characterizes a major thrust of Lainer's thought as establishing the 'insignificance of human action…[or] its complete nullification.'[3] Indeed, Weiss writes:

> The religious anarchy of Mordechai Joseph is not based
> on the concept of individuality of differing natures but on

3

the concept of Divine Will…Mordechai Joseph…takes no account of [the concept of the individual] or of that of the highly personal disposition of mankind, his 'inner form', the 'roots of his soul', as expressed in Cabbalistic [sic] terms, essentially logical concepts from which antinomian propositions can indeed easily be derived.[4]

Not only does this conclusion ignore key texts, but also the terms cited by Weiss (especially 'roots of his soul') and the conceptual world they imply are in fact absolutely central to *MHs*.[5]

Weiss's reading of Lainer as radically disempowering the individual is consistent throughout.[6] He writes dramatically of the 'breakthrough of divine action' which becomes manifest 'in the untrammeled power of absolute compulsion'.[7] Weiss's final sentence sums up the theocentric axis of his reading of Lainer: 'Human salvation begins when man is rendered defenseless before the divine power…' As we will discuss in the afterword to this volume, nearly all of Izbica scholarship follows Weiss's lead to varying degrees.[8] I hope to demonstrate, on the contrary, that Lainer's individualism is rather the most natural and logical manifestation of his nondual acosmic humanism. Lainer's thought has a primarily anthropocentric axis, which intends to empower man, not to enfeeble him.

The essence of my argument revolves around rethinking what a religious master might mean when he proclaims that 'All is God'. It might mean: Since all is God, there is essentially no room for humans. The human is effaced in front of an overpowering divine force. Or one might interpret the same texts very differently. If 'All is God', then human is God as well. In the spirit of the Romantic Zeitgeist in which Lainer wrote—and following the thrust of important kabbalistic traditions upon which he creatively draws—'All is God' can be a highly empowering notion in which the lines between God and humans significantly blur, with provocative implications for normative behavior and psychology.

I suggest the term 'acosmic humanism' for this theological position. Lainer's acosmism is not unique. He merely adopts in extreme form the classic acosmic position of a number of the major Hasidic masters, most notably, perhaps, Schneur Zalman of Liadi.[9] Yet his interpretation of acosmism is very different than that of his predecessors or contemporaries, yielding surprising corollaries, including radical individualism, which we examine

4

here and in Part Two. This radical individualism, which permeates the entire *MHs* corpus, is a powerful and poignant expression of Lainer's anthropocentric focus manifesting the human dimension of his acosmism. In Part Four, we will come to a fuller understanding of Lainer's individualism based on the nature of his acosmism.

The Unique Self, Dignity, and Redemption

For Lainer, every individual is absolutely unique.[10] Lainer's radical concept of uniqueness is rooted in ontology and finds expression in his reading of sacred texts, in psychology, ritual, study, and religious anthropology. He generally refers to uniqueness using one of the following terms: פרטים *peratim* 'individuals', or 'particulars'; פרט נפש ישראל *perat nefesh yisrael* 'a unique individual of Israel'; מדרגתו *madreigato* 'his (unique) level'; מעלתו השייך לו בשורשו *maʿalato ha-shayakh lo beshorsho* 'his stature, intrinsic to him at his root'; מקום השייך לו *makom ha-shayakh lo* 'the place (intrinsically) related to him'; שייך לחלקו *shayakh lehelko* 'related to his (unique) portion'; חלקו *helko* 'his portion'; הטוב השייך לו *ha-tov ha-shayakh lo* 'the good that is related to him'; and שורשו *shorsho* 'his root'.

For Lainer, the phrase לעתיד *leʿatid* 'in the future', denoting redeemed consciousness, is always an indication of ontological significance.[11] In the following passage, Lainer understands the process of *berur* as a crystallizing of uniqueness. He affirms that *leʿatid*, in the expanded consciousness of the eschaton, uniqueness will still remain a demarcating feature.

> ואפילו לעתיד...מדרגות חלוקות, אך מורא רבו לא יהיה אז, כי לא ילמוד
> איש את רעהו, אך כל מה שיחדש כל אחד בד״ת יודיע לחבירו בפנים
> שוחקות, מפני שכל אחד יעמוד מבורר על חלקו בד״ת השייך לו

> Even in the future...[there will be] distinct levels of uniqueness. However, no one will fear his teacher at that time, 'for no longer will a person teach his friend' (Jer. 31:34). Rather, he will tell his friend anything he innovates in the knowledge of Torah, with a laughing countenance, since everyone will be clearly possessed of his own unique portion of the Torah.[12]

This passage contains many key elements that I will discuss below. What is worth noting at the outset is that Lainer posits a distinction between hierarchy and uniqueness. In the eschaton, there will be no hierarchy, and

5

yet uniqueness will remain. We can understand this in terms of similar distinctions drawn in contemporary social science between pathological hierarchy, which is a tool of domination, and holistic hierarchy, which affirms uniqueness as an essential demarcating characteristic of all of reality.[13]

Thus Lainer teaches that even though in the future, מורא רבו *mora rabo* 'fear of one's teacher'—interpreted by Lainer as teacher-student hierarchy—will not exist as it does in our present level of consciousness, this will not erase the distinctiveness of each person's Torah. Indeed, the future will be the time of the ultimate *berur* of uniqueness. However, in this redeemed reality one's unique Torah will not be, as it is at present, a source of hierarchal power. Rather, everyone will share their unique Torah, the product of their singular creativity, with פנים שוחקות *panim sohakot* 'a laughing countenance.'

'Igulim (Circles) and Yosher (Straight Lines)

Another expression of the ultimate ontology of uniqueness is its relation, according to Lainer, to the classic Lurianic categories of עיגולים 'igulim 'circles' and יושר *yosher* 'straight lines.'[14] *Yosher* classically represents the male, more hierarchical dimension of reality and 'igulim the more feminine, interconnected and egalitarian aspect of reality. In Lurianic thought, עליית הנוקבא *'aliyat ha-nukva*[15] 'the ascension of the feminine' is a central feature. This represents the ultimate triumph of the נוקבא *nukva*, of 'igulim, over yosher.[16] However, according to Lainer, even in the world of 'igulim, which will ultimately defeat the world of yosher, uniqueness remains as an important feature.[17]

For Lainer, God's very selection of Israel[18] is bound up in the realization of uniqueness. The divine call to Abraham is refracted through the prism of uniqueness. Abraham realizes that his question is unique only to him and in this very singularity finds God.[19] For Lainer, uniqueness is that which gives human beings their dignity and value.[20] The essence of liberated consciousness is a profound and highly precise understanding of one's own uniqueness.[21] Uniqueness is so essential to Lainer as a demarcating characteristic of the spirit that he has difficulty reconciling himself to the legal notion that a sacrifice can, in particular cases, be offered in partnership between two people. Although he has little choice but to accept such a partnered sacrifice, since it is considered legal in biblical law, his resistance to the concept highlights the centrality of uniqueness in his thought.[22]

6

According to Lainer, any violation of the parameters of an individual's uniqueness is rectified during the Jubilee year, which, in Lainer's thought is the mechanism that allows a person to reclaim not primarily their lost wealth, but rather their lost unique story.[23] Here uniqueness is expressed in the classic lexicon that Lainer uses throughout *MHs*: מעלתו השייך לו בשורשו *ma'alato ha-shayakh lo beshorsho* 'his unique level that is intrinsically related to him in his root or source'. The loss of uniqueness caused by a person's violating the boundaries of their story is how Lainer understands the illicit strivings of the archetypal human being described in Ecclesiastes. Moreover, the illegitimate expansion of one's boundaries cannot hold because it violates the metaphysics of creation. יובל *Yovel* 'Jubilee', in Lainer's reading, is the mechanism set in place by the divine to assure that every individual returns to their root or source story.

Throughout the *MHs* corpus, Lainer reads numerous classical texts as expressing the notion that no individual is ever repeated. For Lainer, this is a demarcating characteristic of the divine universe. The census of Israel in the desert is an affirmation of the radical uniqueness of every individual. מספר *Mispar* 'number' is not a technical means of identification but rather a badge of each individual's metaphysical honor, the expression of their uniqueness.[24] For Lainer, the census in the desert is not aimed at yielding population statistics, that is to say, the final number of the community; rather, it is focused on the act of numbering every individual as the revelation of their uniqueness. Lainer states:

> עניין נשיאות ראש היה כפי מה דאיתא בגמרא אין דעתו של זה דומה לשל
> זה. כי הש״י חלק לכל אחד טובה וחיים בפני עצמו ואין אחד דומה לחבירו.
> ע״כ נאמר שאו את ראש היינו שתעמדו כל אחד על מקום השייך לו

> The idea of 'lifting up the head' (taking census) is in accordance with the Talmud (*bBer.* 58a): 'One person's mind is not similar to another person's mind'. For God apportioned goodness and life to each one in particular, and no one is similar to anyone else. It is therefore written, 'Lift up the head'. That is, every person should be in the place belonging to him.[25]

Every human being is infinitely special; that special quality is his radically unique nature, his unique self, which I have described in other works as one's 'soul print'.[26] While this uniqueness is situated within the metaphysics of community,[27] the trajectory, challenges, and destiny of a soul[28] flow from

7

it alone. Ultimately, no two souls are comparable. Both loneliness[29] and conflict result from the incommunicable nature[30] of uniqueness.

Individuality in Time and Place

It is important to note, however, that according to Lainer, radical uniqueness is not limited to the human soul. It exists for both time and place as well. For Lainer, beyond sacred time demarcated by Sabbath and holidays, a unique nature inheres in each moment in time.[31] A similar notion of radical uniqueness also appears in *MHs* in reference to place, affirming the unique character of every space well beyond the legal formalism of sacred place.[32]

The Unique We, Conflict, and Judgment

Returning to the individual, uniqueness in *MHs* is both broad and specific, meaning that individuals belong to a soul group and at the same time each individual soul is wholly specific.[33] Both the specific and broad soul groups chart the soul's destiny even as they both produce conflict and loneliness in their wake. For example, a soul might be a Judah or a Joseph soul. Each type of soul has a different destiny, and their inability to understand one another yields deep and acrimonious conflict.[34] Furthermore, because each tribe is unique, each must be judged by a different standard.[35]

The nature of divinity—and the reason for the epithet 'the wise one of (divine) secrets'—is precisely the notion of radical individuality.[36] In accounting for the diversity engendered by uniqueness, Lainer quotes the Talmudic idiom, 'These and those are the words of the living God' (*bGitin* 6b), which affirms that contradictory legal opinions can both reflect divine will.[37] Lainer further explains that the unique attributes that are the source of each tribe and soul are the cause of the legal conflicts that permeate the Talmud.[38] In a related vein, he explains that the uniqueness of Solomon and Moses is that they each contain within themselves, and thus know, the uniqueness of every individual in Israel.[39] It is this quality that allows them to judge not only in accordance with the 'general principles of law' but in accordance with the uniqueness of פרט נפש ישראל *perat nefesh yisrael*, each individual soul.

Berur (Clarification) and Uniqueness

The key to realizing a soul's destiny is what Lainer terms the religious path of *berur*, an introspection and contemplation that yields deep understanding of the unique nature of the individual soul.[40] Success in *berur* for Lainer is the demarcating characteristic of the eschaton, while the inability to do so is what produces suffering.[41]

The desire to understand the unique nature of the individual soul was the inner intention of Moses' entreaty to see God's face.[42] God responds, in Lainer's reading, with an affirmation that divinity knows the depth of unique individuality for every person, and that from a divine perspective everyone chooses their unique portion (or, in our terms, is living their story). Once again, in this passage, uniqueness is ontological, rooted in the order of the cosmos 'from the beginning of creation'. The moment of revelation for Moses in this story is in the satori-like realization that every choice made by every person is precisely the choice necessary for the realization of their uniqueness. Moreover, Lainer lays out the interpersonal implication: One who is rooted in their own soul's uniqueness will not need to violate or co-opt or otherwise impinge on חלק חברו *helek havero*, the unique portion of their friend. Lainer uses חלק *helek*, as we noted at the outset, along with other terms, to refer to the radical ontology of uniqueness.

The Desire to Know One's Story

Every person is possessed of a powerful, legitimate, desire to know and understand the contours of their uniqueness.[43] Lainer explains:

נשאת ונתת באמונה...אזהרה לכל נפש מישראל שיחקור בנפשו מה הוא
חלקו ומדרגתו

> 'Have you dealt in good faith?'...is an admonition to each person of Israel to examine his soul and find out what his portion and level may be.[44]

Not living according to the unique contours of one's soul is identified by Lainer as a lack of אמונה *emunah* faith, which is best translated here as integrity. Every person has a measure, which is appropriate to them; it is this חלק *helek*, this uniquely individual portion, that needs to guide their spiritual trajectory both in terms of normative decision and existential

9

tone. As we shall see in Chapter Twelve, the difference between the Judah and Joseph archetypes is far more than a technical relationship to *nomos*, with Joseph (and Levi) being nomian and Judah being trans-nomian.[45] Rather, each of these types has a distinctly different psycho-spiritual and existential tone. Finally, it is important to note that what I term 'soul print' is a dynamic concept for Lainer. A person is not locked in an archetype, and at different times of life may shift from one to another.[46]

The Unique *Mitzvah* (Commandment)

A fundamental idea appearing numerous times throughout *MHs* is that every person has a unique מצווה *mitzvah* commandment: לפרט זה הנפש שייכת זה המצוה 'this particular *mitzvah* is connected to this individual soul'.[47] For Lainer, however, uniqueness is not limited to normative expression. Lainer extends this idea to mean that one has a unique path not only in the world of *mitzvah* but also within the realm of what he calls דברים מותרים *devarim mutarim*—'permitted activities or things',[48] thus implying that uniqueness is much more than even a distinctly individual relationship to nomos. Similarly, Lainer makes clear that אהבה *ahavah* love and יראה *yir'ah* fear are not generic terms; rather, every person has their own unique *ahavah* and *yir'ah* 'that are connected to their own root'.[49] Lainer also suggests in this passage that difference between the generic commandments and one's unique commandment is palpable. In Lainer's nomenclature, the former literally 'weigh you down', while the latter 'lifts you up'.

Uniqueness and Joy

Uniqueness, writes Lainer, is a primary source of joy. In a Hasidic context this is significant, since joy is a crucial telos in Hasidic (and earlier mystical) thought.[50] Contemplation of one's uniqueness, symbolized in Lainer by phylacteries, is the method most effective in healing hubris,[51] even more so than the traditional method of יראה *yir'ah*, fear of God, symbolized for Lainer by ציצית *tzitzit* 'ritual fringes'. The reason is simply that knowing one's uniqueness enables one to be שמח בחלקו *same'ah behelko* 'joyous in one's portion'.[52]

Uniqueness and Sin

Indeed, for Lainer, not living one's unique חלק *helek* is a primary cause of sin, which he also equates with failure.[53] Hence a primary obligation of בירור *berur*, as we have already noted, is the identification of one's unique

10

nature. Conversely, misidentification of one's unique Torah or nature is a root cause of sin in *MHs*.[54] On the Biblical phrase כי יהיה בך איש אשר לא יהיה טהור...ויצא אל מחוץ למחנה 'If there be anyone among you who is impure... he shall go outside of the encampment' (Deut. 23:11-12), Lainer teaches:

כי ענין מכשול הזה בא לאדם מפני שמביט בד"ת שאינם שייכים לו, ולכן נאמר ויצא אל מחוץ למחנה להראות לו שאין זה מקומו כי הוא עומד מחוץ לזה

> This obstacle befalls a person who engages words of Torah that are not his. Therefore it is written that 'He shall go outside of the encampment' (Deut. 23:10)—to show that he was out of place, for he stands outside it.[55]

Lainer explains in this passage that the root source of failure is stepping out of the מחנה *mahaneh*, the encampment. While in the biblical text this refers to the encampment of Israel in the desert, it is understood by Lainer to refer to one's uniqueness or story. Leaving the unique Torah that is connected to one's unique soul is the matrix of failure.

The original fratricide in which Cain kills Abel,[56] the primordial flood[57] of Genesis, the sins of Aaron and Miriam,[58] and the sin of the children of Israel at Refidim[59] are explained by Lainer as stemming from an inability to embrace one's 'soul print', one's own level and uniqueness, thus creating in its wake—in various forms—the need to impinge on the 'soul print' of another. The core sin of גאות *ge'ut*[60] 'hubris' is rooted in 'soul print' misidentification. If one is not living their Torah, then *ge'ut* becomes a way of compensating for, and covering up, that painful truth.

Besides the damage reaching for another person's level can do to the self, it can also do significant interpersonal damage. In Lainer's understanding, when Joshua prays for the level of understanding the Torah that belonged uniquely to Moses, he almost causes Moses' death.[61]

The pain of emptiness, according to Lainer, is the natural result of not living one's soul print. This leaves one vulnerable to sin, particularly to sexual sin, which provides a pseudo-salve for the emptiness. But for one who is connected to their deep story, sexual sin has no foothold. In this way, Lainer explains the assertion in the Talmud that the midwives in Egypt were solicited for sexual favors but did not assent. Not only, says Lainer,

11

did they not assent, but they were not in any way tempted. In Lainer's reading, theirs is the story of people who are not only able to reject the enticement of unredeemed sexuality, but who are not even propositioned because אין זה שייכות להם כלל למי שדבוק בשורשו באמת 'to one who is truly attached to *shorsho* his root, [the possibility of sin] has no foothold in them at all'. [62] *Shorsho* here refers both to God and to a person's integral story, which, as we shall see below, are ontologically identical.

Uniqueness and Healing

Not only is misidentification of a soul's uniqueness a source of pathology, the converse is also true: proper identification is a source of great healing. [63] Lainer writes:

וראה הכהן והנה נרפא נגע הצרעת מן הצרוע. איתא בזה"ק (תזריע מ"ט:) הכהן סתם דא קב"ה היינו שבעת שהשי"ת מביט לפרט נפש מישראל, אז ממילא מתרפא האדם

> The priest will look and see that the plague of leprosy has been healed from the leper' (Lev. 14:3). It is written in the holy *Zohar* (3:49b),' "The priest" without further elaboration signifies God'. That is, when God looks at an individual person in Israel, that person is automatically healed. [64]

The priest in the *Zohar* text cited by Lainer is identified with God. The phrase פרט נפש ישראל *perat nefesh yisrael*, as a synonym for unique individuality, suggests that the priest heals the leper by fulfilling the person's deep need to be seen in all of their uniqueness. [65]

Notes for Chapter One

1 See below, Part Five, 'Lainer and the Romantics'. On these two basic forms of individualism, see Taylor, *Ethics of Authenticity* 25–29.

2 Weiss, 'Determinism', esp. 449.

3 Weiss, 'Determinism' 448. Among scholars who adopt Weiss's interpretation of Lainer as anti-activist, see esp. Lever, *Principles* 139–143.

4 Weiss, 'A Late Jewish Utopia' 214.

5 I believe that Weiss understood—even if he was not willing to acknowledge it—that many Lainer texts run counter to his exaggerated claim. Therefore, he makes a statement that marginalizes that which I argue is central, namely, the place of the individual in Lainer's theology: 'Although the concept of personality as setting a rhythm for individual lifelong acts is not elaborated in the teachings of Mordechai Joseph, nevertheless he does not entirely exclude this as one element in his works'. Weiss acknowledges in his concluding sentence that the notion of 'personal *mitzvah*' does occur in *MHs*, 'although', he adds, 'it does not stem from him', suggesting that this notion is extraneous to Lainer's thought.

6 Weiss, 'A Late Jewish Utopia' 231, 236, and 'Determinism' 452

7 Weiss, 'A Late Jewish Utopia' 242.

8 See Faierstein, *Hands* 53; Elior, 'Temurot' 410; similarly Feigelson, 'The Theory of Mitzvot'. Although Faierstein does devote seven lines to individuality in *MHs*, he sees it as an essentially artificial balance to his theocentric framework, a concession on Lainer's part '[s]ince he wishes to remain within the bounds of Judaism and Hasidic tradition' (*Hands* 54, also 37, 62, 66), from which he might have been excluded, according to Faierstein, as a result of his other radical doctrines.

9 On the acosmic assumption of most of Jewish mystical thought from Joseph Ergas to Abraham Kook, see Ross, 'Musag' 109–112. Also see Ross, 'Shenei' 153–155; Pachter, 'Acosmism and Theism'.

10 On uniqueness as a core construct in *MHs*, in addition to the texts cited throughout, see also *vol. 1* Proverbs s.v. *otzar nehmad*; Rosh Hashanah s.v. *banim*; *vol. 2* Bava Metzia s.v. *mai metzatiha*; Likutim Vayikra, s.v. *lo taki*.

11 On *le'atid* as a synonym for ontology, in addition to the following citation, see *MHs vol. 1* 'Ekev s.v. *vehayah*; Balak s.v. *vihineih*; Hukat s.v. *vayomer*; Ki Teitzei s.v. *zakhor*; Ecclesiastes s.v. *semah*.

12 *MHs vol. 1* Toldot, s.v. *ahi* 1. See also *vol. 1* Tzav s.v. *ha-makriv*. The quote from Jeremiah has been slightly modified in *MHs*.

13 For a discussion of these distinctions, see, e.g., Wilber, *Sex, Ecology* 23–33. On the blanket dismissal of hierarchy, see Taylor, *Sources of Self* 1–10. Taylor argues that we cannot exist without what he calls 'frameworks', which by definition involve 'a crucial set of qualitative distinctions', paralleling what Wilber (35) terms 'value hierarchy'.

14 For a general discussion of 'igulim* and *yosher*, see Pachter, 'Igulim Veyosher'.

15 See, e.g., Vital, *Eitz Hayyim* Shaar Hanukva.

13

16 For another Hasidic reading of the ascension of *'igulim* over *yosher*, see Epstein, *Maor Vashemesh* Beshalah s.v. *vataʾan Miriam*. For a scholarly analysis of the passage, see Polen, 'Miriam's Dance'. An analysis of this passage can also be found in Schneider, *Kabbalistic Writings* 225–273. On *'aliyat ha-nukva* as a core feature of redeemed conciousness, see also Schneur Zalman of Liadi, *Sidur Tefilot Lekol Hashanah* 138–139. On a more general level, two contrasting discussions of the feminine in Lurianic Kabbalah can be found in Jacobson, 'The Aspect' and Wolfson, 'Woman–The Feminine'.

17 *MHs vol. 1* Vezot Habrakhah s.v *vayehi biyeshurun*. For a discussion of the usage of *'igulim* and *yosher* a kabbalistic tradition contemporaneous with Lainer, see Pachter, 'Igulim Veyosher' 65.

18 Lainer, like most Hasidic writers of his time, asserted a particularistic, even chauvinistic world view. See endnotes 91 and 878.

19 See *MHs vol. 2* Psalms s.v. *ashrei adam*; see also *vol. 1* Lekh Lekha s.v. *vayomer*.

20 See, e.g., *MHs vol. 1* Vezot Haberakhah s.v. *yehi Reuven* 2. Uniqueness makes the person דבר שבמנין וחשוב *devar shebeminyan vehashuv*, a legal term indicating that which cannot be nullified by numerical superiority. On the relationship between the concepts of כבוד *kavod* (dignity or gravitas) and uniqueness, see *MHs vol. 2* Behaalotekha s.v. *vayomer*. For a contemporary view on uniqueness and its role in the concept of self, see Taylor, *Ethics of Authenticity* 25–29, 38–40, 62–69.

21 *MHs vol. 1* Maʿei s.v. *kein mateh* 1 and 2.

22 See *MHs vol. 2* Vayikra s.v. *adam*. Also see *vol. 2* Vayikra s.v. *im 'olah*.

23 See *MHs vol. 1* Behar s.v. *vesafarta*. This passage, in contrast with sources adduced throughout Chapter Eight, suggests that human activism cannot reconfigure the boundaries of one's personal story. See our analysis of the idea of personal story in terms of contemporary culture in Gafni, *Soul Prints*, Section Four ('Living Your Story').

24 See *vol. 1* Bemidbar s.v. *vayedaber* 1. In this passage, Lainer asserts at length that the attribute of uniqueness applies only to Israel. This is part of his paradoxical chauvinism: On one hand he radically affirms a broad and sweeping acosmism in which all emerges from the one, while on the other hand he consistently and artificially limits his acosmism to Jews. For further remarks on Lainer's chauvinism, see endnote 878. For the kabbalistic context of this position see Hallamish, 'Yahas'.

25 *MHs vol. 1* Bamidbar s.v. *se'u*. Note that the verb for 'taking census' also means 'lifting up'.

26 See Gafni, *Soul Prints*, esp. 351, where Lainer is referenced. See also the Hebrew edition of *Soul Prints*, which has footnotes not appearing in the English edition.

27 See, e.g., *MHs vol. 2* Kedoshim s.v. *vayedaber* in regard to the tribes who, despite their uniqueness, emerge from שרש אחד 'one root'. Also see *MHs vol. 1* Ki Tavo s.v. *hashkifah* on the metaphysical advantage of the individual being judged within, rather than separate from, the community, as well as *vol. 2* Isaiah s.v. *kol tzofayikh*; Berakhot s.v. *sheloshah she'akhlu* (analyzed on p. 254); and *MHs vol. 2*

Tetzaveh s.v. *vesamta*. Note how unlike this is to the individualism of the British philosophical tradition. A position strikingly similar to Lainer's is expressed by Joseph Soloveitchik in one of the last essays he wrote, 'The Community'.

28 See, e.g., *MHs vol. 1* Hukat s.v. *shim'u* where Lainer asserts that Moses' חלק *helek* was not to enter the land of Israel.

29 On the loneliness of Moses, see *MHs vol. 1*. Devarim s.v. *va'omar*. Moses' לבדו *levado* experience expresses itself in his inability to communicate his inner intention to the people. For a closely aligned reading of Moses, see Soloveitchik, *Besod Hayahid* 204–208.

30 See *MHs vol. 2* Likutim Psalms s.v. *sod Hashem liyerei'av* where סוד *sod* 'secret' is understood not as that which is forbidden to be shared but as that which cannot be shared, at least not through speech. The way to communicate *sod*, which is of the heart, is through the principle of 'that which leaves from the heart will enter the heart'. For a similar reading of *sod*, see Hakohen, *Tzidkat Hatzadik* 149. On *sod* in earlier kabbalistic literature, see Idel, *Absorbing Perfections* 184.

31 See *MHs vol. 2* Behaalotekha s.v. *vaya'asu*. Here Lainer suggests the idea of a time in which it becomes clear to the person that he must act against the 'general principles of law' in order to respond to רצון ה' *retzon Hashem*, 'the [unmediated] will of God'. See Chapter Seven. On the correlation between the soul print of person and time, see *vol. 1* Shabbat s.v. *mai Hanukah*; *vol. 2* Rosh Ha-shanah s.v. *berosh ha-shanah*; Hagigah s.v. *Rav*; Nedarim s.v. *davar zeh*.

32 On the uniqueness of place beyond legal categories, see, e.g., *vol. 2* Likutim Samuel, s.v. *vesamti makom le'ami yisrael*.

33 See, e.g., *vol. 2* Tetzaveh s.v. *vesamta*.

34 See *vol. 1* Vayeishev s.v. *vezeh* (Source 9 in volume 2) and *vol. 2* Emor s.v. *ve'asitem*, where Lainer asserts that overcoming this struggle is a demarcating characteristic of redemption.

35 See *vol. 1* Vayehi s.v. *Gad*. See also *vol. 2* Ki Tavo s.v. *ve'anu*, as well as the ten following comments that begin with 'arur'.

36 *MHs vol. 2* Teztaveh s.v. *vesamta*.

37 See *bEruvin* 14a, Ritva *ad loc.*, for a medieval interpretation asserting ontological pluralism. On pluralism in Talmudic and post-Talmudic sources, see also Sagi, *Elu Ve'elu*.

38 *MHs vol. 1* Vayehi s.v. *Gad*.

39 *MHs vol. 2* Behaalotekha s.v. *im yihyeh* (Source 5 in volume 2). See also *vol. 2* Devarim s.v. *havu* (Source 6).

40 See, e.g., *vol. 1* Psalms s.v. *Elokim*, Toldot s.v. *ahi*, Toldot s.v. *vayeira*, Mikeitz s.v. *vayehi*; *vol. 2* Korah s.v. *vayikah* (Source 20 in volume 2), Joshua s.v. *unetatem*, Isaiah s.v. *va'asim*.

41 *MHs vol. 1* Toldot s.v. *ahi*.

42 *MHs vol. 1* Ki Tisa, s.v. *vayomer ani a'avir*.

43 See, e.g., *MHs vol. 1* Bo s.v. *zot hukat*, Lekh Lekha s.v. *el ha-aretz*, Tzav s.v. *ha-makriv*. See also *vol. 1* Yitro s.v. *lo ta'asun*. According to Lainer, we need to free

ourselves from our parents' stories and find ourselves in the details of our own sacred autobiography. See *MHs vol. 1* Vayeitzei s.v. *vayeitzei*.

44 *MHs vol. 2* Ki Tisa s.v. *shishah parshiyot*.

45 'Trans-nomian' more accurately describes Lainer's thought than the term 'antinomian', which scholars have used to describe *MHs*. In our discussion of law (Chapter Eight and Chapter Ten), we will see that for Lainer going beyond the law is not a rejection of the law. Rather, it is the law itself that sensitizes a person so that they can hear the personal revelation which invites them to transcend it.

46 See *MHs vol. 1* Balak s.v. *ki lo nahash*. In this passage, Balaam praises Israel as being a people in which each knows ערכו *erkho*, their own uniqueness, and hence the moment when they must act according to one type or another.

47 *MHs vol. 2* Psalms s.v. *oheiv*.

48 See *MHs vol. 2* Beshalah s.v. *vayisa*: 'King David, of blessed memory, prayed that God turn his heart, that he receive only things which were clear, permitted, and belonging to his portion. For even something permitted, if not belonging to his portion, would be deemed greed'.

49 *MHs vol. 2* Likutim Sidur Hatefilah s.v. *vayasem belibeinu*.

50 See Shochat, 'Al Hasimhah Bahasidut'. See also Garb, 'Simhah Shel Mitzvah'.

51 *MHs vol. 1* Aharei Mot s.v. *bezot*.

52 *MHs vol. 2* Isaiah *vehayah*.

53 On the identification of failure and sin in *MHs*, see *vol. 1* Yitro s.v. *zakhor*; *vol. 2* Tetzaveh s.v. *ravu'a*, Vayikra s.v. *vayikra*. See also endnote 220.

54 Note however that in many cases sin is understood as en essential expression of being overcome by God and embodying *retzon Hashem*. See especially Sources 40–44 of volume 2, constituting the *Menutzah* sub-cluster.

55 *MHs vol. 1* Ki Teitzei s.v. *ki teitzei mahaneh*.

56 *MHs vol. 1* Bereishit s.v. *halo*. In Lainer's reading, the source of the original fratricide is jealousy, rooted in the failure to identify one's unique soul print. Cain feels that his brother has usurped his *madreigah*, his unique level or rung. Cain, suggests Lainer, is not entirely wrong, 'for if Cain had no claim, then God would not have revealed Himself to him'. Had Cain attempted to embrace his own story, he would have realized that his 'soul print' was distinct from that of his brother. Explaining God's admonition to Cain ('If you do well, it will be lifted up' Gen 4:6), Lainer teaches: שאת "Lifted up" means you will raise yourself higher and higher through your own levels…meaning, if you will serve according to תשוקתך your desire, but not according to the levels of your brother'.

57 *MHs vol. 1* Noah, s.v. *ve'atem*.

58 *MHs vol. 1* Behaalotekha s.v. *vatedaber*. Lainer attributes Miriam and Aaron's sin of slander against Moses to their inability to distinguish between their מדרגה *madreigah*, or soul print, and that of Moses.

59 *MHs vol. 1* Beshalach s.v. *vayavo*.

60 For example, in *MHs vol. 1* Beshalach s.v. *vayavo*, the people, overwhelmed by the greatness of Moses, were unable to sustain their own uniqueness. This was the

source of what Lainer calls their sin of hubris. See also *MHs vol. 1* Yitro s.v. *velo ta'aleh*. There, Lainer suggests that the karmic-like result of hubris, in which one asserts their false superiority over another, is that the other ascends and takes the first one's place (מקום *makom*).

61 *MHs vol. 1* Joshua s.v. *vayedaber*.

62 *MHs vol. 2* Likutim Shemot s.v. *vatir'ena*.

63 For a brief survey and analysis of earlier biblical, Talmudic, and Maimonidean sources that assume a correlation between healing and sin, see Soloveitchik, *On Repentance* 210–213.

64 *MHs vol. 2* Metzora s.v. *vera'ah*.

65 See also texts cited below (p. 51ff, and in endnotes 205 and 219) on healing and *hisaron*. Lainer's interpretation of the story of King Uziyahu, analyzed on p. 52, is particularly important.

Chapter Two
Personal Revelation and the Personalized Torah

A primary manifestation of Lainer's theory of uniqueness is the idea of ongoing personal revelation[1] coupled with the notion that every person has a unique portion, חלק *helek* in Torah. Weiss's presentation of personal revelation fails to see it as part of an overarching theory of personal uniqueness that is woven throughout *MHs*.[2] This is critical, because it underlies Weiss's characterization of personal revelation as anarchic.[3] It is not anarchic at all, but rather responds to a higher order than the 'general principles of law'.

The phrase used throughout *MHs* to describe personal revelation is יאיר לו *ya'ir lo*, 'he will illuminate him', or a similar permutation of the Hebrew term הארה *he'arah* 'enlightenment'. God enlightens a person with direct revelation that either points them in the proper direction or affirms the spiritual integrity of their past choices.

With Abraham, it is the latter. Lainer describes an ongoing conversation between Abraham and God.[4] Abraham suffers from the possibility that he may not have fulfilled the will of God, רצון ה' *retzon Hashem*, on many occasions. For example, he fears that perhaps he should not have saved Lot, because from Lot are born Ammon and Moab, who participate in Jerusalem's destruction. In response God grants him a *he'arah*, a personal revelation, affirming that he acted correctly, 'for indeed the house of David will eventually come forth from Lot'.

In the same passage, Abraham fears he may have violated כבוד שמים *kevod shamayim*[5] the honor of heaven through his child Ishmael. God again responds to Abraham's fear with a personal revelation. In this case, Lainer reveals to us one of the internal mechanisms of such revelations. When Avimelekh and Pikhol say to Abraham, 'God is with you in all you do', Lainer understands 'all' to refer to Ishmael. Though this was not Avimelekh's intention, Lainer suggests, citing a Zoharic dictum, 'da'at knowledge (or, wisdom) is hidden in the mouth',[6] meaning, words may have a divine revelatory status without the awareness of the speaker.[7] Lainer identifies this notion with the Talmudic idea of בת קול *bat kol*,[8] the heavenly voice, which, while inadmissible in legal proceedings, is an important normative guide nonetheless.[9] The critical issue in this passage and many others like it[10] is that the personal revelation comes in response to an individual concerned with their own spiritual status. A revelation of this nature is, by definition, an affirmation of the dignity of individuality. Indeed, according to Lainer, one of the primary purposes of prayer is to provoke such a personal revelation.[11]

Uncertainty

Personal revelation is also critical in the realm of uncertainty.[12] Lainer, discoursing on a Talmudic passage, suggests that there are five distinct realms in which certainty cannot be achieved.[13] In these arenas, in which there is no clear normative guidance from the law—the neutral zones about which Schneur Zalman of Liadi spoke so much[14]—one is to be guided by personal revelation invoked through prayer. This is termed by Lainer, based on the *Zohar*, לחישה *lehishah* 'whisper'.[15] In this sense, personal revelation cannot be validated by a source external to the person. While it is highly directed, it is not directed by the external law, but rather by the internal law determined by the unique contours of the individual soul. Often, this requires not less, but far more from the individual, than the normative law common to the entire community.[16]

It is the religious imperative of the individual to clarify personal revelation. According to Lainer, the inner goal of the binding of Isaac story is for Abraham to move from the יצר הרע *yetzer ha-ra'* evil inclination, disguised as the divine voice, to a clear apprehension of the divine will.[17] According to Lainer's radical reading of the story, though the verse says that God spoke to Abraham, that does not indicate that this is so.[18] Lainer cites the *Zohar*, which states that God spoke to Abraham through אספקלריא דלא נהרא *aspaklariya delo nahara* 'an unclear prism'.[19] Indeed, the source cited by Lainer identifies the name used to refer to God when He talks to Abraham in this passage, אלהים *Elohim*, with the *yetzer ha-ra'*.[20] The entire point of the story is Abraham's need for a clear revelation. The telos of divine service is no less than the ability to properly discern the intent of the divine voice.

However, the ultimate model for personal revelation in response to uncertainty in *MHs* is Jacob. Jacob is considered the most elevated of the patriarchs because he refused to resolve uncertainty other than through direct personal revelation, as seen in Lainer's discussion of Jacob's deathbed blessings.[21] Moreover, even if he already had yesterday a personal revelation about how to proceed in a particular situation, he would not rely on yesterday's revelation but would rather seek personal revelation anew on the same issue. Jacob is posed here in sharp contrast to the other patriarchs 'who expanded God's will בכחם *bekoham* (independently)'. Lainer concludes his discussion by saying that immediate personal revelation is both the promise of prayer and the deep nature of divine providence. It is only a person's 'turning of their face', i.e., their lack of prayer, that prevents divine revelation from illuminating their life in all of its exigencies.

The Individual's Unique *Helek* (Portion) of Torah

So far, the sources we have discussed refer to various modes of revelation other than the Torah itself, to which we now turn. While the public character of the Sinaitic theophany is nowhere formally denied by Lainer[22]—indeed, it is an axiomatic principle—Sinai is just the beginning of the story. Lainer assumes a theory of continuous revelation, which he explicitly relates to his central theme of individuality. God is נותן תורה *noten ha-torah*, constantly giving the Torah in the present and not merely in the past, according to 'what is needed in this moment, in this place, by this *nefesh*'.[23] Each human being in all the particularity of their person, place, and time must receive their own unique revelation.

What will become clearer by the end of this chapter and in Part Three is that the way to access one's unique revelation of divinity—the revelation that speaks to one's unique life—is through the specific prism of one's own unique story. Rather than effacing one's unique self in order allow one's natural divinity to manifest itself, Lainer teaches that it is only by deepening the unique self that a person becomes transparent to their divine nature. Here Lainer steps beyond the intellectual matrices that informed his thought. We will further clarify and sharpen this vital existential/ontological core of Lainer's thought as we proceed.

The Metaphysics of Individuality

Lainer's theory of individuality is rooted not in moving away from the divine center but rather in a radical locating of the human being within the divine matrix. As discussed above, autonomy for Lainer is not a flight from the divine but the realization that self is rooted in, and an expression of, the divine self. Said differently, Lainer's theory of individuality is a direct corollary of the acosmism that lies at the heart of his thought and religious life.

21

For Lainer, radical uniqueness derives from the ontological axiom that every individual, every *perat nefesh Yisrael*, is endowed by God or incarnates as God, a unique dimension of sanctity. God is the direct lineage of every member of the covenant.[24] He goes even further in two major clusters of texts, one of which links the concepts of name and uniqueness,[25] the other of which links the concepts of *retzon Hashem* and uniqueness.[26] Because name and will are the twin pillars of Lainer's understanding of acosmism, we will analyze these sources in Part Three.

Returning to the notion of one's unique Torah, what makes the individual's unique חלק *helek* in Torah ontologically meaningful is the fact that the individual is a *helek* part of God. This is a major motif of Lainer's interpretation of the census at the beginning of the book of Numbers.[27] He makes three major points. First, the counting of each person was to affirm their full uniqueness and infinite value before God. Lainer's second point is chauvinistic in its application, but important in its conceptual basis: The concepts of uniqueness and divine providence are inextricably linked. In Lainer's metaphysics, non-Jews are subject neither to the intimacy of providence nor endowed with the charisma of uniqueness. Third, Lainer moves from a language of providence or *hashgahah* to a language of the mystique of participation. The human being (or more accurately in his language, Israel) is literally a *helek* of God. Uniqueness is rooted in an acosmic metaphysics in which the human being is not merely subject to divine providence but actually participates in divinity.[28] The result of this ontology is the daring, yet obviously necessary, assertion made by Lainer that if one unique soul, נפש בפרט *nefesh biferat*, were to be missing, then divinity itself would be lacking. Lainer interprets the phrase 'This shall be the number' (Hos. 2:1) as meaning that:

שכל אחד יהי' נצרך כי מתוך כלל ישראל ניכר גדולות הש"י ובאם נחסר
אחד מכלל ישראל אז יחסר המזג. כמו שמצייירין צורת המלך על כמה
אלפים טבלאות ואם יאבד אחד מהם צורת המלך חסרה

[E]veryone will be needed, for from all of the people of Israel,
God's greatness can be seen. And if one person is missing
from all of Israel, then 'the goblet would be lacking wine'
(Cant. 7:2). Just as when the portrait of the king is drawn on
many thousands of tiles—if one of them is lost, the portrait
of the king would be lacking.[29]

This passage affirms the radical uniqueness and infinite value and dignity of every individual. Were one unique individual to be חסר *haser*, missing or lacking, then there would be a *hisaron* or lack in God. We shall see below how the concept of *hisaron* is integrally bound up with Lainer's theory of uniqueness. This passage also alludes to Lainer's activist position, which we will more fully illuminate in Chapter Eight.

Faierstein's claim that according to Lainer, humans are not active partners with God, is partly based on his assertion that theurgy is absent in Lainer's thought.[30] Passages like this one seem to show that this is incorrect. Indeed, the idea that any missing individual creates a lack in God, a defacing of the image of the king, is a theurgical idea.[31] What is true is that Lainer's theurgy is—like that of Luria—collapsed into his acosmism.[32]

Uniqueness and Law

Until this point, the antinomian potential implicit in the sources has not led to antinomian conclusions. However, we will see that Lainer's theory of personal uniqueness is inextricably bound to his antinomian impulse, even if—as we shall see in Chapter Seven—both are driven by a third, overarching, desire for the unmediated embrace of the שכינה *Shekhinah*.[33] Yet even at this point in our exploration, we can see how a person's unique מצווה *mitzvah* or *helek*, their portion in Torah, can have normative ramifications. This is true in two ways. First, a person's choices are a function of their uniqueness. Zimri and Pinhas, the daughters of Tzelofhad, all act as they do in the biblical stories because they are connected to and acting out their unique portions of Torah.[34] Second, Lainer, in two daring passages,[35] which to the best of our knowledge have no legal precedent in the classical sources,[36] suggests that one must sacrifice one's life rather than violate one's unique *mitzvah*. Generally, rabbinic sources allow or obligate martyrdom only for three major transgressions: murder, incest, and the denial of God through idolatry.[37] Lainer's extension of the obligation of martyrdom, in light of our construction of his theory of uniqueness, is elegantly simple. Since one's uniqueness is precisely their *helek Hashem* 'portion in God', i.e., their participation in the divinity, to deny that uniqueness, which is expressed through their unique *mitzvah*, is to deny divinity, or, as we have seen, to deface the image of the king. Certainly, this violation is of sufficient gravity to warrant martyrdom.

However, Lainer will further suggest that there is a level of personal revelation that directs one not only to move beyond the realm of law but to nullify the law in response to the higher imperative of one's personal revelation.[38] This major move in Lainer's thought emerges directly from the sources I have presented here. It is not an anarchic idea, as Weiss suggested, but rather a choice guided by a different controlling mechanism than law, by the integrity of each soul's unique contours. Far from anarchic, it is precise and demanding. In fact, it may be far more demanding than the mere strictures of the law.

Unique *Mitzvah* and Unique Torah: The Matrix of Antinomianism

It is in light of these ontologies that we must read the passages that claim that a unique portion of Torah and/or a unique *mitzvah* exists for every person in Israel.

> שערי ציון נקראו הדברי תורה והמצווה השייכת לנפש מיוחד, שזה נקרא
> שערים המצוינים בהלכה שלפרט זה הנפש שייכת זה המצווה ופרט אלו
> דברי תורה כפי מדריגתו, ומשכנות יעקב הם דברי תורה ומצוות בכלל, וזה
> שאמר שהשי״ת אוהב ויקר בעיניו הד״ת הנצרכים לפרט נפש בשעתו יותר
> ממשכנות יעקב

> 'The gates of Zion' refer to the words of Torah and that commandment which belongs to each individual. This is called 'the excellent[39] gates of *halakhah*' (bBer. 8a), for this commandment belongs to this particular individual, and these specific words of Torah are according to his level. 'The dwelling places of Jacob' are words of Torah and the commandments in general. This is why it says that God loves and cherishes the words of Torah that are needed by the individual at a specific time, far more than the dwelling places of Jacob.[40]

Here, uniqueness and personal revelation fully converge. As I have already observed, the term used consistently by Lainer for unique individual and unique *mitzvah* is *perat*.[41] In this passage, however, Lainer connects two critical dimensions: פרט נפש *perat nefesh* the unique individual, and פרט אלו דברי תורה *perat eilu divrei Torah* 'these specific words of Torah', that is, the unique Torah of that individual. Personal revelation to the individual, through the portal of individual uniqueness, is the revelation of one's unique Torah, including that which may move one to transcend and even contradict the law.[42] Lainer terms the law כללים *kelalim,* כללי התורה *kelalei ha-Torah,* or כללי דברי תורה *kelalei divrei Torah.*[43]

Lainer explains that the revelation of *peratei divrei Torah* לאחד יאירו ביותר בהירות יען שהוא גדול מחבירו 'illuminates one individual with more brightness because he is greater than his fellow'.[44] That is to say, the *peratim* are revealed according to the level of the *perat nefesh.*[45] It is through the prism of *perat nefesh yisrael,* the existential uniqueness of one's story, that one is able to access *peratei divrei Torah,* one's personal Torah, through unmediated personal revelation.[46]

According to Lainer, personal revelation cannot only allow one to transcend *halakhah,* it may also cause one to be יחייב לפעמים לעשות מעשה נגד ההלכה 'compelled to act against the *halakhah*'.[47] This is a quality of Judah.[48] Judah, explains Lainer, is unique in that he is connected not merely to the *kelalim* but also to the *perat nefesh.*[49] Indeed, the essence of Judah is being able to access the divine will not merely according to the *kelalim* (the general principles of Torah) but 'according to the *perat*', that is to say, the *unique individual*.[50] That unique Torah, as we have now seen, is far from being anarchic. It is also far from rendering the human being autonomous. Rather, the unique Torah possesses a commanding quality that supersedes all other sources of authority, including the law itself. This means that illumination requires the fostering of deep connection to the part of Torah that is most related to that person.[51] The personal revelation of depth in Torah can only take place, writes Lainer, when the Torah is *shayakh lenafsho,*[52] profoundly related to his unique soul.

In effect there are three stages in Lainer's presentation of individuality. In the first stage, the human being is not yet individuated. The person has not identified their unique *mitzvah,* an expression of their unique part in Torah and their unique individuality. The second level is reached when a person discovers their radical personal uniqueness. The third level is reached when a person is so deeply integrated into the divine that they merge the divine with their separate unique identity. This integration is so profound that separate identity itself collapses and the ontic identity between human and God is realized. It is at this point that a person accesses, through the prism of their radical uniqueness, the unmediated will of God.

This understanding of the stages of individuality has remained unnoted in previous works on *MHs*. As fruitful as this scholarship may be in other regards, it does not explain the mechanics of antinomianism underlying Lainer's thought. These mechanics are uncovered in the relationships between personal revelation, uniqueness, and antinomianism that will be explored throughout this volume.

Notes for Chapter Two

1 See Silman, *Kol*; Rosenberg, 'Hitgalut'. In the section 'Lainer and the Romantics', we summarize these authors' positions and relate Lainer to their models.

2 Weiss, 'A Late Jewish Utopia' 245–248.

3 Weiss, 'A Late Jewish Utopia' 214, 244. Virtually all scholarship focusing on the 'anarchic' nature of his theoretical doctrine ignores the fact that *berur* in the form of Torah and *mitzvot* remained the primary activity and focus of Lainer and his Hasidim. See Seeman, 'Martyrdom' 253–254, for elaboration on this critique.

4 *MHs vol. 2* Vayeira s.v. *vayehi*.

5 For a detailed analysis of the concept of *kevod shamayim* in Izbica, see Seeman, 'Martyrdom' 254, 269–274, esp. 272–273.

6 *Zohar* 2:123a.

7 See also *MHs vol. 2* Vayeitzei s.v. *vayishma*, where Jacob overhears a conversation among the sons of Laban and interprets it as a personal revelation: 'Even though they did not understand what they were saying, nevertheless, Jacob our father understood that God sent these words into their mouth...' Parallel ideas can be found in other thinkers (as well as in the classical rabbinic idea that one could receive a kind of prophetic revelation by inquiring about what verse a child might be studying at the moment). See Nahman of Braslav's discussion of 'divine hints' addressed to the individual (*Likutei Mohoran* sec. 54:2).

8 An identical concept of *bat kol* appears in the work of Lainer's most famous student, Tzadok Hakohen of Lublin. See *Dover Tzedek* 4.

9 *bMeg.* 32a.

10 See *vol. 1* Lekh Lekha s.v. *el ha-aretz*; Vayigash s.v. *vayizbah*; *vol. 2* Hayyei Sarah s.v. *vayosef*; Vayehi s.v. *vayehi*.

11 See, e.g., *vol. 1* Hayyei Sarah s.v. *vayehiyu*; *vol. 2* Vayehi s.v. *vayizbah*. See also *vol. 1* Vayehi s.v. *vayomer*, discussed in the next section.

12 On uncertainty in Lainer's theology, see Faierstein, *Hands* 66–68; Schatz-Uffenheimer, 'Autonomiah' 556. On uncertainty in Hasidism, see Weiss, *Mehkarim* 109–149. On uncertainty in biblical, Talmudic, and mystical sources as a key to modern theology, see Gafni, *Safek* and Ezrahi, *Olamot*.

13 See *vol. 1* Hayyei Sarah s.v. *vayehiyu*.

14 See Hallamish, 'Mishnato' 305–310.

15 On *lehishah* as personal intimate revelation, see *MHs vol. 2* Yitro s.v. *va'esa*, *vol. 2* Ki Tavo s.v. *Hashem he'emarta*. On *lehishah* as a mixture of intimacy and gentleness, see *MHs vol. 2* Ha'azinu s.v. *ha'azinu*. See also *vol. 1* Emor s.v. *emor*. On revelation and *lehishah*, *Zohar Hadash* (Yitro, *Maamar Kol Vedibur*) explains: 'For it would strike each and every one by a whisper, and then he [the person] would speak'. Although this is not a source cited by Lainer's compilers, it would seem to be important for Lainer's linking of *lehishah* and personal revelation.

16 See the discussion of 'martyrdom' for the sake of one's unique *mitzvah* on p.43.

17 See *MHs vol. 1* Vayeira s.v. *veha-Elohim*. See further discussion in volume 3 on

Source 28 (*MHs vol. 2* Vayeira s.v. *vayikra*). See also Gellman, *The Fear* 23–72. Note that Gellman considers Lainer's central concern to be uncertainty, while we consider it to be the nature of personal revelation. The term *hei'ir lo* used in this passage ties it to all the personal revelation passages in *MHs*.

18 This reading is diametrically opposed to that of Maimonides, who writes, '[A]ll that is seen by a prophet in a vision of prophecy is, in the opinion of the prophet, a certain truth…A proof for this is the fact that [Abraham] hastened to slaughter [Isaac] as he had been commanded…' (*The Guide* 3:24).

19 *Zohar* 1:120a.

20 *Zohar* 1:119b.

21 *MHs vol. 1* Vayehi s.v. *vayomer.*

22 It is however implicitly undermined; see *MHs vol. 1* Yitro s.v. *vayehi*; Matot s.v. *vayedaber; vol. 2* Beha'alotekha s.v. *im yihyeh* (Source 5 in volume 2) . See our discussion below that contrasts רצון ה' *retzon Hashem* (divine will that speaks to the individual) with כללי דברי תורה *kelalei divrei Torah* (general principles of law).

23 *MHs vol. 1* Nedarim s.v. *davar.*

24 *MHs vol. 2* Yitro s.v. *va'esa et'hem.*

25 See Chapter Nine, 'Name, Activism and Acosmic Humanism'.

26 See 'The First Quality of Will: Will and Uniqueness' and subsequent sections.

27 *MHs vol. 1* Bamidbar s.v. *vayedaber.*

28 See also *MHs vol. 1* 'Ekev s.v. *'al tomar*, where Israel is described in the verse (Deut. 32:9) by the phrase חלק ה' עמו *helek Hashem 'amo* 'a portion [part] of God is His people'. This is explained by Lainer, in a phrase evocative of the Habad school (Elior, 'HaBaD') as 'they are a *helek*—a part of God—in their depth and root'. For our purposes, what is significant is that *MHs* establishes ontological legitimacy using this metaphysical framework. See also *MHs vol. 1* Bamidbar s.v. *se'u.* We will discuss acosmic metaphysics below in Chapter Five.

29 *MHs vol. 1* Bamidbar s.v. *vayedaber* 1. The parable is of a mosaic.

30 Faierstein, *Hands* 53ff.

31 For obvious examples of theurgical ideas in *MHs,* refuting Faierstein's claim, see *MHs vol. 1* Emor s.v. *velakahta*; Shelah s.v. *beha-sidra* (Source 42 in volume 2); *vol. 2* Terumah s.v. *vayedaber,* Ha'azinu s.v. *ki*; Psalms s.v. *potei'ah*; Yitro s.v. *anokhi.* However, see Idel, *Perspectives* 267–271 on Hasidism's general move away from theurgy.

32 On Lurianic theurgy, see the important work by Menahem Kallus, 'The Theurgy', esp. Ch. 4, secs. D–2 and D–4. On Lainer's reworking of Lurianic doctrine, see the sections 'Luria and Lainer: Provisional Conclusions' and 'Revisiting Individuality in Luria and Lainer'.

33 See section 'Model Four: *Shekhinah*, The Eros of the Will of God'.

34 On the unique 'soul print' destinies and challenges of Zimri and Pinhas, see *MHs vol. 1* Pinhas s.v. *vayar.* See also *vol. 1* Balak s.v. *vehineih* and *vol. 2* Pinhas s.v. *vayomer,* which also discusses the daughters of Tzelofhad, as well as the sources cited in endnote 369.

35 *MHs vol. 1* Va'et'hanan s.v. *ve'ahavta;* Ki Teitzei s.v. *ki yikarei.*

36 However, for a possible midrashic foreshadowing, see 'Strand One: *Mitzvah Ahat* (Unique Mitzvah)'.

37 See *bSanh.* 74a and the classic dispute between Tosafot *(ad loc.)* and Maimonides *(Mishneh Torah* Hilkhot Yesodei Hatorah 5:3). Tosafot rules that while one is *obligated* to give up one's life rather than violate the three major *mitzvot,* one *may* do so for other *mitzvot* if one desires, as an act of extra piety. Of course, the Talmud itself says that when a *mitzvah,* even a minor one, becomes symbolic of Jewish identity in a particular period of persecution, then one must martyr oneself rather than violate that *mitzvah.* For Lainer, a *mitzvah* that expresses one's *unique* identity commmands martyrdom.

38 See, e.g., *MHs vol. 1* Vayeishev s.v. *vayeishev;* Vayeishev s.v. *vayehi;* Mikeitz s.v. *tishma'.*

39 The word *metzuyan* 'excellent' can also have the sense of 'special', which is how Lainer is reinterpreting it here.

40 *MHs vol. 2* Psalms s.v. *oheiv.*

41 See, e.g., *MHs vol. 1* Mas'ei s.v. *kein mateh 2; vol. 2* Psalms s.v. *ashrei; 1* Kings s.v. *ein.*

42 *MHs vol. 1* Vayeishev s.v. *vezeh* (Source 9 in volume 2).

43 See, e.g., *MHs vol. 1* Hukat s.v. *vayis'u; vol. 2* Devarim s.v. *havu.* On the specific term *divrei Torah kelalim* see *MHs vol. 1* Mas'ei s.v. *kein mateh 2.* On the relation of the *kelal* to the *perat* in *devar Torah,* see also *MHs* Ki Teitzei *vol. 2* s.v. *ki teitzei,* where Lainer teaches that only after the *kelal* is internalized in one's heart can one access the revelation of the *perat.* For a view of *kelal* and *perat* that is different than the classical position in *MHs,* particularly in its relation of בינה *binah* to *kelalim,* see *vol. 1* Vayehi s.v. *vayehi* and *vol. 1* Avot s.v. *im ein.* On the more classic under-standing of *binah* in *MHs,* see the section 'The Eros of the Will of God'.

44 *MHs vol. 2* 1 Kings s.v. *ein.*

45 *MHs vol. 1* Mas'ei s.v. *kein mateh 2; vol. 2* Psalms s.v. *oheiv.*

46 On personal revelation to the *perat* that goes beyond the revelation to the *ke-lalim,* see *MHs vol. 1* Shabbat s.v. *mai Hanukah,* discussed below on p. 248ff. On *perat nefesh* as an expression of personal revelation to the unique individual, see also *vol. 2* Isaiah s.v. *vehayah.*

47 *MHs vol. 1* Vayeishev s.v. *vezeh* (Source 9 in volume 2). On the contradiction of the law, see this representative passage, where Lainer clearly affirms the possibility of acting against the law.

48 See Chapter Twelve.

49 The relation between Judah and individuality is a major motif of *MHs.* On Ju-dah and *perat nefesh* see, e.g., *MHs vol. 2* Behaalotekha s.v. *im yihyeh.* Regarding the idea that revelation in and to the *peratim* (i.e., in the unique situation and to the unique individual) reflects the deep will of God and allows the human being to have *tekufot,* see *MHs vol. 2* Ketubot s.v. *darash Bar Kapra* (Source 18 in volume 2).

50 On revelation to the individual, see also *MHs vol. 2* Kedoshim s.v. *vayeda-*

ber; Pinhas s.v. *vayomer*; Birkat Hamazon. On the use of *perat* and *perat nefesh* in the context of personal revelation, see *MHs vol. 1* Vayehi s.v. *vayehi,* and *vol. 2* Tetzaveh s.v. *ravu'a* 2, where Lainer interprets the classical term *hashgahah peratit* ('providence') in terms of the *perat* actually participating in the divine.

51 *MHs vol. 1* Toldot s.v. *ahi.* See also *vol. 2* Vayishlah s.v. *vayishma'* and *vol. 1* Behaalotekha s.v. *vekoh* for the notion of a unique גדר *gader* 'fence' or restriction that a person accepts upon themselves, and *vol. 1* Va'et'hanan s.v. *shamor* on טעם המצווה *ta'am ha-mitzvah,* i.e., the experience and interpretation of the *mitzvah,* as being totally unique to each person (quoted in endnote 334). In addition, *vol. 1* Sukkah s.v. *mahloket* understands a person's מדרגה *madreigah* 'level' as an influence shaping one's interpretation of the law. See also 'The Unique Group, Conflict, and Judgment'. Lastly, see also *vol. 1* Matot s.v. *ish,* where Lainer explains that the differences in interpretation between R. Yohanan and Reish Lakish in Talmudic debates were לפי שורשם *lefi shorsham,* i.e., based upon the respective roots of their souls.

52 *MHs vol. 2* Proverbs s.v. *hokhmah bahutz.*

Chapter Three

The Way of *Hisaron* (Spiritual Pathology)

A critical expression of Lainer's theory of uniqueness is his notion of *hisaron* 'lack' or 'deficiency'. This topic, overlooked by most Izbica scholarship[1] and traditional interpretation, is central to Lainer's thought. In the index to *MHs* prepared by 'Izbica insiders', including a member of the current generation of Lainer's descendants,[2] the topic of *hisaron* is simply not listed. *Hisaron* is so fundamental it is difficult to believe that this omission was not intentional. A possible explanation is the radical and almost shocking nature of the idea, which does not resonate with the contemporary conservative mood in Hasidic circles. The only scholar to mention *hisaron* at all, Faierstein,[3] deals with it only briefly and makes no distinction between the three forms of *hisaron*. Furthermore, he asserts that *hisaron* in Lainer is a replacement for שבירה *shevirah*, the shattering of the vessels, in Lurianic cosmogony.[4] In the next section, I will show that Lainer's notion of חיסרון מיוחד *hisaron meyuhad*, unique lack or deficiency, is most probably based on four different sources: three distinct conceptions of *hisaron* found in Luria and a broader idea of *hisaron* found in many layers of kabbalistic literature.

Lainer speaks about *hisaron* in three primary ways, not exclusive of each other; they are united together in *MHs* into one element that forms an essential part of Lainer's notion of radical individualism. Furthermore, a hidden underlying structure in Lainer's thought—namely, Lainer's adaptation and extension of the Zoharic 'Wisdom of Solomon' genre[5]—illuminates *hisaron* with a fourth meaning as well, having highly significant overtones. In the Zoharic description, the defining image of a redeemed world, such as was said to exist in the time of Solomon, is סיהרא בשלימותא *sihara bisheleimuta* 'the moon in her fullness'.[6] Conversely, *hisaron* may be symbolized by the לבונה בחסרונה *levanah behesronah* 'the moon in its lack' or סיהרא פגימין *sihara pegimin* 'the blemished (or, damaged) moon'.[7] In Lainer's *Weltanschauung*, this language, adopted from the *Zohar*, can refer to a person's 'unredeemed consciousness' that becomes 'repaired' through *berur*. Here, however, we are primarily interested in how *hisaron* operates as part of Lainer's philosophy of radical individualism.

31

Three Readings of *Hisaron*

The first type of *hisaron* precedes the creation of humanity and is inherent in all things. Lainer views this first type of *hisaron* as a general ontological flaw which is built into the fabric of the cosmos. Because it is axiologically prior to humanity, it exists in and applies to all persons equally as well as to all of reality. This form of *hisaron* contrasts starkly with the third form of *hisaron* outlined below. Lainer views this first type of *hisaron* as the catalyst for creation. He teaches that the essential 'lack' in creation that existed before the appearance of humans 'aroused' God to create humanity.[8]

The second type of *hisaron*, which manifests itself on the human level, is also generic, a part of every person's reality in the same way that every person inhales and exhales. This notion of an ontological *hisaron* embedded in the human persona is referred to in one passage as the שורש החסרון הנמצא בלב האדם שממנו בא התפשטות לכל צד 'root of *hisaron* found in the heart of a person that causes the person to expand to all sides'.[9] The expansion described here is the shadow side of the expanded consciousness (*hitpashtut*) that manifests itself in the Judah archetype—what Lainer terms the 'moon in its fullness'.[10] When the person is not in their fullness, however, there exists a great desire to expand to every side in order to fill the emptiness. This kind of *hisaron* is close to the modern existentialist notion of emptiness. The difference, of course, is that for the existentialist,[11] all is emptiness. In contrast, for the Hasid, which is of course whom Lainer addresses, divinity is a reality in which a human being participates if they but remove the filters that deny them consciousness of their core reality.

One subtle example of the second type of *hisaron*[12] is described by Lainer as the fear of להכחיש יופי עבודתו 'damaging the beauty of one's divine service' by entering into uncertainty.[13] Jacob paradigmatically is afraid to let go of the security and safety of his absolute certainty in divine service. Risk is the antithesis of his service. The inability or refusal to take risks in divine service is, perhaps counter intuitively, described by Lainer as lack of love. To love, for Lainer, is to be willing to enter into uncertainty and the moment of *hisaron* that it might engender, for the sake of achieving higher certainty. In describing Jacob's almost desperate desire to avoid uncertainty, Lainer teaches:

בקש יעקב לישב בשלוה היינו להשמר לבל יכנוס בשום ספק כל מעשה
כי כשאדם מנהיג א"ע להסתלק מכל ספק ולשמור מכל מעשה רע אז הוא

בשלוה, וע״ז אמר לו הש״י כי בעוד האדם בגוף אין באפשר להתנהג בכ״כ
שמירה ויראה וענוה כי הש״י חפץ במעשים של האדם כי בעוה״ז צריך
להתנהג באהבה, ומעשה שאינה מבוררת כ״כ

> Jacob desired to live in tranquility, that is, to be careful regard-
> ing all deeds, so as not to enter into uncertainty… Concerning
> this God said, as long as one is in a body, it is impossible to
> behave with such carefulness and fear and humility. For God
> desires human action, for in this world man must act out of
> love and in deeds that are not so fully clarified [and hence
> enter into uncertainty].[14]

Although the person being described in these passages is Jacob, Lainer is
not describing Jacob's personal *hisaron*, unique to him. Rather, according
to Lainer, Jacob in this text is an archetype expressing a generalized fear of
uncertainty which applies to most people.[15]

Hisaron Meyuhad, Unique Shadow

The third notion of *hisaron*, which constitutes the key to Lainer's theory of individuality, is specific and unique. Lainer teaches that every human being has a unique *hisaron* that is their defining characteristic.[16] I
have drawn my teaching on Unique Shadow found in *Awakening Your
Unique Self: Notes on the Enlightenment of Fullness and the Democratization
of Enlightenment*, which significantly evolves shadow from Jung's understanding, from Lainer's sense of *Hisaron Meyuhad* which might be translated as unique lack in the sense of a unique psychological pathology.
What Lainer insists however is that we mythologize the *hisaron* instead
of pathologizing it. This core insight of mythologize don't pathologize
opens up the understanding that one's unique chisaron is the doorway
to their Unique greatness which we have called Unique Self. But we are
getting ahead of ourselves.

The second and third conceptions of *hisaron* are not exclusive; Lainer
sometimes utilizes both understandings in the same passage.[17] This third
notion, which Lainer terms חיסרון מיוחד *hisaron meyuhad*, is a major motif
in Lainer's thought, with few obvious parallels or antecedents in earlier
Jewish thought. Holiness is obtained, writes Lainer in a typical passage,
by כי כל פרט נפש יש לו פרט עבודה השייכת לנפשו שבזה ישלים חסרונו 'doing the
specific service which is related to one's soul that will complete his *hisaron*,

33

or *perat nafsho'*[18] (*perat nafsho*=unique spirit). Implied in this passage and explicit elsewhere is the link between one's unique *mitzvah* or Torah and one's unique *hisaron*. The following passage deals specifically with the curative agency of one's unique Torah:

והחסרון שיש לזה אינו דומה לזה, ע״כ באותה מדה שיודע כל אחד חסרונו בה, צריך להטיף שם תמיד אותו ד״ת השייכים לאותו חסרון

> What one lacks is not similar to what another lacks. There-
> fore, in that attribute where a person knows he is deficient, he
> needs to instill there always those words of Torah relating to
> that deficiency.[19]

Healing is not an ancillary benefit of Torah. According to Lainer, healing the unique *hisaron* with which a person is born is the essential reason for the revelation of Torah:

כי התורה לא ניתנה רק להשלים החסרון...למי שמכיר חסרונו ומוסר נפשו להשלים חסרונו, כי יראה כי באופן אחר אין לו חיים כלל

> For the Torah was only given to make *hisaron* whole…For one
> who recognizes his *hisaron* (understands his unique *hisaron*)
> is ready to give over his life to heal his *hisaron*, for he under-
> stands that [without healing his *hisaron*] he has no life at all.[20]

It is the purpose of a person's life to first identify their *hisaron* and then to identify the unique Torah and *mitzvah* that will heal it.[21] The clear underlying premise is that each person has a different path to walk based on their unique individual nature. The identification of one's uniqueness is thus a desideratum of personal redemption. Lainer often terms the path to redeemed consciousness עולם הבא *'olam ha-ba* 'the world-to-come'.[22] *'Olam ha-ba* is virtually synonymous in *MHs* with בינה *binah* or בינת הלב *binat ha-lev*.[23] *'Olam ha-ba* is, as we will see,[24] the place beyond law in which a person is governed not merely by the national revelation of Sinai but by their personal and particular law which can contradict the national revelation.

For Lainer, much like for the early Hasidic masters, the redeemed messianic experience of *'olam ha-ba* may be obtained even in the present.[25] The way to achieve *'olam ha-ba* is by healing one's unique *hisaron*. Lainer teaches:

חכמת...רומז לעבודה שע״י עבודה...יוכל לרפאות את הקודם...ודעת נקרא
החיים שבא לאדם אחר עבודה שזה נקרא חיי עולם הבא שהוא שלמות הגמור

> 'Hokhmat wisdom' (Isa. 33:6) hints that by means of 'avodah
> service (or work, toil)...one can heal that which is kodem
> prior[26]...and 'da'at knowledge' is called 'life',[27] since it comes to
> a person after 'avodah, for this is what is called 'the life of the
> world-to-come', i.e., complete perfection'.[28]

In elaborating on Lainer's theme, Tzadok Hakohen, his premier student
and a source for many of his teachings, identifies 'olam ha-ba with a person's recognizing and living their inner uniqueness.[29] The midrashic passage[30] on which Tzadok comments there deals with whether or not a person
sees their friend in 'olam ha-ba. The answer is no, which Tzadok takes to mean
that the essence of 'olam ha-ba is the infinite uniqueness of the individual; this
essence is by definition incommunicable. Naturally then, says Tzadok, a person does not see their friend in 'olam ha-ba.[31]

This interpretation, of course, resonates with Lainer, who often defines
berur as the clarification of uniqueness that brings a person to 'olam ha-ba.
'Olam ha-ba is beyond law for Lainer because once a person arrives at 'olam
ha-ba–consciousness, they have achieved a level of clarity and purity at
which they can trust the law of their own soul.

The 'olam ha-ba theme unfolds in a classic passage that has largely been
overlooked, in which Lainer dramatically reinterprets the story of King
Uziyahu,[32] related in Kings and Chronicles.[33] In the simple reading of the
Chronicles story, Uziyahu is a highly successful king who becomes arro-
gant. He oversteps his bounds by seeking to enter the Holy of Holies to
perform the ketoret or incense service. He is challenged by the priests and
struck by God with leprosy. Succeeded by his son Yotam during his lifetime, he remains in isolation until his death in a place referred to by the
text as בית החפשית beit ha-hofshit. Lainer, creatively interpreting a verse in
Proverbs, completely rereads this story. He understands the verse שממית
בידים תתפש והיא בהיכלי מלך semamit bayadayim titapes vehi beheikhalei melekh
'A lizard by its hands grasps [the wall] and it [is already] within the palace
of the king'[34] as referring to Uziyahu, who became a leper when he tried to
enter the inner sanctum of the Temple. The lizard represents hisaron and
in particular symbolizes anger and violence. In order to heal[35] this hisaron,
which was unique to his story, Uziyahu was willing to risk his life and

enter the Holy of Holies. Even though this was clearly a violation of the law, Lainer writes that this was a situation of פיקוח נפש *pikuah nefesh* 'saving a life', in which any risk is acceptable.

Of course, Lainer is broadly interpreting saving a life to refer also to a spiritual, existential threat. The Holy of Holies, like the Garden of Eden,[36] is apparently a place beyond *hisaron*, and the incense is a source of joy. According to Lainer, had Uziyahu been able to do the service of the incense, his joy would have healed his sadness and he would have reached a redeemed Edenic state, beyond *berur*, i.e., *'olam ha-ba*. By entering the Holy of Holies in violation of the law, he was responding to the higher law of his soul that sought the cure for its *hisaron*. By the very act of entering the Holy of Holies, he achieved a level of *berur*, which brought in its wake a profound freedom. This is why the text tells us that Uziyahu lived out his days in *beit ha-hofshit*, which literally means 'the house of freedom'. The house of freedom, which Lainer calls in this passage *hashlamah* 'completion', is the place beyond the law that the priests were unable to understand.[37] Thus, even though Uziyahu was not allowed to complete the offering, he still achieved *'olam ha-ba*–consciousness.

It is in healing one's unique *hisaron* that one achieves בנין עדי עד *binyan 'adei 'ad*,[38] or eternally present reality, another term that to Lainer indicates the place of freedom, of ultimate good and life, where a person responds to the divine call of their unique individual nature, beyond the boundaries of the law.[39] Lainer states: ומעתה לא היה אצלם שום חסרון וא״כ אין שייך להם ד״ת 'Now that they had no more *hisaron*, Torah was no longer relevant to them'.[40]

Of course, all this directly correlates with the radical notion we encountered earlier in Lainer, namely, that one must forfeit their life rather than violate their *mitzvah meyuhedet* 'unique commandment'. Just as one must accept martyrdom rather than violate one's unique *mitzvah*, one must similarly risk one's life and enter the Holy of Holies in search of the cure for one's unique *hisaron*.[41] It is clear why, according to Lainer, the great good that God grants a person is the direct personal revelation that makes a person aware of their unique *hisaron*.[42]

We can generally divide Lainer's approach to unique *hisaron* into what we propose to term a 'conditional' versus a 'dialectical' model. While in some passages it appears as if the healing of *hisaron* is a prior condition for attaining enlightened consciousness (הארה *he'arah* or עולם הבא *'olam ha-ba*), at other times the relationship between *hisaron* and redeemed consciousness seems far more paradoxical. This is the sense that one gets from the conclusion of the passage about Uziyahu. Yotam the son of Uziyahu is described as follows: 'ויעש הישר בעיני ה' ככל אשר עשה עזיהו אביו רק לא בא אל היכל ה' 'Yotam did that which was straight in the eyes of God, like everything which his father Uziyahu did; only he did not come into the chamber of God' (2 Chron. 27:2). Classical biblical commentary reads this simply to mean he did not sin like Uziyahu his father, who illicitly entered the Holy of Holies.[43] Lainer, turning the text on its head, reads the word *rak* 'only' as a critique of Yotam: שלמדרגה הזאת לא בא ...והוא מיעוט '[rak] means an limitation...[for Yotam] did not attain this level [of his father Uziyahu]'. If he had offered incense like his father, then בא לחיי עוה"ב מיד 'היי 'he would have immediately attained the life of the world-to-come'.

Tzadok Hakohen is much more explicit in his transmission of this teaching in the name of his teacher Lainer. He writes:

> They said, 'yeast in the dough: a lot is difficult, a little is
> appropriate' (bBer. 34a), as I heard (i.e. from Mordechai
> Lainer) in regard to Yotam, about whom it is said, 'only he
> did not come to the chamber of God' (2 Chron. 27:2); this is
> his *hisaron*; that he had no *hisaron* at all and indeed it is said:
> 'More precious than wisdom and honor is a little foolishness'
> (Eccl. 10:1)[44] that is, everyone must have a little foolishness...
> and this is perfection.[45]

Foolishness and yeast are both identified with *hisaron*. Lainer's teaching is understood in its most paradoxical sense: the *hisaron* of Yotam was that he did not have any *hisaron*! As Tzadok, Lainer's student, describes later in this passage, the need to be בקשר אחד עמו *bekesher ehad 'imo*, to be wholly 'connected' to one's *hisaron*, is what leads one toward redeemed consciousness.

This idea of *hisaron meyuhad* is of course a direct outgrowth of Lainer's radical individualism. He states:

> והנה התנהגות הש"י עם האדם אשר באותו הטובה שנתן בהמדה, במדה
> הזאת עצמה ברא בו חסרון, ע"כ לא יוכל הטובה לצאת לפועל קודם
> שיתרפא חסרונו...ואז יושע

> Indeed, God's treatment of a person is that in the attribute
> in which He set that [unique] goodness, in this attribute

37

itself He creates the deficiency. Therefore, the good cannot
be realized until the deficiency is healed…and then he will be
redeemed.[46]

Lainer makes clear that one's unique *hisaron* is a direct reflection of one's
soul print, as we have termed it.[47] The former is the gateway to the latter.
In the conditional model, it is only by healing this *hisaron* that one can access the good of one's individual soul.[48] This concept of unique pathology
and cure is essential to Lainer's understanding of the *homo religiosus* and
the nature of religious service incumbent upon this person. The essence of
perfection comes from the healing of *hisaron*.[49] Likewise, when the priest
looks at an individual with leprosy, that gaze—identified by Lainer with
the gaze of God—is curative, its purpose being no less than this healing.[50]

A Phenomenology of *Hisaron*

Stepping back from an analysis of the threefold typology of *hisaron*, we can
also approach *hisaron* from a phenomenological perspective. What emerges is that *hisaron* is the catalyst for many of the greatest values in Lainer's
theology. *Hisaron* is the catalyst for creation itself. It also catalyzes תשוקה
teshukah (passionate) 'desire' for דברי תורה חדשים *divrei Torah hadashim*[51]
'new and original Torah'. Furthermore, *hisaron* catalyzes תשוקה שאין לו גבול
teshukah she'ein lo gevul[52] 'infinite desire', an extremely high, if not the highest, value[53] in Lainer's hierarchy.

All of this suggests a certain preoccupation and even fascination with
hisaron, central to *MHs*. In seeking to develop a phenomenology of
hisaron in *MHs*, the fact that *hisaron* is identified with sin in many passages, while at the same time it is understood to be a critical catalyst for
growth and unfolding, is highly significant. When Isaac encounters his
hisaron, it paradoxically creates within him new *teshukah* for *divrei Torah*.[54]
Even more dramatically, he explains in this same passage, as a direct result
of Solomon's marriage to the daughter of Pharaoh, אשר זאת היה נחשב אצלו
לחסרון 'which was considered for him a *hisaron*', new *teshukah* was engendered in Solomon. This is considered by Lainer to be a great accomplish-
ment. All *hisaron* has a צד טוב *tzad tov* (positive dimension). Each type
of sin or *hisaron*—adultery, anger or anything else—has a dimension of
holiness.[55]

Hisaron and Uniqueness

By far the most critical affirmation of the centrality of *hisaron* in *MHs* is its structural role in Lainer's system. The primary way to identify one's unique soul portion, something for which one must forfeit one's life rather than violate it, is through one's unique *hisaron*. One's *hisaron* is, paradoxically, the very essence of one's uniqueness. Clearly, *hisaron* for Lainer is not just a sin or lack requiring discipline, but a unique psycho-spiritual dynamic in the soul that must be actively courted and engaged. It is through this engagement that religious growth and fulfillment occur. *Hisaron* must be addressed in a process Lainer calls 'healing'. Healing has a number of stages. First, one must become aware of one's unique *hisaron*. This occurs through a unique personal revelation to the individual that grants them insight. Once the *hisaron* is recognized, it can be healed in a process that Lainer often terms בירור חסרון *berur hisaron*. This can take place through a person's unique *mitzvah* or unique portion of Torah, which has the specific mystical or psychological properties necessary to heal one's unique *hisaron*. It also might happen through a more general process of *berur* that is psychospiritual or mystical in nature. This process on occasion may require that the person perform an עבירה לשמה *'aveirah lishmah* 'sin for its own sake', as in the case of Uziyahu.

Notes for Chapter Three

1 See Weiss in 'A Late Jewish Utopia' and 'Determinism', Elior in 'Temurot', Schatz-Uffenheimer in 'Autonomiah', and Seeman in 'Martyrdom'.

2 *MHs vol. 2* Index 327–383. Elhanan Reuven Goldhaber, one of the editors, is a direct descendant of Mordechai Lainer.

3 *Hands* 56–57.

4 *Hands* 56. Though Faierstein offers no real conceptual or textual matrix to support his assertion, I think Faierstein's core intuition is correct. *Shevirah* is one of the strands that informs Lainer's theory of unique *hisaron*, and while no explicit source may be adduced from Lainer for this connection, his student Tzadok Hakohen writes (*Dover Tzedek 4*):
In the order of creation there needed to be the first 'kings that died' (a code for *shevirah*) and only then the fixing, in the sense of (*bGit.* 43a), 'A person only stands firm upon the words of Torah if he has first failed in them'…and so it is with the individual *adam perati*.
However, it is key to note that while Tzadok reintroduced the *shevirah* myth, Lainer leaves it out entirely. See the sections 'Luria and Lainer: Provisional Conclusions' and 'Revisiting Individuality in Luria and Lainer'.

5 See volumes 2 and 3 of this work. See also the section 'Model Five: The Wisdom of Solomon'.

6 E.g., *Zohar* 1:149b (Source 14 in volume 3), 3:297a (Source 23 in volume 3); 3:181b. See Lainer's use of the first example in *MHs vol. 2* Proverbs s.v. *ki va'ar* (Source 11 in volume 2).

7 E.g., *Zohar* 1:181a, adduced in Tishby, *Wisdom* 403.

8 *MHs vol. 1* Bereishit s.v. *vayomer*. See also *vol. 2* Bereishit s.v. *veha-nahash*.

9 *MHs vol. 1* Proverbs s.v. *refa'ot*.

10 *MHs vol. 2* Proverbs s.v. *ki va'ar* (Source 11 in volume 2).

11 See Barrett, *Irrational Man* 23–43. See also Kaufmann, *Existentialism*, esp. the introduction.

12 On the idea of a generic ontological *hisaron* on the human level, see *MHs vol. 1* Lekh Lekha s.v. *harimoti*. Regarding generic *hisaron* on the human level, see *vol. 1* Proverbs s.v. *refa'ot*. See also *vol. 2* Lekh Lekha s.v. *vayomer*, where Lainer discusses circumcision as an agent for rectifying *hisaron*. See also *vol. 2* Vayeishev s.v. *vayehi*.

13 See *MHs vol. 1* Vayeishev s.v. *vayehi Er* regarding Jacob's fear of uncertainty. See also *vol. 1* Toldot s.v. *vaye'ehav*.

14 *MHs vol. 1* Vayeishev s.v. *vayeishev*.

15 The contrasting archetype in Lainer's thought is the Judah archetype. See Chapter Twelve. It is worth noting that the Judah persona is the only consistent archetype in *MHs*. In contrast, Jacob is characterized differently in different passages. Sometimes Jacob's unwillingness to enter into uncertainty is viewed as a positive model (see the section 'Uncertainty'). At other times, as in the passage adduced here, this is viewed as a deficiency.

16 See e.g. *MHs vol. 2* Yitro s.v. *vayishma‘* and *vol. 1* Vayeitzei s.v. *shem*, s.v. *vatomer*.

17 On the Hasidic tendency to have different strands of thought within one passage, see Green, 'Rethinking' 12. Green discusses the tendency in Hasidic writings for both the personal God and impersonal acosmism to appear in the same paragraph or even in the same sentence. In our case, of course, we are not dealing with logically exclusive ideas. Rather, as I shall show, Lainer combines two distinct understandings to develop a complex idea of *hisaron*. See, e.g., *MHs vol. 1* Bereishit s.v. *vayomer el ha-ishah*.

18 *MHs vol. 2* Sukkah s.v. *'inyan lulav*.

19 *MHs vol. 1* Ha'azinu s.v. *kise'irim*.

20 *MHs vol. 1* Shabbat s.v. *ve'amar*. See also *MHs vol. 2* Ki Tavo s.v. *ve'anu*.

21 On Torah as a healing force for *hisaron*, see also *vol. 1* Bereishit s.v. *vayomer el ha-ishah* and Vayeitzei, s.v. *vatomer*. For a different approach to the healing of *hisaron* in *MHs*, see the notion of עבודה *'avodah* 'work' (activism) as healing *hisaron*, particularly עבודה...בכל כוחו *'avodah...bekhol koho* 'service with all of his strength', in *MHs vol. 1* Korah s.v. *ve'avad*, and *vol. 1* Bekhorot s.v. *mashrei desakina*; *vol. 1* Vayeitzei s.v. *vatomer*. On the healing power of the unique *mitzvah* in relation to *hisaron*, see *vol. 1* Proverbs s.v. *ner mitzvah*.

22 See *MHs vol. 1* Isaiah s.v. *kol tzofayikh*. While this text seems to put *'olam ha-ba* consciousness in the עתיד *'atid* 'future', this is because the verse interpreted is a future vision. *'Olam ha-ba* refers to a state of consciousness available in this reality. (See endnote 212.) In particular, *'olam ha-ba* refers to an act emerging from *binat ha-lev* (an incarnation of the divine will). Similarly, the phrase *le'olmei 'ad* refers to an act that has absolute ontological value in that it is an incarnation of divine will. See also the section 'Activism Passages not Linked with Name'.

23 *Binah* 'understanding' is the *sefirah* in the kabbalistic system often referred to as the higher *Shekhinah*, which is also often termed in kabbalistic literature *'olam ha-ba*, or *hayyim*. For a discussion of this linkage in earlier kabbalistic literature, see Scholem, 'Shekhinah' 176. See also the close association between *tzadik* and *'olam ha-ba*, which is important to our discussion, in Chapter Four below.

24 In the sections 'The Eros of the Will of God' and 'Freedom and Law'.

25 On the messianic fulfillment within the present historical reality in early Hasidism, see Idel, *Messianic* 229–234. Also in this regard, see Idel's discussion of the white and black fires in Hasidic sources, *Absorbing Perfections* 64.

26 This phrase in Lainer almost always refers to unique *hisaron*. See e.g. *vol. 1* Bereishit s.v. *vayitzmah*.

27 In various passages, cited earlier and in the remainder of this section, the healing of *hisaron* brings 'healing', 'the good', and 'life', all of which are synonyms for the expanded consciousness of *'olam ha-ba* within the present reality. See next note.

28 *MHs vol. 2* Isaiah s.v. *vehayah*. It is clear in this passage, and many like it, that according to Lainer, one can move beyond the *mitzvot* even in this world. Indeed, that is the desired goal of service in this world. As described above, *'olam ha-ba* refers to a state of consciousness and not a particular future time. In Faierstein's

words, 'A person who has completed his own clarification can be said to be living in the messianic period. In effect, the messianic and pre-messianic periods are not absolute temporal opposites but relative to each individual' *(Hands 96)*. Note also in *MHs vol. 1* Behaalotekha s.v. *mei'ayin* and *vol. 1* Mas'ei s.v. *kein mateh* 1, where the state of consciousness termed 'the land of Israel' is said to contain the quality of *'olam ha-ba*.

29 *Tzidkat Hatzadik* 149. The theme of the entire passage, a *locus classicus* in *Tzidkat Hatzadik*, is a theory of radical individualism that echoes Lainer's major themes. Tzadok's remarks on *'olam ha-ba* appear in the context of this discussion. The preceding paragraph states, 'Every person has a root...of their own...as the sages said, "Just as their faces are different"... and the faces attest to interiority [which is unique in each person]' *(Tzidkat Hatzadik* 149).

30 *Shemot Rabbah* Exod. 52:3.

31 In other sources, Tzadok is more traditional in deferring the state of *'olam ha-ba* to some future eschaton. See the sources adduced by Lever, *Principles* 74. There are, however, other Tzadok texts that suggest a different direction (Lever, *Principles* 103–105).

32 *MHs vol. 1* Proverbs s.v. *semamit.*

33 2 Kings 15 and 2 Chron. 26.

34 Prov. 30:28.

35 On healing and *hisaron* in *MHs*, see *MHs vol. 1* Metzora s.v. *uva*; Vayeilekh s.v. *vayeilekh; vol. 2* Metzora s.v. *vera'ah.*

36 See *MHs vol. 2* Bereishit s.v. *hein ha-adam*, where the Garden of Eden is presented as a place of total *berur*, beyond sin. Sin in *MHs* is sometimes used interchangeably with *hisaron*; see, e.g., *MHs vol. 1* Toldot s.v. *vayeilekh*; Tazria s.v. *adam; vol. 2* Behaalotekha s.v. *uveyom*. On the possible identity between *kishalon* 'failure', which is also associated by Lainer with sin, and *hisaron*, see *vol. 1* Naso s.v. *ish.*

37 The priest is related to the archetype of Aaron and the tribe of Levi, who are consistently presented in *MHs* as the foil to the Judah archetype. Lainer describes them as seeing only the גוון *gavan* (the surface) and not לעומק *le'omek* 'in depth'; therefore, they cannot respond directly to the will of God nor can they violate general principles of law. On the Levites, see, e.g., *MHs vol. 2* Ki Tavo s.v. *arur ha-ish* (Source 43 in volume 2); on Aaron see *MHs vol. 2* Va'eira s.v. *vayikah* (Source 15 in volume 2).

38 See *MHs vol. 1* Tetzaveh s.v. *ve'eileh* 2, where Lainer describes בנין עדי עד *binyan 'adei 'ad*—a *terminus technicus* in *MHs* for the place of unmediated divine will—as the level one achieves through healing one's *hisaron*.

39 Lainer concludes the passage by saying that had Uziyahu performed the service of the incense, he would have achieved *'olam ha-ba* immediately. Clearly *'olam ha-ba* is being used by Lainer as state of consciousness and not merely a description of a faraway eschaton. While this is typical of Hasidic literature, unique to Lainer is the freedom with which he expresses the antinomian implications that *'olam ha-ba* brings in its wake.

40 *MHs vol. 1* Shabbat s.v. *ve'amar.*

41 On the requirement of radical commitment, which Lainer calls נפש מסירות *mesirut nefesh,* in healing *hisaron,* see also *MHs vol. 1* Shabbat s.v. *ve'amar.*

42 *MHs vol. 2* Bereishit s.v. *bereishit* 2. On the gift of awareness of *hisaron,* see also *vol. 2* Vayeishev s.v. *be'inyan* and Shemot s.v. *vaye'anhu.*

43 David Kimhi (Radak) *ad loc.* See also Rashi *ad loc.,* who similarly reads the verse as praising Yotam; he writes אין בו דופי *ein bo dofi* 'had no defect'.

44 See *Zohar* 3:47b which, playing on the ambiguity of the Hebrew word מן *min* (which can be interpreted as either 'than' or 'which comes from'), rereads the verse 'Greater is wisdom *than* foolishness' as 'Greater is wisdom *which comes from* foolishness' (Eccl. 2:13).

45 *Tzidkat Hatzadik* 158.

46 *MHs vol. 1* Vayeitzei s.v. *vatomer.*

47 See, e.g., *vol. 2* Proverbs s.v. *refa'ot;* Sukkah s.v. *'inyan lulav.*

48 See also *MHs vol. 1* Ha'azinu s.v. *ha-tzur.* This link finds clear echo in Tzadok; see, e.g., *Resisei Layla* 13; *Tzidkat Hatzadik* 49, 70.

49 *MHs vol 2.* Isaiah s.v. *vehayah,* discussed above, p. 52.

50 *MHs vol. 1* Metzora s.v. *vera'ah.*

51 *MHs vol. 1* Toldot s.v. *vayeishev* (Source 3 in volume 2).

52 *MHs vol. 2* Ki Teitzei s.v. *ki teitzei* 2 (Source 26 in volume 2).

53 Lainer equates *teshukah* with *hayyim* in several places; *hayyim,* to Lainer, means the full consciousness of the divine life force. See, e.g., *vol. 2* Ki Teitzei s.v. *ki teitzei* 2 (Source 25 in volume 2). *Hayyim* is virtually synonymous with the redeemed consciousness of *'olam ha-ba* which animates all reality. See discussion at endnote 207. For more on *teshukah,* see Chapter Eleven.

54 *MHs vol. 1* Toldot s.v. *vayeishev* (Source 3 in volume 2).

55 This idea is also common in early Hasidism. See, e.g., Menahem Nahum of Chernobyl on אהבה רעה *ahavah ra'ah* ('evil' or fallen love) in *Meor Einayim* 123, 62a.

PART TWO

Precedents for the Theory of Uniqueness
in *Mei Hashiloah*

Chapter Four
Introduction and Overview

In Part One, we investigated radical individualism and uniqueness in *MHs*. To fully understand the originality of Lainer's theory of uniqueness, and specifically his notion of *hisaron meyuhad*, we must inquire into two distinct areas. First we need to establish a general intellectual history of the Jewish textual sources of uniqueness, and see how it may have shaped Lainer's thought. Second, we need to gain a general understanding of the kabbalistic backdrop to the notion of *hisaron*. These inquiries will show that Lainer combined the traditions of uniqueness and *hisaron* to form the theory of *hisaron meyuhad*, moving significantly beyond each individual tradition.

In Part Two, we will outline those sources in classical Jewish texts that form four strands of thought, uniquely combined in *MHs*, which we propose as the major intellectual matrix underlying Lainer's concepts of radical individualism and *hisaron meyuhad*. Lainer understood himself to be heir to a tradition of individual uniqueness in rabbinic and post-rabbinic sources that ran as a crosscurrent to the dominant emphasis on the centrality of community in classical Jewish thought.[1] This tradition, which we term 'personal myth',[2] is a significant strand of Jewish intellectual history, although it is often obscured by the dominant 'national myth' in which community plays the central role.

Some important sources for the matrix of this tradition of personal myth have been collected by Louis Jacobs in his *Religion and the Individual*.[3] However, while Jacobs explicitly formulates his task as the identification of the Jewish intellectual crosscurrents to community, Jacobs does not significantly address what is critical to the idea of the individual, which is the notion of uniqueness itself.[4] Neither Lainer nor any of the formative strands discussed below are mentioned by Jacobs.

These four strands are independent but often interconnected in Jewish thought.[5] The first strand is the normative tradition of the 'unique *mitzvah*', rooted in rabbinic thought. The second strand is the hermeneutic tradi-

47

tion of the unique individual as the interpreter of revelation. This tradition has some Talmudic roots,[6] but was substantively transformed and developed in sixteenth-century Safed by Luria, his colleagues, and disciples. We will term this the 'one-letter' school. The third strand is the theology of 'raising the sparks', also explored in great nuance and detail by Luria in sixteenth-century Safed. The fourth strand is the theory of prophecy. The first three strands are on occasion explicitly alluded to by Lainer, but they are more often implicit in his formulation, and form part of his 'intellectual furniture.'[7]

Strand One: *Mitzvah Ahat* (Unique Mitzvah)

The concept of each person having a unique *mitzvah* critical to their personal redemption is, as we have shown, a major motif in *MHs*.[8] The source for this concept is explicit in the Talmud. Before looking at the rabbinic sources, however, two qualifications are necessary. Our purpose in adducing these sources is neither a literary nor historical nor conceptual analysis of the sources in and of themselves. Rather, we are interested in seeing the sources from the perspective of Lainer (and his kabbalistic predecessors) and understanding his elliptical references in *MHs* to the traditions they represent. For example, the Talmudic idea of 'a *single mitzvah*' may not be an expression of an ontology of uniqueness.[9] This reading of *mitzvah ahat* is a later development that was overlaid on the Talmudic sources by the kabbalistic readers.[10] Thus, we do not mean to suggest that any of the examples here serve as formal sources for Lainer; rather, they are seeds from which he developed his own very original position.

The *Mishnah* teaches, כל העושה מצווה אחת מטיבין לו ומאריכין לו ימיו ונוחל את הארץ 'Anyone who does one *mitzvah*... good is done for him, his days are lengthened and he inherits the land'.[11] The Jerusalem Talmud understands this to mean: 'One who was ייחד מצווה *yiheid mitzvah* (i.e., chose a specific *mitzvah*), never violating it...'[12] Both sources are understood by Azikri, for example, to mean that not all *mitzvot* are equal[13]; it is possible for a person to form a special relationship with a unique *mitzvah* of their choosing which will have unique redemptive power in their lives. The Talmud,[14] in an agadic passage adduced by Lainer,[15] records a conversation in which the question posed is, אבוך במאי זהיר טפי 'With what was [a particular sage's father] especially careful?'[16] The Talmud calls this זהיר טפי *zahir tafei*, indicating extra love and care in regard to a specific *mitzvah*. This particular *mitzvah* is understood to have stood the person in good stead in the

48

world-to-come. Here may well lie the literary seed that foreshadows the relationship between uniqueness and the world-to-come in Lainer.[17]

A *midrash* adds a new dimension to the idea of the *mitzvah ahat* which has explicit resonance in *MHs*: 'Anyone who does not take for himself one *mitzvah* for which is he is willing to give up his life *moser nafsho*, this also is vanity.'[18] As we have seen, Lainer argued similarly, without adducing a source, that a person must give up their life מוסר נפשו (*moser nafsho*) not only for the three cardinal sins listed in the Talmud, but also for their unique *mitzvah*.

In the medieval period, the redemptive power of *mitzvah ahat* merited dramatic formulations from unexpected sources like Maimonides,[19] echoed by Joseph Albo,[20] who suggests that through one's unique *mitzvah*, one merits *'olam ha-ba* 'the world-to-come'. Lainer makes a similar suggestion, although for him, *'olam ha-ba* is primarily a level of consciousness,[21] attainable in this world.[22] This idea finds an important echo in the kabbalistic tradition as well. In the *Raaya Mehemana* section of the *Zohar* it takes on a more holographic significance:

> When a person fulfills one *mitzvah* and no more, and he
> does it out of love and fear for the Holy One, blessed be He,
> the ten *sefirot* dwell with him because of that [*mitzvah*]. And
> anyone who fulfills one *mitzvah* properly; it is as if he fulfilled
> all two hundred and forty-eight positive commandments,
> for there is no commandment that does not include all two
> hundred and forty-eight.[23]

This holographic notion is also echoed in Elazar Azikri, who writes in this regard:

> Even though one is obligated...in all of the *mitzvot*, neverthe-
> less he should uphold one *mitzvah* with great passion and
> consistency, for the totality of Torah which the 613 com-
> mandments is called the tree of life...and one who holds a
> branch firmly, holds the entire tree.24

The notion of *mitzvah ahat* established a strong foothold in later Hasidic thought[25] through Azikri as well as through three other influential writers: Isaiah Halevi Horowitz,[26] Aron Brekhiah of Modena,[27] and Hayyim

Yosef David Azulai, better known as the Hida.[28] All of these writers were important in the dissemination of many core kabbalistic ideas. The idea of *mitzvah ahat* had substantial resonance in some of the canonical Hasidic masters in the first generation of the movement,[29] as well as in the works of some of Lainer's contemporaries. The Baal Shem Tov, like Azikri, picks up on the holographic reading of the *Zohar*:

> He who fulfills one *mitzvah*…with love, which is the attaching to him, and grasped in this *mitzvah* a *helek* part of divinity; indeed all of [God] is in his hands, as if he fulfilled all the *mitzvot*, which are the totality of His unity, a *partzuf shalem* complete divine face[30], as it were.[31]

This particular formulation, which we have seen now in three major mystical works, does not separate the individual from the larger whole but rather sees singular realization as a means of integration with the greater whole.[32]

Another one of the early masters, Moshe Hayyim Efrayim of Sudilkov, seems to limit the privilege of choosing one's unique *mitzvah* to the צדיק *tzadik* (spiritual master).[33] This, of course, emerges from the heavy emphasis on the *tzadik* that characterizes his writings, and is one of the most striking contrasts to Mordechai Lainer's more egalitarian expression of the same idea that can be found in Hasidism. It is no accident that Lainer in his affirmation of individuality almost completely effaces the role of the *tzadik*.[34]

Strand Two: The Hermeneutic One-Letter Tradition

The second major source for Lainer's theory of unique individuality, which we will term the hermeneutic one-letter tradition, emerges directly from the notion of *mitzvah ahat*. This tradition is rooted in the sixteenth-century kabbalistic schools of Safed. Although the *mitzvah ahat* and the one-letter frameworks are in some sense entirely different, the post-Lurianic Hasidic masters, including Lainer, essentially conflated the themes. Both frameworks are understood as expressing the individual's unique portion in Torah and *mitzvah*. Two short articles that address the concept of *mitzvah ahat* assume, one implicitly[35] and the other explicitly,[36] that the one-letter tradition is essentially a kabbalistic garment for the *mitzvah ahat* tradition. This conflation is not altogether accurate. The *mitzvah ahat* tradition is normative, while the one-letter tradition is hermeneutic and deeply rooted in the complex systems of Lurianic Kabbalah; what they share in common, however, is the matrix of unique individuality in which they are rooted.

This distinction is important in terms of our discussion because Lainer's original contribution to the concept of uniqueness is rooted in part in his extension of the assumptions specific to the Lurianic one-letter theorists. This will become clearer in Part Four, where we discuss the sources of acosmic humanism. Once we establish both the principle of Lainer's acosmic humanism and the centrality of will in his system, we will revisit the Safed one-letter theorists and see in what ways Lainer shares their theological world view and in what ways he moves significantly beyond them.

Here, however, we must content ourselves with analyzing the essential claims of these thinkers. The Safed hermeneutic tradition was first noticed in modern scholarship and analyzed briefly by Gershom Scholem.[37] Moshe Idel subjected the same core sources, with some important additions, to a second, subtler analysis.[38] Our key interest lies not with Idel's and Scholem's hermeneutical issues, but in the way these sources provide a foundation for conceptions of individual uniqueness present in Mordechai Lainer's thought.

It is important to note at the outset that, as Louis Jacobs has pointed out,[39] the idea of uniqueness is already found in the rabbinic sources. In the following midrashic text, which may prefigure the Lurianic one-letter tradition, the theme is the divine voice and specifically the power of that voice:

> Scripture says: 'The voice of the Lord is with power' (Psalms 29:4), not with 'his power' but with power, that is to say, according to the capacity of each individual...each person כפי כחו *kefi koho* 'according to his strength'.[40] R. Yosi ben Hanina says: If you are doubtful of this, then think of the manna that descended with a taste varying according to the taste of each Israelite...Now if the manna, which is all of one kind, became converted into so many different kinds to suit the capacity of each individual, was it not even more possible for the voice, which had power to vary according to the capacity of each individual, [to do so as well], so that no harm should come to him?[41]

Here we have a position that flirts with the idea that the nature of divine power implies the infinity of the divine voice, not least in terms of the human experience of that voice. Hearing a voice of revelation that violates one's unique individuality is harmful. The power of the divine voice is that it has the ability to project itself in a way that can be heard differently by every person.

Such an expression of pluralism might be based on two very different but complimentary understandings, the first being the limited nature of the receiver and the second being the infinite nature of the giver. Because the receiver of revelation is limited, each face of the Torah[42] is a partial expression that can only be made whole in relation to all other interpretations. Alternately, what may seem to be contradictory 'faces' or interpretations can all have ontological legitimacy and truth.[43]

The Lurianic theorists adopted a far more daring and sophisticated hybrid version of both approaches, arguing for the ontological congruence between the nature of the text and the nature of the interpreter. Just as there are six hundred thousand letters in the Torah, there are six hundred thousand souls in Israel, and every soul corresponds to a different letter. In this regard, Scholem cites a series of sources from the Safed school[44] that affirm what Scholem calls the 'infinite meaning' of the Torah. Luria writes:

> Consequently there are six hundred thousand aspects and meanings in the Torah. According to each one of these ways of explaining the Torah, the root of a soul has been fashioned in Israel. In the Messianic age every single man in Israel will read the Torah in accordance with the meaning peculiar to his root...[45]

This passage actually implies much more than the infinity of the meaning of Torah suggested by Scholem; it also suggests a parallel infinity between interpreter and text.

Helpful in expanding the full intent of the text is a key citation from Hayyim Vital.[46] This passage became the basis for later recensions of Lurianic material in two key works, *Emek Hamelekh*[47] and *Hesed LeAvraham*,[48] both critical in spreading key Lurianic ideas, including the one-letter notion, to a wider audience:

Know that the totality of souls is six hundred thousand
and not more. And the Torah is the source of the souls of
Israel for from it they were hewn and in it they are rooted.
Therefore in the Torah there are six hundred thousand
interpretations...[49]

Vital goes on to say that in each of the four levels of interpretation[50] there
are six hundred thousand interpretations. The text continues, '...it emerges
that from every interpretation there was formed a soul and in the future
every soul in Israel will merit to know the interpretation through which
he was formed'. What becomes clear here is that it is not merely that every
soul is unique and therefore capable of producing a unique interpretation.
Rather, Vital says that the souls of Israel are both rooted in, and created
by, the Torah. Each unique interpretation yields a unique soul.[51] Continues
Vital:

> In the end of days every single person in Israel will grasp and
> know all of the Torah in accordance with that interpretation
> that is aligned with the root of his soul, for through this
> interpretation he was created and brought into being.

In effect, redemption is the realization of uniqueness; indeed it would not
be inaccurate to express Vital's idea by saying simply that uniqueness *is*
being. In Part Four, we will deal more fully with the underlying assumptions
of these sources. For now, we note that uniqueness is much more than
the subjectivity of the receiver or even the infinity of divine power that
produces unique interpretation. Rather, uniqueness itself is ontologically
prior to the text.

Vital continues in the same passage:

> Every night when a person gives over his soul...and ascends
> on high; he who merits to ascend on high is taught the unique
> interpretation upon which the root of his soul depends...
> However, it is all in accordance with his deeds on that day[52]...
> Similarly, on that night they would teach him a specific verse
> or portion, for his soul was illuminated with that verse on
> that night and on another night his soul might be illuminated
> with a different verse...the verse to which the root of his soul
> was essentially related...[53]

In this dramatic formulation, Vital affirms that uniqueness is the very illumination upon which the soul depends. Vital here also refers to another dimension of uniqueness which has clear resonance in Lainer: that which results from the interface of the individual with the realm of time. This sense of uniqueness becomes clearer in another text by Vital: 'The worlds change each and every hour, and there is no hour which is similar to another...'[54] In our context, just as the individual has a 'soul print', so too does each period of time have its own quality and demand something unique of each person. In the third generation of Hasidism, we see what is perhaps the clearest formulation of these parallel tracks of uniqueness, of the human being and time, in the writings of Menahem Mendel of Vitebsk:[55]

> From the day God created the world until the end of all generations, there is no day which is equal to another...and no two moments which are not distinct, and no two people equal to each other...for if [every one was not unique] what need would there be for each one?[56]

As we have seen, the uniqueness of time is a core axiom of Lainer in his discussion of personal revelation and uniqueness.[57] These ideas of interpretation and time, as they appear in these pre-*MHs* writers are, in and of themselves, anomian in character. It remained to Mordechai Lainer to apply these very same ideas in a radically antinomian context.[58]

Returning to Vital, it is important that this idea of radical uniqueness is not merely a theoretical construct, but a practical part of the lives of Luria's students. Indeed, guidance in realizing their uniqueness was one of the primary teachings that Luria gave to his inner circle of students.[59] Vital writes:

> My teacher (i.e., Luria) every evening would look at the students who stood before him, and see what verse was especially shining in the forehead of the person...And he would explain to him some of the interpretation of the verse which was 'related to the root of his soul'. And before that person would sleep, he would *mekaven* direct his intention to the interpretation of this verse [partially explained to him by Luria] and he would read with his mouth the verse out loud[60] so that when his soul ascended...other things would be taught [in regard both to his unique soul destiny and the interpretation of this

verse] and he would ascend to very great levels...and through this the soul would be purified.[61]

Not only was individual uniqueness an integral part of Lurianic theology, it also was a *kavanah* 'intention' taught, apparently by Luria himself, to his inner circle of students as part of their daily mystical ritual.[62] Abraham Azulai, a later compiler of Lurianic thought, suggests that not only must each person engage their uniqueness through the prism of their unique interpretation, but they are also obligated to reveal that interpretation to the community. Azulai writes: 'For every individual soul has a unique dimension of Torah, which cannot be revealed by anyone other than that specific soul.'[63]

All of this has clear resonance in the inner Zeitgeist of the Hasidic world inhabited by Lainer. Two examples will suffice to show us that the one-letter theorists of Safed thoroughly penetrated the Hasidic consciousness.[64] Yitzhak Yehuda Safrin of Komarno writes:

> All the letters of the Torah...are what cause change. For there is no day similar to another, and no righteous person similar to another, no creature similar to another...And all creations were created...by the letters...And in the midst of the letters there is divine energy חיות *hiyut*..., but the suckling יניקה *yenikah* [of no two people] is the same and the תיקון *tikun* fixing/healing of no two is the same.[65]

Here we find the concept of uniqueness, both of time and person; the fundamental idea that the letters themselves are the agents of creation, each creating a manifestation of their own unique interpretation. The last phrase in the passage is particularly interesting: 'and the fixing/healing of no two is the same'. Here we find a conflation of the Lurianic one-letter theory and the Lurianic theory of *tikun*; they are assumed to have the same ontological matrix of radical uniqueness. We find a similar conflation in Pinhas of Koretz. He writes, 'It is in the writings that every person should intend לתקן *letaken* (to heal/fix) the root of his soul, for the *yesh* is wisdom, as it says, "Wisdom from *ayin* will be found", and everyone has their own [unique] root of wisdom.'[66] Again, we see in Pinhas a conflation of the hermeneutic theory of uniqueness and the soul root theory of uniqueness which is at the heart of the Lurianic theology of *tikun*.

This brings us to the third strand of thought informing Lainer's theory of uniqueness, the theory of individualism that lies at the core of the Lurianic theory of *tikun*. It is clear that the hermeneutic one-letter theory is but a counterpoint to the theory of *tikun*.

Luria and Lainer: Provisional Conclusions

Before we turn to this third strand, however, it may be in order to draw some provisional conclusions in regard to the theory of uniqueness in Lainer. It is clear from our outline of Lainer's theory of uniqueness in Part One that it is, at least in part, rooted in the *mitzvah ahat* and one-letter traditions. The *mitzvah ahat* tradition is both referred to by Lainer directly, and implicitly in virtually every other statement on uniqueness. Similarly, Lainer refers directly to the one-letter tradition: 'It is known that all the souls of Israel are in their root attached to God, each and every one in the letters of the Torah'.[67] More important than these references, though, is that the *mitzvah ahat* and one-letter traditions clearly form the matrix from which Lainer develops his twin ideas that every person has a unique *mitzvah* and a unique Torah, and that the identification and *berur* of one's unique *mitzvah* and Torah is essential to one's personal redemption.

Yet, Lainer is doing far more than adapting and restating earlier principles and traditions. Lainer moves significantly beyond the Lurianic traditions that informed his theory of uniqueness. The first difference is simply one of emphasis, which, however, should not be underestimated. The idea of personal redemption[68] based on a person's embracing of their individuality is a dominant motif in *MHs*. The theme of the unique individual appears to be more present and central in *MHs* than in the Lurianic writers or in any other Hasidic work.

Second, Lainer's formulation is profoundly humanistic and existential in both tone and content, unlike either the unique *mitzvah* or one-letter traditions. Idel, in evaluating the one-letter tradition rooted in Lurianic writers, characterizes it in this way:

> There is nothing modern here; no special veneration of the uniqueness of the individual. The soul is conceived of as but part of the greater spiritual reservoir of souls, which are no more and no less than sparks of the divine essence which descended into the world and will return to their divine source

at the end of time…It would be salient to see authenticity as a value [in what we have termed the one-letter Lurianic school]…rather than a search for originality.[69]

Idel's characterization, in our estimation, refers to two major issues. The first issue is the overwhelmingly technical and complex nature of the Lurianic system. Technicality is the defining characteristic of Luria's theology. It would not be inaccurate to refer to the complex Lurianic system as a kind of spiritual technology with particular functional goals for the repair of the broken cosmos. If one were to read Luria 'extremely', one might suggest that the human being is very much a cog in a machine. A cog is absolutely unique with respect to the machine that cannot function without it—yet it is hard to celebrate the existential individuality of a cog.

The second issue is what we might term the nature of the Lurianic system's theocentrism.[70] The entire focus of the system is the repair of the divine anthropos. There is room to dispute—on metaphysical grounds—the characterization of Luria as strictly theocentric. The Lurianic system assumes a substantive identity between God and human which is the axis upon which the great Lurianic system of כוונות *kavanot* is based. However, in the realm of narrative and myth, rather than ontology and metaphysics, Idel's characterization stands. The issue is, what is the tenor of the narrative that informs the mood of the human being? What stories are being told and how do those stories inform the person's existential fabric? These are the questions Idel is addressing. In Luria, that narrative is about 'fixing' God; in Lainer, it is about 'fixing' the human.

Like most kabbalistic thinkers after Joseph Ergas, whose interpretation of Luria became normative,[71] Lainer was an acosmist. Yet unlike Luria himself, or other post-Lurianic interpretations of Luria—*Habad*, for example[72]—Lainer's acosmism became the basis for his humanism. His radical individualism is not of a merely technical nature. While he does not embrace a naïve celebration of the individual characteristic of some strands of Romanticism,[73] he does celebrate originality. For Lainer, individual uniqueness is the source of joy.[74] This is how he understands the well-known rabbinic maxim, *same'ah behelko*, 'to be joyous in one's portion'. Joy comes from individual uniqueness. Uniqueness extends its realm beyond the limited sphere of *nomos* to include *devarim mutarim*, the realm of the mundane. Emotional life, one's love and fear, must be an expression of one's individuality. Lainer's teachings on the biblical census are a paean to human dignity and grandeur rooted in individuality. His vocabulary to describe unique individuality, which he uses constantly, includes words such as התנשאות *hitnas'ut*, a kind of exaltation of the individual, and מדוגל במעלתו *medugal bema'alato*, which carries the sense of being publicly adorned by one's uniqueness. He describes the unique individuality as the great gift of *tovah* and *ḥayyim*, of 'good' and 'life', that God grants every person.

The third contrast between Lainer and Luria is that in the Lurianic narrative, the focus of *berur* (the process of purification) is God, i.e., it is on the scattered sparks of divinity that fell. In contrast, according to Lainer, the particular goal of *berur* in many passages is the person's clarification of their uniqueness, namely, to be מבורר על חלקו *mevurar 'al ḥelko*.[75] Furthermore, *berur* is accomplished not primarily by Torah, *mitzvot*, and *kavanot* as in Luria, but by a much more personal process of introspection. For Lainer, *berur* is knowing the nature of one's own soul.

Lainer represents a move beyond those schools of hermeneutics to which Idel refers because he embraces a decidedly Romantic orientation.[76] People who embrace their individuality and who have undergone *berur* can, according to Lainer, trust their deepest primal impulses even and especially למעלה מדעתו *lema'alah mida'ato*, beyond their rational intellectual faculties.[77] This is, of course, a distinctly Romantic orientation. Lainer's proto-modern existential affirmation of the unique individual is perhaps best summed up in his teaching[78] that the deep healing of a person is affected by their being *seen* in their individuality. Moreover, to be *seen* in one's unique individuality is to be *seen* by God. As opposed to the Safed school which, according to Idel, emphasized authenticity over originality,[79] according to Lainer, authenticity is to be found only in originality.

The fourth difference between Lainer and the Lurianic sources that informed him lies in the antinomian formulation of individuality found in *MHs*. The idea that one's personal revelation of Torah comes not through transcending one's existential uniqueness but rather through embracing it is original to Lainer. It is precisely the experience and knowledge of one's *perat nefesh* that allows one to access personal revelation, even revelation which contradicts and supersedes law at Sinai.[80]

Here again, Lainer, in Romantic fashion, went much further than any of the Safed one-letter theorists would dare venture. That is not to say, however, that Lainer's theories do not emerge directly from the Safed one-letter theorists. In Chapter Fourteen, by analyzing more fully the underlying metaphysical assumption of the one-letter school in Safed, we will demonstrate that Lainer's innovation emerges directly from the metaphysical assumptions that underlie the hermeneutic principles of much of kabbalistic hermeneutics in general and the Safed school in particular. At the same time, he moves significantly beyond them. It is important to note this, both normatively, as we have already seen, and conceptually, as we will illustrate in Part Four.

We can best understand Lainer's uniqueness by contrasting his 'hermeneutic of the individual' to the three preceding distinct stages in the history of kabbalistic hermeneutics.[81] In the thirteenth century, the hermeneutic focus was on the infinite meanings of the Bible; these were thought to be implicit in the Bible's canonical status. In the sixteenth century, the *Zohar* was granted such status and therefore infinite meanings were ascribed to it. Finally, in the eighteenth century, Hasidic homilies were sometimes able to attain canonical status immediately upon being uttered, and certainly upon publication. Of course, the reason for this latter development, as Idel points out,[82] is the canonical status of the *tzadik* himself.[83]

I suggest that in Lainer we find a fourth stage. The canonical status that earlier Hasidism had only been willing to grant the *tzadik*, Lainer granted, at least in potential, to every individual. An individual who attained such status was termed by Lainer a 'Judah persona'.

It is worth noting at this stage the potentially antinomian implication of Lainer's radical individualism. Idel points out that such an implication, which was at least theoretically present in the kabbalistic hermeneutics of the Lurianic school, was attenuated in the Lurianic school by its 'conservative attitude to the interpreter'.[84] It is precisely such an attitude that was overturned by Lainer's ascription of a virtually canonical status to the individual, as we will demonstrate in the section 'Model Three: The *Tzadik* and the Democratization of Enlightenment'. The Hasidic apotheosis of the *tzadik* became the much more radical and messianic apotheosis of the unique individual. This is, as we will show, an essential part of Lainer's understanding of the Judah archetype.

In Lainer's understanding, then, all limitations on the interpreter naturally fall by the wayside. For Lainer, it is not merely that the individual can reveal a unique understanding of the infinite text which they manifest; nor even is it that only the individual's words in and of themselves can become canonical text. Rather, it is that this is so even when these words contradict the normative dictates of the law. In effect, for Lainer, the individual—at least in potential—*becomes the text*. The דברי חולין *divrei hulin* (mundane talk) and words that come from an unconscious place[85] can have canonical status superseding the law of Sinai.

The fifth characteristic that distinguishes Lainer's individualism from the earlier strands that formed it is the relationship between the individual and the community. Louis Jacobs, in discussing this issue, states categorically that in the Jewish tradition, 'the individual is never seen in isolation from the community'.[86] Idel, in describing what would seem to be a potentially isolating tendency in the affirmation of individual uniqueness implicit in the kabbalistic hermeneutics of the Lurianic thinker, apparently confirm Jacobs' conclusion:

> Interpretation is not an expression of the separation of the individual from the group or community, or an idiosyncratic vision which sets him apart, an act of creativity or individuality particular to him, in the way the Romantics would understand it...the singularity of voice does not imply an insularity of discourse.[87]

We have seen passages in *MHs* that seem to suggest that a similar analysis might hold true for Lainer.[88] These texts seem to indicate an integrated and holistic interpenetration between the unique individual and the community. Uniqueness and the diversity it engenders, writes Lainer, express and do not violate the larger unity.

Indeed, as Idel points out, for the Lurianic kabbalist, it is a metaphysical principle that each soul contains all other souls. And yet, while Lainer would certainly subscribe to this doctrine in theory,[89] Lainer's emphasis on uniqueness also breaks this mold entirely. The essence of individuality in Lainer is that it may potentially be necessary to make decisions that will violate the norms of the community and whose motivation or rationale will be utterly incommunicable to people. In a series of virtually identical passages running throughout *MHs*, Lainer turns on its head the simple reading of a mishnaic dictum requiring that a person's actions should be both תפארת לעושיה *tif'eret le'osehah* and תפארת לו מן האדם *tif'eret lo min ha-adam*.[90] Simply read, this means that an action must meet two criteria

60

if it is to be deemed appropriate: It must be beautiful *le'osehah* for the one who does it and beautiful *min ha-adam* to people, i.e., in relation to the broader community.

Lainer, however, understands this as referring to two distinct typologies of the individual.[91] In a deliberately counter intuitive reading meant to indicate that one must seek עוׁמק *'omek* beyond the גוון *gavan* (depth beyond the surface),[92] Lainer interprets: 'Beautiful for the person who does it really means that it is acceptable to the community. Beautiful for the community really means quite the opposite'. Even if a person is subject to censure by the community and cannot explain their act, they must be responsible לאדם *la'adam*, explains Lainer, i.e., to the צורת אדם *tzurat adam*, to their higher unique and incommunicable self. While ideally one should endeavor to meet both standards, Lainer makes it clear that according to him, the latter is the higher model of the individual. For such an individual, when the standards of community and unique individuality clash, the community must be forsaken and they must withdraw into their own insular, incommunicable place. Lainer points out that this is a great source of acrimony, conflict, and even hatred between the individual and the rest of the community. Thus we see that unlike the tradition which forms him, for Lainer, the singularity of voice does indeed lead, almost inevitably, to insularity and isolation from the community.[93]

It is worth noting that in one of the Lurianic sources we adduced above, it was the obligation of each person to reveal their unique Torah to the community.[94] The axiomatic assumption is that this was both possible and desirable. In contrast, a defining characteristic of extreme individualism is the incommunicability of personal essence.[95]

Despite these clear distinctions between Lainer and the Safed school that preceded him, we must not overstate the differences. Lurianic individualism is undergirded by the old tradition of *mitzvah ahat*, which is clearly a formative influence on Lainer's thought in this area. While a Romantic individualism of the kind manifested by Lainer does not characterize the Lurianic school, it still remains the place where the idea of individualism crystallized.[96] Idel's notion of the rejection of originality in Safed in favor of authenticity therefore seems to be an overstated dichotomy.[97]

Much of the distinction between Luria's and Lainer's differing understanding of the individual can be illuminated by, but not reduced to, the periods in which they lived. Luria's individualism reflects major currents in Renaissance thought,[98] while Lainer reflects the Romantic Zeitgeist. In Renaissance thought, the individual was just starting to emerge. The discarded image of the medieval period,[99] to borrow C. S. Lewis's phrase, was just beginning to be replaced by a new order.

In the medieval period, each individual had a clear place in the order of things, but this was not a very grand place. Obligation and duty to one's rigid social station were very much the order of the day. A person was viewed as having little effect on the unfolding of the universe; in Judaism, medieval scholars like Maimonides represent this school of thought.[100]

The Renaissance introduced the idea of self.[101] Peter Abbs[102] points out that the word 'self' did not take on its modern meaning in the Oxford English Dictionary until 1674, in the same general epoch as what Werblowsky has termed the Safed Revival.[103] As a matter of fact, Italian Jews who came in contact with Renaissance culture at its center in Italy were not insignificant in the shaping of the Safed community.[104] In a gradual but ultimately significant shift from the medieval period to the Renaissance, people are granted a central role in the unfolding of the cosmic drama. But an individual was not generally conceived of as separate from or in rebellion against the higher order of things. Rather, a person had a grand role to play within the larger harmonies. So, while the self did emerge, the individualism of the Renaissance is for the most part the reworking and upgrading of the role of the individual within the larger rational, spiritual, and even cosmic systems. A person has a glorious role to play, effecting and even creating the order of things, but is still a cog. People are not, for the most part, discrete worlds unto themselves. A person is not a 'particular' who exists only in their rejection of the neoclassicisms that hold him or her.

This is very different from the Romantic period,[105] where, partially in response to the Enlightenment, there was a tendency to see the individual as the center of all life. This was a rebellion against rules, old forms, hierarchies, and all aspects of neoclassicism. This rebellion permeated all areas of thought, from politics to art and music. The individual was celebrated, not as part of a broader whole, but as transcending the general rules of society, culture, and law. It is the 'particular' and 'primal' human, the 'natural' human who is able to transcend the shackles of reason and access a higher self, who is the hero of the Romantic period. For a Romantic, the concept of a given world order was virtually meaningless. People needed to discover their own unique, primal, and idiosyncratic subjectivity.

While we do not want to fall into the trap that has been labeled the periodization of history,[106] it seems that both Luria and Lainer, even if not directly influenced, were at least in part informed by the Zeitgeist of their respective times.[107] In Luria's theory of individuality, the human assumes a central and grand role. At the same time, humans find their place—even if it be a celebrated place[108]—within a larger divine order. In the Jewish context, this means that a person is fully bound by normative law. Indeed, law, Torah, and *mitzvot* are primary methods of accomplishing the *berur*, the healing of God that, according to Luria, is incumbent on humans. While there is a move beyond law in Luria's system, namely, in his elaborate system of *kavanot*,[109] these are a series of intentions and unifications that accompany and deepen normative performance but in no way override it. Lurianic individuals, like Renaissance individuals in general, may be unique and significantly anomian, but they are virtually never antinomian.

For Lainer, however, the individual stands—at least ideally—outside and even against the system. The individual rejects the general (*kelalei divrei Torah*) and embraces concrete particularity (*peratim; peratei divrei Torah*) as sacred. As we shall see more clearly in Part Three and Part Four, will and the trans- or supra-rational become the ideal. The reason for this is simple: the individual is to a large degree apotheosized, reaching a kind of divine status. For our purposes here, it is sufficient to note that while the Lurianic human functions within the system in a central role, Lainer's ideal human is realized by transcending the system in response to their own *tzurat adam*.[110] In this sense Idel is correct in seeing nothing 'modern or Romantic' in the Lurianic persona.

It is clear, however, that the transition from Luria to Lainer involves not only rupture but also real continuity.[111] The idea of originality and not merely authenticity, as Idel would have it, does seem to have its origins in rabbinic and kabbalistic thought. This idea is expanded significantly in the kabbalistic hermeneutics of Lurianic Kabbalah. However, it crystallizes in its most exquisite form in the theological anthropology of Mordechai Lainer.

Strand Three: Soul Sparks and *Tikun* (Repair)

We now turn to the third strand of thought, which informs Lainer's notion of the unique individual in general terms, as well as being an important basis for his notion of the individual: the idea of *hisaron meyuhad*, which we outlined in detail in Chapter Three. This strand is the Lurianic theory of *tikun* and soul sparks to which we have already alluded. In the Lurianic myth,[112] after the breaking of the vessels, sparks are scattered throughout reality. The sparks must be redeemed and returned to their proper place within the divine anthropos. The redeeming of the sparks is considered an act of *tikun*, best understood as the repair of the divine structure. It is noteworthy that the language used by Luria throughout *Shaar Hagilgulim* to describe the flaw needing repair is *hisaron*. *Hisaron* for Luria and those who follow his teachings is a word associated with evil, sin, and ontological flaw. The intellectual history of the word *hisaron* is beyond the purview of this book. It would appear, however, that Lainer, in part, drew inspiration for his concept of *hisaron* directly from Luria.

Three major types of *hisaron* are mentioned in *Shaar Hagilgulim*; each resonates in Lainer. Luria's general theory of *hisaron*, and the particular expression of unique *hisaron*, is the third strand incorporated into Lainer's theory of uniqueness. By outlining the three types of *hisaron* here, we will see that Luria's theory of *hisaron* and raising the sparks is really one with his theory of uniqueness. We will also see that Luria, preceding Lainer, incorporated into his theory of uniqueness the old rabbinic tradition of *mitzvah ahat*. This will clarify how deeply Lainer's theory of uniqueness and unique *hisaron* is indebted to Luria.

The first type of *hisaron* is ontological. The goal of existence, in Vital's language, is תיקון חיסרון *tikun hisaron* repair of the cosmic flaw.[113] It reflects the essentially fallen state of reality after the shattering of the vessels. Luria calls this state גלות השכינה *galut ha-Shekhinah* 'the exile of the Divine presence'.[114]

The second type of *hisaron*, which Luria often conflates with the first, is caused by the fall of the primordial Adam's soul.[115] Once the initial stages of בירור *berur* [116] (the gathering and clarifying of the sparks from the shards of the fallen vessels) were almost completed, a second cosmic shattering was occasioned by Adam's sin. Adam's fall resulted in a new dispersion of sparks throughout reality. Here, however, begins Luria's theory of uniqueness. Each soul in the world, according to Luria, is capable of a unique tikun 'repair' of hisaron. The nature of this tikun is determined primarily by the organ or limb in Adam's soul that is that particular soul spark's source. Luria teaches: 'When a person is born his soul must מברר mevarer clarify[117] those sparks that are connected to the part of Adam Kadmon (the primordial human) soul from which he fell... And this is the purpose of a person's birth in this world'.[118] The systems for identifying the precise tikun that can be effected by each individual are far more intricate than we can present here; for our purposes, it is sufficient that according to Luria, each individual possesses not only infinite value and worth, but also has an utterly unique role to play in the cosmic drama.[119] Indeed, for Luria, as for Lainer in his wake, the infinite value, dignity, and adequacy of the individual is rooted directly in the individual's uniqueness.[120] The individual is called on לתקן letaken 'to fix' the very unique hisaron that only that person is capable of fixing.

However, a third type of hisaron exists that demands the form of tikun most extensively addressed in Shaar Hagilgulim. This type of hisaron, like the second kind, is a hisaron meyuhad. It focuses on the particular flaws—occasioned by sin or by the failure to perform a particular mitzvah—for which a person undergoes גלגול gilgul 'transmigration'. Like the second type of hisaron, this type is unique to every individual.

Of course, the uniqueness discussed in the Lurianic theory of sparks is not distinct from the uniqueness discussed in the Luria's kabbalistic hermeneutics. Indeed, Vital often conflates the two. Both frameworks are based on the same core myth that there are six hundred thousand root souls at each level of existence. On the hermeneutic level, this translates into six hundred thousand different interpretations at all four levels of interpretation.[121] In terms of soul sparks, this is manifested as six hundred thousand root souls for each organ of Adam's soul. Each root soul itself, however, divides into another six hundred thousand sparks, and so on. What emerges in the correspondence between unique soul sparks and unique Torah intepretations is a highly complex and sophisticated system of distinctions that affirms the radical uniqueness of each individual soul.

This interpretation of the soul spark theory in terms of radical uniqueness is grounded in a shared ontology between the hermeneutic myth of uniqueness and the soul spark myth of uniqueness in the Lurianic system. Evidence of this shared ontology can be found in the following passage which comes from Nahar Shalom, a commentary on Vital's Eitz Hayyim by one of the primary exponents of Lurianic Kabbalah, Rabbi Shalom Sharabi. Sharabi here assumes that the six hundred thousand souls tradition functions identically in both myths. Indeed, Sharabi moves seamlessly from one myth to the other:

> The order of divergence of the [five levels] of each soul of… every one of the 613 great root souls, which diverge to the 613 פרצופים פרטיים *partzufim peratiyim* specific faces or configurations of each entire limb, is [connected] to primordial Adam…And from these *[partzufim]*…diverge the [five levels] of every root soul, which [themselves] divide into six hundred thousand. And these are called 'sparks' rather than 'roots'.… And each *partzuf* includes the 613 *mitzvot*, each entire one of which is *mitzvah ahat* out of the 613 general *mitzvot*, diverges, and is divided into six hundred thousand times 613 [for each one of the sparks]….And from the light of the body of the Torah shine and spread six hundred thousand types of interpretations; they shine and diverge…to each of the six hundred thousand *partzufim*…according to the [five] soul levels…[122]

In another passage, Vital writes that a person might need to be reincarnated either because they have not fulfilled a particular *mitzvah* (what he calls a מצווה פרטית *mitzvah peratit*), thus fostering a unique *hisaron* in need of *tikun*, or—as Vital concludes the passage—because they did not study the unique interpretation connected to their soul spark.[123] In the same passage, Vital writes that a person who is a reincarnated soul might need to only fulfill a particular *mitzvah* or particular *mitzvot* (the concept we have referred to as *mitzvah ahat*).

We see from this text that Vital fully absorbed the Talmudic idea of uniqueness (*mitzvah ahat*), which we examined earlier, into the Lurianic conception of uniqueness and transmigration. We further see that in these passages, three traditions are conflated: the unique *mitzvah* tradition, the one-letter Safed hermeneutic tradition, and the Lurianic soul spark tradition. According to Vital, the soul spark tradition was not merely functional. Rather, it was deeply rooted in the matrix of uniqueness.

The technical term used often by Vital to refer to what we would call the unique individual is נשמה פרטית *neshamah peratit*.[124] This is not the שורש נשמה *shoresh neshamah*[125] 'root soul', but rather, as we have seen, one of the

600,000 sparks deriving from each root soul. Vital's *neshamah peratit*—the unique individual spark that needs to fix its unique *hisaron*—evokes Lainer's phrase פרט נפש ישראל *perat nefesh yisrael*. Other terms used by Lainer to designate individual uniqueness, notably שייך לו בשורשו *shayakh lo beshorsho* 'related to him in his root', are common in *Shaar Hagilgulim*[126] and other Lurianic texts.

Now we can easily sketch the parallel between the forms of *hisaron* in Lainer and Luria that we asserted at the beginning of our discussion. In Lainer, as in Luria, we noted three types of *hisaron*. The first type of *hisaron* is the ontological *hisaron* that precedes humanity. Lainer's source for this is what Luria calls the *hisaron* occasioned by the primal shattering of the vessels. The second type of *hisaron* in Lainer, as we saw, is the unique *hisaron* of every individual מיום הולדו *miyom hivaldo* 'from their day of birth', i.e., not catalyzed by sin. Lainer's source for this is the second form of *hisaron* in Luria, namely, the *hisaron* occasioned by the fall of primordial Adam's soul, causing a unique *hisaron* in every human being correlated with a particular one of primordial Adam's limbs. The third form of *hisaron* in Lainer is that fostered by sin, paralleled by the same idea in Luria.

At this point it is clear that Luria's theory of transmigration and *hisaron*, developed in great detail in *Shaar Hagilgulim* and other Lurianic writings and rooted in the matrix of uniqueness, is both conceptually and linguistically a key strand (the third, in our enumeration) informing the theory of uniqueness in Lainer.

Revisiting Individuality in Luria and Lainer

Yet, as we noted in our initial discussion of individuality in Lainer and Luria,[127] it is clear that here as well, Lainer and Luria are not discussing precisely the same thing. Lainer certainly received the categories of unique *hisaron* and their matrix of transmigration from Luria, but he transforms them, changing their mood, tenor, and substance.

Before outlining the distinctions, it is worth noting that not only was Lainer aware of the Lurianic concept of transmigration and its implications for personal *tikun*—this in itself is not remarkable, since any Hasidic master would be—but he explicitly references this set of ideas in explaining his theory of uniqueness. One passage explicates the eight words describing our relationship to Torah in the morning blessing preceding the *shema*, to which Lainer draws a parallel to the eight garments of the high priest.[128] His comment on the word לשמוע *lishmo'a* 'to listen' is relevant here:

לשמוע הוא נגד המעיל, היינו שהאדם ישמע ויטה אזן ליסודו וישרשו כמו שדרש בגמ' (שמות רבה מ:ג) על פסוק איפה היית ביסדי ארץ איפה שלך איך היה באדם הראשון, וע"י שהאדם יבא על יסודו מזה יבין מה שתיקן כבר בעולם ומה צריך עוד לתקן...כדאיתא בזוה"ק המעיל הוא ברזא דגילגולא

'To listen' corresponds to the tunic. That is, a person should listen and incline his ear to his foundation and *shorsho* his root as the Talmud interpreted in regard to the verse, 'Where were you when I created the land?' (Job 38:4): 'Where was your portion in *adam ha-rishon* the first human?' And through a person coming to understand his foundation, from this he will understand what he has already fixed in the world, and what he still needs to fix...as it says in the Holy *Zohar*, 'The tunic is the secret of transmigration'.[129]

What is important about this passage is not merely that it echoes the Lurianic themes, but also that it is virtually the only such passage in the entire *MHs* corpus.[130] This indicates that Lainer did not merely receive the Lurianic doctrine of uniqueness and *hisaron* with its emphasis on transmigration, but that he transformed it as well.

Lainer's first transformation is, of course, the almost total divestiture of the apparatus of transmigration. Lainer understands an individual's unique *hisaron* almost solely in terms of the person's framework in this world.

The second transformation is in the nature of the *hisaron*. Similar to what we saw in the section 'Luria and Lainer: Provisional Conclusions' with regard to the general transition from Luria to Lainer in terms of uniqueness, Luria's *hisaron* is of a technical nature, while according to Lainer, *hisaron* has a broader, existential nature. For example, in a classic passage we analyzed in the section '*Hisaron* and Uniqueness', the unique *hisaron* of Uziyahu was a certain kind of sadness or depression. It was only by dealing with his depression that Uziyahu could attain a measure of what Lainer refers to as healing and freedom, even though in doing so Uziyahu performed actions that isolated him from his community. Furthermore, instead of referring to either the shattering of the vessels or the particular limb in primordial man with which a soul spark might be associated, Lainer almost always uses the term חיסרון מיום היוולדו *hisaron miyom hivaldo*[131] the 'lack from the day of your birth'. This is not a mythical apparatus; rather, it means something like the existential challenge of one's life, which can only be met by walking through one's personalized and unique spiritual pathology.

Third, unlike Luria, according to Lainer, the *tikun* of *hisaron* does not necessarily take place through Torah and *mitzvot* or their deepening in anomian *kavanot*. As evidenced in the source cited about Uziyahu, healing *hisaron* may well demand radical antinomian behavior.

Fourth, according to Lainer, the fixing of *hisaron* is more an internal introspective process than a formal technical procedure as it seems to be for Luria.

Fifth, other than the exceptional passage we cited that referred directly to transmigration, Lainer rarely uses the formal Lurianic word *tikun* in describing the healing of *hisaron*, but prefers the word healing (that is, R.F.A. ה.פ.א.). While clearly this word is already used in biblical texts and is adopted extensively in later literature about repentance, Lainer's switch from *tikun* to healing[132] may be indicative of a more existential sense, as compared to Luria's technical tone.[133]

Sixth, whatever the formal metaphysics might be (that is, even if we assume an acosmism in both Luria and Lainer in which the entire world is technically just divine autobiography), nevertheless, the tone of Luria's *hisaron* myth differs substantively from that of Lainer. In Luria's conception, certainly in regard to the first two forms of *hisaron* (those that result from the shattered vessels and Adam's fall), it is clear that the *hisaron* is something that needs healing in God. Even in the third form of Lurianic *hisaron*, the trauma of sin is so intense precisely because it is so traumatic to the divine anthropos. In contrast, according to Lainer, the whole concept of *hisaron* revolves around the human being. *Hisaron* is personal; it is related to the unique life of the person, with no obvious divine anthropos waiting to be healed in the background. Luria's conception of *hisaron* is profoundly theocentric while Lainer's is markedly anthropocentric.[134]

The final difference lies in the relationship between *hisaron* and uniqueness. For Luria, uniqueness is an adjective describing the type of *hisaron* that needs to be fixed. According to Lainer, recognition of uniqueness is itself part of the healing of *hisaron*. For example, according to Lainer's original reading, when the priest sees the person in their uniqueness, being seen is in and of itself healing.[135] In another passage, Lainer teaches that only one's unique *mitzvah* can heal *hisaron*.[136] As we have seen, according to Lainer, *berur* of *hisaron* is to a large extent the *berur* of uniqueness. This *berur* heals *hisaron* and brings one to the expanded consciousness of *'olam ha-ba*, where one participates in divinity.[137]

Having noted these differences, it remains for us to affirm that the Lurianic matrix remains the major formative influence on Lainer's theory of uniqueness and on his notion of *hisaron meyuhad*.

We need to examine one more aspect of the influence of Luria's 'raising the sparks' theory on Lainer. We will focus on some passages from the first generations of the Hasidic movement which were in all probability bridge texts between them. The first passage, representing a whole genre of sources, comes from the Baal Shem Tov's grandson, Efrayim of Sudilkov. He writes:

> I have heard from my grandfather that all that belongs to a man, be it his servants and animals, even his household effects—they are all of his sparks which belong to the root of his soul, and he has to lift them up to their upper root.[138]

Another passage reads: 'Every single individual in Israel must go to such places as contain sparks from the root of his own soul, in order that he might free them'.[139] These passages were adduced by Scholem as part of his well-known and often acrimonious debate with Tishby over the messianic tendency, or lack thereof, in early Hasidic sources.[140] For Scholem, these sources, in contrast with their Lurianic predecessors, prove both the messianic character of Luria and the non-messianic character of Hasidism.[141] We are not concerned with that debate here; we rather wish to call attention to Scholem's comments contrasting these sources with their Lurianic antecedents in terms of their more personal and intimate nature.[142]

Although we believe that Scholem somewhat overstates the Hasidic transformation of Lurianic sources,[143] his core point remains valid. For Luria, the issue of raising the sparks has a far more generalized nature than for the early Hasidic thinkers. This is why the line between the redemption of the sparks of Adam's soul unique to each person, and the more general redemption of the *Shekhinah*, is often blurred.

The Hasidic sources that Scholem calls personal and intimate might be termed by us 'autobiographical'. These sources suggest that every significant meeting along a person's life path—be it with an animate or an inanimate being—is part of a person's sacred autobiography.[144] The structures of individuality implicit in Luria's theory of raising the sparks are far more sharply expressed, in strikingly existential terms, in Hasidism, as seen above. A similar personal, intimately individual, Hasidic expression is found in another text also hotly debated in terms of its messianism: a quote from the Baal Shem Tov relayed by Menachem Nachum of Chernobyl. These sources are critical to us because they are the canonical Hasidic traditions inherited by Mordechai Lainer and the Hasidic bridge to the original Lurianic texts. As in the texts cited above, we are interested not in the question of messianism but in noticing the very sharply defined theory of individuality.

> Each and every one in Israel has to repair and to prepare the
> part of the stature of Messiah (קומת משיח *komat mashiah*)
> which belongs to his soul, as is well known, since Adam is an
> acronym for Adam David Messiah. The stature of Adam is
> from the beginning of the world unto its end, as all the souls
> of Israel were included in him. Afterward, his stature was
> diminished by the sin. So too will the stature of the Messiah
> be [formed] of all the souls of Israel, which are 600,000 in
> number, as before the sin of Adam. This is the reason why
> each and every one of Israel has to prepare that part which
> is the aspect of the Messiah that belongs to his soul.[145]

Clearly Menahem Nahum of Chernobyl, writing in the same early period as the texts adduced above, offers here a reworking of Luria's 'raising of the sparks' not dissimilar to that of Lainer. As Idel points out, the difference between *Meor Einayim* and the Lurianic sources it reformulates is that in *Meor Einayim*, the goal of the rebuilt 'stature of the Messiah' is not the fixing of the divine anthropos, but what Menahem Nahum terms at the beginning and the end of this passage 'the unification of speech and thought'.[146] According to *Meor Einayim*, the Messiah is, at least in part, 'the everlasting unification of speech and thought'.[147] Idel, expanding Scholem's characterization of the Hasidic sources, argues that while Luria is fundamentally theocentric, Menahem Nahum must be regarded as more anthropocentric. Texts like this one provided Lainer with a strong intellectual matrix for his central tenet: the radical uniqueness of every individual. Yet, while we can establish that these modernized Hasidic versions of Luria's theories seem to have contributed to the development of Lainer's conception of individuality, it is important to note that he moves a very important step beyond even them.

First, individualism, as noted above, is far more pervasive a theme in *MHs* than in any of these other sources. Second, Lainer strips away all of the mythical elements. Neither the 'stature of the Messiah', nor the figure of a messiah in the classical sense, nor any discussion of raising sparks, appear in his teachings in any significant way. All of this is part of Lainer's acosmic humanism. Third, Lainer introduces the idea of antinomianism, which, as we saw, stemmed from the concept of unique individualism, in a way that appears nowhere else. Fourth, Lainer introduces the theme of the natural insularity of the ideal individual who must sometimes separate from the mainstream community because of the inherent incommunicability of their ideas and actions. Finally, as far as we know, Lainer's existentially reformulated idea of *hisaron meyuhad* has no parallel elsewhere in Hasidic literature.

Hisaron, Tikun, and Kabbalistic Theories of Evil

Hisaron, as we noted above, is a byword for ontological imperfection, sin, and especially evil. At this point we examine the final strand of thought which must have influenced Lainer's original theory of *hisaron meyuhad,* what Moshe Idel has termed 'the kabbalistic fascination with Evil'.[148] In the thirteenth century, Kabbalists understood evil not as privation in the Plotinian sense[149] but as an ontological reality rooted in the Godhead.[150] In the *Zohar,* this culminated in some strands of thought encouraging or even viewing as absolutely necessary an engagement with evil, not only for the purpose of its eradication, but also for its healing and transformation.[151] Indeed, the ability to engage and transform evil was viewed as a unique characteristic of the spiritual elite.

In the Lurianic period, the fascination with evil was part of a larger dynamic that led to the development of normative כוונות *kavanot* (intentions), which demanded that a person enter the realm of the קליפות *kelipot* (husks—the source of evil) on a regular basis, for example, in the daily נפילת אפים *nefilat apayim* prayer (literally, 'falling on the face').[152] This fascination broke

72

normative boundaries completely in the Sabbatean movement.[153] In the Hasidic movement, engagement with the יצר הרע *yetzer ha-ra'* (evil inclination), the raising of alien thoughts in the writing of the Magid of Mezerich,[154] the transformation of evil in the writing of Schneur Zalman,[155] and the raising of fallen love in the writing of Menahem Nahum of Chernobyl,[156] can all be seen as manifestations of the kabbalistic fascination with evil. This fascination was part of the intellectual furniture that Lainer inherited from his kabbalistic forbearers and it finds expression throughout Lainer's writings. Lainer's basic predilection reflects the *Zohar* teaching that evil must be engaged with not only in order to be eradicated,[157] but also in order to be transformed.[158] Like the earliest strands in the Spanish Kabbalah, Lainer insists on the ontological priority of darkness.[159] Darkness is the אור בהיר *or bahir,* the light that is so clear and pure that it cannot be seen and which is therefore called darkness.[160] Moreover, light is revealed specifically through the darkness,[161] i.e., good is revealed through what appears to be evil. Lainer suggests, based on a passage from the *Zohar,* that to know the good that comes from evil is the very secret of faith.[162] The power of this path of *hisaron* is so potent that once one understands the secret of one's *hisaron,* light is transformed into darkness and redemption is instantaneous. Lainer exults in poetic description: יתהפך ברגע אחד...ויעלה בבת אחת להתהפך מחושך לאור 'He will be transformed in a single moment... He will rise in a blink to be transformed from darkness to light...'[163]

Hisaron, which is often identified with רע *ra* 'evil' is, as we have seen, also the great catalyst to תשוקה שאין לו גבול *teshukah she'ein lo gevul* [164] 'desire without bounds', as well as to all other goods affirmed by Lainer.[165] *Hisaron* is also identified with כשלון *kishalon* failure, yet, as Lainer reminds his reader often, citing a rabbinic dictum, 'A person only stands firm upon the words of Torah if he has first failed in them'.[166] All this expresses Lainer's fascination with *hisaron.*

Most central, however, in Lainer's perception of evil is his radical acosmism, which moves him to exclaim time and again that God will מברר הכול לטוב *mevarer ha-kol letov* 'clarify that all is for the good'. This, in Lainer, does not express a classic theodicy that claims that evil is justified because it is sometimes necessary for the good. Rather, according to Lainer, all of evil is, in its more profound reality, *already* good.[167]

This belief naturally predisposed Lainer to emphasize those strands in Kabbalah that are not only concerned with destroying evil, but are also fascinated by evil, particularly with its great, if hidden, spiritual power. Finally, Lainer asserts[168] that one must not eradicate but integrate the darkness. This is the purpose of the journey to the desert, beyond one's personal boundaries, which, according to Lainer, each person must undertake:

כי ענין נסיעת ישראל במדבר ממסע למסע, הוא שיצאו חוץ לגבולם
למקומות השוממים והשובבים להכניע כל הכוחות השובבים הנקראים נחש
שרף ועקרב וצמאון, ולהוציא משם הקדושה, וכן האדם בנפשו יש לו כוחות
שובבים שרוצים להחטיאו והם מעלמין דאתחרבו, וצריך האדם להכניעם
להקדושה, וזה נקרא נסיעה

> Israel…went out beyond their boundaries to the desolate and primal places to subjugate the primal forces that are called snake, viper, scorpion and thirst, and to bring the holiness out of there; so too a person has primal powers in his own soul that desire to make him sin, and these are from the worlds that have been destroyed,[169] and a person must integrate them into the sacred, and this is called a journey.[170]

At this juncture, having closely read Lainer's texts and reconstructed the intellectual history that informed him, we can draw some conclusions about how he originated his theory of uniqueness, particularly in terms of *hisaron meyuhad*. Lainer weaves together the different mystical-intellectual traditions we have outlined in a highly original fashion in order to form his concept of *hisaron meyuhad*.

First, *hisaron meyuhad* is in effect Lainer's unique interpretation of the old Lurianic tradition that says that each person has their own letter in the Torah. Writes Lainer:[171]

כידוע שכל נפשות ישראל המה בשורש דבוקים כל אחד ואחד באותיות...
התורה

> [I]t is known that all the souls of Israel are in their root, each and every one, attached to the letters of the Torah.[172]

This tradition itself, as we have seen, was in part formed by the rabbinic unique *mitzvah* tradition expressed throughout the generations.

It is also the hermeneutic expression of the theory of unique individuality that lies at the heart of the Lurianic notion of raising the sparks. This is the first strand woven into Lainer's notion of *hisaron meyuhad*. Second, Lainer is heir to the kabbalistic tradition of fascination with evil; this topic appears in many of its classical forms throughout his writings. This tradition as well is woven into his theory of *hisaron meyuhad* as a central category of his thought.

We need to remember that in the Hasidic adaptation of the Lurianic image, one who raises the sparks unique to their soul fixes the *qomah* 'stature', or figure, of the messiah. In Lainer's reformulation, anyone who heals their *hisaron meyuhad* moves to an expanded *'olam ha-ba*–consciousness.[173] Personal revelation is apprehended through the prism of uniqueness. The key to the prism of one's uniqueness is one's letter in the Torah, which in Lainer's combining of the older kabbalistic traditions is one's *hisaron meyuhad*.

Strand Four: Prophecy and Uniqueness

We now arrive at the fourth and final strand, which we term the 'prophetic soul print' tradition. In four separate passages in *MHs*, it is clear that Lainer is both aware of and conducting a provocative dialogue with this tradition. What is foreshadowed here and will be clear by the end of Part Four is that this tradition is actually far more central to Lainer than might appear to be the case given the paucity of texts referring to it directly in *MHs*. In fact, it may be part of one of the most refined and daring expressions of Lainer's theory of individualism, fully merged with his mystical conception of acosmic humanism.

'Even prophecy requires great *berur* [to know] if it is truly from God',[174] says Lainer. Once *berur* is completed, one moves into *'olam ha-ba*[175], that is, the consciousness of the Judah archetype. Before looking at this prophetic level shared by Moses, Solomon, and the Judah archetype, let us examine how Lainer views the non-Mosaic prophetic experience. He states:

שכל הנביאים המה פרטי נפשות ואין השי"ת מאיר להם רק כפי בחינת
נפשם וזה נקרא במראה אליו כפי שורש בחינת נפשו, וגם זה ההארה אינו
מפורש לפניו היטב

[A]ll the prophets are individual souls, and God illuminates
to them according to the contours of their [unique] souls.

75

This is described as 'in a vision unto him *eilav*'[176]—[meaning] according to the root of the dimensions of his soul, and even this illumination is not made clearly explicit for him…[177]

The biblical passage which Lainer cites, 'in a vision I will make myself known unto him, in a dream I will speak with him', contrasts other prophets with Moses. Moses is described as 'trusted in all my house' and Moses' prophecy as being received 'mouth-to-mouth…without riddles'.[178] The key word in Lainer's reading of this verse is אליו *eilav* 'unto him', which Lainer interprets to mean that the vision of every other prophet comes 'according to his unique soul'. When Lainer says above that non-Mosaic prophecy is 'not explicit', he is also referring to the Talmudic tradition that Moses sees through a clear prism,[179] while all the other prophets see through an unclear prism.[180] In regard to the other prophets, this means that their vision is refracted in an inherently subjective way through the unique lens of what we have termed their 'soul print'.

As we outline this tradition, we will see both the traditional sources that Lainer was drawing on, and the places where, in a highly dramatic manner, he parts with tradition in order to assert the radical importance he ascribes to unique individuality, even where the classical Jewish tradition seems to abandon the principle, namely in the case of Moses.

The Talmudic and midrashic authors are well aware of the subjective aspect of prophecy based on the persona of the prophet. The Talmud states, 'No two prophets prophesy in the same style'.[181] Similarly, the respective prophecies of Isaiah and Ezekiel, which differ in tone and substance (for example, the number of wings ascribed to the angels), are understood as a reflection of their personal histories: Ezekiel is 'a village dweller who saw the king [and is thus more overwhelmed] while Isaiah is a 'city dweller'.[182] *Midrash Rabbah* to Song of Songs is even more dramatic in affirming the uniquely personal active participation of the prophet in crystallizing the prophetic message:

> The prophets said to Jeremiah: What did you apprehend
> [that prompted you] to say, '[Who does not fear you,] King
> of the Nations?' (Jer. 10:7). All the other prophets call him
> 'King of Israel' and you call him 'King of the Nations'. He said
> to them: 'I heard Him [say], 'A prophet for the nations I have
> appointed you' (Jer. 1:5), so I said 'King of the nations'. [183]

In an even more provocative version of the same *midrash*, it is God who says to Jeremiah, 'You call me king of the nations. Am I not king of Israel?'[184] All these texts are understood as expressions of the core idea that prophecy is refracted through the prism of the prophet's unique perception. It is in this sense that Lainer's student Tzadok Hakohen interprets Ezekiel's vision: 'Understand that the secret of a likeness of "a man" upon the throne, [beheld] by Ezekiel, is that this man is Ezekiel himself'.[185] In another formulation of the same idea Tzadok writes, 'The likeness of a "man" upon the throne is the perception of the soul by the soul'.[186]

At this point we turn to Lainer's second reference to the 'soul print' tradition of prophecy. Because prophecy is refracted through the unique individuality of the prophet, it requires *berur* to ensure that one's action comes not from external motives, but from the deepest place of essential self. It is in this sense that, as we quoted above, 'Even prophecy requires great *berur*'.[187]

The context of this passage is a general discussion of the *berur* required by every person in order to ascertain the true nature of one's inner desire (*teshukah*) unclouded by other considerations. Failure to perform such *berur* is identified by Lainer with idolatry and prevents one from accessing the divine will.[188]

As we have seen, the divine will for an individual is accessed through the prism of one's uniqueness, which brings one to the state of *'olam ha-ba*–consciousness. Since the experience of prophecy is similarly expressed through the personal uniqueness of the prophet, that uniqueness must be purified in the same way to ensure a nondistorted manifestation of prophecy. Thus, writes Lainer,[189] although the people knew that Jeremiah was a true prophet, they were afraid that he had an ulterior agenda for telling them to remain in the land of Israel. According to Lainer, Jeremiah takes their accusation to heart and performs an inner process of *berur* to ensure that the prophetic voice emerges from his clarified self and not his distorted self. Tzadok, explaining the teaching of Lainer on this Jeremiah story,[190] writes as follows:

> If the prophet does not clarify the [self-interested] rela-
> tionship entirely, then, because of the relationship, he may
> imagine that it is the voice of God [that he hears], and it is
> not. The [possibility] of error is there because in reality, it is

77

actually his own voice [that the prophet hears]. Only [in true prophecy does] he perceive and know that it is the voice of God speaking from within himself.[191]

What emerges from these sources is the unique contribution of what Lainer calls the פרט נפש *perat nefesh* (the unique individuality of the prophet) towards prophecy. A prophet is one who has achieved a level of *berur* that allows God's voice to speak, undistorted, through and from within himself. These are not descriptions of prophetic channeling in which the prophet, emptied of self, becomes a vehicle for the 'downloading' of objective divine information. Rather, a mystical apprehension of spirit conveys experience and/or information through the uniquely individual and subjective person of the prophet. Said simply, in Lainer's reading of the classic prophetic tradition, unique individuality is the conduit for the prophetic experience.

Moses, Uniqueness, and Prophecy: A Radical Reading of Revelation

All of the sources thus far dealing with prophecy concern the general category of prophets; they exclude Moses, who is said to be in a category by himself. Heretofore, while Lainer and Tzadok may have had particularly sharp formulations in terms of uniqueness, they reflected the general sense of the sources. In regard to Moses, however, the radical nature of Lainer's position, as well as that of Tzadok, becomes most apparent.

The midrashic literature distinguishes Mosaic from non-Mosaic prophecy by suggesting that Moses' prophecy is associated with the word זה *zeh* 'this', as in זה הדבר אשר צוה ה' 'this is the word that God commanded',[192] while the other prophets are associated with the word כה *koh* 'thus', as in כה אמר ה' 'thus spoke God'.[193] 'This' is understood to mean a clear apprehension, whereas 'thus' is understood to express 'likeness',[194] indicating a process of imagination and association on the part of the prophet.

The dimension of imagination in prophecy is, in most sources, connected to verse 12:11 in Hosea, וביד הנביאים אדמה 'By the hand of the prophets I am imagined'.[195] Imagination that clearly emerges from the unique persona of the prophet is considered a positive and desirable quality; indeed, this is the quality that generates prophecy.[196] A representative passage on this question is found in the following *midrash*[197]:

> Said R. Yudah: Great is the power of the prophets in that
> they imagine the likeness of the divine might as the form of
> a man, as it is said, 'I heard the voice of a *man* between [the
> banks] of Ulai'.[198]

Imagination, however, is also what is said to be absent from the prophecy of Moses. It is precisely this absence, which—in many texts, but most powerfully in Maimonides[199]—accounts for the qualitative superiority of Moses' prophecy. The general understanding, as we discussed above, is that Moses' prophecy occurred through a 'clear lens', and that it lacks the personal subjective dimension that defines all other prophecy. It has unique clarity and, therefore, authority. Maimonides, a most vocal proponent of this tradition, writes, 'The obligatory call to the Torah…derives solely from that level of perception [unique to Moses]. Therefore, according to our outlook, there neither was nor will be any Torah other than the one Torah which is the Torah of Moses our teacher'.[200]

The eternal nature of Torah rests on this qualitative distinction between Moses and other prophets. Because Moses sees through a clear prism, he can transmit a Torah with binding authority on all generations. Simply stated, three conclusions may be drawn about the prophecy of Moses: First, it is free of the distorting quality of imagination. Second, it is the voice of God and not the voice of the prophet who is speaking. Finally, as a corollary of the first two, Mosaic prophecy is eternally valid and not merely temporal.

What is critical for our purposes is that Lainer, as we shall see, while affirming the qualitatively higher nature of the prophecy of Moses, nonetheless disagrees with all three distinctions.

At this point we come to the third passage in *MHs* relating to uniqueness and prophecy. Lainer alerts the knowing reader of his radical intention with his citation and interpretation of the *midrash* distinguishing Moses from the other prophets based on the respective usages of *zeh* and *koh*.

כל הנביאים היה שליחתם לישראל...כפי העת והזמן וכפי כח השגתם...
כן התנבאו, ועלה ברוח נביאתם אשר דבר נבואה הלז יהיה לעולמי
עז, אך באמת נמצא שנוים כפי ערך דור ודור, וע"ז הוסיף עליהם משרע"ה
להתנבאות בזה הדבר, היינו שהוא השיג כל דבר לפי שעתו ומקומו והבין כי
הנבואה אינה רק לזמן ולאחר זמן יחפרוץ הקב"ה בענין אחר

79

All the missions of the prophets for Israel…were according to the time and according to the power of their grasp of their prophecy, and it occurred [to them] in their prophetic inspiration that that particular prophecy would be eternally valid. However, truly there are changes according to the character of every generation, and in this aspect Moses went beyond them, prophesying with '*This* is the matter'—meaning that Moses grasped everything according to its time and place, understanding that prophecy was only temporal, and that after a time God would desire something else.[201]

In overturning the classical midrashic reading, Lainer asserts that the qualitative distinction of Moses' prophecy was not in its eternal nature but rather in Moses' realization of its limited and temporal nature. According to Lainer, because the divine will is dynamic, prophecy can only express the divine will at a particular moment or place. Conversely, the weaker quality of the other prophets is expressed by their false belief that their prophecies should be eternal. All of this is alluded to, Lainer explains, by Moses use of the expression '*zeh hadavar*' in regard to vows. The nature of a vow, which is a prohibition imposed by one upon oneself, is that it is temporary. The language of *zeh* used by Moses in his prophecy underlines that it too is limited and temporary in nature.

Lainer's radical understanding of Moses' prophecy hinges on his interpretation of the phrase *bekolo shel Moshe*, which appears in the Talmud. Before we turn to *MHs*, we need to understand the exegetical field within which Lainer is operating. The verse under discussion is משה ידבר והאלהים יעננו בקול 'Moses would speak and God would answer him in a voice'.[202] This verse immediately precedes the theophany in the biblical narrative, and classical exegetes either understand it as referring to events before the theophany,[203] or find some way to interpret the verse to ensure that the Ten Commandments issue from God and not Moses. Rashi,[204] for example, cites the rabbinic tradition that this phrase refers not to the first two commandments, which the Israelites received from God directly, but to the latter eight which Moses received from God and then transmitted to the people.

A Talmudic passage which seeks to understand this verse in the context of a seemingly unrelated issue becomes the focal point of Lainer's interpretation.

R. Simeon b. Pazi said: From where do we learn that the translator is not permitted to raise his voice above that of the Torah reader? Because it says, 'Moses would speak and God would answer him in a voice'. The words *bakol* 'in a voice' do not [appear to] add meaning. What then does 'in a voice' mean? [It means God answered] in the voice of Moses.[205]

In the simple reading of this Talmudic passage, the subject of the biblical verse is indeed the theophany itself; Moses is the reader while God seems to be relegated to the role of the translator. When God answers Moses with 'Moses' voice' it means that God the translator did not raise his voice louder than Moses the reader.

The medieval Tosafists and Alfasi,[206] however, were disturbed by the possible reading of the text as antithetical to classic Jewish doctrine, which holds that the Ten Commandments emanated from God and not Moses. They therefore reread it to say that God is the reader and Moses the translator. The phrase the 'voice of Moses' is interpreted to mean that God speaks in a voice like the voice of Moses, specifically, in a voice that is equal in volume. Lainer explicitly rejects the opinions of the Tosafists and Alfasi, one of the few times that such an outright rejection of an earlier authority is recorded in *MHs*.[207] After he rejects these opinions, he states:

והענין בזה כי באמת משה היה אומר עשרת הדברות לישראל אך...
בשורש הדבר שיחקקו הד״ת בלבות ישראל זה היה מאת הש״י שהיה
חוקק בלב כל אחד ואחד כפי רצונו ית'. וזה הענין אשר הש״י כביכול נקרא
מתורגמן, היינו אחר שיצאו עשרת הדברות מפי משה לישראל חזר הקב״ה
וחקק אותם בלבם

The matter of this [passage] in truth is that Moses would say the Ten Commandments to Israel, even though in the root of the thing, which was the words of Torah becoming engraved in the hearts of Israel, this came from God, who would engrave in the heart of each and every one, according to His blessed will. And this is the sense in which God is called, as it were, the translator. That is, after the Ten Commandments came out of the mouth of Moses to Israel, God would go back and engrave them in their heart...[208]

In Lainer's radical reading, it is Moses who speaks the Ten Commandments, Moses who is the source of divine revelation! This is the ultimate prophetic experience, in which the voice of God and the voice of the prophet have become in essence identical.[209]

A fourth Lainer teaching about the radical nature of 'soul print' prophecy can be found in the work of his student, Tzadok Hakohen:

וידבר אלהים את כל הדברים האלה לאמר. שמעתי דבסיני היה דבור ממש, דוידבר אלוקים וגו' היינו ע"י ה' מוצאות הפה דבני ישראל, וזה ברור ואמת דכל נבואה היינו ע"י קול הנביא עצמו כמו שכתוב (ברכות מה.) בקולו של משה, ואז היו כל ישראל מדרגת נבואה ששמעו דבר ה' כנודע והיינו ע"י דיבורים דאין קול בעולם זולת ה' מוצאות הפה ונאמר (שיר ה ו) נפשי יצאה בדברו וגו' שכללו כל חלקי נפשותם להש"י אז

> I heard (i.e., from Mordechai Joseph) that at Sinai there was actual speech. For [where it states] 'And God spoke' (Exod. 20:1), this means [it happened] through 'the five issuances of the mouth' of the children of Israel, and this is clear and true, for all prophecy is through the voice of the prophet himself, as [the Talmud] wrote: *bekolo shel Moshe* 'through the voice of Moses'.[210] And at that time, all of Israel were on a level of prophecy, for they heard the word of God, as is known, and this was by means of spoken words…[F]or there is no voice in the world other than 'the five issuances of the mouth', and it is said, 'my soul issued forth when he spoke' etc. (Cant. 5:6)— for they integrated all the parts of their souls in God then.[211]

Here we see that while Lainer and Tzadok certainly affirm some distinction between Moses and the other prophets, it is a different sort of distinction than the fundamental one posited by most of the tradition. In effect, Tzadok is saying that all prophecy is like the 'voice of Moses'—they are, in a profound sense, one and the same. Lainer, as cited by Tzadok, does not make an essential distinction between Mosaic and non-Mosaic prophecy. The phrase that the Talmud interprets as the voice of revelation, בקולו של משה *bekolo shel Moshe* 'in the voice of Moses', is taken to refer to Moses *and* the other prophets. Lainer believes that *both* emanate from the voice of the prophet. Moreover, all the people according to Tzadok are at this level of prophecy at the theophany of Sinai, and the commandments issue in their voices, in actual speech, not just in the voice of Moses but of all six hundred thousand souls. Moses becomes the guarantor that it is possible for God's commandments to be spoken by everyone in their own voice.

Our reading is complemented by the following passage in *MHs*. In the text with which we began our discussion of prophecy,[212] Lainer discusses Mosaic prophecy in two very different ways.

אבל במשה רבינו פה אל פה אדבר בו, היינו שבשעת התגלות הוא רואה הדבור מפורש יוצא מפי השי״ת באתוון גליפין, ומראה ולא בחידות שהוא כלל כל נפשות ישראל, לכן מראה לו השי״ת כל חילוקי דעות שנמצא בישראל, וזה נקרא ולא בחידות, היינו לא דעה אחת לבד רק כל הדעות, כי משה רבינו היה כלל כל הששים רבוא נשמות מישראל

> Concerning Moses, however, it is written, 'I speak with him mouth-to-mouth', that is, at the moment of revelation he sees clearly the word coming from God's mouth in formed letters: [hence] 'a vision, and without riddles', for he is the totality of all the souls of Israel. Therefore, God shows him all the different opinions of Israel, which is described as 'without riddles', that is, not one opinion alone, but all the opinions. For our teacher Moses incorporated all six hundred thousand souls of Israel…

First, Lainer says that Moses sees the words explicitly coming out of God's mouth as engraved letters. However, this is a dogmatic flourish that covers his real position.[213] Mosaic prophecy is not characterized by an objective transmission in which the unique individual self is lost. Lainer explains that Moses is unique because his soul includes all the souls of Israel. The uniqueness of Moses is such that it is integrative of all perspectives and thus not distorting. Functionally, Moses' voice is the equivalent of all the Israelites' voices together. As a result, Moses is not blinded by his uniqueness, unlike the other prophets, whose uniqueness is the prism that refracts and focuses (i.e., both constricts and makes clear) their prophecy. Throughout the passage, Lainer moves seamlessly from Moses to the Judah archetype and Solomon, showing that the Judah persona is the carrier of Mosaic prophecy. These all participate in divine intuition, which allows them to transcend the general principles of law and access the will of God, even if it contravenes the normative law whose source is the Mosaic prophecy itself.

Since the Mosaic revelation was in fact only reflective of a particular time and place, as Lainer stated above, it is naturally subject to displacement in the event that one accesses an unmediated divine revelation. Such a revelation would indicate that the dynamic will of God wants something other than what is enjoined by the old law. Of course, if this is so, then it makes perfect internal sense for the Judah figure to be able to override the general principles of law set up in the Mosaic revelation.

The final source we will adduce here is another citation from Tzadok Hakohen, which transmits a teaching from Lainer.[214] On first reading this text seems like a recapitulation of Maimonides[215] (i.e., Moses is 'wisdom' while the other prophets are 'imagination'), a favorite tactic of Tzadok before revealing a radical position that moves far beyond Maimonides.[216] He begins by saying that Moses is a clear prism while the other prophets are unclear prisms, prophesying with the quality of *koh*; Moses is wisdom while the other prophets are imagination. However, in his concluding paragraph, Tzadok shifts directions and clarifies his deeper intention. Following the tradition of his teacher, Tzadok explains (against Maimonides) that there is imagination in the prophecy of Moses. It is not that Moses, in being wisdom, becomes an empty vessel divested of voice, heart, and imagination. On the contrary:

> While for most prophets prophecy is 'on the heart', for Moses
> it is 'in the heart'…[his uniqueness is that] his essential soul
> and heart *were* Torah, thus the Torah is called by his name…
> Moses is 'on the inside'[217]—[that is to say] all of Moses, (even)
> the inside of Moses,…is made of Torah.[218]

Moses is in effect inside God concurrently with God's being inside Moses. Other prophets' uniqueness, mediated by their imagination, is both what allows for prophecy, and, at the same time, what separates them from God. In contrast, in the case of Moses, his uniqueness and his דמיון *dimayon* 'imagination' are fully merged with חכמה *hokhmah* 'wisdom'. A key phrase in the aforementioned passage is 'the Torah is called by his name'. As we shall ultimately see[219], this phrase indicates an identity of will between Moses and God. Thus he merges with God, and the Torah emanates from Moses, who is one with God.

Lainer and his student Tzadok hold that the distinction between Moses and other prophets is not that Moses simply becomes an empty channel free of any distortion due to Moses' nature. Rather, Moses is distinguished from other prophets by the inner nature of Moses himself, which is so radically מבורר *mevurar* 'clarified' that the voice of Moses and the voice of God become one. This is an expression of romantic consciousness at its most ecstatic: in the depth of human individuality—that is to say, in ultimate subjectivity—lies God.

The *Shekhinah* Speaks Through the Voice of Moses

In this section we will continue to explore the depth of Lainer's theologically provocative idea that the Torah was given by a Moses who is merged with God; not in the voice of God, but in the voice of Moses. Our focus in this section is exclusively on the phrase 'the *Shekhinah* speaks through the voice of Moses'.

The Torah is held by tradition both to be the word of God and to have been authored by Moses. This conundrum has been addressed in various ways in the history of Jewish thought. Particularly problematic is the authorship of the book of Deuteronomy.[220] On one hand, tradition holds that it must be the word of God as it is one of the five books of the law received by Moses on Sinai. At the same time, the Deuteronomy text itself begins with 'And these are the words which Moses spoke', which imputes some real level of authorship to Moses. The *Zohar* in several places implicitly offers a resolution with the pregnant if ambiguous phrase 'The *Shekhinah* speaks through the voice of Moses'.[221] This phrase suggests two very different understandings. The first understanding, reflecting the theocentric model adopted by many Hasidic readers, is that Moses was so completely effaced that he became a kind of channel for the divine voice. Hence the Torah is the word of God and not that of Moses. The Magid of Mezerich, for example, writes in the name of the Baal Shem Tov:

> The world of speech is the world of consciousness. It is as if the *Shekhinah* contracts herself in order to dwell within the speech. This is the meaning of the *Sefer Yetzirah* statement that 'they were places in the mouth', [and this is the meaning of the phrase] 'God, open my mouth' (Psalms 51:17)...that is the *Shekhinah*...And he is merely like a *shofar*...for the *shofar* only emits the sound that is blown into it, and if the blower separates from the *shofar* it does not emit voice.[222]

85

In a related text, a student describes his master, the Magid of Mezerich, as teaching, 'It is not he himself who speaks, [rather it is as] if the *Shekhinah* were speaking from his throat'.[223]

A similar understanding that the *Shekhinah* talking from the throat of Moses indicates the effacement of the person in order to allow the divine voice to be channeled clearly is sharply formulated by Kalonymus Kalman, teacher of the Seer of Lublin, an important direct source in Hasidism of Lainer's spiritual lineage.[224] He writes, describing the *tzadikim* 'saying Torah'[225], that 'the *Shekhinah* rests on them and the *Shekhinah* talks through their throat, and those *tzadikim* do not know afterwards what they said... for the *Shekhinah* talks through their throat'.[226] Both Weiss and Piekarz read the Hasidic sources adducing this adage as supporting a radically theocentric instrumental model in which the *tzadik* is the empty vessel: in Piekarz's phrase, the *tzadik* is 'the medium' through which the divine voice flows.[227]

This phrase is particularly important, for while the *Zohar* may have used it to explain the attribution of divine authorship to a book which presents itself as the word of Moses, it was greatly expanded by many Hasidic authors. In the first stage of Hasidic thought, Moses 'saying' the book of Deuteronomy was generalized to include the *tzadik's* 'saying Torah'.[228] Then in the second stage, the *tzadik* saying Torah was expanded to include all the words of the *tzadik*.[229] Finally, in *MHs*, the concept of 'the *Shekhinah* talks through his throat' was expanded from the *tzadik* to include the Judah archetype, which in theory could be accessed by any person.[230]

The first two readings of the *Shekhinah* speaking from the throat of Moses are rooted in a decidedly theocentric orientation; in both, Moses' attainment comes through his effacement.[231] The last expansion by Lainer is radically different: in *MHs*, the *Shekhinah* speaking comes through the *intensification of individuality*, rather than through its effacement.

This then is the second possible understanding of 'the *Shekhinah* speaks in the voice of Moses': Moses is not effaced, but rather Moses is so completely present that his voice and the voice of the *Shekhinah* blur into one. In this sense, as we saw earlier, Moses is an expression of the Judah archetype who is characterized by התנשאות *hitnas'ut*, the perfected one, the righteous one or the master, one of Lainer's terms for the radical uniqueness through which one participates in their ontic unity with God.[232]

86

Based on Lainer's and Tzadok's reading of Mosaic prophecy,[233] outlined above, it seems reasonable to suggest that their reading of the *Zohar* would be equally empowering. However, we do not need to rely on conjecture, because in another passage, Tzadok explicitly reads the Zoharic text on the *Shekhinah* speaking through the voice of Moses in precisely in this fashion, cited as explanation of the nature of the divine revelation of Deuteronomy.[234]

In this passage, Tzadok discusses the distinction between שיחה *sihah*, casual conversation, and תלמוד תורה *talmud Torah*, speech which is engaged in the sacred act of study. However, he draws this distinction only in order to undo it, suggesting that while one must begin with formal intention, this is to allow one to arrive at a level where even one's unconscious words are ד"ת גמור *divrei Torah gamur* 'fully words of Torah'. This, as we shall explore in Chapter Twelve, is the defining quality of Lainer's Judah archetype. Lainer teaches: 'Even if [his words] appear to be *divrei hulin* idle words, they are from God'.[235] Tzadok explains this idea using a Talmudic passage[236] that interprets a verse in Psalms to mean, 'In the beginning [when a person studies Torah] it is *Hashem's* Torah, but then it becomes his Torah'. Tzadok explains that this second level in which it becomes 'his Torah' is achieved when a human being realizes his ontic identity with the Torah. 'His very kidneys' become Torah, according to Tzadok. Tzadok here alludes to a concept which we will show below to be one of the most important underlying structures in Lainer's theology; that is, the ontic identity between human and God, and between the name of man and the of God. This ontic identity is the meaning, according to Tzadok, of the Zoharic claim made in interpreting the Talmudic passage that 'Moses said [the words of Deuteronomy] on his own'.[237]

> ...for the *Shekhinah* spoke through his throat...and this is called words that come from the heart, as it says in the Song of Songs, 'My heart is awake', for God is the heart of Israel... this is [indicated in] the language of 'These are the words he spoke' (Deut. 1:1), supraconscious words...For this is the level of the *Shekhinah*, which spoke through the throat of Moses... that is, from [Moses] himself...and so Moses said, 'I am not a man of words' (Exod. 4:10), for he was the husband of the *Shekhinah* (i.e., erotically merged with the *Shekhinah*). Thus, all of his words were the Torah of God...the highest level of the level of *sihah* conversation...Thus, all of his conversations are words of Torah'.[238]

87

As in the Tzadok passage we analyzed at the end of the previous section, here again Moses is described not as being effaced, but as speaking from the depth of himself. According to both Lainer and his student Tzadok, when one reaches the depths of עצמו 'atzmo himself, (i.e., selfhood), one realizes one's identity with the divine and all one's words become Torah. The ontological level of 'atzmo, according to both Lainer and Tzadok, emerges from the level of consciousness termed by the *Zohar*, 'The *Shekhinah* talks from the throat of Moses'. In the giving of the Torah through Moses, the ontic identity between the authentic voice of Moses and the voice of the *Shekhinah* is revealed. This position is indicative of the nature of acosmic humanism, which is the defining characteristic of Lainer's thought.[239] All of these themes will be seen below to be fully developed in Lainer's theology.

What emerges from the above is that, according to Lainer, the principle of acosmism does not efface the individual, but rather empowers the individual, because the human is a part of God as well. The divine voice finds expression in the voice of the unique individual, modeled, as we saw above, by the prophet who manifests God's voice through the clear prism of his *perat nefesh* unique individuality.

Notes for Chapter Four

1 This tradition was 'inherited' from Lainer by no less central a figure than Abraham Kook. See the section 'Lainer and Abraham Isaac Hakohen Kook'.

2 For previous uses of the term 'personal myth', see Keen, *Hymns*. See also Idel, *Perspectives* xi–xx, where Idel characterizes ecstatic Kabbalah in terms of personal myth. However, uniqueness in the sense that Lainer uses it is not a theme in ecstatic Kabbalah.

3 Jacobs, *Religion*. For example, he adduces a Talmudic passage (*bBer*. 58b) identifying the divine as the 'wise one of secrets', explaining that even though 'no two minds are alike', God nonetheless knows the secret of every person. See *Religion* 6. This passage is cited by Lainer in *MHs vol. 2* Teztaveh s.v. *vesamta*, discussed on p. 30.

4 The primary concerns of the sources adduced by Jacobs are themes of individual value, worth, and dignity.

5 The first three strands interlock in the sources to a highly significant degree, as I will point out below. The fourth is more independent, overlapping only occasionally with the other strands.

6 See Scholem, 'Revelation' 292–293.

7 The term was suggested to me by Haym Soloveitchik. When I asked him for his opinion on the intellectual influence of kabbalistic thought on his father Joseph Soloveitchik, his response was that scholars sometimes need to search less for direct citations and more for what he called 'intellectual furniture'. Such was the case, Soloveitchik suggested, with his father's rather massive adaptation of kabbalistic categories (personal communication, Jerusalem 1996).

8 See section 'Unique *Mitzvah* and Unique Torah: The Matrix of Antinomianism'.

9 I am indebted to Johanna Weinberg for this important caveat.

10 Some of the primary sources are cited in Berlin's *Haemek* Toldot She'ilta 19:4; see discussions in Sperber, 'Al Yesod' and Hallamish, 'Mitzvah'.

11 *mKid*. 1:10.

12 *yKid*. 19a, adduced in Berlin, *Haemek* Toldot She'ilta 19:4. See also *bMak*. 24a for a similar formulation suggesting that one *mitzvah* chosen by a person as their unique *mitzvah* has redemptive power.

13 See Azikri, *Sefer Haredim* 71, 72.

14 *bShab*. 118b.

15 *MHs vol. 1* Proverbs s.v. *ner mitzvah*. Lainer cites this passage as a source for the idea of the unique *mitzvah*.

16 *bShab*. 118a.

17 See section 'Hisaron and Uniqueness'.

18 *Midrash Kohelet*, commenting on the verse 'He who loves money will not be satisfied by money' (Eccl. 5:9) (not in printed edition; adduced in Berlin, *Haemek* Toldot She'ilta 19:4).

19 Maimonides, Commentary to Mishnah ad mMak. 3:17.

20 Albo, *Sefer Ha'ikarim* 3:29.

21 See the section '*Hisaron Meyuhad*', esp. endnote 212.

22 The idea of unique *mitzvah* appears in *Sefer Hasidim* as well. He seems to view it in more pragmatic terms: 'Better to have one *mitzvah* done properly than many done improperly' (Yehudah ben Shmuel Hehasid, *Sefer Hasidim* 529).

23 *Zohar* 3:124a.

24 Azikri, *Sefer Haredim* 61a.

25 Hallamish, 'Mitzvah' 228–229.

26 Horowitz, *Shenei* 38 col. 4, 49b, adduced in Hallamish.

27 Modena, *Maavar Yabok* Siftei Renanot Ch. 31, adduced in Hallamish, 'Mitzvah'.

28 *Petah Einayim*, commentary to *mAvot* 5:23, adduced in Hallamish 'Mitzvah'.

29 See, e.g., Polnoye, *Toldot Yaakov Yosef* Yitro 182a; Braslav, *Likutei Mohoran vol. 2 (Tinyana)* sec. 63; Alfasi, *Sihot HaRan* 185.

30 *Partzuf* is a term used throughout the Lurianic corpus. On the relationship of Luria and Hasidism, see Elior, 'Historical' esp. 317, where Elior discusses terminological and conceptual affinities between Hasidism and Luria. See also Idel's critique of Elior's 'overemphasis' on the Lurianic influence in understanding the Hasidic Zeitgeist (Idel, *Messianic* 221–234, esp. n. 58). For a brief overview of the various configurations of the *sefirot* which are designated *partzufim*, see Jacobson, *Mikabalat* 31–52.

31 Polnoye, *Toldot Yaakov Yosef vol. 1* Yitro 182a.

32 See also the passages from *Meor Einayim* that we discuss in the context of the hermeneutics of uniqueness (p. 92ff). There as well, the issue is the implicit integration into the community through the affirmation of uniqueness.

33 Degel Mahaneh Efrayim Va'et'hanan 68a.

34 See Chapter Twelve for a discussion of the Judah archetype who replaces the role of the *tzadik*; this is one of the major innovations in Lainer's thought.

35 See Sperber, 'Al Yesod' 118, 119. Sperber begins the article with a citation from Zusia of Onipol expressing the one-letter tradition and then uses the unique *mitzvah* tradition as its source.

36 See Hallamish, 'Mitzvah'.

37 See, e.g., Scholem, 'The Meaning' 65.

38 Idel, *Absorbing Perfections* 81–110.

39 Jacobs, *Religion* 120.

40 For a treatment of the topic of God's voice in relation to the nature of revelation, see Scholem, *The Messianic Idea* 282–303, esp. 293–302.

41 *Shemot Rabbah* 5:9, adduced by Jacobs, *Religion* 120. For other rabbinic sources on the different perceptions of revelation in accordance with the capacity of each person, see *Pesikta DeRav Kahana* 12:5. See also Idel, *Absorbing Perfections* 95 and Handelman, *Slayers* 61.

42 On the 'faces' of revelation see Scholem, *Revelation* 297; Idel, *Absorbing Perfections* 518 n. 74; see also Gafni, *Safek* 331–360; *Mystery* 14–17; *Soul Prints* 43–45.

43 See Sagi, *Elu Ve'elu*, on the Talmudic phrase 'These and these are the words of

the living God', for a detailed analysis of these possibilities in the Talmud and its commentaries.

44 Scholem, 'The Meaning' 65 n 1.

45 Luria, *Sefer Hakavanot*, adduced by Scholem, 'The Meaning' 65 n. 1. The source of this correspondence between interpretations and letters predates Luria. See Nahmanides' sermon, 'Torat Hashem Temimah' vol. 1, 162. Nahmanides states: 'Creation was with differing faces to the extent of six hundred thousand, and this number included all opinions, and they said, it was worth receiving the Torah in order that all the opinions be received'. See also Idel, *Absorbing Perfections* 518 n. 75.

46 Scholem himself refers to this text without citing it ('The Meaning' 65 n 1).

47 Bacharach, *Emek*, see endnote 302. On this kabbalist, see Liebes, 'Lidemuto'.

48 Azulai, *Hesed*, see endnote 302. On this kabbalist, see Tishby, 'Yahaso'.

49 Vital, *Shaar Hagilgulim* Introduction 17.

50 The four levels of interpretation often parallel the four worlds of the Kabbalah. See Scholem, 'Leheker'. See also Scholem, 'The Meaning' 50–63; Idel, *Absorbing Perfections* 661 and references cited there.

51 See Idel, *Absorbing Perfections* 98 n. 96. Idel suggests a similar reading with an emphasis on hermeneutics; he cites it as copied in *Emek Hamelekh*. This text is also cited by Scholem (*On the Kabbalah* 65 n. 1).

52 In Azulai and Bacharach, the phrase 'on that day' is left out.

53 Note that the term שייך אל שורש 'the root of his soul' is borrowed by Lainer from Luria to refer to uniqueness.

54 Vital, *Eitz Hayyim* 15a. In the continuation of the passage, Vital links the uniqueness of time to astrological considerations and then says: '...These changes are taking place at each and every moment, and in accordance with these changes... the sayings of the book of the *Zohar* are changing [too], and all are the words of the living God'. Similarly, Luria himself says that 'in each and every moment the [meanings] of the passages of the holy *Zohar* are changing' (*Zohar Hai* vol. 1 3a). This view is incorporated into the teachings of the founder of the Hasidic movement, the Baal Shem Tov, who is reported to have said, 'The book of the *Zohar* has each and every day a different meaning' (Sudilkov 98). See *Perspectives* 248, 249 nn. 247–250 and *Absorbing Perfections* 101–102, nn. 98–101, where these sources are adduced in the context of different issues.

55 Vitebsk, *Peri Haaretz* Vayeishev 3. On the theology of Menahem Mendel, see Hallamish, 'The Teachings'; see also Safran, 'Maharal'.

56 See also Elimeleh of Lishensk, who discusses the 'root' of a generation. (*Noam Elimelekh*, vol. 1 3b). On the uniqueness of time among contemporaries of Lainer, see Alter, *Sefat Emet*, Hayyei Sarah 24:1. In several years of commentary on the verse 'Abraham was old', he deals with what we call the soul print of time.

57 See the section 'Individuality in Time and Place'.

58 In this respect, I disagree with Magid's characterization of Lainer as a soft antinomianist (*Hasidism* 205, 255) While it is true that Lainer does not reject law in its entirety and even regards it as the key to his system, he does break the

fundamental identity between law and the will of God. *Nomos*, in that context, becomes instrumental.

59 On Luria's guidance of his students in terms of identifying their unique souls, see Vital, *Shaar Ruah Hakodesh* 14; the important material adduced by Benayahu, *Sefer Toldot HaAri* 156–157; Fine, 'The Contemplative', esp. 75.

60 On the role of orality in kabbalistic ritual see Idel, *Absorbing Perfections* 470–481.

61 Vital, *Shaar Hagilgulim* Introduction 17.

62 Taking full stock of this text helps us avoid the common problem of privileging doctrine over ritual in assessing theological ideas.

63 Azulai, *Hesed* Ma'ayan 2 Nahar 21. See also Idel, *Absorbing Perfections* 96 n. 75, who cites a different passage in Azulai on the nexus between the number of letters in the Torah and the number of Israelites. In regard to the inability of anyone other than that soul related to reveal that interpretation to others, see Bacharach, *Emek* 41d, adduced in Scholem, *The Meaning* 65 n. 1, and in *Absorbing Perfections* 96.

64 See also Alter, *Sefat Emet, vol.* 3 85d: 'God placed in the souls of Israel illuminations…so that in every generation they could find new illuminations, that were always in their root', cited in Idel, *Absorbing Perfections* 519 n. 86.

65 See Safrin, *Sefer Heikhal Haberakhah vol.* 5 31:19.

66 Shapira, *Midrash Pinhas* 24a.

67 *MHs vol. 1* Bo s.v. *vezot hukat.*

68 On personal redemption in early Hasidism, see Nigal, Introduction 39–50 in Hakohen, *Tzafnat Paaneah.* In terms of Lainer and the later period of Hasidism, see Faierstein, 'Personal' 212–214.

69 See Idel, *Absorbing Perfections* 98–99.

70 See Idel, *Messianic* 212–247.

71 See Ross, 'Shenei' 153 n. 1.

72 See, e.g., Hallamish, 'Mishnato', esp. 112–135; Elior, 'The Paradigms'; *Torat HaElohut.* See, however, Idel's critique of Elior, particularly in regard to Schneur Zalman of Liadi (Idel, *Hasidism* 122–124). His critique notwithstanding, one could hardly apply our term 'acosmic humanism' to Habad.

73 *Berur*, which is in part a clarification of intention and desire, is a long and arduous process that belies any sort of romantic naiveté on Lainer's part. See Chapter Ten. See also Seeman, 'Martyrdom', which focuses throughout on the complex 'ritual work' ('avodah – including also psychological and emotional work) necessary for clarification.

74 See Chapter One for discussion of the ideas summarized here and in following paragraphs.

75 On the shift in the understanding of the term *berur* from Lurianic to Hasidic sources, see Jacobson, *Mikabalat* 110. According to Jacobson, this is an expression of Hasidism's less mythic structure of and its immanentism.

76 For further discussion see on 'Lainer and the Romantics'.

77 See sources cited in Weiss, 'Determinism' 447 n. 1.

78 See the section 'Uniqueness and Healing'.

79 See p. 72.

80 See Chapter Two and the section 'Freedom and Law'.

81 Elaborated in Idel, *Absorbing Perfections* 106.

82 See especially Idel, *Absorbing Perfections* 105, and (in 'On Oral') 471, 474.

83 This perception of the *tzadik* was very widespread in Hasidism, particularly in the court of one of the most important predecessors to Lainer in Polish Hasidism, the Seer of Lublin. On the conception of the *tzadik* in Lublin, see Elior, 'Bein'. See, however, Idel's partial critique of Elior's understanding of the Seer and, in particular, the dialectical quality of *yesh* and *ayin* (Idel, *Hasidism*, 112, 123, 310, nn. 41, 42).

For a more detailed bibliography of the *tzadik* in Hasidism, see the section 'The Democratization of Enlightenment'.

84 *Absorbing Perfections* 102–108.

85 Whatever the king, the Judah archetype, says, becomes the word of God. It remains for us to show that according to Lainer, anyone can embody this archetype. See Chapter Twelve.

86 Jacobs, *Religion* 6.

87 See Idel, *Absorbing Perfections* 99.

88 See Chapter One.

89 See e.g. *MHs vol. 2* Devarim s.v. *havu*; Isaiah s.v. *kol tzofayich*.

90 *mAvot* 2:1.

91 *MHs vol. 1* Vayeishev s.v. *vayehi*. See also *vol. 1* Bo s.v. *vayehi hoshekh*, *vol. 1* Bemidbar s.v. *bemidbar*, *vol. 2* Kedoshim s.v. *vayedaber*.

92 On *'omek* and *gavan* see Elior, 'Temurot', esp. 413ff.

93 Note however that part of the necessary *berur* before performing any action is to clarify how this action will affect the community. See *MHs vol. 1* Kedoshim s.v. *ish 'imo*. In addition, Lainer suggests that one who has transcended *mitzvah* and entered the place beyond commandments must nonetheless fulfill the commandments for the sake of the community. See *MHs vol. 1* Vayeira s.v. *ve'atah* and *vol. 1* Mishpatim s.v. *va'avadetem*. These positions provide some balance in Lainer's system.

94 See p. 70.

95 A classic description of unique individuality by Lainer states: 'Each person feels a unique taste in the *mitzvah* that his friend does not feel'. Taste, of course, is the paradigm of incommunicability (*vol. 1* Va'et'hanan s.v. *shamor*). See Chapter Twelve on the Judah archetype, where we shall see that the concept of insularity and incommunicability is in large part related to Lainer's insistence on the primacy of will in defining the essence of the *homo imago dei* and the nature of the individual. Will, by its very nature, is incommunicable, as opposed to Sophia/wisdom. On the incommunicability of will and its relation to individuality in Hasidic

literature, see the brief but important remarks by Joseph Soloveitchik, *Reflections* 98–106. The Hasidic idea of סוד *sod* being not that which is forbidden to communicate but rather that which is incommunicable is attributed to Simcha Bunim of Przysucha, Lainer's teacher. See the sources adduced by Idel in *Absorbing Perfections* 181–185.

96 See Idel, *Absorbing Perfections* 104.

97 See Idel, *Absorbing Perfections* 98–99. Idel himself qualifies his analysis of individuality in the Safed school, recognizing the emergence in Luria's Safed of 'a new emphasis on the individual that deserves separate study'. However, in his next sentence, he claims that authenticity as opposed to originality was the issue in Safed.

98 Of course, these were the only currents of thought in the Renaissance. Obviously, Renaissance thought was far more complex and diverse. This characterization of the Renaissance is what Ken Wilber has termed an 'orienting generalization'. See Wilber, *Sex, Ecology* 1–20. For our purpose, this is more than sufficient. See endnote 344.

99 Lewis, *The Discarded*.

100 Note however, that in the kabbalistic world, the concept of theurgy, which affirms human influence on the cosmos, formed not in the Renaissance but in the medieval period. See Faierstein, 'God's'. Idel has explored some of the possible lines of influence going from Kabbalah to the Renaissance which may give order to these intertwining timelines. See e.g. *Absorbing Perfections* 489–492. An in-depth study outlining the different sensibilities of medieval, Renaissance, and Hasidic theurgies is very much needed.

101 See Morris, *The Discovery*, esp. 88. See also Jacob Burckhardt's classic study, *The Civilization* 81.

102 Abbs, *The Development* 130–132.

103 Werblowsky, 'Safed', esp. 7.

104 See Idel, 'From Italy'; see also Ruderman, 'The Italian'; Werblowsky, 'Safed' 7.

105 See Taylor, *Sources of the Self* 305–390. See also Ken Wilber's incisive analysis of Romanticism in *The Eye* 151–164 and *The Marriage* 90–102.

106 See Werblowsky, 'Safed' 7.

107 On the development of the concept of self from Plato through the Renaissance and Romantic periods and into modernity, see Taylor, *Sources of the Self*, esp. 211–368.

108 On the development from the Middle Ages to the Renaissance of the concept of the human role, see Faierstein, 'God's'.

109 On the difference between Lurianic *kavanot* and the Hasidic move to a more anthropocentric prayer concept, see Etkes, 'HaBesht', esp. 435–437; see also Weiss, 'The Kavvanot'.

110 See Chapter Twelve.

111 On rupture and continuity in kabbalistic thought, see Idel, *Perspectives* xi–xx. See also Idel, *Absorbing Perfections* 5 and Scholem, 'Religious'.

112 See Vital, *Eitz Hayyim*, where the core of the Lurianic myth is outlined. For

the classic scholarly statement of the Lurianic myth, see Scholem, 'Isaac Luria'. See also Jacobs, 'The Uplifting' 99–126 and Tishby, *Torat*. On Idel's challenge of what he terms Scholem's historical 'proximism' in explaining the Lurianic myth, see Idel, *Perspectives* 264 –267; also see Idel, *Hasidism* 6–9. See also Kallus' more recent challenge to Scholem's and Tishby's reading of the Lurianic myth, 'The Theurgy' 29–69.

113 Vital, *Shaar Hagilgulim* Introduction 5.

114 On *galut ha-shekhinah* in Luria see, e.g., Vital, *Shaar Hagilgulim* Introduction 21; Scholem, *Major Trends* 275–276, *Messianic* 137. On exile in Luria, see also Scholem, 'Isaac Luria', esp. 249–250.

115 This conflation appears clearly in Vital, *Eitz Hayyim* Shaar 48 Shaar Hakelipot 3. On the conflation of the two falls, also see Scholem, 'The Neutralization' 187. On the Lurianic corpus and its layers of texts, see Avivi, *Binyan* 77–91.

116 Note that Lainer's dependency on Luria for *hisaron* and his transformation of this concept is closely paralleled by a similar process with respect to *berur*.

117 For Luria, this word is often synonymous with *tikun*.

118 Vital, *Eitz Hayyim* Shaar Nun Perek 3.

119 For a fairly detailed exposition of the ideas of unique soul roots and sparks, soul families, and their interrelationships as expressed in *Shaar Hagilgulim*, see Scholem, 'Gilgul'. For the post-Scholem scholarly literature on transmigration, see Hallamish, *Mevo* 223–246.

120 For a clear linkage of value and uniqueness in Lainer see *MHs vol. 1* Bamidbar s.v. *vayedaber* 1 and s.v. *se'u*.

121 On *pardes* and the four levels of interpretation, see the sources cited in endnote 289.

122 Sharabi, *Nahar Shalom* 10b.

123 Vital, *Shaar Hagilgulim* Introduction 16.

124 On the term פרטי *perati* to indicate unique individuality, see Vital, *Shaar Hagilgulim* Hakdamot 1, 6, 11, 36, 39, esp. Hakdamah 6. See also Sharabi, *Nahar Shalom* 10b, 22b; Vital, *Shaar Hakavanot* Derushei Halailah Derush 10; *Shaar Hapesukim* Vayeira s.v. *vatahar vateiled; Shaar Hamitzvot 'Ekev, mitzvat birkat ha-mazon*. On the specific term *neshamah peratit*, see Vital, *Shaar Maamarei Razal bEruvin*.

125 Note, however, that Lainer's student Tzadok Hakohen uses *shoresh nishmato* to describe unique individuality, without the very specific Lurianic connotation. See, e.g., *Tzidkat Hatzadik* 149. The same is true of the term *shorsho* in *MHs*.

126 See, e.g., Vital, *Shaar Hagilgulim* Hakdamah 17. *Madreigato, helko*, and *ma'alato*, are also standard terms in *Shaar Hagilgulim*. See *Shaar Hagilgulim* Hakdamah 5, 11–13, 18–20, 35–38 for various examples of these usages.

127 See section 'Luria and Lainer: Provisional Conclusions'.

128 *MHs vol. 1* Tetzaveh s.v. *ve'eileh* 2.

129 See *Zohar* 2:94a–114a, the section of the *'Saba demishpatim'*, on the 'secret of transmigration'.

130 The other references to reincarnation in *MHs* concern the specific incarnations of Zimri-Shekhem and the Shimon-Dinah-Shekhem triangle. *See vol. 1* Vayishlah s.v. *vayavo*, Matot s.v. *vayiktzof* and Pinchas s.v. *vayar*.

131 The term is used in countless passages; see, e.g., *MHs. vol. 1* Bereishit s.v. *vayatzmah*.

132 On the use of healing in *MHs* instead of *tikun* in passages dealing with *hisaron*, see, e.g., *MHs vol. 1* Bereishit s.v. *vayatzmah*; Vayeitzei s.v. *vatomer*; Vayeilekh s.v. *vayeilekh*; vol. 2 Metzora s.v. *uva*; Metzora s.v. *vera'ah*;. On healing as a meaning of *tikun* see also Jacobson, *Mikabalat* 53.

133 When Lainer does use the word *tikun*, it is often in the context of a citation from Luria. See, e.g., *MHs vol. 1* Behaalotekha s.v. *vaya'as*. See also Ki Teitzei s.v. *ki teitzei* where, while Lainer does not cite Luria directly, the sentence about *tikun* concluding *lo yidakh mimenu nidakh* is almost a direct quote from Luria. See *Shaar Hagilgulim* Introduction 15. Note also that Lainer almost always uses *tikun* to refer to *tikun* of that which occurred in the past.

134 Etkes, taking issue with Weiss and Schatz-Uffenheimer, views the abandonment of Lurianic *kavanot* as an innovation of the Baal Shem Tov, and as internally tied to the Besht's notion of ecstatic prayer. Ecstatic prayer, unlike Lurianic *kavanah*, has as a major goal תענוג *ta'anug* 'pleasure', including the pleasure of the devotee, thus expressing, according to Etkes, a decided anthropocentric shift in Hasidism, away from Luria's more theocentric axis (Etkes, 'HaBesht' 422–454, esp. 435–37).

135 *MHs vol. 2* Metzora s.v. *vera'ah*.

136 *MHs vol. 1* Proverbs s.v. *ki*.

137 See Part Three.

138 Sudilkov, *Degel Mahaneh Efrayim* 38a, adduced in Scholem, 'The Neutralization' 189.

139 Polnoye, *Ketonet Pasim* 35a–35b, adduced in Scholem, 'The Neutralization' 189. See other sources there and in 'Gilgul' 244–250, esp. 248, where Scholem quotes a different (though nearly identical) part of the same passage.

140 See endnote 48. In this context, Scholem is engaged in a polemic with Tishby where Scholem's interest is to define as Hasidic and non-Lurianic the idea that raising the sparks is related to each person's uniqueness. However, when engaged in a polemic with Buber, where Scholem's interest is to root the Hasidic predilection for uniqueness in a broader intellectual context, he insists that the fundamental idea of uniqueness is rooted in Luria and not Hasidism. Scholem writes:

> Buber's interpretation stresses the *uniqueness* of the task
> facing each individual. 'All men have access to God but each to a
> different one'. This is certainly true but it is not a new statement of
> *personal* religion introduced by Hassidism [*sic*]. Rather, this idea
> comes originally from the Lurianic Kabbalah, i.e., from the very
> gnosis at which Buber in his later writings looks so askance. It holds
> that *each individual* is enjoined to raise the holy sparks which belong

specifically to his holy root in the great soul of Adam, the common soul root of all Mankind. For at one time every soul and every root has its *special place* in the soul of Adam. All that Hassidism did was to formulate this theory in a popular manner and thus give it an even more personal turn. (Scholem, 'Martin Buber' 246, italics added)

For an analysis of Scholem's relationship to Buber and Tishby, see the understated description by Sara Ora Heller Wilensky ('Joseph' 11, 12).

141 See Scholem, 'Devekut'. Idel critiques Scholem's view that *devekut* is an emergent feature of Hasidism, *Perspectives* 35–58. He also critiques Scholem's reading of Luria as overly messianic, *Messianic* 169–175.

142 In addition to above sources, note Scholem's examination of 'the strictly personal and intimate cast' ('Gilgul' 248) of the Hasidic position on redeeming the sparks, discussed in 'Gilgul' 244–250.

143 Scholem argues that Jacob Joseph of Polnoye's 'personal and intimate descriptions of raising the sparks' (Scholem's phrasing), which Jacob Joseph attributes to Luria, are merely his transformation of Luria, having little to do with the Lurianic school itself. (See 'Gilgul' 248–249.) This claim is not fully borne out by the sources. For example, Vital, in his discussion of raising the sparks, explicates the necessity of performing *berur* on one's own קליפת העשייה *kelipat ha-ʿasiyah* (the husk of one's own world of action) (*Shaar Hakavanot* Shaar Nefilat Apayim, Derush 3). Vital refers precisely to the concept of raising the sparks of one's personal environment. Moreover, as we have pointed out, individualism is also an important factor in Luria's thought.

144 Abbs, *The Development* 130–132.

145 Menahem Nahum of Chernobyl, *Meor Einayim* 166–167; see also 110. For a scholarly analysis of this text, see Tishby, *Studies in Kabbalah* vol. 2, 509–510.

146 Idel, *Messianic* 231–236.

147 For a general discussion of speech and thought, albeit in the more quietistic schools of Hasidism, see Schatz-Uffenheimer, *Hahasidut* 110–128.

148 Personal communication (Jerusalem, Aug. 2002).

149 See *Plotinus*, Enn. 1:8, 'evil…appears in the absence of any form of good'.

150 See, e.g., Idel, 'Hamahshavah'; Farber, 'Kelipah'. Also see Pedaya, 'Pegam'; Dan, 'Samael'.

151 See Wolfson, 'Light', esp. 87–94. More generally, see Liebes, 'Hamashiah' 219–221; 'Hamitos', esp. 449–479; 'Keitzad', esp. 66–68. Wolfson's reading should be contrasted with Scholem and his school, who tended to view evil in more Gnostic and dualistic terms. See, e.g., Scholem, *Major Trends* 235–239, and 'Sitra'; Tishby and Lahover, *Mishnat Hazohar* vol. 1 138–150; 295–298.

152 See Vital, *Shaar Hakavanot* 47a; see also the discussion about Luria and *nefilat apayim* in Jacobson, *Mikabalat* 38–52

153 See Scholem's classic essay, 'Redemption'. For a more nuanced pictured of the Sabbatean theology incorporating virtually all post-Scholem scholarship, see

Elqayam, 'Sod'.

154 See, e.g., *Magid Devarav LeYaakov* sec. 232.

155 See, e.g., Hallamish, 'Mishnato' 374–382.

156 Meor Einayim 62a.

157 The aspect of eradicating evil also finds limited expression in *MHs*. In passages which take this stance, Lainer discusses הפרדה *hafradah* 'separation' of the evil from the good. Although this is not quite eradication, it is also not transformation. See *vol.1* Bamidbar s.v. *zot hukat*; *vol. 2* Va'eira s.v. *vehifleiti*; see also *vol. 1* Mikeitz s.v. *mikeitz 1*.

158 Not surprisingly, a key passage cited by Wolfson (*Zohar* 2:108b; Wolfson, 'Light' 91–92) to prove his thesis that there is a thread in the *Zohar* about positively engaging evil for the sake of its transformation is also one of the few *Zohar* passages cited almost in its entirety in *MHs* (*vol. 1* Gilyon Tzav s.v. *ve'inyan*).

159 See *MHs vol. 2* Likutim Malakhi s.v. *az*, where Lainer transforms the concept of קליפה קודם לפרי *kelipah kodem leperi* 'the husk (or shell) comes before the fruit', which was understood ontologically in early Kabbalah (Farber, 'Kelipah'), into a principle governing what one might call, along with Buber, an I–thou human relationship.

160 See *MHs vol. 2* Likutim Isaiah s.v. *yotzer or*. See also *vol. 1* Metzora s.v. *zot*.

161 See *MHs vol. 1* Behukotai s.v. *vezeh*, where Lainer discusses the revelation of the dark from within the light and links it thematically to what we will term the Judah archetype.

162 *MHs vol. 2* Vayishlah s.v. *atah*.

163 *MHs vol. 2* Korah s.v. *ketiv*.

164 *MHs vol. 1* Toldot s.v. *vayeishev* (Source 3 in volume 2); *vol. 2* Ki Teitzei s.v. *ki teitzei 2* (Source 22 in volume 2).

165 See the section 'A Phenomenology of *Hisaron*'.

166 *bGit.* 43a; see *MHs vol. 1* Vayeitzei s.v. *ha-aretz*; Yitro s.v. *zakhor*; Naso s.v. *ish*; Devarim s.v. *ahad asar* (Source 12 in volume 2).

167 See, e.g., *MHs vol. 1* Bamidbar s.v. *zot hukat*, where Lainer affirms that no evil can ever touch the essence of the 'deep life' of Israel. See also *vol. 1* Ki Teitzei s.v. *ki yihyeh*.

168 *MHs vol. 2* Behaalotekha, s.v. *uveyom*.

169 See *Bereishit Rabbah* 9:2 68; *Zohar* 2:34b. See Scholem, 'The Kabbalah of', esp. 194–195, 248–251. See also the additional nuances and texts in Idel, 'Hamahshavah' 359–360.

170 *MHs vol. 2* Behaalotekha s.v. *bayom*.

171 In the work of Lainer's student Tzadok Hakohen, the one-letter theory is explicit: '...all of Israel have a portion (*helek*) in Torah...everyone's [ontological] foothold is in their letter in the Torah and a Sefer Torah that is missing a letter is invalid'.

172 *MHs vol. 1* Bo s.v. *zot hukat*.

173 For a extensive list of sources on *'olam ha-ba* and its relation to unmediat-

ed divine will, see also Liebes, 'Hamashiah' 219–221; 'Hamitos', esp. 449–479; 'Keitzad', esp. 66–68. On *'olam ha-ba* in Lainer, see above p. 51ff.

174 *MHs vol. 1* Kedoshim s.v. *veilohei maseikhah.*

175 See section '*Hisaron* and Uniqueness'.

176 Num. 12:6

177 *MHs vol. 2* Behaalotekha s.v. *im yihyeh* (Source 5 in volume 2). Here Lainer weaves the ultimate prophetic achievement of Moses with that of the contemporary halakhist who has achieved a level of intuition which Lainer calls *emet le'amito* (the truth unto its deepest truth); this level allows him to settle disputes of the most ordinary kind. See Cluster 2 in volume 2.

178 Num. 12:7–8.

179 b Yevamot 49b.

180 See also *MHs vol. 1* Vayeira s.v. *veha-Elohim* and *vol. 2*; also Vayeira s.v. *'ikar,* where Lainer links the non-explicit nature of prophecy with the image of an unclear prism.

181 *bSanh.* 89a; Shimon, *Yalkut Shimoni* Kings 221; see also Loew, *Hidushei Agadot* loc. cit. and Albo, *Sefer Haikarim* 3:9.

182 *bHag.* 13b. The number of angels' wings is not an insignificant issue in prophetic vision. For attempts at explanation, see *bHag.* 13a and commentary *ad loc.* For alternative explanations see, e.g., Shimon, *Yalkut Shimoni* Ezekiel 338; Maimonides, *The Guide* 1:43–49; and Loew, *Netzah Yisrael* Ch. 22.

183 Shir Hashirim Rabbah 29:9.

184 Midrash Tehilim 93:1.

185 Hakohen, *Dover Tzedek* 4 191.

186 Hakohen, *Kedushat Hashabbat* Essay 7, 37; see also Luzzatto, *Daat Tevunot* 186, 138; *Shaarei Ramhal* Pit'hei Hokhmah, Petah 7.

187 *MHs vol. 1* Kedoshim s.v. *veilohei maseikhah.*

188 See, e.g., *MHs vol. 2* Ki Tisa s.v. *elohei maseikhah* 1 (Source 4 in volume 2). This is a recurrent theme for Lainer, who consistently identifies idolatry with the general rules of Torah in contradistinction to the immanent will of God. See below, 'Acosmic Humanism and Idolatry'.

189 *MHs vol. 1* Kedoshim s.v. *veilohei maseikhah.*

190 Tzadok explicitly attributes the teaching to Lainer elsewhere, in *Tzidkat Hatzadik* 22.

191 Hakohen, *Dover Tzedek* 4 161.

192 See, e.g., Num. 30:2.

193 See, e.g., Exod. 11:4.

194 For *koh* as likeness see, e.g., *Sifrei* to Num. 30:2; see also Mandelkern, *Veteris* 532 s.v. *koh.*

195 See, e.g., Shimon, *Yalkut Shimoni* Isaiah 385; also *Mekhilta* Exod. 20:2; *Yalkut Shimoni* Exod. 385; Halevi, *Hakuzari* 4:3; Maimonides, *Mishneh Torah* Hilkhot

Yesodei HaTorah 1:9; Luzzatto, *Daat Tevunot* 180.

196 On imagination and prophecy, see Maimonides, *The Guide* 2:36–38. See also Halevi, *Hakuzari* 4:3; Ibn Halawa, *Rabeinu Bahya* to Num. 12:6 s.v. *bamareh*; Loew, *Gevurot Hashem* Introduction 2–3; Levi Isaac of Berdichev, *Kedushat Levi* to Gen. 15:1; Hakohen, *Tzidkat Hatzadik* 203–205.

197 *Bemidbar Rabbah* 19:3; see also *Tanhuma* 6; *Pesikta DeRav Kahana* 4; Maimonides, *The Guide* 1:46.

198 Daniel 8:16.

199 See Maimonides, *The Guide* 2:35; 'Hakdamah Leperek Helek' Yesod 7; *Mishneh Torah* Hilkhot Yesodei HaTorah 7:6. See also *Mishneh Torah* Hilkhot Yesodei HaTorah 1:9–10, 2:8; *The Guide*, 1:21, 37, 54, 64.

200 Maimonides, *The Guide* 2:39, see also Maimonides, *Commentary to Mishnah* ad Hulin 7:6.

201 *MHs vol. 1* Matot s.v. *vayedaber*.

202 Exod. 19:19.

203 See, e.g., Nahmanides, *Commentary* and Ibn Ezra *ad loc.*

204 Exod. 19:19 *ad loc.*

205 *bBer.* 45a.

206 *ad bBer.* 45a.

207 Another example is *MHs vol. 2* Behaalotekha s.v. *im yihyeh* (Source 5 in volume 2). Here, Lainer rejects the simple reading of the relevant Talmudic passage (*bYoma 26a*) because it violates his sense of the Judah archetype.

208 *MHs vol. 1* Yitro s.v. *vayehi*.

209 For an earlier interpretation of the Talmudic phrase 'the voice of Moses' in this manner, see Abulafia, Oxford Manuscript 123 e. Heb. 264b, adduced in Idel, *The Mystical* 43, esp. n. 14.

210 *bBer.* 45a, quoted below.

211 *Tzidkat Hatzadik* 229. We analyze more of this passage in volume 3, Part Two.

212 *MHs vol. 2* Behaalotekha s.v. *im yihyeh* (Source 5 in volume 2), discussed above, p. 69.

213 This pattern is discussed above; see p. 21.

214 Hakohen, *Tzidkat Hatzadik* 204.

215 On the difference between Mosaic and non-Mosaic prophecy according to Maimonides, see, e.g., Wolfson, 'Hallevi' 49–82. Also see Macy, 'Prophecy'.

216 See Pariz, 'HaKohen'.

217 Tikunei Zohar 209a.

218 See also *MHs vol. 1* Vayehi s.v. *uvedam*, where the same passage from *Tikunei Zohar* is discussed.

219 See the section 'Called by the Name of God' in Chapter Nine, esp. discussion of the *MHs* passages where Jacob's acts are 'called by his name', p. 197ff.

220 On the authorship of the book of Deuteronomy see, e.g., Heschel, *Torah Min Hashamayim vol. 2* 71–143; 166–219.

221 On the origin of this phrase, see Hyman, *Otzar* 524; cf. Weiss, 'Via Passiva' n. 38. For its Zoharic expression, see *Zohar* 1:267a, *Zohar* 3: 26a, 219a, 306b; see also Hakohen, *Tzidkat Hatzadik* 163. Further discussion can be found in Piekarz, *Bein* 92 n. 3, and especially in 'Via Passiva' 71–84.

222 Mezerich, *Or Haemet* 1b; cf. Schatz-Uffenheimer, *Hasidism* 191, *Hahasidut* 112; see also Mezerich, *Hayyim Vahesed* 34a.

223 Zhitomir, *Or Hameir* Rimzei Rakia 2b; cf. Weiss 'Via Passiva' 79. For similar readings see Epstein (Kalonymus Kalman of Krakow, disciple of Elimelekh of Lizhensk), *Maor Vashemesh* 1 44a, and see extensive citations of extant material in Hasidism interpreting this phrase similarly in Weiss, 'Via Passiva' 72–79; Schatz-Uffenheimer, *Hasidism* 201–203, *Hahasidut* 119–121.

224 On the relationship between the theologies of Mordechai Lainer and the Seer of Lublin, see Elior, 'Temurot'.

225 On the significance of this description of Hasidic teaching, see Idel, *Absorbing Perfections* 470–481.

226 Epstein, *Maor Vashemesh* Bo 152.

227 Weiss, 'Via Passiva'; Piekarz, *Bein* 82–103.

228 Zhitomir, *Or Hameir* Rimzei Rakia 2b; cf. Weiss, 'Via Passiva' 79.

229 See, e.g., Zeev Wolf of Zhitomir, who writes 'and all the details of his speech are the words of the *Shekhinah* speaking from his throat' (Zhitomir, *Or Hameir* Rimzei Rakia Tetzaveh 70c). See also Tzvi Elimelekh of Dinov, who writes, 'it cannot be that the words of the *tzadik* will not be fulfilled, and even that which he says unintentionally, for the *Shekhinah* speaks through his voice' (*Igra Dekalah* Vayeishev 144c).

230 See the section 'The Democratization of Enlightenment' in Chapter 8.

231 Both sources are gathered by Joseph Weiss and Rivka Schatz-Uffenheimer in their classic studies of *via passiva* and quietism in Hasidism. See further discussion below, *p. 117ff*.

232 On *hitnas'ut* (exaltation coming from being in one's uniqueness) as a core quality of the Judah archetype, see *MHs vol. 1* Bemidbar s.v. *se'u*. Compare this with the more classic Hasidic position (Piekarz, *Bein* 96 n. 53), where *hitnas'ut* is seen as being mutually exclusive of realizing one's divine 'Moses' nature.

233 In both, the prophet is empowered; contrast this to a more classic Hasidic view of prophecy (see Piekarz, *Bein* 83).

234 Hakohen, *Tzidkat Hatzadik* 183.

235 *MHs vol. 1* Shoftim s.v. *shoftim* 2 (Source 7 in volume 2). See further discussion there and below, p. 302.

236 *bA. Zar.* 19a.

237 *bBer.* 45a—the same passage Lainer comments on in the text cited above.

238 Hakohen, *Tzidkat Hatzadik* 183.

239 Mendel Piekarz does not explicate this idea; however, he critiques what he views as the tendency of scholarship to equate acosmism with mystical quietism or passive attitudes (*Bein* 101).

PART THREE

Acosmic Humanism in the Religious Theology
of Mordechai Lainer of Izbica

Chapter Five
Overview

In this part of the book, we explore in detail the term we have used to characterize the unique religious theology of Mordechai Lainer of Izbica, acosmic humanism. Acosmism is a well-worn category in the scholarship of Hasidism and Kabbalah.[1] The acosmic reading of the verse אין עוד מלבדו *ein 'od milvado* 'there is none beyond God alone'(Deut. 4:35) understands it to mean not merely that there are no other gods besides the one divine being or force, which is a kind of numerical assertion. More dramatically, there are absolutely no other beings, things or subjects that exist independently or outside of the divine being or force.[2] A core feature of acosmic consciousness is what is often referred to as יחוד *yihud*. *Yihud* is the absolute and substantial divine unity in all of existence, or, in other words, the understanding and experience that all is interconnected and part of the One.[3] While this kind of acosmic understanding is already to be found as early as Azriel of Gerona,[4] it becomes a core feature of kabbalistic thought in the Lurianic flowering of Kabbalah during the 'Safed Revival'.[5] This belief, as Tamar Ross has pointed out, was taken by virtually all kabbalistic teachers from Joseph Ergas and onward to be an essential feature of Luria's thought.[6]

The acosmic notion that *altz iz Got* 'all is God'[7] can naturally yield one of two very different religious models. We might term these the theocentric model and the anthropocentric or humanistic model. In the first model, the human is virtually effaced. In the second model, the humanistic reading central to Lainer's thought, the human is paradoxically empowered, for if all is God, then the human is God as well.[8]

Joseph Weiss, who initially did the most to interpret Hasidism in terms of self-abnegation, annihilation, and passivity (i.e., the theocentric model),[9] suggests two versions of the theocentric model in early Hasidic sources, particularly with regard to the mystic's ecstatic experience of self-negation.[10] In the first version, the mystic becomes an instrument of God 'on which God exercises his exclusive activity'. All that the human does is the work of God, 'a work in which man has no share'. In the second version, the mystic achieves total self-annihilation. In this reading, which Weiss views as even more radical, the negation of man's capacity is synonymous 'with the denial of personal existence altogether'. Both versions of the theocentric model are, according to Weiss, really part of the same overall phenomenology, 'variations on the same theme'. The only difference is that while in the first reading, the dominant theme is human passivity, in the second reading, the dominant theme is human nonexistence.[11] These themes, central to Weiss's major writings on Hasidism, are the prism through which he reads *MHs* as well.[12]

Much of early Hasidic thought tends to a greater or lesser extent towards Weiss's theocentric model.[13] In this understanding, the fundamental human posture is one of self-abnegation, often termed ביטול היש *bitul ha-yesh* 'the nullification of what is' or nullification of the illusion of separate existence.[14] The true reality of אין *ayin* in the nomenclature of Habad Hasidism is a reality in which one has achieved total *bitul* (self-nullification), causing the illusion of *yesh* to be fully dissipated. Elior explicitly interprets Habad's acosmism, expressed in its absolute demand of *bitul ha-yesh*, as being what she terms a highly 'theocentric orientation' well beyond 'the bounds of traditional Kabbalistic esoterism' as well as 'ordinary religious praxis'.[15]

In contrast, the term *bitul* virtually never appears in *MHs*, and, while similar language and constructs occasionally do appear in terms of exile and redemption,[16] the difference in orientation between Lainer and the theocentric model is profound. On one hand, Lainer accepts the fundamental distinction between the divine and human perspectives—classically termed מצידו *mitzido* 'from his side' and מצידינו *mitzideinu* 'from our side'.[17] Furthermore, he assumes, in line with the Habad axiom and against Lithuanian Kabbalah (expressed paradigmatically in the thought of Hayyim of Volozhin),[18] that the essential goal of worship is to move from the human to the divine perspective.[19] However, he differs radically in the corollaries of his acosmic assumption. Lainer's is the ultimate expression of what we have termed the anthropocentric/humanist model. The unique corollary of his acosmism is the sense of humanism and radical freedom that permeates his writing.[20] For Lainer, the empowering conclusion of acosmism is the felt ontic identity between the human and God.

The word Lainer uses to describe the empowerment born of acosmism is תקופות *tekufot*.[21] Literally, this refers to a kind of forcefulness born of personal power. In *MHs*, it refers to the personal audacity, determination, and freedom born of acosmism. The realization of this ontic identity is, for Lainer, linked with human empowerment, the affirmation of human dignity and radical human freedom, and the virtual apotheosis of human intuition. These are the qualities that lie at the heart of acosmic humanism. In Lainer's thought, freedom is realized after בירור *berur*—a process of spiritual clarification.[22] Its primary manifestation is the ontic identity of human will and God's will.

According to Lainer, the human being is a prism who, when clarified through *berur*, refracts the unmediated divine will. This divine will is not merely theoretical; according to Lainer, it can and must override the imperatives of the old revelation that took place at Sinai. For Lainer, the Sinaitic revelation is naturally overpowered after one realizes the ontic identity of the human and God, a realization that can only be achieved though a process of *berur*. The old revelation is rendered momentarily obsolete; it cannot reveal the divine will in 'this moment'[23] and is superseded by the new divine revelation whose seat, like that of the original Sinaitic revelation according to Lainer, is none other than the clarified human will that becomes a prism for the will of God.[24]

The achievement of this stage of consciousness is explicitly termed by Lainer as הארה *he'arah* 'enlightenment'.[25] *He'arah*, according to Lainer, is ahistorical. It is fully accessible even within the present pre-eschaton reality. While in theory this is true of other Hasidic schools as well, including Gur and Habad, it is a far more prominent feature of Lainer's thought, in part because he effaces more fully than any other Hasidic master the distinction between eschaton and pre-eschaton reality. According to Lainer, enlightenment is achievable not only by the צדיק *tzadik*, but by every human being, in the present. We shall refer to this as the 'democratization of enlightenment'; it lies at the core of Lainer's thought. Lainer demonstrates the extreme seriousness that he attributes to this idea by drawing normative conclusions of a radically antinomian nature which, according to the dominant strain in Lainer, are fully actionable in the present reality.

Notes for Chapter Five

1 For an outline of acosmism in Hasidic theology, see Elior, 'HaBaD' 160–164. Elior defines acosmism in Habad as the belief that 'from the divine viewpoint the world is lacking any distinct or discrete existence'.

2 The tension between God as a personal being or a cosmic principle is sharply highlighted in the *Zohar* (2:64b), which creatively reads Exod. 17:7 'Is God (*YHVH*) in our midst or not (אין *ayin*)?' to mean, 'Is God a personal force or divine nothingness?' On the idea of *ayin* as emptiness or nothingness, see Matt, 'Ayin'. This tension, which runs throughout the mystical literature, has been noted by Arthur Green in terms of Hasidic texts ('Rethinking') and Aryeh Kaplan in terms of kabbalistic texts (*Inner 97*). Kaplan's works are not academic in nature, but they are useful nonetheless. We note Idel's comment (personal communication, 1998) that even though Kaplan's love for the material sometimes causes him to interpret texts erroneously, his general understandings are perceptive and valuable.

3 See Elior, 'HaBaD' 159, 163, 164.

4 According to Idel (personal communication, 1990).

5 See Werblowsky, 'Safed'.

6 See Ross, 'Shenei' 155–162. See also Pachter, 'Acosmism and Theism'. Of course, the acosmic assumption appears in the mystical expression of every theistic system. In Christianity, the example of Meister Eckhardt is striking. See Baumgardt, *Great* 34 and 81 n. 74. On Islamic expressions, see Schimmel, *Mystical*. For Eastern approaches to acosmism, see Moore, *History*, vol. 1 273ff, where he cites the Chandogya Upanishad 111:14, and Zaehner, *Mysticism* 129–152. See also Huxley, *The Perennial* 14–35.

7 On this phrase in Hasidism, see Loewenthal, 'Reason' 122.

8 A not entirely dissimilar set of models is suggested by E. R. Dodds in distinguishing between different models of ecstasy: 'The Plotinian ecstasy, unlike the Philonic…is presented less as an abnegation of the selfhood than as the supreme realization' ('Parmenides' 142; cf. Weiss, 'Via Passiva' n. 5). To contextualize Izbica's notion of power within the various models of power in Jewish mystical thought, see Garb, 'Hakoah'.

9 'Via Passiva'. It is not impossible that Weiss's apparent misreading of Izbica as radically theocentric was influenced by his prima facie orientation to Hasidism as a *via passiva*. The alternative reading to Weiss would be rooted in a kind of 'identity mysticism' in which the human being's ontic identity with God is experienced as empowering and not effacing. Weiss, however, ruled out such a position in Hasidism with dogmatic certainty: 'Needless to say, "identity-mysticism"…has no place at all in Hasidic literature' (Weiss, 'Via Passiva' 87).

10 'Via Passiva' 84.

11 Green critiques Weiss's tendency to typologize Hasidic texts in an overly rigid fashion. See Green, *Tormented* 318–23 and n. 53; see also Green, 'Hasidism: Discovery' 121. Green further critiques the typologizing of Habad versus Braslav Hasidism in Weiss's important article 'Contemplative'. For additional evidence

supporting this critique of Weiss, see Idel, 'Universalization' 47.

12 Weiss's antipersonalistic attitude comes dramatically to the fore in comparison with his teacher, Scholem. Weiss ('Via Passiva' 88) accepts Scholem's rejection of *unio mystica*. However, unlike Scholem, who uses that rejection to reclaim the personal and individual moment in the mystical *deveikut* experience, Weiss takes no such step, asserting instead that the goal of the mystic is still 'to eradicate…self-hood in its various expressions'.

13 The relevant sources in Hasidism were first read as a genre by Weiss ('Via Passiva'). Schatz-Uffenheimer further developed Weiss's intuitions in *Hasidism*. Idel, however, has taken issue with this characterization of Hasidism (*Hasidism*, esp. 133–146). Nevertheless, as Seeman has noted, ('Martyrdom' 253, n. 3) *MHs* is a highly idiosyncratic work that does not lend itself to analysis using Idel's models.

14 On this Hasidic concept, see the following by Elior: 'Iyunim' 157–166; *Torat HaElohut* 178–243; 'HaBaD' 181–198.

15 Elior, 'HaBaD' 158. For a somewhat different reading of Habad, see Hallamish, 'Mishnato' 129. See also in this regard Yoram Jacobson, 'Torat', esp. 350.

16 See, e.g., *MHs vol. 1* Vayigash s.v. *vayigash eilav* 2, and *MHs vol. 2* Toldot s.v. *vaya'al*.

17 See Ross, 'Shenei' 157ff. On the distinction between *mitzido* and *mitzideinu* in *MHs*, see, e.g., *vol. 2* Isaiah s.v. *ve'amar* 2 and *vol. 1* Vayikra s.v. *'al kol* (Source 26 in volume 2), where the term used for *mitzideinu* is *tefisat ha-adam*. See also *vol. 1* Vayeishev s.v. *vayeishev*; *vol. 2* Psalms s.v. *vayemalei*; Ecclesiastes s.v. *mah yitron* 2, and finally *vol. 2* Likutim 2 Taanit s.v. *biyemei*, where Lainer understands *teshuvah* 'repentance' as the move from *mitzideinu* to *mitzido*.

18 For a reading of the Lithuanian Kabbalists on this issue, see Ross, 'Shenei' 167–168 and Pachter, 'Acosmism and Theism'. See also Lamm, *Torah Lishmah* and Etkes, 'Shitato'.

19 See, however, *vol. 2* Ki Teitzei s.v. *lo ta'ashok*, where Lainer suggests that the goal of worship is not to move from the human to the divine perspective but to maintain both perspectives simultaneously. This concept will become clearer in our discussion in Chapter Thirteen of paradox as a major category of thought in *MHs*.

20 On the fundamental principles of humanism and their theological implications, see Werner, *Humanism*.

21 Avraham Leader suggests that *tekufot* in *MHs* is a Hebrew rendering of the Yiddish *tekifus*. Cf. Ben Dor, 'Normative' n. 26. *MHs* texts on *tekufot* can be found in the section 'Empowering Acosmism and *Tekufot*'.

22 See our discussion of *berur* in Chapter Ten.

23 See, e.g., *MHs vol. 1* Mas'ei s.v. *kein mateh* 2; see further discussion below in the section 'Freedom and Law'.

24 See our discussion of revelation in Lainer at the end of Chapter Three. See also Magid, *Hasidism* 205–248.

25 Lainer is one of several Jewish thinkers who use the term 'enlightenment', contrary to the modern claim that this idea is foreign to Jewish texts. See Kamenetz, *Stalking*, Ch. 1.

Chapter Six

The General Themes of Acosmic Humanism

In this chapter we will outline, in broad strokes, the defining themes of acosmic humanism. In chapters Eight through Twelve, these themes will be subject to a closer conceptual and textual analysis.

First Major Theme: Acosmism and Uniqueness

The first central expression of acosmic humanism is the theme of radical individualism that runs throughout *MHs* which we have already analyzed in detail. Lainer's theory of unique individuality, and thus of individual dignity, is fully rooted in his acosmism. In Lainer's words, if any individual is lost then צורת המלך *tzurat ha-melekh* (the form of the King) is lacking…for all of Israel are a *helek* of God'. Each individual is possessed of *hitnas'ut*, a princely or exalted ontological status, each is חשוב בעיני הש״י *hashuv be'einei Hashem*, 'important (i.e., ontologically) in God's eyes', and מדוגל *medugal*, 'distinctive', a special expression of the divine.[1] This is in distinct contrast to the often impersonal nature of *unio mystica* (the state of being in which a person realizes their supreme identity with the Godhead).[2]

Second Major Theme: Empowering Acosmism

The second major expression of Lainer's acosmic humanism is its distinctively empowering nature. This is expressed in his notion of תקופות *tekufot* (personal audacity and determination), which, as we have already noted, is a defining characteristic of the enlightened person.

Third Major Theme: Affirmation of Human Activism

A major corollary of the empowering *tekufot* dimension of Lainer's acosmic humanism lies in his affirmation of human activism.[3] Here the essential paradox of Lainer's theology affirms that once a person has achieved full *berur*, human action does not become irrelevant (as Weiss suggested). Rather, the notion of human action independent of God becomes absurd. The result, however, is not an effacing of human dignity and activism, but

111

rather radical human empowerment through the realization of the ontic identity between human and divine action. In this reading, post-*berur* human activism is radically affirmed as one attains one's full power in the realization of one's ontic identity with the divine. The individual's action and divine action are identical.

Fourth Major Theme: The Ontic Identity of Name and Will

The fourth major theme expressing Lainer's acosmic humanism is the identification he assumes in many passages between the name of God and the name of the human. This is how we read—against the implicit assumption of previous scholarship—Lainer's common refrain that human actions are 'called by the name of man'. This is not, as has been assumed, a kind divine consolation prize to the human whose actions in fact have no ontological efficacy, but rather a veiled expression of his true position: that the name of God and the name of the human are, on some level, identical. This theme is grounded in the centrality of *ratzon* in Lainer's theology, and on the identity of wills as a primary manifestation of the ontic identity between human and God.

Fifth Major Theme: The Ontological Dignity of Desire

The fifth major expression of Lainer's acosmic humanism is his affirmation of the ontological dignity of *teshukah* (inner experience or stirring of human desire). In contradistinction to other contemporaneous major strains of Jewish thought,[4] Lainer affirms that the experience of *teshukah*—after the clarification effected by *berur* to insure that the *teshukah* is an expression of *'omek* 'depth' and not merely *gavan* 'surface or superficial' *teshukah*— is a primary mediator of divine revelation.

Sixth Major Theme: *Lema'alah Mida'ato* (The Suprarational)

The sixth expression of Lainer's acosmic humanism, having a distinctly European Romantic cast, is his affirmation of the state of receptivity beyond normal awareness, which he terms *lema'alah mida'ato* (the suprarational), as a primary mediator of divine revelation. The 'God-voice' speaks through the human being, especially when the person transcends the confines of reason and thought. Lainer, however, is profoundly aware

112

of the danger inherent within this Romantic agenda, which dominated the Zeitgeist of his age.[5] Therefore, Lainer tempers his affirmation with an insistence that one cannot rely on the authenticity of the God-voice unless one has first successfully completed a process of *berur*. While, as we shall see, *lema'alah mida'ato* has important antecedents in Habad literature,[6] Lainer radicalizes it and brings it to antinomian conclusions that are explicitly rejected by the Habad masters.

Seventh Major Theme: The Human Being as a Source of Revelation

The seventh expression of Lainer's acosmic humanism is his assertion, already noted, of the human being per se as the source of divine revelation that may override earlier divine revelations including that of Sinai. The old revelations were addressed to a different time and place and what remains of them is only their formulaic expression in the legal codes. These legal codes are nonetheless critical, for as we shall see, it is paradoxically the norms of *mitzvah* contained in them that effect the necessary *berur* to enable one to access the unmediated divine revelation.[7] Lainer affirms that the human being can be trusted to hear the voice of revelation through the agency of human will. Lainer's operating assumption is that the divine nature of revelation is precisely what makes it not eternal, but rather subject to change at any time. Therefore, the new revelation, which is unmediated by law and mediated rather through the agency of human will, and which becomes ontologically identical to the divine will, overrides the old revelation.

Eighth Major Theme: The Judah Archetype and the Democratization of Enlightenment

The eighth expression of Lainer's acosmic humanism is his democratization of the concept of enlightenment.[8] While for some earlier Hasidic masters and older Kabbalists, the *tzadik* alone was identical with God, Lainer transfers the Hasidic apotheosis of the *tzadik*, rooted in ancient Hebrew mystical texts, to—in theory—every individual. In effect, Lainer can be viewed as one of the latest expressions of the old Hebrew tradition of apotheosis. In Lainer's nomenclature, every individual, at least at some point in their spiritual path, participates in what we have termed the Judah archetype, whose primary characteristics are *tekufot* (personal audacity and determination), and *hitpashtut* (a sense of expansiveness, both in consciousness and in action).

Conclusion

Many other minor motifs in Lainer's thought express his acosmic humanism. These include his affirmation of the legitimacy of תרעומת *tir'omet*, his affirmation of the central importance of risk and uncertainty as core characteristics of his ideal religious archetype, the nature of תשובה *teshuvah* 'repentance', and the paradoxical nature of sin. All of these are corollaries of his central intuition: his highly paradoxical acosmic humanism. We will return to the themes we have outlined in Chapter Eight. In Chapter Seven, we will get a general overview of the theological structure of Lainer's thought which forms the foundation for the themes which characterize his work.

Notes for Chapter Six

1 *MHs vol. 1* Bemidbar s.v. *vayedaber* 1; see also s.v. *vayedaber* 2.

2 See the section 'Post-*Berur* Consciousness vs. *Unio Mystica*: The *Berur* and *Bitul* Models'.

3 For a discussion of the place of activism in an acosmic Hasidic school that had great influence on Lainer, see Lowenthal, 'The Apotheosis'. See also Hallamish, 'Torat'.

4 E.g., the Musar school. For a sophisticated treatment of this school, see Ross, 'Hamahshavah'.

5 See our discussion of Taylor and Lainer in relation to Romanticism in Part Six.

6 See Loewenthal, 'Reason'. Significant distinction between the usage of this term in Izbica and Habad is worthy of a separate study.

7 See our discussion of law in the section 'Freedom and Law'.

8 For texts and discussion see 'The Democratization of Enlightenment', p. 169 below.

Chapter Seven
Texts of Acosmic Humanism

In this chapter, we study some of the representative passages capturing the theology of acosmic humanism in Lainer's thought. First, we will examine his acosmism itself, adducing and analyzing some of the key sources in *MHs* that discuss unity consciousness. Second, we will adduce and analyze clusters of texts related to the humanistic corollaries of acosmism that we outlined in the previous chapter. Before turning to the texts, however, a methodological caveat is in order. The strands of thought forming Lainer's acosmic humanism are interwoven. Often one source contains five or six different strands woven together. For the sake of clarity, we will, to the extent that it is possible, treat each strand independently. This will mean that occasionally we will return to an idea several times, not, we hope, in a repetitive way, but rather seeing it from the perspective of a new issue in *MHs*, which will deepen our grasp of its meaning and resonance in Lainer's system.

One: Acosmism, Unity Consciousness, and Redemption

The essential metaphysical unity of reality is a recurring theme in *MHs*. The realization of unity consciousness is defined by Lainer as redemption; the failure to achieve unity consciousness is exile.[1] Lainer is also aware of the erotic quality of unity consciousness. A veritable mantra in *MHs* for unity consciousness is the eros-laden text from the Song of Songs תוכו רצוף אהבה *tokho ratzuf ahavah* 'its inside is lined with love' (Cant. 3:10).[2] Lainer uses this verse often to signal the ontic identity between God and Israel. In one passage, Lainer states: 'Israel are attached in their souls to God, for "its inside is lined with love" '.[3] The phrase 'Israel are attached to God' is a synonym in *MHs* for the ontic unity between human and God, which is the essence of unity consciousness. In another example, Lainer says that the verse means that '"inside" the heart of Israel "it is lined with love" '.[4] Therefore, explains Lainer, even if an action was not fully clarified, God testifies in reference to that action that it is as if it had been fully clarified.

For Lainer, redemption is a natural function of the essential ontic union between human and God, expressed in the old kabbalistic dictum, 'Anyone who breathes, breathes from himself'—which in the kabbalistic tradition means that God's act of creation imbued divinity into human beings.[5] Interpreting the verse 'You will be holy, for I am holy' (Lev. 19:2) in this light, Lainer suggests that redemption is part of the natural order of things because of the ontic identity of God and Israel. 'You will be holy' is a promise rather than an instruction, rooted in the divine law of nature.[6] Hence, according to Lainer, the efficacy of God's redemptive promise is rooted in acosmism.

The Experience of Interconnectivity

A key feature of union is the experience of interconnectivity of the discrete individual with the all. *MHs* understands the *Zohar's* comment that Noah did not ask for mercy for his generation after being informed by God of the impending flood as indicating that Noah was deficient in his desire for union. After the flood,

נתן הקב״ה בלב כל הברואים שירצו באחדות כמו אברהם שביקש על סדום,
ומשה אף שאמר לו הקב״ה ואעשך לגוי גדול אמר מחני נא

God placed in the heart of all creatures a desire for union, just like Abraham, who prayed for Sodom, and Moses, who despite God saying to him 'I will make you a great nation' said, 'Erase me from your book' (Exod. 32:32).[7]

According to Lainer, the desire for union is built into the very fabric of the cosmos. Based on a passage in the *Zohar*,[8] Lainer uses the term תיאובתא דנוקבא *tei'uvta denukva*, the passionate yearning of the feminine, to express the desire for union, explaining, 'everything yearns towards its root'.[9] One can apprehend the divine will by going back to one's root, for one 'reaches naturally for the divine will even when it is beyond his reason'.

Acosmism and *Mikdash* (The Jerusalem Temple)

In another passage, Lainer explains that as a result of interconnectivity, which is the defining characteristic of union, 'יהיה שוכן אצלם רצונו ית בהתגלות מפורש לעיני כל 'the will of God dwells in them in explicit revelation for all'.[10] This passage describes the Temple in Jerusalem, which is a primary symbol of unity consciousness throughout *MHs*. In particular, the incense is understood by Lainer, following the *Zohar*, as a symbol of unity consciousness: קטורת רומז רמז שיש חיבור והתקשרות...וכל נפשות ישראל מתאחדים ועל ידי זה נתאחד כל הבריאה 'The incense alludes to the reality of *hibur* joining and *hitkashrut* connectedness...All the souls of Israel are in union, and, through this, all of creation is in union...'[11]

The incense expresses an important corollary of union to which we will return in our discussion below, namely, the reality that God is תוך כל המעשים שנעשו מבריאת העולם ועד סופו 'within every action from the beginning of creation until its end'.[12] Or, in another passage:

אם היה לבו מתנמנם ופוסק רגע...לא היה מועיל כל השתדלות בזה,
שבמקום המקדש...שהוא מורה לישראל שאין שום הויה בעולם רק השי"ת
לבדו...וכדאיתא במדרש (בראשית רבה ג:י) ויהי ערב ויהי בקר יום אחד
זה יום הכפורים

[T]he place of the Temple...teaches Israel that there is no *havayah* existence in the world except God alone...as it says in the *Midrash* (*Bereshit Rabbah* 3:10):' "There was evening and there was morning: *yom ehad* one day"—this is Yom Kippur'.[13]

According to the *midrash* that Lainer cites, the choice of the word *ehad* indicates union, in contrast to the word ראשון *rishon* 'first', which would have been more natural to the text. *Ehad* alludes to Yom Kippur, whose essence is union. Yom Kippur, the ultimate and paradigmatic Temple ritual, corrects the false imagining of a person that they 'have any power of existence outside of God'. Rather, as Lainer states in many passages, the person is literally a 'part of God'.[14] The key word is *helek*, 'a part of'. The essential nature of all of reality, including the person, is 'partness'.[15] In other words, the person, and all of reality, participates in God.

The prooftext for this, cited repeatedly by Lainer in reference to the individual's participation in divinity, is כי חלק ה' עמו *ki helek Hashem 'amo*.[16] This is read by Lainer literally to mean, 'His people are a part of him'. This refers to participation mystique. The person does not exist merely in relation to God; rather, the person actually participates in God.

For Lainer, of course, the Temple means not only the Temple in Jerusalem but the 'deep point of the heart' which is the human realization of unity consciousness.[17]

Participation Mystique

Much of ritual is explained by Lainer as a method of recovering consciousness of the participation mystique, which is an essential goal of religious service. Circumcision, for example,[18] is explained by Lainer as שיהיה גם בהגוף רשימה שהוא לחלקו של השי״ת 'a sign also in the body that the individual is a part of (i.e., participates in) God'.[19] In a highly typical passage,[20] Lainer states that the source of the concept of participation mystique is an old kabbalistic tradition. Lainer comments on the Talmudic text that suggests two different formulations upon seeing a sage: the first upon seeing a Jewish sage and the second upon seeing a gentile sage.

Before discussing Lainer's argument, it is important to note that according to Lainer, Jewish birth is synonymous with the metaphysical reality of ontic participation in the divine.[21] Thus, according to Lainer, to be Jewish is to be 'part of', literally, to participate in God. Therefore, he explains that when seeing a Jewish sage the blessing is אשר חלק *asher halak*, 'who gave part (apportioned) of his wisdom to flesh and blood'. In contrast, upon seeing a gentile sage, the language is not *halak* but rather נתן *natan*, meaning who 'gave' his wisdom. The difference is crucial. The word *halak* comes from the same root as *helek* 'part', ח.ל.ק., *H.L.K.* This is the root used by Lainer to describe the acosmism which informs the realization of participation mystique as the essential religious service. 'The non-Jewish sage receives wisdom from God but is separated from divinity'. In the gentile sage scenario, the wisdom, 'is separated from God's domain completely' as opposed to the Jewish sage's acosmic reality about which is written, 'God, Torah, and Israel are one'.[22] What this means, according to Lainer, is that the human being substantively participates both in Torah and in God, which are essentially identical:[23] 'The language of חלק *H.L.K.* means that in truth, a person and his חכמה *hokhmah* are attached to God כי חלק ה׳ עמו יעקב חבל נחלתו "for the *helek* of God is His people, Jacob is the lot of His inheritance"' (Deut. 32:9). This is, of course, somewhat reminiscent of the intellectual *unio mystica* suggested by Abulafia.[24]

Two: The Reality of Love in Lainer's Theology

Lainer's acosmism emerges out of his conception and experience of a reality suffused with divine love. The dominant motif in Lainer's conception of the divine is neither Spinoza's cold and impersonal *dei natura* nor even Abulafia's intellectual mysticism.[25] Reality for Lainer is not impersonal; it is, rather, a vitally alive acosmic divinity coursing through all of being. God is תוך כל המעשים *tokh kol ha-ma'asim*,[26] animating all of reality. According to Lainer, when a prophet eavesdrops on God's internal conversation, it is found to be entirely about God's love for Israel.[27] In turn, the human being's love of God is the portal through which an individual accesses the ultimate oneness of the acosmic reality of divinity. Lainer states regarding the biblical phrase כל קדשיו בידך 'All of his holy ones are in your hands' (Deut. 33:3):

הוא לשון נוכח היינו העושים מאהבה הם ביד הש"י ולנגדם מפורש הנוכח

> This is the language of unmediated presence, that is to say, those who act from love are in the hand of God, and directly before them the presence is made explicit.[28]

In particular, the unmediated divine will is accessed though love, i.e., a perception of the acosmic nature of reality:

והישר בעיניו תעשה. ישר מורה שתעשה פקודתו באהבה וחיבה, ותבין לכוון עומק דעתו ית' לעשות יותר ממה שנצטווית...לפנים משורת הדין

> 'Do that which is *yashar* straight in His eyes'—*yashar* teaches that you should fulfill His assignment with love and embrace, and understand how to intend the depth of His consciousness, to do more than you were commanded...beyond the letter of the law.[29]

To 'intend God's will' according to Lainer, means specifically to intend the unmediated will of God as it is incarnated in the human will.[30] It is for this reason that David, a central manifestation of the Judah archetype who accesses the unmediated will of God, is associated with love: דהע"ה שנולד במדת אהבה כידוע והיה מדוגל בה 'King David...was born in love, as is known, and was distinguished by [love]'.[31] Similarly, Solomon's ability to intend the unmediated will of God is closely linked to his identification with the quality of love.[32] Also similarly, the quality of *tekufot*—sacred audacity and determination characteristic in *MHs* of the empowering acosmism defining Lainer's Judah archetype—is rooted in love.[33] In all of this, Lainer, at least in part, follows his teacher's teacher, the Seer of Lublin, who, as Elior has already pointed out, draws a direct line between the love of God and the antinomian impulses of the *tzadik*.[34] Lainer, as we shall discuss below, extends this idea beyond the *tzadik* to include every person in potential. Lainer expresses this conception of love in many passages by citing, almost as a mantra, a verse expressing his acosmic view affirming the ontic identity between human and God waiting to be realized: the verse from the Song of Songs which describes the wedding bed (אפריון *apiryon*) of King Solomon as תוכו רצוף אהבה *tokho ratzuf ahavah* 'its inside is lined with love' (Cant. 3:9-10).[35] Lainer interprets this verse to mean that the inside of all of reality, even where it might appear harsh, is divine love. Inside reality, sin does not exist; all participate in divinity. In choosing this verse as one of his basic prooftexts for acosmism, Lainer seeks to characterize the universe—in contrast to the cold necessity of Spinoza's *dei natura*[36]—as being animated by divine love.

For Lainer, as for earlier Kabbalists, love is a virtual synonym for ontic unity.[37] In the *Zohar*, which Lainer is drawing on, *apiryon* generally refers to the ספירה *sefirah* of מלכות *Malkhut*, that is, the שכינה *Shekhinah*.[38] Lainer is in effect saying that the inner nature of reality is *Shekhinah*, whose animating characteristic is love. In fact, Lainer suggests that Solomon's wisdom—which is virtually identical with intending the 'depth of the will of God'—is rooted in the world order based on the Song of Songs,[39] the great love song of the Hebrew canon. In this passage, the world ordered by love is identified with Solomon and contrasted with a world ordered by law, identified with Moses. Lainer's preference for the Solomon model is clear. Love is the essential manifestation of the divine acosmic principle.[40] Lainer even teaches that God's name is love.[41] This is highly significant because, as we shall show below, according to Lainer, the human and divine names at some point converge into one. Living in the presence of this love and being suffused by it is the essential goal of religious service. Redemption itself is simply love revealed.[42]

To recapitulate, the driving force behind the human-divine conjunction of wills is love, both from the perspective of God and from the human perspective. The motivating force of love moves the creative process to unfold from the divine a human being who is part of the Godhead. The motivating force of love also allows human beings to perceive the depth of the divine will. The human love of God is, in effect, a shift in perception in which one steps beyond one's normal ego and realizes one's supreme identity with the Godhead.

Three: Shadows of Union and Activism

Lainer goes to great lengths to insist that the acosmic system does not run by blind necessity. The unity of his acosmism remains relational. The opposite model, in which all runs by necessity, is represented by the Tower of Babel and Amalek,[43] which are primary symbols in *MHs* for the shadow side of union. Lainer terms this אחדות נגד רצונו *ahdut neged retzono* 'union against His will'.[44]

The Tower of Babel is perceived as the foil to the *beit ha-mikdash*, the Holy Temple in Jerusalem and the archetype of union. The people of Babel desire (as a function of their consciousness of union) that יראה *yir'ah* (fear of God), which symbolizes the religio-ethical consciousness of law, *mitzvah*, and human struggle, should be natural to them so that they should no longer need עבודה *'avodah* worship, or, in the context of *MHs*, activism. The first shadow side of union is the undermining of human activism. This negation of the activist posture implicit in *mitzvah*, law, and human struggle is termed by Lainer אחדות נגד רצונו *ahdut neged retzono* 'union that is a violation of the divine will'. The idea that acosmism yields a quietist or anti-activist position in which the human being is fundamentally passive is explicitly rejected by Lainer here and in many other passages.[45] This is one of the many affirmations of human activism in *MHs* which we discuss below. As we shall see, this idea is essential to Lainer's religious ideal. The second shadow side of union is the implication of a Spinoza-like determinism in which both the basic freedom of divinity and the living intimacy of relationship and prayer to God would be lost.[46]

In the following passage, Lainer explicitly rejects such a reading. This passage, like the passage adduced above on 'union against his will', assumes a foil-like relationship between the Temple and the Tower of Babel:

כי כוונת בית המקדש הוא כדי שיתאחדו שם כל ישראל ביחד כאיש אחד
ובלב אחד וע"י זה יהיה שוכן אצלם רצונו ית' בהתגלות מפורש לעיני כל.
כך היה כוונת דור הפלגה נמי לעשות עיר ומגדל, כדי שיתאספו שם יחד
ויתאחדו כלם כאחד בלב אחד, וע"י זה האחדות יהיה מוכרח רצונו ית'
לשכון אצלם...היינו שהיו רוצים שזה הרצון שיהיה שוכן בבית המקדש
יהיה שוכן אצלם בהכרח. אמנם החילוק הוא שגבי ישראל בבית המקדש
היה מקום המקדש גבוה מכל העולם, כדאיתא בגמ'...וזה מורה שישראל
מסתכלין תמיד רק לרצונו הפשוט ית' ואינם רוצים בשום הכרח ח"ו כלל,
אבל העיר והמגדל היו בונים במקום בבקעה שהוא נמוך מכל העולם ובארץ

123

שנער שהוא נמוך מכל הארצות וכדאי' בגמ'...כי כל כוונתם היה בזה
הבנין כדי שלא יגיע להם כליון כמו במתי מבול, כי כל חפצם היה ליקח
את רצונו ית' ביד חזקה שיהיה שוכן אצלם למען יהיה להם קיום הויה
בהכרח בחוצפא כלפי שמיא, ולכן הראה להם השי"ת הגם שאמת ויציב
הדבר שבמקום שהברואים מתאחדים ביחד בלב אחד שוכן ביניהם רצונו
ית', אבל זאת האחדות והחיבור ביחד תלו נמי ברצונו ית' במקום שחפץ
השי"ת לשכון שם הוא מאחד את הלבבות ושוכן ביניהם אבל אין זאת ביד
אדם לאחד את הלבבות מהברואים, כי ברצונו ית' אין שום הכרח ח"ו, לכן
האחדות שהם היו עושים נגד רצונו ית'

For the purpose of the Temple was that all of Israel should
unify there together…and through this the will of God would
dwell in them explicitly and openly. This also was the intention of the generation of the dispersion in making a city
and tower…[The difference, however, is that the generation
of the Tower of Babel intended] that through their union,
God would dwell among them as a matter of necessity… as
opposed to Israel, who always look towards the simple will
of God, without any desire, God forbid, to force at all…for
the entire desire of [the builders of the Tower of Babel] was
to take God's will with a strong hand in order that it would
dwell in them so that they would have existence by virtue of
necessity, with impudence towards the heavens…for there
is not any necessity in the will of God…so their union was
against His will.[47]

The builders of Babel were also lacking what Lainer terms in several other passages הכרת הנותן *hakarat ha-noten* (a recognition, and relationship,
with the Giver, or, a recognition of the good of the Giver).[48] As we have
mentioned, Lainer's thought is not based on a blind and impersonal determinism of the Spinozan variety; rather, its basis is relational. Indeed,
this relationship, like all of reality, is animated by divine love as indicated
by the mantra-like verse he uses to describe his acosmic view: 'Its inside is
lined with love'.

Notes for Chapter Seven

1 See, e.g., *vol. 2* Yitro s.v. *anokhi*. In other texts, Lainer suggests not only that exile is a result of lack of union in the psychospiritual sense; in addition, historical exile is a result of the violation of unity among the people. See, e.g., *vol. 1* Vayehi s.v. *ve'atem*.

2 Song of Songs 3:10. For a more precise understanding of this verse and its role in Lainer's theology, see the section 'Two: The Reality of Love in Lainer's Theology'.

3 *MHs vol. 1* Hukat s.v. *vayikah*.

4 *MHs vol. 2* Naso s.v. *yisa*.

5 *MHs vol. 2* Kedoshim s.v. *kedoshim 2*. *MHs* gives the source for this dictum as *Sefer Hakaneh* and quotes it in Aramaic as מאן דנפח מתוכו נפח *man denafah mitokho nafah*. The source is actually Sefer Hapeliah s.v. *sha'al Moshe leMeta"t*, where the dictum is stated in Hebrew: מי שנופח, משלו הוא נופח *mi shenofei'ah, mishelo hu nofei'ah*. On the history and development of this dictum and its acosmic implications, see Hallamish, 'Limekoro'. On Lainer's use of this dictum in relation to the idea of choicelessness that is central to his concept of acosmic humanism, see *MHs vol. 2* Bereishit s.v. *vayapel*.

6 For Lainer this idea is expressed in the verse: 'For as the rain or snow drops from heaven and returns not there, but soaks the earth and makes it bring forth vegetation, yielding seed for sowing and bread for eating, so is the word that issues from My mouth...' (Isa. 55:10–11).

7 *MHs vol. 2* Noah s.v. *vayomer*. On interconnectivity as a fundamental feature of unity consciousness, see also *MHs vol. 1* Vayikra s.v. *adam; vol. 2* Vayak'hel s.v. *vayak'hel*.

8 *Zohar* 1:85b.

9 *MHs vol. 2* Vayeira s.v. *vayikra* (Source 28 in volume 2).

10 *MHs vol. 2* Likutim Noah s.v. *vayomru*.

11 *MHs vol. 2* Ki Tisa s.v. *vayedaber Hashem el Mosheh lekh reid* (Source 21 in volume 2).

12 *MHs vol. 1* Shemini s.v. *vayehi*.

13 *MHs vol. 2* Tetzaveh s.v. *ravu'a 2*. For other passages referring to the Temple in terms of acosmic humanism, see p. 252ff and sections 'Acosmism and *Mikdash* (The Jerusalem Temple)', 'The Paradox of Human Activism: Levels of Consciousness' and 'Model Five: The Wisdom of Solomon'.

14 See, e.g., *MHs vol. 1* Bemidbar s.v. *vayedaber*.

15 On the idea that all of reality being a part of a greater whole is a basic characteristic of all of being, see philosopher Ken Wilber's citation and explanation of Arthur Koestler's terms 'holon' and 'holarchy', indicating that everything that exists is a 'whole part'. Wilber, *Sex, Ecology* 40–59.

16 See sources using the concept of *helek* in the section 'The Individual's Unique *Helek* (Portion) of Torah'.

17 *MHs vol. 2* Behaalotekha s.v. *uveyom*.

18 On the mystical symbolism of circumcision, which serves as a backdrop to

Lainer's reading, see Wolfson, 'Circumcision and the Divine Name'.

19 *MHs vol. 2* Hayyei Sarah s.v. *vayosef*. On unity consciousness in the participation of Israel in God, see also *MHs vol. 2* Avot s.v. *Akiva*; Likutim Ha'azinu s.v. *ki yadin*.

20 *MHs vol. 2* Berakhot s.v. *tanu rabanan ha-ro'eh*.

21 See sources cited above, p. 127ff, where the phrase 'Israel are attached to God', used to describe the Jewish people, is an expression of acosmism.

22 *MHs vol. 2* Berakhot s.v. *tanu rabanan ha-ro'eh*. Lainer cites this epigram (as most Hasidic masters do) as a Zoharic text. See below for discussion of this issue.

23 See section 'Model Two: God, Torah, and Israel are One'.

24 On the relationship of *unio mystica* to Lainer's theology, see below, 'Post-*Berur* Consciousness vs. *Unio Mystica*: The *Berur* and *Bitul* Models'.

25 While in Abulafia's thought, love is also the essential animating force, it is closer to Maimonidean or Aristotelian love than to erotic embrace of the *Shekhinah*, which, as we shall see, underlies Lainer's thought. However, Abulafia scholars may well disagree with this. On love in Abulafia see Idel, *The Mystical* 39–43, 50, 104, 113, 119, 127–129, 132–137, 155.

26 *MHs vol. 1* Shemini s.v. *vayehi*.

27 *MHs vol. 2* Ki Tisa s.v. *vayedaber Hashem el Mosheh panim el panim*. The phrase *einah poseket* 'does not stop' indicates the ontological status of this love:

> The Holy One showed [Moses] that God's love for Israel does not stop even for a moment…When God bestows prophecy on the prophet…he assuredly sees God's love for Israel, therefore [Moses] wanted to know and listen to what God was saying to Himself, and he heard Him saying 'Peace to His people'.

28 *MHs vol. 1* Vezot Haberakhah s.v. *kol*. In *MHs*, the terminology of מפורש *meforash*, explicit, and נוכח *nokhah*, present or presence, almost always refers to accessing the unmediated will of God. On the theme of hands, see the section 'The Suprarational and the Unconscious'.

29 *MHs vol. 1* Beshalah s.v. *vayomer* 2. In this particular passage, Lainer's exegesis is anomian and not antinomian.

30 See the discussion in Chapter Eight.

31 *MHs vol. 1* Vayikra s.v. *'al kol* (Source 26 in volume 2). On David and love, see also *vol. 1* 2 Kings s.v. *ben sheteim 'esrei shanah*. In both of these passages, David is contrasted with the idolatrous king of Israel, Manasseh. Lainer portrays Manasseh sympathetically as one who is born into such omnipresent *yir'ah* that he loses his experience of choice. His desperate desire is to experience himself as free from *yir'ah* and capable of dignified choice. While David is as overwhelmed by God as Manasseh, he is overwhelmed by *ahavah*. The distinction is that for David, this is liberating; he is filled with *tekufot* (audacity and determination) by his love, and by the knowledge that he is a direct manifestation of divine will.

32 On Solomon as a primary model of the ability to intend the will of God

through the religious path of the Song of Songs (i.e., the path of love), see two key complementary passages in *MHs*: *vol. 2* Behaalotekha s.v. *im yihyeh* (Source 5 in volume 2) and *vol. 1* Shoftim s.v. *shoftim* 2 (Source 7 in volume 2).

33 *MHs vol. 2* Shelah s.v. *ve'asu.*

34 See Elior, 'Temurot'. This is a recurrent theme in the section of this article discussing the theology of the Seer of Lublin (383–402).

35 On the 'inside of reality' being *ratzuf ahavah* 'lined with love', see, e.g., *MHs vol. 2* Yitro *va'esa et'hem* 2; see also *MHs vol. 2* 2 Samuel s.v. *vayosef*; Psalms s.v. *gal 'einai*. For other formulations of the idea of love as the inner essence or ultimate goal of reality, see, e.g., *MHs vol. 1* Tzav s.v. *veheirim*; Emor s.v. *beyom ha-shabbat*; Shelah s.v. *beha-sidra* (Source 42 in volume 2).

36 See Buber, *Spinoza* 90–112, who writes specifically about Spinoza's relation to Hasidism. On Spinoza's determinism, see Yovel, *Spinoza* 417–418, 449.

37 See, e.g., Idel *(Perakim 81)*, who cites from Abulafia the idea often repeated in Hasidic literature that אחד *ehad* and אהבה *ahavah*, unity and love, each have a numerical value of 13, and add up to 26, the numerical value of *YHVH*, God's name of love.

38 See *Zohar* 1:29a, and 2:127a–128a. See also 1:38a; 82b; 2:127b. For discussion of these sources, see Melila Hellner-Eshed, 'Al Sefat' 74–76.

39 *MHs vol. 1* Shoftim s.v. *shoftim* 2 (Source 7 in volume 2).

40 See, e.g., *MHs vol. 1* Tetzaveh s.v. *ve'asita, vol. 2* Ki Tisa s.v. *vayedaber, vol. 2* Aharei Mot s.v. *ve'al.*

41 *MHs vol. 2* Ki Tavo s.v. *ki tekhaleh.* On the correlation between the name of God, the name of Israel, and divine love, see importantly *MHs vol. 2* Likutim s.v. *va'et'hanan.*

42 See, e.g., *MHs vol. 2* 'Ekev s.v. *vehayah.*

43 On Amalek, see *MHs vol. 1* Beshalah s.v. *Hashem yelaheim.* Amalek is described as employing unity consciousness to justify evil, 'for without the will of God it could not be done'. On the Tower of Babel, see below, next paragraph. These symbols are also discussed at some length in the section 'The Paradox of Human Activism: Levels of Consciousness'. See p. 218ff.

44 *MHs vol. 2* Noah s.v. *vayomer.*

45 See also *MHs vol. 1* Shemini s.v. *vayehi* on the potential dangers of unity consciousness. Lainer reads the 'Four Who Entered Pardes' tale in the Talmud as well as the biblical story of Nadav and Avihu as paradigms of the potential shadow side of unity consciousness.

46 In fact, this type of determinism is attributed to Lainer by much of Izbica scholarship. See, e.g., Weiss's classic article, 'Determinism' 441–453. See also Faierstein (who follows Weiss), *Hands* 27–28. On Spinoza's determinism, see Yovel, *Spinoza* 417–418, 449.

47 *MHs vol. 2* Likutim Noah s.v. *vayomru.*

48 See, e.g., *MHs vol. 1* Berakhot s.v. *asur; vol. 2* Ecclesiastes s.v. *ra'iti;* Isaiah s.v. *ha'aniyim;* see also discussion on p.226.

Chapter Eight
The Will of God and Radical Freedom

In the next four chapters, we will begin our analysis of the twelve defining features of acosmic humanism. These features incorporate the themes we listed in Chapter Six as well as the theological foundations we have just examined. Our focus in this chapter will be the interaction between the will of God and the will of the individual that leads to to the emergence of radical freedom. The themes of this chapter include empowerment, the merging of human and divine will, trust in the individual as source of revelation, and supraconscious action.

Empowering Acosmism and *Tekufot* (Personal Audacity and Determination)

It is not the empowering humanistic nature of Lainer's teachings per se that make his theology unique; rather, it is the fact that this humanism is rooted specifically in Lainer's acosmism. Hence it is fair to call this empowering quality the first defining feature in Lainer's acosmic humanism.

We will begin our exploration with three representative passages that highlight the empowering nature of Lainer's version of acosmism. Each one draws on different strands of Lainer's acosmic weave that will be analyzed more fully below.

The overt issue in the first passage is Pharaoh's question, cited in the *Midrash:* מי מתקיים על מי אני על אלהי או אלהי עלי 'Am I on my God or is my God on me?', to which Pharaoh is answered, אתה על אלהיך 'You are on your God'.[1] This means, according to Lainer, that Pharaoh's thoughts and will are his own; however, once he thinks a thought, he receives divine aid towards its fulfillment. However, this is only true of Pharaoh, who is Lainer's model for non-acosmic thought. Lainer continues:

אבל בישראל אינו כן כי ישראל הם מרכבה לשכינה וכפי רצונו ית' כן
יתנהגו...וכמו אברהם אבינו ע"ה אחר נסיון העשירי, ויצחק ויעקב
כשנשלמו...וזה נרמז בגמ' (שבת ס"ט) המהלך בדרך ואינו יודע מתי שבת

רב הונא אמר מונה ששה ימים ומשמר יום אחד, חייא בר רב אומר משמר
יום אחד ומונה ששה. כי ששת ימי המעשה הם השתדלות האדם ושבת
היינו הסיעתא מהש״י, ורב הונא מדבר באדם שנשלם בכל, שלבו נמשך
אחר רצון הש״י אז מותר לו לעשות השתדלות ואח״כ יבקש מהש״י שיגמור
בדעתו, אבל בעוד שאין האדם בשלימות אז צריך לקבל עליו עול מלכות
שמים קודם כל מעשה, ואם יסכים לו הש״י אז יעשה

But this is not the case for Israel, for Israel are the *merkavah*
'chariot' for the *Shekhinah* (a synonym for acosmism in
Izbica), and in accordance with God's will, they take action…
This is like Abraham after the tenth test and Isaac and Jacob
after they were completed…This is what is alluded to in the
Talmud: 'If one was walking in the desert and did not know
when the Sabbath was, R. Huna says, count six days and then
keep one day for Sabbath, and Hiya Bar Rav says, keep one
day for Sabbath and then count six days', for 'the six days of
work' mean *hishtadlut* human effort (activism) and 'Sabbath'
means the aid of God. Rav Huna is speaking of a person who
is perfected in everything, whose heart is drawn after the will
of God. Such a person is thus permitted to act through human effort and then afterwards petition God that God should
finish his action. However, a person who is not perfected
should accept [upon himself] the yoke of heaven before
any action, and if God approves it, then he may act.

According to Lainer, once one has achieved *sheleimut* (a level of complete-
ness), one is empowered to act with audacity, knowing that both one's
thought and action are a manifestation of divine will. Israel acts in this
context: when they have a thought, they can assume that it is a direct
expression of the will of God. Being the chariot to the *Shekhinah* expresses
some level of human-divine merger and identity. The human is empowered
to act even before accepting the yoke of divine kingship because the acosmic
matrix ensures the divinity and therefore value and dignity of human action.

It is worth noting as well that in the beginning of the passage, Lainer refers
to the possibility of one being a chariot to the *Shekhinah* as limited to the
עתיד *'atid*, the eschaton, while in the second half of the passage it becomes
a genuine option in the pre-eschaton reality for one who has lost their way
in the desert and needs to determine when to observe the *shabbat*.

In our second passage, Lainer writes that divine will includes not only specific deeds that God wants from the human, but also שרצון הש״י הוא שיתפשט
קדושתו ועבודתו בלבות ישראל, עד שיתפשט גם על קנינים השייכים להאדם שלא יוכלו
לעשות דבר שלא כדת 'that God's will should suffuse His holiness and service
in the hearts of Israel, until it suffuses even into property connected to each
person, so that they could not do anything [with it] which is not proper'.[2]
However, Lainer states that this should not engender fear in the heart of a
person that they cannot fulfill the divine will. Rather, ימסור האדם כל יסודותיו
וכחותיו להש״י שהוא ישלוט בהם ברצונו ית׳ וממילא יהיו כל קניניו טובים ולא יגיע מהם
שום היזק 'a person should give over all one's power and faculties to God, so
that God will rule him in accordance with His will, and ipso facto all his
posessions will be good, and no harm will come to him on account of them'.
Rather than causing fear, this should create in a person what Lainer calls
ישוב הדעת yishuv ha-da'at, a deep sense of ease and equanimity, knowing
that ונותן עצות לאדם שיבא לכל הד״ת בנקל '[God] shows him how to come to all
of the divrei Torah in ease'. In this passage, we see that acosmic consciousness, the giving over of self to God, returns to the human being a sense of
profound ease and balance in which the fulfillment of Torah flows easily
and naturally. When one identifies with God's ratzon as animating not only
the person but even all of his property, it creates a flow in which a person
acts beneikal, transcending טרדה tirdah, anxiety and fear.[3]

The third passage highlights the centrality of freedom as a demarcating
characteristic of Lainer's acosmic humanism. The Jubilee year represents,
says Lainer,

שאז שולט רצון הפשוט ואז יתעורר בלב כל נפש מישראל רצון הפשוט, לכן
אין שום שעבוד על שום נפש מישראל

[a time] when ratzon ha-pashut simple desire (or, will) rules,
and when simple desire will be awakened in the hearts of each
soul in Israel. Therefore there can be no shi'abud servitude (or,
subjugation) over any soul in Israel.[4]

The Yovel, which is classically identified by the Kabbalists as the sefirah of
Binah,[5] is understood by Lainer as the spiritual consciousness in which
the identity of human and divine will is revealed.[6] The simple will of God
is aroused, not only in the spiritual elite, but in the heart of every soul in
Israel. The acosmic identification of the human and the divine brings in its
wake total freedom.

The notion that acosmism is not effacing of the human being but rather profoundly empowering is designated by a formal term that is a *terminus technicus* Lainer uses to express this empowering notion throughout *MHs*. The term is תקופות *tekufot*, which literally connotes some form of strength or power. For Lainer, *tekufot* means the personal audacity and determination that courses through a person as a function of their participation in the divine, or in other words, acosmic humanism. The understanding of *tekufot* as an expression of acosmic humanism is explicit in many passages throughout *MHs*. For example, Lainer states, תפילין...מורה על דביקות, שישראל דבוקים בהשי״ת, כי תפילין מורה על תקופות אור הנמצא בכל פעולות ישראל 'Phylacteries...express *devekut* (attaching to God), for Israel are attached to God, and phylacteries express *tekufot*, the [divine] light found in all the actions of Israel'.[7]

Light is also a theme in the next passage, which connects *tekufot* with messianic consciousness. Lainer, basing himself in part on sources in both the Talmud and *Zohar*, interprets the קשת *keshet* 'rainbow' that appears to Noah after the flood in terms of *tekufot*:

וזה שנאמר בזוה״ק (בראשית עב:) לא תצפה לרגלי דמשיחא עד דתתחזי קשתא בגוונין נהורין, היינו שיהיה התקופות מהש״י בולט ומפורש נגד עיניך אז תצפה לרגלי דמשיחא

> This is the intention of the *Zohar* (1:72b) which says, 'Do not expect to see the feet of the Messiah until you behold a brightly-colored rainbow', that is to say, until *tekufot* from God emerges and spreads out before your eyes.[8]

This messianic quality of *tekufot*, is, Lainer states, also found in the שמע *shema'* prayer. *Tekufot* is a function of acosmism. Although Lainer does not explicitly explain the *shema* prayer in terms of acosmism, such an understanding of the *shema* prayer is commonplace in the mystical tradition and is especially prevalent in Luria and post-Lurianic sources.

A key concern in *MHs* is the 'King of Israel', which for Lainer is synonymous with the Judah archetype of sovereignty. The Judah archetype, as we shall see in Chapter Twelve, is the personification for Lainer of acosmic humanism. 'Great *tekufot*' is almost the defining quality of the king. In the next passage, the tremendous power of the king is contrasted with the enlightened receptivity of the sage:

ונקודת התלמיד חכם הוא שמכיר שאין שום כח מעצמו רק מהש"ת, אפילו
כח תפלה...כי גם כל מעשינו פעלת לנו, והיינו שהכל בידי שמים, ונקודת
המלך ישראל הוא תקופות גדול עד שכל מה שבלבבו יעשה, כי מה שעולה
בלבבו הוא בטח רצון הש"י, וזה הוא מדרגה גדולה שלא נצרך לשום עצה
משום נביא...ושם היה ענין עמוק...כי מלך כל היוצא מפיו הם דברי
אלהים

> The essence of the sage is that he recognizes that there is no
> independent power [in the human being]. Rather, all is from
> God, even the power of prayer...'for even in all our actions
> you acted in us' (Isa. 26:12). This is the meaning of, 'All is in
> the hands of heaven [even the fear of heaven]'; and the essence
> of the king of Israel is great *tekufot*, so much so that he may
> do everything in his heart, for anything that arises in his heart
> is certainly the will of God. This is a great spiritual level, for
> he requires no guidance or prophet, and this is very deep...
> Regarding the king, whatever comes out of his mouth are the
> words of the living God.[9]

The sage is someone who 'recognizes' the reality of acosmic humanism,
while the king is someone who has fully realized acosmic humanism to the
extent of embodying God's will. In this quintessential statement of acosmic humanism, the king realizes his ontic identity with the divine to such
an extent that any desire that arises in his heart is ipso facto affirmed to
be God's will, and anything that the king says is considered God's word.
Without understanding the notion of acosmic humanism in *MHs*, one
might very well read the beginning of the passage as theocentric, undermining and effacing the dignity and efficacy of human action. Lainer's
position is, paradoxically, not theocentric but rather an anthropocentric
acosmism that empowers the human being. This is but one more representative example of Lainer's acosmic humanism.[10]

The notion of *tekufot* in *MHs* is in no sense limited to the king. Acosmic humanism and therefore *tekufot* can, at least potentially, be realized
by every person. This becomes clear in the following striking passage,
in which Lainer identifies *shabbat* with *berur*.[11] *Berur*, as we have seen and
will explore more fully below, is the spiritual work of clarification in which
one engages before achieving the enlightenment[12] of unity consciousness.
The ultimate clarification achieved by *berur* is the realization of unity
consciousness:

אדם שהוא קדוש ושלם בכל הבירורים שנמשך אחר רצון השי״ת שלא
יבא בלבו שום דבר רק ברצון השי״ת שמשפיע לו על זה נאמר וכל היתדות
למשכן ולחצר סביב נחשת, נחשת מורה על תקופות שאדם הנשלם צריך
להיות תקיף בדעתו שלא יעזוב שום רצון לריק, כי כשיבא לו רצון בטח הוא
רצון השי״ת

> [Regarding] a person who is holy and completed in all of his
> [process of] *berur* (i.e., beyond the level of *shabbat*), who is
> drawn after the will of God, there will not come into his heart
> any will which is not the will of God, whose will is flowing to
> him…This is symbolized in the Tabernacle by copper. Copper
> expresses *tekufot*, for the completed person needs to have great
> audacity. He must not treat any arousal of will as superfluous.
> [He must give expression] to every will that arises, for when a
> will arises in him it is certainly the will of God.[13]

In fact, in another passage, Lainer makes every person's felt experience of
tekufot the litmus test of whether an act is or is not the will of God.[14]

Acosmism and Uniqueness

A second defining feature of Lainer's acosmic humanism is the marked
emphasis on unique individuality as the path to enlightenment. What is
unique in *MHs* is not merely that Lainer underscores the absolutely critical need for each person to identify and then embrace their unique individuality—what we termed in Chapter One their 'soul print'—it is rather
that he understands uniqueness as a function and expression of acosmism.
In this second sense as well, Lainer's acosmism may be termed acosmic
humanism.

One of the key words used by Lainer to describe the idea of a unique 'soul
print' possessed by every individual is *ḥelek*.[15] Crucially, *ḥelek* is also the
key term that expresses Lainer's theory of acosmism. 'Israel who are a *ḥelek*
(part of God) are attached to God in their root'.[16] This concept of *ḥelek* is
the source of uniqueness.

ומ״ש והי׳ מספר נאמר על פרטי נפשות בישראל שיהיה כל אחד
מספר,היינו דבר שבמנין ויהיה חשוב בעיני השי״י...כי כל ישראל חלק השי״י,
כמ״ש (דברים לב:ט) כי חלק ה׳ עמו. וכל אחד אחוז במדה אחת ממדותיו
של הקב״ה

134

[C]oncerning every unique, individual person in Israel…every one [has his own] number, that is to say, in the *minyan* count, and he will be [uniquely] valuable in *Hashem's* eyes…for all of Israel is a *helek* 'part' of God, as it is written, 'for God's *helek* portion is His people' (Deut. 32:9). Every single one is attached to (and personifies) a unique dimension of all the dimensions of God.[17]

The human being, or in Lainer's limited acosmism, the Jew, is a *helek* of God. Consequently, each person is possessed of unique individuality. Each person is a prism that refracts a unique face of the infinite divine. Lainer links individual uniqueness with his acosmic theology:

ואתם תהיו לי ממלכת כהנים, היינו שלשלת יחוס, ויחוסם יתחיל מהשי״ת בעצמו, כי השי״ת הוא אביהם, ומהשי״ת ישתלשל הקדושה דרך האבות עד לנו, וכן בפרט כל נפש מישראל מקבל מהשי״ת קדושה המיוחדת לנפשו בפרט

'And for me you will be a kingdom of priests'—that is, a chain of lineage. The lineage begins with God Himself, for God is their father and from God holiness unfolds through the patriarchs unto us, and so it is in regard to every unique individual, [who] receives unique holiness for his individual soul [deriving directly from God].[18]

Uniqueness, however, according to Lainer, is not only a function of acosmism. It is also the portal through which to realize unity consciousness: the acosmic nature of reality. One of the key code words in *MHs* for unity consciousness is 'olam ha-ba, the world-to-come. The world-to-come, for Lainer as for many of the Hasidic masters,[19] refers not merely to a future eschatological reality but to a stage of consciousness that inheres within the present. It is accessed, not as a reward after death, but through an internal shift in perception during life.[20] What is different in Lainer's thought is that one accesses 'olam ha-ba, that is to say unity consciousness, through the prism of uniqueness. For Lainer, the door to the unique One is through uniqueness. Prima facie, in a mystical system one needs to abandon personal uniqueness in order to access the One. Indeed, such an impersonal cast is the dominant tone of important Hasidic masters who preceded and in many ways influenced Lainer, including the Magid of Mezerich and Schneur Zalman of Liadi.[21] The level of 'olam ha-ba is accessed not by abandoning but by identifying and deepening one's unique individuality. Writes Lainer:

וזהו רק קודם שיתברר לאדם חלקו השייך לו בשורשו, כי לכל נפש שייך מצוה מיוחדת שעל ידה יגיע לעוה״ב כפי המצוה וכפי אשר יקיימה וזה עיקר לאל נפש

> For every individual has a *mitzvah* that is connected to his unique root, and it is through this unique *mitzvah* that he achieves *'olam ha-ba*, the world-to-come.[22]

In a similar vein, we saw in Part One that one of the fundamental expressions of Lainer's theory of the unique individual is that every person possesses a unique *hisaron*. We saw that, according to Lainer, the process of *berur* 'clarification' involves the identification of one's unique *hisaron*, and that when one heals one's unique hisaron, one achieves *'olam ha-ba*.[23] Moreover, the very identification of one's uniqueness is itself essential in healing *hisaron*.[24] Again we see that uniqueness is connected directly with the unity consciousness, which is the essential nature of *'olam ha-ba*. The emphasis on radical uniqueness is thus a key feature in Lainer's acosmic humanism.

Acosmism and Will

A third major feature of Lainer's acosmic humanism is the centrality of will. According to Lainer, the essence of acosmism means the ontic identity between the will of God and the human will. Lainer takes two distinct steps in this direction. First, he identifies the essence of divinity as will.[25] Second, he posits the identity of human and divine will. Of course, he does not assume that the identity of wills is naturally expressed in the world. Like many of the great spiritual thinkers whom Leibniz called the perennial philosophers,[26] he assumes that some sort of process is necessary to realize the supreme identity of the human being and the Godhead. Lainer terms his particular version of this process *berur*. *Berur* is, fundamentally, the clarification of will needed to bring the will of God and the human will not into mere alignment, but to conscious realization of their ontic identity. Indeed, for Lainer, the will of God in many if not most decisions is not dictated by the 613 *mitzvot* in the Torah.[27] Lainer states this explicitly in the following passage:

שאף אדם נזהר לקיים כל השלחן ערוך עדיין הוא בספק אם כוון לעומק...
רצון השי״ת, כי רצון השי״ת הוא עמוק עמוק מי ימצאנו

> Even if one were to fulfill the entire *Shulḥan Arukh* (Code of
> Jewish Law), one would not be sure if they had intended the
> depth of God's will, for the will of God is very very deep, 'who
> can fathom it'.[28]

One can access the will of God through הרגשה *hargashah* 'feeling' and תביעת
הלב *tevi'at ha-lev*,[29] the uniquely receptive nature of the individual's heart,
which, according to Lainer, are reliable guides. Human feelings and heart
murmurings are accurate antennae because they themselves are part of
God. This is the beginning point of Lainer's acosmic humanism.

According to *MHs*, it is the radically unique, fleeting, and subjective human
will that is identical to divinity, and not some intellectualized abstraction
of will. It is the full-blooded and engaged human being with the person's
ephemeral nature, frailty, and subjectivity, whose will, when sufficiently
clarified, is identical to the will of the eternal God. The human being is
endowed with the ability to access the unmediated will of God, refracted
through the prism of one's own will. Ultimately, Lainer's understanding is a
clear affirmation of human dignity and adequacy, and a central expression
of his acosmic humanism.

The human can access or intend the unmediated will of God because the
human being participates in divinity. במקום שהברואים מתאחדים ביחד בלב אחד
שוכן ביניהם רצונו ית' 'Wherever people unite themselves together, with one
heart, then the will of God dwells among them';[30] אז יהיה לב ישראל מקושר
בהש״י מבלי שום נטיה 'The heart of Israel is bound up in God without any de-
viation'.[31] 'Israel are attached to God' and therefore manifest *retzon Hashem*
in all their actions.

This paradoxical notion of acosmic humanism expresses a 'raising' of the
conception of a human being that is virtually 'beyond the human ability
to grasp'.[32] The verse Lainer uses in this passage to explain the ontological
status of the human being is כי כאשר ידבק האזור אל מתני איש כן הדבקתי אלי את
כל בית ישראל 'As the girdle attaches to the loins, so have I attached to me
the whole house of Israel'.[33] According to Lainer, this reality is what gives
a fully realized person the ability to incarnate the divine will.[34] Lainer is
not speaking about mere obedience to the divine will. Once a person has

achieved *berur*, their every human action is fully animated by the divine will. This happens not through an intense study of the Jewish law; Lainer states that one can fulfill the entire Code of Jewish Law and still not apprehend the divine will.[35] Rather, a person must רק יביט להשי״ת בכל פרט מעשה ולפי העת מה שהשי״ת חפץ לעשות ולכוון רצון השי״ת בכל עת 'look to God in every specific action, according to the specific time, [to know] what God desires to do, and to intend the will of God in every moment'.[36] The blurring of human and divine will is so complete for Lainer that he not only declares that the will of God is in fact the internal will animating the human being, he also—consistent with his internal logic—reverses the equation. Interpreting the verse 'God is my *helek*',[37] he states,...רצון ישראל הוא רצונו יתברך וכן ישראל רואים שכל מעשם הוא רק לברר שרצונם הוא רצון השי״ת 'the will of Israel is the will of God...and the entire spiritual work of Israel is to clarify that their will is indeed the will of God'.[38]

Because members of Israel have true existence, they participate substantively in the divine will, in what Lainer often refers to as חיים *hayyim* 'life',[39] while the nations of the world, who do not participate substantively in the divine, have no true existence and thus are paradoxically able to act against the will of God.[40] In another passage, Lainer presents the underlying ontology of his conception of will: רק רצון השי״י הוא הנמצא ואין נמצא אחר זולתו 'The only true existent is the divine will and there is nothing (i.e., no will) besides'.[41]

These sources ground Lainer's humanism in his understanding of the person as the incarnation of the divine will.[42] In another passage, he explains the midrashic tradition that sees Jacob expressed in the symbol of a בית *bayit* 'house', in the following manner:

כי אין האדם יכול להרים את ידו ורגלו בלתי רצונו ית' כמו בית שהוא מוקף
כן האדם מוקף שלא יוכל לעבור רצון הש״י

> For a person cannot lift his hand without the divine will. Just as a house is encompassed by God, so is the person encompassed, so that they cannot transgress the divine will.[43]

The Hebrew term used by Lainer that we have translated as 'encompassed' is מוקף *mukaf*, a reference to the classic kabbalistic idea of 'light which surrounds'. In Lainer's reading, this light surrounds the human being and creates a kind of 'energy field' in which the human will flows in unison with the divine will.[44]

The Qualities of Will and the Freedom of the Individual

The fourth feature we will analyze is the most powerful expression of Lainer's humanistic interpretation of his acosmism: the very dramatic freedom accorded by his system to one who realizes the identity of wills between the personal and the divine. According to Lainer, not only can one incarnate the will of God in the arenas of living that are beyond the purview of the law, but even with respect to the law itself. In the following sections we will examine in detail the several features of will which lead to Lainer's most important innovation: the radical freedom of the post-*berur* individual to contravene the law.

The First Quality of Will: Will and Uniqueness

For Lainer, the will of God is not an abstract or general category. He is concerned, as we have noted above, with a very specific type of will, namely, that of the unique individual. It is that will, which, as a direct corollary of acosmism, incarnates the will of God. The word used throughout *MHs* to describe the expression of the divine will beyond the lesser category of *mitzvah* is almost always *perat*, which, as we saw in Part One, is a *terminus technicus* in Lainer's writings for uniqueness on all levels.[45] It is through the portal of *perat* that one accesses the unmediated will of God. No less important in *MHs* is the term *helek* 'part', which is a key word expressing both individual uniqueness[46] (i.e., every person has a unique *helek*) and acosmism (i.e., God's people are a *helek* of God).[47] Or, in another passage:

כי עוד בתחלת הבריאה הודיע השי״ת לכל פרט נפש את חלקו...ודעת
נקרא החיים שבא לאדם אחר עבודה שזה נקרא חיי עולם הבא שהוא
שלימות הגמור

> At the beginning of creation God made known to every
> *perat nefesh* individual soul his *helek* unique part...and
> 'knowledge'is called life, which comes to a person after *'avo-
> dah*, for this is called the life of the world-to-come which is
> complete wholeness.[48]

Hayyim and the world-to-come,[49] achieved after *berur*, are for Lainer virtually identical with the will of God fully incarnate and manifest in the individual.[50]

The Second Quality of Will: Eros and the Will of God

A second defining quality of the will of God, and an innovative aspect of Lainer's acosmic humanism in general, is its erotic and even seductive cast.[51] Lainer explicitly explains 'being drawn after the divine will' in terms of seduction: ולהתפתות לטוב זה הוא מדה טובה שנשתבחו בה ישראל שנמשכין אחר השי"ת 'To be seduced towards the good—this is the good quality with which Israel are praised, for they are drawn after God'.[52] Broadly speaking, one's heart is either drawn after superficial pleasure נמשך לבו אחר הנאות עצמו *nimshakh libo ahar hana'ot 'atzmo* 'pleasures for oneself'[53] or after higher pleasure נמשך לבו אחר רצון ה' *nimshakh libo ahar retzon Hashem*, the pleasure of 'the will of God'.[54] *Nimshakh libo ahar retzon Hashem*, '[Having] one's heart drawn after God's will', describes the stage after *berur*, when the will of God is קבוע בלב *kavu'a balev*, i.e., implanted in the human heart, is a state in which the will of God becomes an integral part of the interior psychology of the human being. At this level, one is able to access in a regular manner *retzon Hashem*.[55]

Being drawn after the will of God is a grounding experience,[56] characterized according to Lainer by both pleasure and joy.[57] The phrase itself echoes Song of Songs, משכני אחריך ונרוצה *mashkheini aharekha venarutzah* 'Draw me after you and we will run' (Cant. 1:4).[58] This connotes not merely an intellectual apprehension of the divine will, nor even a stage of illumination in which one realizes the ontic identity between the human and divine wills. Rather, the phrase is erotic, clearly evoking the image of one drawn after, entranced, and seduced by the divine will. Lainer's basic idea is that everyone is seduced; wisdom, however, is in knowing whom to trust as the seducer. Joshua's greatness is that he trusts Moses to seduce him.[59]

The Third Quality of Will: Radical Freedom

A third characteristic of will in Lainer's writings is that a person who realizes the identity between their personal will and the will of God (post-*berur* consciousness) attains radical freedom. In the passage about the Jubilee year discussed above, Lainer emphasizes 'in *Yovel* (redeemed consciousness)…there can be no subjugation over any soul in Israel'.[60] Similarly, the seventh year of שמיטה *shemitah* 'no authority can subjugate him'. *Yovel* and *shemitah*, which in classical kabbalistic symbolism are respectively *Binah* and *Malkhut* (both symbols for God's will),[61] hold in them the energy of radical freedom. In another passage we will analyze further

below, Lainer states:מי שלבו נמשך אחר רצון הש״י בשלימות וכשיפול במחשבתו...
[O]ne whose heart is completely drawn שום דבר היא רק מרצון הש״י שהשפיע לו
after the will of God—whatever occurs to him [he may do], for whenever
anything falls into his mind it is the will of God'.[62] Lainer also states that in
that state: 'אז מותר להתפשט, כי אז הכל רצון ה then it is permissible to expand,
for all is the will of God',[63] and אז יוכל האדם להתפשט ולילך בכל ענינים שירצה...
כי ה' עמו 'he can expand and go forward with anything he wants, for God
is with him….'[64] In all of these sources, the common humanistic thread is
radical freedom, attained when an individual realizes their *ratzon* as *retzon
Hashem*.

Thus far we have seen five defining characteristics of Lainer's acosmism: its
existentially empowering nature, the radical emphasis on the individuality
and uniqueness, the absolute centrality of will, its erotic cast, and its valu-
ing of freedom as the religious ideal. At this point we need to analyze in
greater depth the relationship between law and freedom, which emerges
from the centrality of will, because it is the foundation of Lainer's acosmic
humanism.

Freedom and Law: *Kelalim* (General Principles) and *Peratim* (Particulars)

As we have seen, the human being through unmediated revelation of God
can also incarnate God's will in overriding the law. This is because the law is
but the codification of the will of God that once was. As long as it remains
unchallenged by a superseding revelation, the law stands and is binding.
Once, however, there is a personal revelation of God's will, unmediated by
law, then, if the person who receives the revelation has achieved post-*berur*
consciousness, they can trust the reliability of the revelation and thus it
may override the law. In this view, human will itself is the primary source of
revelation. It is difficult to imagine a position that could be more affirming
of human adequacy and dignity.

There are many perspectives one might bring to bear in analyzing the
sources related to this idea in *MHs*. The prism of legal theory (Ben Dor),
notions of human autonomy (Schatz-Uffenheimer and Elior), theories of
revelation (Weiss), or philosophies of will (Weiss and Faierstein) are perspectives that each contribute to our understanding. However, our argument is that none of these perspectives represents a primary concern for
Lainer. Rather, his concern is the fostering of a person who realizes their

141

ontic identity with the divine, and through that realization becomes totally free. This is the perspective that we use to approach the sources below.

Lainer draws a fundamental distinction between two modes of divine will. The first mode of revelation is general and public; the second is personal and intimate. Each one is expressed through a different modality of revelation, as Lainer explains in interpretation of a verse in the Book of Samuel:

אמר אלקי ישראל לי דבר צור ישראל מושל באדם צדיק מושל יראת
אלקים, וכמו שביארו ז"ל צדיק מושל ביראת אלקים אמר אלקי ישראל,
היינו הכללים של ד"ת והם הרמ"ח מצות עשה ושס"ה מצות ל"ת אשר ניתנו
בכל נפש מישראל שוה בשוה. לי דבר צור ישראל, לי היינו להבעל תשובה
לזה מדבר הש"י בפרט ונותן לו תקופות

'Said the God of Israel; spoke the rock of Israel to me' (2 Sam. 23:3)…'Said the God of Israel'—These are the general principles of Torah, the 248 positive commandments and 365 negative commandments that were given (revealed) equally to every person in Israel. '[S]poke the rock of Israel to me'—'to me' means to the *ba'al teshuvah*, to this one God speaks individually and gives him *tekufot* audacity.[65]

Both the general principles and the specific will of God are forms of revelation. The second and higher form of revelation is constantly changing in accordance with 'the place, the time, and the person'.[66] The first should lead us to the second. Lainer clarifies that this is the explicit nature of the written Torah, explaining that laws about endogamy and the inheritance come at the end of Numbers because just as they were temporary, applying only to the generation of the desert, so too the revelation of the entire Torah is temporary:

לא על הלחם לבדו יחי' האדם כי על כל מוצא פי ה' יחיה האדם, לחם היינו
ד"ת כללים הנצרכים לכל עת בכל נפש לכל עת מבלי שום שינוי ותמורה והם
התרי"ג מצות והעיקר הוא להבין בד"ת בכל זמן מה רצון ה' מה רצונו בכל
רגע לפי העת והזמן ומד"ת יצא אור ללבות ישראל שיבינו עומק רצון ה' כפי
הזמן, ועי"ז נכתב הפרשה הזאת אחר סיום כל התורה בכדי להבין לישראל
כי מכל התורה יוצא פרטים לכל עת ולכל זמן וכל ד"ת הם עצות בכדי שיבין
האדם באיזה דבר הש"י עתה ויעסוק בה

142

'Not by bread alone does a person live, but by everything that comes out from the mouth of God does a person live' (Deut. 8:3). 'Bread' means the general principles of Torah needed all the time, for every person, without any changes, and these are the 613 commandments. And the essence [is not the commandments but rather] is to understand through the words of Torah, at all times,… what God's will is in every moment in accordance with the nature of the time. And from Torah, light goes out to the hearts of Israel, so that they understand the depth of the divine will according to the time. It is for this reason that this section comes after the end of the Torah (i.e., at the end of Numbers, which is the last of the narrative books): in order to teach the children of Israel that from the entire Torah emerge *peratim* particulars (i.e. particular guidance), for each time and period; and [to teach] that all the words of Torah are *eitzot* guidelines, so that the person should understand what God desires now, and be engaged in it…[67]

From this passage and others like it, it is clear that for Lainer, the national revelation of the Torah, the 'bread' of life, even according to its 'objective' meaning, is limited in authority. Its deeper meaning is subjective and specific to each individual.

Bread, like *mitzvah*, is a basic staple of living. However, it does not always represent 'that which comes out from the mouth of God'. It is rather what God had to say at a particular time, speaking through the interiority of the human being.[68] Notwithstanding the suggestion of one important scholar, Nahum Rakover, to the contrary,[69] Lainer makes clear in many passages that *retzon Hashem*, i.e., revelation 'from the mouth of God', is virtually synonymous with one 'whose heart is drawn after the will of God', or, using another parallel term, one who acts according to *binat ha-lev*.[70]

In a classic form of kabbalistic hermeneutics,[71] which is relatively unconcerned with literary context, Lainer interprets the verse 'The children of Israel made the Passover sacrifice in its time' as follows: במועדו מורה על מקום שהשי״ת מאיר מפורש לעיני האדם שם מותר לעשות אפילו נגד כללי דברי תורה' '"In its time" refers to a situation when God reveals himself explicitly to the eyes of the person. Then he is permitted to act against the general principles of Torah'.[72] Lainer understands the twenty-eight instances in which the word עת *'et* 'time' is mentioned in the book of Ecclesiastes in a similar manner.

According to Lainer, the general principles of law are insufficient to guide a person in knowing when it is 'a time for birthing, a time for dying,…a time for breaking down, a time for building,…a time for war, a time for peace':

כל הכ״ח עתים...רומזים שלא יסמוך האדם על כללי ד״ת לבד רק יביט
להשי״ת בכל פרט מעשה ולפי העת מה שהשי״ת חפץ

All twenty-eight 'itim 'times'…hint that a person should not rely on the general principles of Torah alone. He should only look to God in every *perat ma'aseh* specific action, [to know] what God desires according to the *'et* specific time…[73]

Of course, the revelation to which Lainer refers here takes place not on the stage of history but in the recesses of the human spirit. He makes explicit in any number of passages in *MHs* that such a revelation may override the law. For example, he writes that:

ושורש החיים של יהודה הוא להביט תמיד להש״י בכל דבר מעשה אע״פ
שרואה האיך הדין נוטה עכ״ז מביט להש״י שיראה לו עומק האמת בהדבר
כי יוכל להיות אף שהדין אמת הוא לפי טענות בעלי דינים אך אינו לאמיתו
כי פן יטעון אחד טענה שקרית כמו שמצינו בקני׳ דרבא, וכמו כן נמצא בכל
ענינים, וזאת הוא שורש החיים של יהודה להביט לה׳ בכל דבר ולא להתנהג
ע״פ מצות אנשים מלומדה אף שעשה אתמול מעשה כזו מ״מ היום אינו
רוצה לסמוך על עצמו רק שהש״י יאיר לו מחדש רצונו ית׳ וענין הזה יחייב
לפעמים לעשות מעשה נגד ההלכה כי עת לעשות לה׳ כו׳.

The root of life of Judah is that…[a person] must look to God in every action or issue. Even though he knows how the law inclines, nonetheless he looks to God to show him the depth of truth in the matter …and not to be guided merely by commandments of men as taught. Even though he may have acted this way yesterday, nonetheless, today he does not want to rely on himself (i.e., on what he thought was God's will yesterday). Rather, he desires that God grant him a new revelation of His will. This means that he is sometimes compelled to act against the *halakhah* (law), for '[There is a] time to act for God [by nullifying your Torah]' (Psalms 119:126).[74]

It is clear in these passages that a person can have the ability to ascertain the divine will even when this contradicts the Torah.

144

Lainer understands very well that revelation requires interpretation. In another passage he points out the Hebrew letters common to the words *halom* 'dream' and *lehem* 'bread', explaining that bread is the raw data of revelation, which, like a dream, must be interpreted by the individual in accordance with place, time, and person.

כל ענייני עו״הז הם כחלום הצריך פתרון...ומי שאוכל פשוט כבהמה, אינו משיג מהלחם רק חיי עו״הז והמבין כי מוצא פי ה׳ הוא המחי׳, זה ישיג חיי עולם

> The matters of this world are like a *halom* dream that requires interpretation...One who simply eats [bread] like an animal only achieves the life of this world from the *lehem* bread (*halom* is composed of the same letters as *lehem*), but one who understands that 'whatever comes out from the mouth of God' is what gives life, he will achieve eternal life.[75]

Bread, as we saw in the passage from Masʿei cited above,[76] represents *kelalei divrei Torah*, the law. The world-to-come (which is also the *sefirah* of *Binah*) represents the unmediated will of God.

In another passage, Lainer, using the categories of the Talmudic passage he is analyzing, compares the different permutations of the Torah to three different geographic areas (*yishuv* settlement, *midbar* desert, and *yam* sea), and to the three necessary components of a meal (bread, salt, and *serif*, sharp condiments).[77] To explain the necessity of salt and *serif* together with bread, or, in the second image, the necessity of *midbar* and *yam* in relation to *yishuv*, Lainer cites a Zoharic passage that 'the light is only recognized through being hidden'. Since bread represents the general principles of law, while salt indicates what is beyond the parameters of law, the two together embody Lainer's understanding of law and norms in contrast with unmediated divine will.[78]

The passage sheds light on a profound aspect of Lainer's antinomian project. The importance of accessing unmediated divine will for Lainer lies not only in the specific will disclosed, but also in the way that this potential to access divine will enlivens the entire system of law. This is the meaning of salt completing the meal, or *midbar* and *yam* completing the world.[79] This completes our present discussion of radical freedom in *MHs*.

145

Radical Rereading

The beginning section of the passage on bread, salt and *serif* also gives us occasion to look at a fifth feature of Lainer's acosmic humanism, which is his use of the concept of permutations, the idea that different levels of the Torah express themselves in the different permutations of the letters and words of the Torah. Lainer is one of the first to actualize the antinomian potential that Scholem and Idel identified in this concept.[80] While this is not a major motif in *MHs*, its appearance is particularly important because in discussing this concept, Lainer suggests an understanding of the relation between law and God's unmediated will that does not appear anywhere else. Lainer sets up the two major expressions of divine will in contrast to each other:

היינו שהשי״ת הציב בעוה״ז גוונים ולבושים והכל הוא לבושים שנתלבש
בהם רצונו ית׳, ובזה הוא עבודת האדם ע״י הלבושים

> God established *gevanim* surfaces and *levushim* garments in this world, and all are garments in which the will of God is clothed, and this is the service of God through garments.

Immediately following, in reference to the second order of divine will, Lainer states, והשי״ת נתן בו חכמה לכוון לרצון השי״ת בכל רגע דבר בעתו ובאמת הכל נברא בדברי תורה 'and God placed in him wisdom to intend the will of God in every moment, דבר בעתו *davar b'ito* "a thing in its time" (Prov. 15:23), and all is in truth created through words of Torah'. This is, of course, a classic Judah archetype text. Lainer then explicates the underlying metaphysics of his position:

כי כ״ב אותיות מד״ת יכולים להצטרף לכמה צירופים וסדרים וכל מה
שיש בכל העולמות הכל נכלל בתורה, וכל מה שהאדם מחדש דבר אפילו
בעניני עוה״ז גם כן הוא מהתורה שמכוון לצרף האותיות שנבראו בהם אלו
הכוחות באלו העניינים

> For the twenty-two letters of the Torah can be arranged in many different permutations and orders. All that exists in all of the worlds, all is included in the Torah (i.e. in its permutations). Everything new that a person originates, even in matters of this world, is also from the Torah, for he intends to combine the letters that created these powers in these specific ways.

146

The fundamental concept that different permutations of the letters and words of the Torah reflect seemingly different wills of God is of course deeply rooted in older kabbalistic traditions. The difference is that for Lainer, that which may be true in the eschaton for the entire community, is already true in the pre-eschaton for those who have undergone *berur* and attained the redeemed consciousness of the Judah archetype. Realizing the antinomian implications of his position, Lainer, as he often does, inserts a more conservative idea in the midst of the passage: 'and our sages knew all of the permutations even in the matters of this world'. However, at the end of the passage, he affirms the radical implication of his words.

In another antinomian passage where Lainer refers to permutation, he re-reads God's prohibition of the tree of knowledge in the Garden of Eden by repunctuating Genesis 2:17-18: 'In the future *le'atid*…there will be a permutation of the verses [so that the verse will read], "From all trees in the garden you shall eat and from the tree of knowledge of good", and after that [as a separate verse], "And evil you shall not eat"'.[81] The Garden of Eden is a primary symbol for redeemed consciousness in Jewish thought,[82] while the tree of knowledge is the beginning of prohibition, whose consequence requires God to establish a normative law. In Lainer's reading, the prohibition is transformed into a positive commandment *le'atid*. However, as we saw in the previous text, this transformation can be realized in the present by individuals through the process of *berur*.

Revelation and Trust

A sixth feature of Lainer's acosmic humanism is his trust in the individual's capacity to receive revelation. This humanistic vein is evident in these sources on three distinct levels. First, the human being is addressed by God not only as part of the nation; rather, every individual is worthy of such address. This is the natural corollary of Lainer's radical individualism, which we analyzed earlier. Without such revelation, a person may keep the entire law and not fulfill the will of God.[83] Second, not only is the individual addressed, but the individual is capable and trustworthy to attain a sufficient level of clarity—through the process of *berur*—that they can rely on and act even in antinomian fashion. Third, and perhaps most dramatic, the divine voice communicating divine revelation to a person is equated with the depth of the individual person's humanity, what Lainer calls צורת האדם שבו *tzurat ha-adam shebo* 'the form of man within him'.[84]

This is made clear by Lainer in many texts. One such teaching, which we examined above,[85] interpreted תפארת לו מן האדם *tif'eret lo min ha-adam* to mean beautiful (and true) according to the deep form of the human being within the person. Even when an action is appropriate in the eyes of the community, it may violate this inner center. Lainer suggests that the question of whether to prefer the general principles of law or the inner voice of personal revelation, in a situation where one must choose between the two, is in fact a Talmudic argument between the schools of Beit Shamai and Beit Hillel. Lainer informs us that 'great tzadikim', spiritual masters, have adopted the Beit Hillel position that the human being can incarnate the will of God and from that place achieve total freedom (i.e., the realization of acosmic humanism), which is, according to Lainer, the posture of the Judah archetype.[86]

In these passages, the full trust and affirmation of human ability and dignity derives directly from the ontic identity between the human being and God. In this sense, Lainer is highly optimistic, which is a classic feature of humanistic thought.

The parameters of Lainer's confidence in the human ability to clearly receive and correctly interpret the internal voice of God are not entirely clear in *MHs*. According to legal scholar Nahum Rakover, two aspects of this concept in *MHs* dramatically limit its normative application.

Rakover argues that, according to Lainer, one may only violate the law if one has first purified oneself from any נגיעה *negi'ah* (personal agenda involving the issue).[87] This is the first limitation. The second limitation suggested by Rakover in his presentation of the relevant *MHs* texts is that one can only act against the law בדיעבד *bedi'avad* 'post facto', in response to a reality thrust on the person.[88] However, one cannot proactively initiate a situation where one will violate the law in order to fulfill *retzon Hashem*. Both of these limitations would limit the empowering humanism of Lainer, and a number of texts in *MHs* do support these readings.[89] However, Rakover's blanket conclusions do not take into account a number of other significant passages in *MHs* which indicate that a person can access the unmediated will of God and act on it even if they have a *negi'ah*, i.e., a personal agenda that has not been fully resolved. These sources recognize that even though *berur* is generally the requirement for accessing the will of God, full *berur* is not always possible and yet a person may still access *retzon Hashem*. *MHs* definitively allows violating the law in response to the call of the divine will speaking from a person's heart in some passages *even* when there is a *negi'ah* (personal agenda) that has not been מבורר *mevurar* (clarified). For example:

שאפילו במקום שנדמה להאדם שיש לו נגיעה בזה הדבר...לא ישגיח על
זה כיון שמפורש נגדו רצון השי״ת והיא תפארת לו מן האדם, שבצורת אדם
שלו מכוון לרצון השי״ת המפורש נגדו

> Even in a place where it seems to a person that he has a *negi'ah* (personal agenda) ...he should not heed it, since God's will is clear before him. This is *tif'eret lo min ha-adam*, that his *tzurat adam* (the inner form of his humanity) intends God's will ...[90]

Rakover was therefore hasty in categorically limiting the applicability of Lainer's radical doctrine of acosmic humanism. Lainer is prepared, at least according to some passages, to trust the person's ability to correctly discern the will of God even in the face of an unresolved personal agenda, and to demand that the person proactively seek out the will of God as a spiritual path in which one realizes their ontic identity with divinity. In fact, the sources in most of the discussions in *MHs* convey no sense of post facto justification; rather, they indicate an active stance in which the human being proactively seeks to know the will of God even when it violates the law.

Rakover was similarly inaccurate in his second limitation. Lainer suggests that accessing the will of God is the way of Judah and that careful adherence to the law is the way of Joseph. While, in one set of passages, Judah does not initiate his antinomian action—rather, it is foisted upon him, as in the story of Judah and Tamar[91]—in most Judah sources this is not the case. Usually the way of Judah is presented as the way of *binah*, the response to a particular form of revelation. This is presented as a proactive spiritual path and not a de facto response to imposed crisis. For example, Lainer distinguishes between the *tzadik* (righteous person) and the *yashar lev* (person with a heart of integrity):

אור זרוע לצדיק היינו שדברי תורה מאירים להצדיק שמכלכל דרכיו על
פי כללי התורה ולא יסור מהם. ולישרי לב שמחה ישרי לב נקרא מי שלבו
נמשך אחר רצון השי״ת, אף שעל הגוון נתראה שלפעמים יסור מדרך
התורה, גם זה הוא ברצון השי״ת

> 'Light is sown for the *tzadik*' (Psalms 97:11)—this means that the words of Torah give light to the *tzadik*, that he charts

149

his way based on the general principles of the Torah and will not deviate from them…while *yishrei lev* 'the straight of heart' (Psalms 97:11)…is one whose heart is drawn after the will of God. Even though *'al ha-gavan* superficially it seems that he sometimes strays from path of Torah, this also is God's will.[92]

In fact, not only is it permitted in specific cases to violate the law post facto, there are times when one must transcend the law by violating it, in response to a higher revelation of the divine will. In Lainer's words:

בשעה שמבורר לאדם על דבר שעתה הוא עת לעשות לה׳ כמו אליהו בהר הכרמל אז מהצורך להפר כללי ד״ת ורק להתנהג עפ״י בינה שהש״י מבין לאדם

At a time when it becomes clear to a person (through a process of *berur)* that 'it is time to act for God' (Psalms 119:126)…it then becomes necessary for the person to violate the general principles of Torah (i.e., the law) and be guided by *binah* alone, which God causes the person to understand.[93]

Binah, as we have already noted, is synonymous with the unmediated will of God. Finally, it is clear that the sources cited above in this section, which suggest that after *berur* is completed one is totally free to do 'as he wants', all assume that being 'drawn after the will of God' is not a post facto concession but rather a realized spiritual ontology engendering radical freedom in the individual.

Whether responding to the will of God that transcends law is an intentional proactive path or a post facto allowance seems to be related to different models of revelation that might inform a person's understanding of the unmediated will of God. However, what is critical for either model of revelation is that it is interpreted by the individual without any guidance or external authority directing his interpretation. In both models of revelation, there is real danger of misinterpretation. Lainer nonetheless explicitly affirms in these sources the human hermeneutic ability, rooted as it is in the ontic identity between man and God. We will now examine the two models of revelation.

Lainer describes two very different ways that the revelation of the divine will might take place. The first we term the 'overwhelmed' model and the second we term the 'intimate whisper' model. In the first model, a person is overcome by passion and is completely unable to control their desire. If a person's best efforts at control fail, the person can then understand that the sin they have performed was in fact not a violation of the will of God but rather its fulfillment. A person's being forced to give up control is one modality that reveals *retzon Hashem*. In this modality, we are clearly talking about a post facto scenario. Here, however, the need to trust human wisdom and spiritual intuition is enormous. The human is, after all, a genius when it comes to self-deception. In fact, according to Lainer, the conflict between Pinhas and Zimri revolved around this issue.[94] Did Zimri do everything possible to assert control, so that—paradoxically—his inability to do so could be understood as a revelation of divine will? Zimri answered this question in the affirmative while Pinhas answered it in the negative. To further add to Lainer's provocative reading, he concludes that Zimri correctly read his interiority and that Pinhas was wrong.

The second model of revelation disclosing the will of God to the individual comes in the form of subtle personal hints provided by the divine universe as the mechanism for revelation of the God's will. This does not mean that, according to Lainer, God left signs along the road of the world. Rather, according to Lainer, the verse 'You shall listen to [God's] voice' (Deut. 30:2) means that the voice of revelation is the intimate personal voice of the divine, which Lainer terms קול פנימאה הנמצא בכל דבר 'the inner voice in everything'.[95] Clearly, such an inner voice requires a human act of hermeneutics to decipher it. For Lainer, the act of interpretation itself is self-fulfilling.[96] This makes sense when we consider that the human capacity to interpret the hints is really rooted in the divine nature of the human being. Thus understood, the interpretation of the dream that wells from the human center is in effect the voice of divine revelation.[97] This can occur in the form of an overheard conversation,[98] in the voice of a coach driver inviting a person to ride,[99] etc.

In both models—revelation lacking control and revelation via what Lainer refers to as a בת קול *bat kol*, a divine echo or hidden voice—the human individual as the hermeneutic agent remains the central player, never ceding the stage to a transcendent divine entity who guides human beings, even benevolently, on their path. It is the individual who engages in the complex and confusing process of deciphering the voice of God as it echoes in their heart. Lainer's confidence in the human to perform this great hermeneutic task is grounded in his belief in the ontic identity between the human and divine wills. This is another humanistic corollary of Lainer's acosmism.

Acosmic Humanism and Idolatry

A seventh feature of Lainer's acosmic humanism is his unique understanding of idolatry. Lainer, in several passages, suggests that to follow the general principles of the law without ever reaching towards the unmediated will of God is idolatry.[100] This provocative analogy makes perfect sense according to the ontology of acosmic humanism. If we understand that the person incarnating the will of God is the primary manifestation of the divine existence, then listening to *binat ha-lev* and to 'the heart that is drawn after the will of God' is the realization of the acosmic reality. Conversely, to remain trapped in the general principles of law is a denial of the acosmic reality, or, in other words, a denial of 'the only true existent in which all else is included'. Therefore worship of a non-acosmic God who merely gives rules is equivalent to the worship of false gods who are less than the full reality of the divine.[101]

The Democratization of Enlightenment

At this point we turn to an eighth defining feature of Lainer's acosmic humanism, already alluded to in our in our discussion above: its democratic or egalitarian nature. The unmediated will of God is, at least in potential, accessible to anyone.

Contemporary readers of *MHs*, including Bezalel Edwards (author of the only English translation of *MHs* to date[102]), have tried to forcibly interpret Lainer's understanding of the ability to access unmediated divine will as limited to the patriarchs and their like, a very restricted spiritual elite. Edwards writes as follows in regard to this genre of passages in *MHs*:

> It could easily be misunderstood as being antinomian, that God forbid the Torah is not absolute and we may choose to act based on our own perception of what God wants…Of course it is not a way to make anything permitted, as only a fool would interpret it, and some fools in our generations have.[103]

In his next sentence, Edwards tries to explain when it does apply: 'It is relevant [only] when we find examples of our forefathers seemingly "breaking" the Torah, when in fact they are doing the will of God'.

Edwards is simply wrong, ignoring the *MHs* text itself. The nature of Lainer's presentation generally makes it clear that his words are not limited to any special elite or any particular group. In some sources this is implicit;[104] in others, he states it clearly. Not only is achieving this intimacy with the divine will the purpose of the covenant,[105] it is a state already achieved on the deepest level by every single person:

היינו בכל רגע ורגע יודע כל נפש מישראל מקטון ועד גדול מה שהש״י חפץ עתה וביבינו ע״פי בינת לבבם שעתה רצון הש״י הוא כך, ולא על פי כללים

> In every single second, every person in Israel, *mikaton ve'ad gadol* from the young to the old, understands what God desires now. They are able to understand through the *binah* of their hearts, that now, such is the will of God, and not [guide themselves merely] based on the general rules of law...[106]

The egalitarian nature of Lainer's theology affirms the full dignity of every person, who, independently of any other channels, always has the potential to access the will of God.

At the same time, Lainer distinguishes between broad typologies and their applicability at different times in the life of the individual. In terms of the latter, Lainer states that 'at a particular time' one may correctly experience oneself as one who can access the unmediated will of God, while at other times one may feel enjoined to follow the general principles of law revealed to the community as whole. Hence, ושניהם אסורים שלא במקומם הראוי להם 'Each one is forbidden in the place not appropriate to them'.[107] It is clear from this passage and virtually all the passages dealing with the will of God that Lainer is addressing every person, who at times may realize acosmic consciousness and be animated by the unmediated will of God, while at other times they may live guided by and in obedience to the will of God as mediated through the law.[108] In terms of typologies, Lainer fundamentally distinguishes throughout his writings between the Judah and Joseph typologies. The Judah type, however, is not limited to the *tzadik* or the scholar. The non-elitist character of Lainer's theology will come into even sharper focus through the texts and analysis we will bring to bear below in regard to the Judah archetype. The possibility of living one's life in the way of Judah is theoretically open to every person, even if a person might only live the way of Judah at particular stages, or even only at specific moments, in their life.

153

Three Qualities of Consciousness

At this point we note the ninth, tenth and eleventh characteristics of Lainer's acosmism: *hitpashtut*, no-boundary consciousness, and the suprarational unconscious. Each of these three characteristics supports the humanistic cast of Lainer's acosmism. All three appear repeatedly in the passages in which Lainer describes the ability to incarnate the will of God after the process of *berur* has been completed. All three are expressions of the radical freedom engendered by a person's realization of their identity with the divine will.

Hitpashtut (Expanded Consciousness)

The ninth characteristic that emerges from the post-*berur* state of consciousness is what Lainer calls התפשטות *hitpashtut* (expansion), the expansion of human consciousness and normative actions beyond the boundaries that remain necessary in pre-*berur* consciousness:

> כל זמן שלא נחקק ונקבע בלב האדם קדושת הש״י...צריך לצמצם עצמו
> בכל עניניו ושלא להתפשט רצונו...וכאשר יפנה האדם לד״ת עד שיחקקו
> בלבו ויקבעו בו, אז יוכל האדם להתפשט ולילך בכל ענינים שירצה כי ה'
> עמו

> Until a person has engraved and established firmly in his heart the holiness of God...he must constrict himself in all his affairs not to expand His will ...However, once a person has engraved and firmly established [the holiness of God] in his heart, he may expand and act in his affairs as he desires, because God is with him...[109]

When this passage is read in conjunction with the rest of *MHs*, it is clear that Lainer does not mean to say that God is with the person in an external, dialogic sense. Rather, the person manifests God; therefore, they may expand beyond the normative boundaries even of the law, for their desire is naturally the will of God. Lainer makes the point explicitly in another passage. After describing all that was prohibited to Noah, Lainer concludes by stating:

> וכל זה הי' הי' עצות לנח קודם שנשלם איך יסתיר עצמו, כי מיד כשיצא מן
> התיבה שאז הי' השלמתו אז עשה היפך מאלו הדברים כמ״ש וישת וישכר

154

וכעס על חם ולא עבר על מדותיו, כי כשאדם נשלם אז מותר להתפשט, כי
אז הכל רצון ה'

'All'... That was before he was completed (i.e., through the
process of berur)...but once a person is completed, it is permissible to expand, for then all is the will of God.[110]

According to Lainer, after berur, one attains expanded consciousness, i.e.,
identity with retzon Hashem.[111] This then expresses itself normatively in
one's right to 'expand' according to whatever one desires,[112] in accordance
with binat ha-lev, the understanding of one's heart.[113] What is embedded
in the term 'hitpashtut' is the suggestion that the acosmic consciousness
engenders an existential expansion of personal identity, and not its nullification. This of course yields a very different existential mood and fosters
a different religious typology than that engendered by the early Hasidic
theology of ביטול bitul, self-nullification.[114]

No-Boundary Consciousness

The tenth characteristic of Lainer's acosmism is the state that Wilber and
others refer to as 'no-boundary consciousness'.[115] Lainer terms this לא גבול
lo gevul or אין גבול ein gevul, both of which literally translate as 'no-boundary'. No-boundary consciousness is a natural result of participation in the
infinite and a feature of all acosmic nondual systems. A boundary is finite
and limited; no-boundary must be infinite and divine. Referring to specific
qualities found in the 'nations of the world', Lainer states:

כל כחות האו״ה אצלם הוא בגבול ולזאת יתפזרו ישראל לבין האומות כדי
שיקבלו כל כחותם שנמצא אצל כל אחד מהשבעים אומות, ואצלם יהי' בלי
גבול כי הם דבוקים בהש״י ג״כ בשורשם ולא בשום גבול

All the qualities of the nations of the world are within a
boundary (limited)...but when [they become part of] Israel
they are without any boundary, for Israel are attached to God
in their root without any boundary...[116]

In Hasidic exegesis,[117] the biblical verse referring to the future expansion
of physical boundaries of the land of Israel is a natural opportunity for
an acosmic reader to discuss no-boundary consciousness in the realm of
spirit. The verse reads: 'When God will extend your boundaries and you

will say let us eat meat, …in accordance with the desire of your heart you shall eat meat' (Deut. 12:20). Lainer comments:[118]

לא נאמר שיצאו חוץ לגבולם רק שגבולם יתרחב, כי באמת משם הוי'
היינו...אשר בחר בישראל אין שום גבולין רק מותר להתפשט בכל
הטובות, אך משם א"ד"נ"י...מזה נצמח כל הגבולין...שיתן בך כח עבודה
כ"כ עד שיסתלקו ויסירו הגבולין מאתך עד שתוכל גם לאכול בשר ולא תצא
חוץ לגבולך

It does not say that they will go out beyond their boundaries, only that their boundaries will expand. For in truth, from the perspective of name *YHVH*…there is no boundary…Rather, it is permitted to expand in all the good. However, from [the aspect of] the name *ADNY*…all the boundaries are generated…until the power of *'avodah* spiritual work that is given you is so great that the boundaries will flee and be removed from you …until you can eat meat and that will not go outside your boundary.[119]

Lainer suggests that the name *YHVH* is the face of no-boundary consciousness in the divine, the nondual conception of God in which the goal of service is to expand one's perception in order to realize that one actually participates in God. In contrast, the name *ADNY* is the more classical, binary, dual conception of dialogical relationship between human and God. We will return to this identification of the *YHVH* name of God with no-boundary consciousness below. We will see that the concept of name—both divine and human, in Lainer's reading—will significantly deepen our understanding of Lainer's theology of acosmic humanism.

According to Lainer, the concept of no-boundary awareness affects the core experience of all of religious life. In Lainer's discussions of prayer,[120] repentance,[121] and the study of Torah,[122] he suggests that each of these has two different modalities: that of 'boundary' and that of 'no-boundary'. To illustrate the profound difference between the modalities, let us briefly examine the most complex of the three: repentance.

Repentance 'within boundaries' would, according to Lainer, suggest the classic form of repentance outlined by Maimonides, in which one first recognizes one's sin, then regrets it, and, finally, commits to never repeat it.[123] Repentance in no-boundary consciousness is entirely different. In

Lainer's conception, one who returns motivated by love—which, for Lainer, is repentance from the level of no-boundary consciousness—has let go of regret and can embrace the sin itself as the will of God.[124] The essence of the idea of תשובה *teshuvah* 'beyond boundaries' is thus an expansion of consciousness to a place where a person realizes that everything that happened needed to happen. It could not have been otherwise, nor would a person want it to be otherwise, for it was the will of God even if it was a sin relative to the general principles of the law.[125]

This conception is, of course, a very powerful affirmation of human value and dignity even in the face of overwhelming evidence of sin. It obviously flies in the face of the classical concept of sin and repentance that dominates Jewish thought. However, in contradistinction to how *MHs* is presented by Gellman, Weiss, and Elior,[126] Lainer does not fully abandon the classical notion of repentance and sin. It appears in one important strand of his writing, and perhaps in others.[127] We will return to this claim in our discussion of paradox in *MHs* in Chapter Thirteen.

The Suprarational and the Unconscious

The eleventh characteristic of acosmic humanism in this cluster is strikingly similar to one aspect of Romantic philosophy.[128] Lainer states that human beings incarnate the divine will and therefore can trust and act on their desires, even *lema'alah mida'ato*.[129] *Lema'alah mida'ato*, literally 'above his דעת *da'at* awareness', connotes for Lainer both the transrational and the unconscious. He calls this דבר עמוק *davar 'amok* 'a deep matter'.[130] This terminology is related to the dialectic in Izbica between עומק *'omek* 'depth' and גוון *gavan* 'surface'. *'Omek* refers to the nondual understanding of reality that is beyond intellect and law, while *gavan* is the normal, dual understanding of reality that expresses itself in law and intellect. In *MHs*, this type of language almost always indicates a teaching about the dialectics of acosmic humanism.

The ability to access the transrational realms—*lema'alah mida'ato*— is explicitly and consistently linked to *binah*, the quality through which one incarnates the unmediated will of God.[131] In this vein, Lainer interprets the wine libations as symbolizing the idea that even *lema'alah mida'ato* Israel fulfills the will of God.[132] This ability is more than an intuitive quality of the mind; post-*berur*, it inheres in the body itself. Interpreting the phrase 'with the wisdom of his hands' (Psalms 78:72) Lainer states:

157

זה רומז שנמצא בידים בינה למעלה מדעת האדם שיכול לכוון כרצון השי"ת
בלי דעתו כלל לא יחטיא המטרה

This hints that in the hands there is found *binah* an understanding that is beyond a person's intellect, which can intend
the divine will without his mind at all [so that] he will not
miss the mark.[133]

Or, in another passage:

שהאדם מטה לבו לאיזה ד"ת, ימשך גם כל גופו ואבריו אחר הלב לפעול
מעצמם אף בלי דעת כפי אשר יוטבע בלב

[W]hen a person inclines his heart to any words of Torah,
his entire body and his limbs will be drawn after the heart
to act on their own accord, even *beli da'at* without awareness
(unconsciously)'.[134]

Here and in other passages, Lainer discusses what is beyond *da'at* not only
in terms of the transrational, but also the unconscious. Similarly, in a third
passage, Lainer states that after *berur* one can intend the will of God אף בלי
יגיעה ואף בעת שינה'without any effort and even during sleep'.[135]

In the post-*berur* state, unconscious action is wholly affirmed: היינו מקום
שהאדם עושה בלי דעת כלאחר ידו לזה גם יסכים הקב"ה לטוב'This is the place where
a person acts *beli da'at* unconsciously, *kele'ahar yado* automatically; also to
these actions God will agree';[136] or in a variation on this theme, שנקבע דברי
תורה בקביעות שאף שלא מדעת יפעל בו הד"ת'Once Torah has been established
permanently [in the heart] then even *shelo mida'at* unconsciously it works
in him';[137] or, in yet another formulation: אף מתוך שכחה'even out of forget-
fulness'.[138]

Once the human identity with God is realized, then all human action, in
both the transrational or supra-conscious realms, and the unconscious
realms, can be understood as expressions of *retzon Hashem*. Of course, like
no-boundary consciousness, the affirmation of the human ability to fulfill
retzon Hashem even *lema'alah mida'ato*[139] is predicated on acosmism; in the
recurrent language of Lainer, both states flow from the ontological reality
that Israel הם דבוקים בה''are *devukim* attached to God'.[140]

Notes for Chapter Eight

1 *MHs vol. 1* Mikeitz s.v. *vehineih.*

2 *MHs vol. 1* Terumah s.v. *vayedaber.*

3 This theme recurs in many passages; see, e.g., *vol. 1* Behukotai s.v. *im* 3 and *vezeh.*

4 *MHs vol. 2* Mishpatim s.v. *sheish shanim.*

5 See *Zohar* 2:183a, adduced and annotated in Tishby, *Wisdom* vol. 1 354–355.

6 See sections 'Acosmism and Will' and 'The Qualities of Will' below.

7 *MHs vol. 2* Bo s.v. *beparashah.* On phylacteries as an expression of acosmism, see also *MHs vol. 1* Ki Tisa s.v. *vehikhritu.*

8 *MHs vol. 1* Noah s.v. *vehayah.*

9 *MHs vol. 2* Tetzaveh s.v. *ravu'a* 1.

10 For parallel passages on acosmic humanism through the prism of the king and the Judah archetype, see *MHs vol. 1* Vayikra s.v. *'al kol* (Source 26 in volume 2) and *vol. 1* Shoftim s.v. *shoftim* 2 (Source 7 in volume 2).

11 This is consistent with his understanding of *shabbat* in *MHs vol. 1* Rosh Hashanah s.v. *yom tov,* which we adduce and analyze in the section 'The Paradox of Human Activism: Levels of Consciousness.'

12 *He'arah* 'enlightenment' is the word used consistently both by Lainer and Tzadok Hakohen to describe the unity consciousness which is achieved after the process of *berur* has been completed. The topic of *he'arah* was initially treated by Weiss, 'A Late Jewish Utopia' 209–248. For different usages of *he'arah* in *MHs,* see, e.g., *vol. 1* Vayeira s.v. *vayeira eilav;* Gilyon Beshalah s.v. *vayasa';* *vol. 2* Lekh Lekha s.v. *vayomer;* Vayeishev s.v. *vayehi kemeishiv;* Shemot s.v. *vayei'anhu.*

13 *MHs vol. 2* Vayak'hel s.v. *vayak'hel* 2. On acosmic humanism and *tekufot* see also *MHs vol. 1* Balak s.v. *ki lo nahash,* vol. 2 Shelah s.v. *nesakhim;* s.v. *'al 'inyan.*

14 *MHs vol. 2* Vayikra s.v. *im 'olah.*

15 See Chapter One for sources on uniqueness, in which *helek* plays a central role.

16 *MHs vol. 1* Beshalah s.v. *nikheho.* See also *vol. 1* Hayyei Sarah s.v. *vayosef,* Toldot s.v. *vaye'ehav,* 'Ekev s.v. *'al tomar;* vol. 2 Hayyei Sarah s.v. *ve'eileh.*

17 *MHs vol. 1* Bemidbar s.v. *vayedaber,* see also *vol. 1* Bemidbar s.v. *se'u:* 'God gave every person a *helek,* part of good and life, and no person's *helek* is similar to his friend.'

18 *MHs vol. 2* Yitro s.v. *va'esa* 2.

19 On the spiritual as opposed to historical nature of redemption in Hasidism, see Scholem, *Major Trends* 329; *The Messianic Idea* 176–202; Schatz-Uffenheimer, *Hahasidut* 168–179; Tishby, *Hikrei vol. 2* 475–519; Wolfson, *Along* 88–109; Idel, *Messianic,* 1–37 and 212–247.

20 See section 'Hisaron and Uniqueness.'

21 See, e.g., Idel's discussion of *unio mystica* (*Perspectives* 59–73).

22 *MHs vol. 1* Ki Teitzei s.v. *ki yikareh* and *vol. 1* Va'et'hanan s.v. *ve'ahavta.*

23 See, e.g., *MHs vol. 1* Tetzaveh s.v. *ve'eileh* 2.

24 See, e.g., *MHs vol. 1* Proverbs s.v. *mayim 'amukim.*

25 *MHs vol. 2* Yitro *s.v. lo ta'asun*. For a general discussion of will and its relation to divinity in Jewish mysticism, see Ish-Shalom, *Haguto* 77–97.

26 See Huxley, *The Perennial*.

27 *MHs vol. 1* Pesahim *s.v. R. Simlai*. Although the term *retzon Hashem* is not used in this passage, it is clear in context that Lainer is referring to the necessity of accessing divine will in making decisions as opposed to relying on guidance based in *halakhah* or *mitzvot*. Lainer writes that a human being is unable to make life decisions merely based on *taryag mitzvot*.

28 *MHs vol. 2* Behukotai *s.v. im* 2.

29 *MHs vol. 1* Pesahim *s.v. R. Simlai*.

30 *MHs vol. 2* Likutim Noah *s.v. vayomru*. The topic under discussion is the Temple in Jerusalem. For Lainer, Temple-consciousness is synonymous with acosmic humanism.

31 *MHs vol.* Pinhas *s.v. ki*. On the enmeshment of Israel and divinity as the basis of Israel's ability to access *retzon Hashem*, see also *vol. 1* Ki Tavo *s.v. et Hashem he'emarta*.

32 *MHs vol. 2* Yitro *s.v. va'esa*.

33 Jer. 13:11.

34 The word 'incarnate' most closely captures the sense of *MHs*. On the term 'incarnational', see endnote 7.

35 *MHs vol. 2* Behukotai *s.v. im* 2.

36 *MHs vol. 2* Ecclesiastes *s.v. mah yitron* 2; for parallel passages, see, e.g., *vol. 2* Berakhot *s.v. amar Rabah yigmor*.

37 Psalms 16:5.

38 *MHs vol. 2* Psalms *s.v. Hashem menat helki*.

39 *Hayyim* is most often a synonym for the *sefirah* of *binah*, referred to in the *Zohar* as the 'higher *Shekhinah*'. On the term *hayyim* see, e.g., *MHs vol. 2* Vayeira *s.v. ki 'atzor* (Source 1 in volume 2); Bo *s.v. vayomer* 1. On the identification of *hayyim* with post-*berur* consciousness in which a person attains 'the world-to-come, which is perfection', see also *MHs vol. 2* Isaiah *s.v. vehayah*. The world-to-come, like *hayyim*, is usually a kabbalistic synonym for the *sefirah* of *binah*. See also *vol. 1* Hukat *s.v. zot hukat*.

40 See Hallamish, 'Yahas'.

41 *MHs vol. 1* Psalms *s.v. ki hineih*.

42 See, e.g., *vol. 2* Bo *s.v. vayomer* 1.

43 *MHs vol. 1* Pesahim, *s.v. ve'amar*.

44 On *or makif* in *MHs* in various guises, see *MHs vol. 1* Pesahim *s.v. ve'amar; vol. 2* Bereishit *s.v. eileh toldot*; Ha'azinu *s.v. yesovevenu*. On *or makif* in Hasidic literature and Habad writings, see, e.g., Hallamish, 'Mishnato' 50-61. A comparative study of the idea of *or makif* in Habad and Izbica, though beyond the parameters of this work, would be worthwhile.

45 See e.g., *MHs vol. 1* Ki Tisa *s.v. elohei maseikhah* (Source 27 in volume 2); Vayehi *s.v. vayehi; vol. 2* Ecclesiastes *s.v. mah yitron* 2.

46 See the section 'The Individual's Unique *Helek* (Portion) of Torah'.

47 See the section 'Acosmism and *Mikdash* (The Jerusalem Temple)'.

48 *MHs vol.* 2 Isaiah s.v. *vehayah.*

49 On *hayyim,* see endnote 598. On the world-to-come, see the section 'Hisaron Meyuhad'.

50 See also *vol.* 2 Behaalotekha s.v. *im yihyeh* (Source 5 in volume 2), where Moses, as function of his being an archetype of acosmic humanism, is able to judge according to the uniqueness of every individual.

51 We understand *eros* here in the way that Yehudah Liebes did in his article 'Zohar Ve'eros'. Liebes sees the idea of eros unpacked by Plato as a major motif in Zoharic discourse. *Eros* in this sense evokes a quality of presence, interiority, sensuousness of intellect and yearning. On the precise relationship between the erotic and holy on the one hand, and the sexual on the other hand, see Gafni, *Mystery.* For more specific discussion on desire, see Chapter Eleven, 'The Way of *Teshukah'.*

52 *MHs vol.* 2 Proverbs s.v. *lakahat.* The remainder of this passage describes one who allows himself to be seduced to the will of God even as he is discerning and avoids seduction to the 'transient goods of this world'.

53 *MHs vol.* 1 Ha'azinu s.v. *ha-tzur.*

54 See *MHs vol.* 2 Isaiah s.v. *vehayah.*

55 On the concept of *retzon Hashem kavu'a balev* see, e.g., *MHs vol.* 1 Emor s.v. *vahaveitem* (Source 24 in volume 2).

56 In Lainer's terms, it is נייחא *neiha,* bringing a sense of comfort, ease, and equilibrium. See, e.g., *MHs vol.* 2 Ki Tavo s.v. *vehayah,* where *neiha* indicates the full realization that what appears as sin comes from God's will. See Source 15 in volume 3 for use of the same term in the *Zohar.*

57 See *MHs vol.* 2 Va'eira s.v. *vayikah* (Source 15 in volume 2), where Lainer interprets the verse 'to the straight of heart is joy' (Ps. 97:11) as referring to one who intends the will of God.

58 Imagery from the Song of Songs is connected to the Wisdom of Solomon genre and connotes the highest stage beyond *berur* in which the human being consciously incarnates the will of God. See, e.g., *vol.* 1 Hukat s.v. *zot hukat; vol.* 2 Va'eira s.v. *vayikah* (Source 15 in volume 2); Proverbs s.v. *lakahat;* Likutim Zohar s.v. *shama'ti.*

59 *MHs vol.* 1 Shelah s.v. *beha-sidrah* (Source 42 in volume 2).

60 *MHs vol.* 2 Mishpatim s.v. *sheish shanim.*

61 See e.g. *Zohar* 2:183a, adduced and annotated in Tishby, *Wisdom* vol. 1 354–355.

62 *MHs vol.* 1 Balak s.v. *ki lo nahash.*

63 *MHs vol.* 1 Noah s.v. *eileh.*

64 *MHs vol.* 1 Behukotai s.v. *im* 2. See further exploration of these themes below in the section 'Three Qualities of Consciousness'.

65 *MHs vol.* 1 Vayigash s.v. *vayigash* 1.

66 On revelation connected to these categories, see e.g. *MHs vol.* 2 Aharei Mot

s.v. *vekhol.*

67 *MHs vol. 1* Mas'ei s.v. *kein mateh* 2.

68 On the voice of revelation being interior, see the passages already cited above: *MHs vol. 1* Yitro s.v. *vayehi*; Matot s.v. *vayedaber*; vol. 2 Behaalotekha s.v. *im yihyeh* (Source 5 in volume 2). See also section 'Personal Revelation and the Personalized Torah', and Weiss, 'A Late Jewish Utopia' 215–219.

69 *Ends* 76–82.

70 See, e.g., *MHs vol. 2* Va'eira s.v. *vayikah* (Source 15 in volume 2) and *vol. 1* Hukat s.v. *vayis'u.* With respect to the latter passage, Rakover (*Ends* 78–81) incorrectly interprets the argument between the *tana kama* and R. Nathan as revolving around a distinction between ascertaining God's will intellectually, based on *binah*, and emotionally, based on one's 'heart being drawn after the will of God'. This interpretation, however, is a misunderstanding because Lainer is not using *binah* in the intellectual sense.

71 For an extended discussion of kabbalistic hermeneutics, see Idel's *Perspectives* 200–249 and his more recent *Absorbing Perfections* 26–136. See also Wolfson, 'Beautiful'.

72 *MHs vol. 2* Behaalotekha s.v. *vaya'asu.*

73 *MHs vol. 2* Ecclesiastes s.v. *mah yitron* 2.

74 *MHs vol. 1* Vayeishev s.v. *vezeh* (Source 9 in volume 2). This passage also introduces Lainer's terminology for higher truth 'for it is possible that the law is true *emet…*but not *le'amito* "unto its innermost truth", as we found with Rava's cane'. We will have occasion to further examine this passage and other passages that concern the case of Rava's cane in the Wisdom of Solomon sources (volume 2, Cluster 2).

75 *MHs vol. 1* Mikeitz s.v. *tishma'.*

76 *MHs vol. 1* Mas'ei s.v. *kein mateh* 2.

77 *MHs vol. 2* Berakhot s.v. *heivi'u lefanav.*

78 *MHs vol. 1* Vayikra s.v. *'al kol* (Source 26 in volume 2).

79 Note the end of the section 'Model Four: *Shekhinah*, The Eros of the Will of God', where we suggest that his antinomianism is less radical than it might otherwise seem.

80 In different worlds the Torah can manifest very different normative implications, hence the antinomian implications of this doctrine. See Scholem, 'The Meaning' 65–72. Idel (*Absorbing Perfections* 353) outlines four basic doctrines of the nature of Torah, all suggesting that the Torah of this eon is a limited temporal expression and that a higher level Torah will emerge at some point in the future. See also Scholem, *Origins* 460–475; *Sabbetai Sevi* 313–314, 811–814; *On the Kabbalah* 77–81; Liebes, *Sod* 47, 292–293, n. 236.

81 *MHs vol. 1* Bereishit s.v. *vayetzav.*

82 See Rosenberg, 'Hashivah'.

83 *MHs vol. 2* Behukotai s.v. *im* 2.

84 *MHs vol. 2* Behaalotekha s.v. *vaya'asu.*

85 *MHs vol. 1* Vayeishev s.v. *vayehi.* See analysis on p. 78.

86 See Chapter Twelve.

87 *Ends* 76–82.

88 *Ends* 76.

89 On both the requirement to be without personal *negi'ah* and the view that acting against the law in fulfillment of *retzon Hashem* is only post facto and not a proactive possibility, see, e.g., *MHs vol. 1* Shelah s.v. *vayehi* and Vayeishev s.v. *vayehi*. Lainer also suggests in these passages that one must fulfill both the law and *retzon Hashem*.

90 *MHs vol. 2* Behaalotekha s.v. *vaya'asu*. See also *vol. 2* Naso s.v. *yisa*. See also in this regard a genre of passages in *MHs* which revolve around the theme of Israel being *'devukim'*, cleaved to God, e.g., *vol. 2* Shelah s.v. *vehikriv* (Source 32 in volume 2)

91 *MHs vol. 1* Vayeishev s.v. *vayeishev*.

92 *MHs vol. 2* Va'eira s.v. *vayikah* (Source 15 in volume 2). See also *MHs vol. 1* Mikeitz s.v. *vehineih*, where being drawn after God's will is an ontological reality realized after the process of *berur* is completed and not as a post facto allowance.

93 *MHs vol. 1* Hukat s.v. *vayis'u benei Yisrael*.

94 *MHs vol. 1* Pinhas s.v. *vayar Pinhas*.

95 *MHs vol. 1* Nitzavim s.v. *vehayah*.

96 *MHs vol. 1* Mikeitz s.v. *tishma'*, citing *bBer.* 55b, 'All dreams follow the mouth [that interprets]'.

97 *MHs vol. 1* Mikeitz s.v. *tishma'*. See above, p. 159. This principle, of course, is also applied to everyday events (and not just dreams) in *Midrash*, and even more generally in *Hasidut* (see p. 38 along with endnote 139), though not with Lainer's unique cast.

98 *MHs vol. 2* Vayeira s.v. *vayehi*.

99 For this particular example, see *MHs vol. 2* Rosh Hashanah s.v. *lo havei yadei*.

100 See, e.g., *MHs vol. 1* Yitro s.v. *anokhi* 1 (quoted in endnote 1535 to volume 2); Ki Tisa s.v. *elohei maseikhah* (Source 27 in volume 2); Va'et'hanan s.v. *va'asitem*; *vol. 2* Ki Tavo s.v. *arur ha-ish* (Source 43 in volume 2).

101 On acosmic humanism and idolatry, see also our discussion on the relationship between voluntarism and necessity, p. 218ff. Another major theme is Lainer's positive evaluation of paganism—see brief discussion on p. 234. This theme is treated in detail in Cluster 5 of volume 2.

102 *The Living Waters.*

103 *The Living Waters* 330 n. 60. See also Rakover, *Ends* 76–82.

104 See, e.g., *MHs vol. 1* Hukat s.v. *vayis'u*.

105 See *MHs vol. 2* Mishpatim s.v. *vayikah* (discussed briefly on p. 246).

106 *MHs vol. 1* Balak s.v. *ka'eit*.

107 *MHs vol. 1* Balak s.v. *ki lo nahash*.

108 See also *MHs vol. 1* Shabbat s.v. *amar Rav*; *vol. 2* Berakhot s.v. *heivi'u lefanav*, where the ability to intend to the will of God in every moment is a faculty that can be realized, at least in potential, by every person.

109 *MHs vol. 1* Behukotai s.v. *im* 2.

110 *MHs vol. 1* Noah s.v. *vekhol*.

111 On *hitpashtut* as a function of identity with *retzon Hashem*, which occurs only after *berur*, see, e.g., *MHs vol. 1* Lekh Lekha s.v. *vayiven, vol. 1* Hukat s.v. *vayis'u, vol. 2* Ki Tisa s.v. *shishah, vol. 2* Vayak'hel s.v. *vayak'hel* 2.

112 *MHs vol. 1* Behukotai s.v. *im* 2; see also Chapter Twelve. Against Weiss ('Determinism' n. 10), we note that *hitpashtut* means the breaking of old boundaries, whether in the direction of expansion or contraction. On drawing a new boundary in the direction of contraction, see, e.g., *MHs vol. 1* Emor s.v. *vahaveitem* (Source 24 in volume 2), where *hitpashtut* occurs in a limiting rather than an expansive direction.

113 See, e.g., *MHs vol. 1* Ki Tisa s.v. *elohei maseikhah* (Source 27 in volume 2); *vol. 2* Vayigash s.v. *vayigash* 2.

114 On the anti-existentialist mood of early Hasidic theologies of *bitul*, see Schatz-Uffenheimer, *Hasidism* 65–79.

115 The best modern treatment of nondual thought and its implications for the concepts of boundary and no-boundary consciousness in both Eastern and Western approaches remains, to the best of our knowledge, Ken Wilber's *No Boundary*.

116 *MHs vol. 1* Vayeira s.v. *ki 'atzor* (Source 1 in volume 2). On the linkage between Israel as participating in the divine and no-boundary consciousness, see also *vol. 1* Beshalah s.v. *nikheho*.

117 On hermeneutics in Kabbalah in general, including extensive material on Hasidism, see Idel, *Absorbing Perfections*.

118 *MHs vol. 1* Re'eh s.v. *ki yarhiv*.

119 *MHs vol. 1* Pesahim s.v. *bayom*.

120 *MHs vol. 1* Berakhot s.v. *lo yitpalel*.

121 *MHs vol. 2* Taanit s.v. *biyemei Rabi Zeira*.

122 *MHs vol. 2* Berakhot s.v. *amar Raba*.

123 See Maimonides, *Mishneh Torah* Laws of Repentance Ch. 1 and 2; for an analysis of these elements of repentance in Maimonides, see Soloveitchik, *On Repentance*.

124 *MHs vol. 2* Taanit s.v. *biyemei Rabi Zeira*. See also *vol. 2* Shelah s.v. *'al 'inyan*.

125 For an analysis of this conception of repentance in Lainer, see Rosenberg (Shagar), 'Teshuvah' 193–219. See also Bartov, 'Sin'.

126 Gellman, *The Fear*; Weiss, 'Determinism'; Elior, 'Temurot'.

127 See, e.g., *MHs vol. 2* Korah s.v. *ketiv*.

128 On Lainer and Romanticism, see also pp. 23, 74ff, and sections 'Secular Influences' (in the introduction to volume 1) and 'Lainer and the Romantics' below. See also Taylor, *Sources of Self* 305–390.

129 For an opposing thread in *MHs*, see *MHs vol. 2* Berakhot s.v. *amru*, which indicates that *lema'alah mida'ato* and its equivalents belonged to an earlier religious era, very possibly the era corresponding to paganism in the pre-rabbinic period. In contrast, the rabbinic period sees the will of God incarnate in ישוב הדעת *yishuv*

ha-da'at, i.e., the settled equilibrium of human *da'at*.

130 See, e.g., *MHs vol. 1* Shoftim s.v. *shoftim* 2 (Source 7 in volume 2).

131 *MHs vol. 2* Psalms s.v. *uvitevunot kapav*, quoted in ths section below.

132 *MHs vol. 2* Shelah s.v. *vehikriv* (Source 32 in volume 2). See also *vol. 1* Berakhot s.v. *kol hanevi'im*.

133 *MHs vol. 2* Psalms s.v. *uvitevunot kapav*.

134 *MHs vol. 1* Proverbs s.v. *kemayim*.

135 *MHs vol. 1* Devarim s.v. *ahad asar yom*.

136 *MHs vol. 1* 'Ekev s.v. *shegar*.

137 *MHs vol. 2* Likutim s.v. *ha'inyan*.

138 *MHs vol. 2* Shelah s.v. *vehikriv* (Source 32 in volume 2).

139 Lainer often links the two. See, e.g., *MHs vol. 2* Berakhot s.v. *amar Rav*.

140 *MHs vol. 2* Shelah s.v. *vehikriv*; s.v. *'al 'inyan*.

Chapter Nine

Name, Activism and Acosmic Humanism

All is in the Hands of Heaven: A Humanist Agenda

We now turn to the twelfth characteristic of Lainer's acosmic humanism: its profoundly activist nature. Weiss suggests that for Lainer, the presence of divine will overwhelms the human being. The result of this, according to Weiss, is what he calls the undermining of human activism: מיעוט דמותה של כל עשייה אנושית...וביטולה הגמור 'the diminished significance of human action...[or] its complete nullification.'[1] As we have already seen, quite the opposite is true. Lainer sets up human freedom as the central defining characteristic of his religious anthropology.

It is easy to understand how Weiss arrived at his reading of Lainer. Lainer often conceals his true position in *MHs*. Moreover, he will often state a more conventional orthodox theocentric position at the beginning of an explanation, and only by implication let his more radical acosmic-humanist position be known at the end.[2] Another method Lainer uses is to express a theocentric position through a dramatic re-reading of a rabbinic adage, which upon closer examination is revealed to be a cover for his genuine acosmic-humanist position.[3]

One text that is critical to the question of human activism is cited by Weiss as a model of this structure. Lainer takes the well-known rabbinic dictum, 'All is in the hands of heaven except for the fear of heaven', and stands it on its head, so that it means, 'All is in the hands of heaven, *even* the fear of heaven'. This appears, prima facie, to support the most extremely theocentric reading of Lainer, first outlined by Weiss.[4]

However, a more careful reading of the concept of 'the hands of heaven' in *MHs* leads to very different conclusions. First, in our reading of *MHs*, 'All is in the hands of heaven, even the fear of heaven' refers to the specific level of consciousness that we have referred to in the introduction to this volume as *shabbat*-consciousness.[5] In *shabbat*-consciousness, one moves beyond the illusion of self-sufficiency to the realization that all is done by

God, i.e., 'all is in the hands of heaven'. However, this phrase itself is understood by Lainer to already imply the third level consciousness that we have termed *mikdash*-consciousness or Temple-consciousness. In *mikdash*-consciousness, as we shall see below, one realizes the ontic identity of human and divine wills. This is the empowering realization of acosmic humanism.

Indeed, when Lainer suggests that 'All is the in the hands of heaven, even the fear of heaven', he is really obfuscating his true position. A careful analysis of some less cited *MHs* passages which address the relationship between human hands and divine will suggests that within Lainer's radical reading of the rabbinic dictum, his true position is that 'the hands of heaven' are ontologically identical with 'the hands of the human'. This is the point we will demonstrate here and it is precisely the point made throughout this entire book.

In an important passage which we examined above,[6] Lainer teaches that the phrase 'with the wisdom of his hands' (Psalms 78:72) indicates the level of *lema'alah mida'ato*: נמצא בידים בינה למעלה מדעת מדעת האדם שיכול לכוון כרצון הש"ית בלי דעתו כלל לא יחטיא המטרה 'in the hands one finds *binah* understanding, beyond the intellect (or, awareness, consciousness) of a person, which can direct [itself] according to the divine will without one's awareness—it will not miss the mark (or, sin) at all'.[7]

The level of *binah* is of course the third level, at which human and divine will merge. There is an intentional blurring here in which human hands paradoxically express the divine will, i.e. the hands of heaven.

It is worth reading out of chronological order for a moment to cite Lainer's student Tzadok Hakohen, who, in a teaching received in part from Lainer, makes this explicit. In describing the highest level of soul (the level of *yehidah*), he writes:

> [Those on the highest level] are, in their essence, the will of
> God and merged with [God's will]…[And regarding this
> level] the idol-worshipers recognized, and said, 'It is through
> the strength and power of my own hands' (Deut. 8:17)…that
> is, all is in the hands of man and not the hands of God…but
> Israel look to divine help…However, in the end it becomes
> their Torah,[8] as it says, 'And the earth was given to human-
> kind' (Psalms115:16)…[T]his is the level of Solomon…who
> was called by the name of God. [9]

Earlier in this passage, Tzadok states that this level is the place where the human has the 'power to save himself'. In effect, an individual, animated by the divine, becomes their own redeemer. This language closely parallels *MHs*:

ועלו מושיעים בהר ציון, שהם נקראו מושיעים שיושיעו את עצמן כיון
שיכירו שכל פעולתם הוא מהשי״ת

'The saviors will go up to Mount Zion' (Obadiah 1:21)—they are called saviors, that is, they will save themselves, because they recognize that all of their actions derive from God...[10]

The key, as Lainer says in the beginning of the passage, is not to think שפעולותיו יעשו לו את הכל כי שם נסתר אור השי״ת 'that his [independent] actions will do everything for him, for there [in the material world] the light of God is hidden'.

Here again, it is not that human agency is irrelevant. In fact, one may legitimately call human beings *moshi'im* or redeemers. Rather, one must realize that one's redemptive act is animated by the divine energy—in the metaphor of Lainer, illuminated by the divine light. In describing redeemed consciousness, Lainer speaks in terms of self-redemption. A person becomes their own savior. The key to this audacious claim is that the nations of the world, who believe that all strength and power are in their hands, are essentially correct. The drive to make this claim is rooted in the highest level of spiritual consciousness. Their mistake is that they do not realize that their hands have power only because of the ontic identity between their hands and the hands of God.

This concept of the evolving enlightenment of God through the vehicle of the human being is an underlying theme throughout *MHs*. In effect, the human, who shares in divine ontology, is the visible expression of the evolving Godhead.[11]

This conclusion is supported by a careful analysis of the all of the passages related to hands in *MHs*. When Lainer stands the rabbinic dictum 'All is in the hands of heaven except the fear of heaven' on its head by re-reading it as 'even the fear of heaven', this initially appears as a move away from human autonomy to a radically theocentric position where the human being has no autonomy, even over his own interiority. As we have begun to show, however, what Lainer really is intending is a profoundly humanistic perspective in which 'the hands of man' realize their ontic identity with 'the hands of heaven'. In effect Lainer refers to the three levels of consciousness.[12]

Level one is the illusion of some degree of human independence where the 'fear of heaven' is controlled by human choice and autonomy and is therefore beyond the reach of 'the hands of heaven'. This corresponds to the classic understanding of the dictum, 'All is in the hands of heaven except the fear of heaven'. The second level of consciousness, the one upon which Weiss focuses virtually all of his attention, is the theocentric level. At this level man realizes that 'all is the in hands of heaven' and that human choice and autonomy is but an illusion. This is the level to which Lainer alludes when he re-reads this rabbinic dictum as 'All is in the hands of heaven even the fear of heaven'.

Level two theocentricism however, is the not the apex of religious consciousness. At the third and highest level of religious consciousness, nondual acosmic humanism, one realizes the ontic identity between 'the hands of heaven' and 'the hands of man'. By tracing the 'two hands' theme, we can see how the idea that *hakol biyedei shamayim'* is another strand in the fabric of Lainer's underlying theory of acosmic humanism. This is the esoteric teaching of *MHs*.[13]

The significance of this theme crystallizes in a set of interlocking passages unnoted by previous authors. These passages, which revolve around King David, clarify that the statement 'All is in the hands of heaven, even the fear of heaven' actually points to the state of post-*berur* consciousness, in which 'the hands of heaven' are 'the hands of man'.

These passages reflect the Talmudic distinction, based on biblical verses, between God's creation, which is the result of 'one hand' of God, and human activism, which is the result of 'the two hands' of God. The following example begins as an explanation of the verse 'Your hands made me and established me; make me understand and I will learn Your commandments' (Psalms 119:73):

כתיב (ישעיה מ כו) שאו מרום עיניכם וראו מי ברא אלה וגו' והיינו כשיביט
האדם לכוחות השמים וצבאיהם יוכל להבין כי ה' ברא אלה ומזה מתחייב
מאוד יראה, אכן בצדיקים איתא בגמ' (כתובות ה.) גדולים מעשי צדיקים
יותר ממעשה שמים וארץ, דאלו בשמים וארץ כתיב (ישעיה מח יג) אף ידי
יסדה ארץ וימיני טפחה שמים, ואלו במעשה צדיקים כתיב (שמות טו יז)
מקדש ה' כוננו ידיך בשתי ידים

170

It is written, 'Lift your eyes up and see who created these...'
(Isa. 40:36), meaning that when a person looks towards the
powers of the heavens and their hosts, he can understand
that *Hashem* 'created these'. And from this he will bring
upon himself intense *yir'ah* fear. So therefore concerning the
righteous, [it says] in the Talmud, 'The work of the righteous
is greater than the creation of heaven and earth. For regarding heaven and earth it is written, *yadi yasdah aretz* "Even My
hand founded the earth, and the heavens were spanned by
My right hand" (Isa. 48:13), while regarding the work of the
righteous it is written, *mikdash Hashem* (sic) *konanu yadekha*
"Your hands established the sanctuary of God (Exod. 15:17)"
' (*bKetubot* 5a)—with two hands.[14]

The *aggadah* itself foreshadows the essence of Lainer's thought: 'Your
hands', that is, God's hands, <u>are</u> the hands of the righteous—in other
words, human deeds are God's actions. It comes as no surprise that the
paradigmatic expression of *ma'aseh tzadikim* is the building of the *mikdash*.
The Temple, as we have seen, is the place where acosmic humanism finds
clearest expression in this world.[15] Lainer here uses the *aggadah* to distinguish between the heavens, created with one hand, which induce יראה *yir'ah*
fear, and מעשה צדיקים *ma'aseh tzadikim* the work of the righteous, which are
greater than the heavens. *Yir'ah*, of course, is a code word in Izbica for
'*avodah*, for *kelalei divrei Torah*, and '*olam ha-zeh*, the unredeemed world,
and for pre-*berur* consciousness.[16] The level beyond *yir'ah* is אהבה *ahavah*
love, *retzon Hashem* and post-*berur* consciousness, and it is represented
here as the work of the righteous, denoted by the verse 'Your hands established the sanctuary of God'. The plural 'hands', i.e., both hands, indicates a
higher level of spiritual consciousness. David, who transcends *yir'ah*—the
quality of the heavens—embodies this quality, as he says 'Your hands made
me and established me'.

All of this is linked by Lainer back to *Shekhinah*-consciousness, symbolized by the moon, as explained in the continuation of this passage.[17]

This theme plays itself out in a long but essential passage which is one of
the closing texts of the first volume of *MHs*.[18] Here, David's lack of fear is
explicitly related to his ontic unity with God's will:

כשבא לו תוקף מרצון הש״י בלבו היינו אות ה׳ אחרונה תיכף סמוך לבו לא
ירא עוד רק נכון לבו בטוח שחשקו ורצונו אינו נוטה מרצון הש״י רק זה
הוא רצון הש״י

[W]hen empowerment came to [King David] from the will
of God within his heart, signified by the last *heh* [of the divine
name], he immediately relied on his heart; he was no longer
afraid; his heart was steadfast, certain that his desire and his will
could not stray from God's will, for exactly this was God's will.[19]

In the continuation of the passage, Lainer equates the sure knowledge that
David's desire is God's desire with the 'two hands' theme and with the third
stage of consciousness:

ולעתיד ישלוט השם ע״פ צירוף...של דהע״ה...בתחל׳ י״ק״ר״ק א״נ״ק״ת״ם
היינו בעוד שלא זכה האדם לבא לשורשו וחלקו בד״ת הוא נואק בצעקה
תמיד להש״י לעזרו מן רצונות ומחשבות זרות המציקים לו ומנגדים
ומבלבלים אותו להרידו ממקומו, אח״כ כשזוכה לישועת הש״י ומתחיל
לבא למקום חפצו זהו פ״ס״ת״ם פס מורה על הרחבה כמו יהי פסת בד
כו׳ שנרחב לו מהמציקים ואויביו נופלים תחתיו, אח״כ פ״ס״פ״י״ם היינו
שמשתדל להרחבת גבול לא מן המציקים לו, רק בשפע רב שמשפיע לו
הש״י בשתי ידים, אח״כ ד״י״נ״ס״י״ם היינו שזוכה להתנשאות בנשיאות
ראש

In the future God will rule according to [the names that derive
from] the combination [of letters coming from] King David...
[The first name refers to a time] when a person has not merited to arrive at his root and portion in the Torah; he cries out
with a constant call to God to save him from the desires and
strange thoughts that disturb him, and oppose him and con-
found him, lowering him from his place...After that, when he
merits God's salvation and begins to approach his desire, this
is [the second name which indicates] *harhavah* extension...
for [his place] is widened for him beyond disturbances and his
enemies fall under him (or, it). After that, [is the level of the
third name, when] he strives to expand boundaries, not because of [needing to overcome] those disturbances, but rather
through the *shefa' rav* great effluence that God showers upon
him with two hands...After that [the fourth name is when]
he merits *hitnas'ut* exaltation, raising high [his] head...[20]

Relating to the names of God that are based on the permutations of the letters of the biblical verses comprising the priestly blessing, Lainer suggests that one name refers to the period in a person's life before they have identified their unique *helek* (vocation), i.e., what we have termed 'soul print'.[21] The second name refers to the period in a person's life after they have identified their soul print. The first name is an existential cry of distress from lack of participating in and living one's own story. The second name affirms the humanistic nature of Lainer's acosmism.

The third and fourth names refer to the time when one's story is comprehended as coinciding completely with the divine will, culminating in התנשאות *hitnas'ut*, exaltation of the unique individual. Divine redemption occurs when a person expands into the parameters of their story; God flows into the person with a great effluence. This flow is from God's two hands, 'the hands of heaven'. The phrase used to describe this stage is הרחבה *harhavah* (widening or extension), which is a term that has clear associations in *MHs*. We saw that Lainer interprets the verse כי ירחיב ה' אלקיך את גבולך 'When God will extend your boundaries'[22] as referring to the no-boundary consciousness that one can attain when one realizes the acosmic nature of the universe.

In the process described above, expansion to no-boundary consciousness paradoxically coincides with affirmation of the unique individual's ontic identity with God. 'Two hands' signifies redemptive consciousness and נשיאות ראש *nesi'ut rosh*, the experience of being raised up or exalted by God, a term that in *MHs* is covalent with radical individualism and uniqueness.[23] In other words, realizing that we are all part of the great quilt of the divine does not nullify the reality that we are each unique patches in the quilt. This is what it means, according to Lainer, to receive God's 'two-handed' divine effluence.

In Lainer's theology, unique individuality and absorption in divinity merge. The continuation of the passage spells this out:

והענין מדות התנשאות הוא באמת למעלה מן השכל...האיך מנשא שני
צדיקים בדור אחד וכ"א זוכה שחלקו מתנשא על כל ראש ואין שני לו,
והשני כמו כן מתנשא ואין שני לו כמו משה ואהרן שהי' כ"א מהם חד
בדרא...וזהו בדרך נס

173

[The nature of] this quality of being raised up truly transcends reasoning…How can two righteous people be exalted in one generation, [even though] each one merits that his portion be lifted up above all, and there is no one comparable to him, while the other is also lifted up, and there is no one comparable to him, as with Moses and Aaron, for each one was unique in that generation…[T]his is a kind of miracle.

The concept of *hitnas'ut*, which is indeed paradoxical, defines Lainer's system. Lainer is aware of the apparent contradiction between his acosmism and the individuality that defines his humanism, and therefore says that this is beyond reason. Two people can each be 'the most unique'. As we will see, it is the Judah archetype who can access this consciousness that exists beyond reason.[24]

The next passage begins with the same Talmudic teaching that the plural 'hands' indicates the precedence of the deeds of the righteous over the creation of heavens and earth. Lainer appropriates the *aggadah* in the following manner:

העניין בזה כי בריאת שמים וארץ היה כדי שיכיר האדם שהשי״ת נמצא
בעולם, ואם היה מפורש זאת בהתגלות, אין שום מקום לפעולות אדם לכן
הסתיר השי״ת זאת והלביש זאת בלבושים ולכן נדמה שעולם כמנהגו נוהג
ואינו נראה הכרת השי״ת מפורש, רק ע״י מעשה המצות אז נתראה התגלות
אור השי״ת בעולם, וכל זה הוא שהשי״ת חפץ להצדיק לבריותיו, לכן נתן
מקום שע״י פעולות ישראל נתגלה זאת

The point of this is that the creation of heaven and earth happened in order that a person would know that God is in the world, and were this clearly revealed, there would be no place for the work of man. God therefore concealed this, clothing it in garments. It therefore seems as if the world behaves in its customary fashion (i.e., according to the natural order), and the recognition of God is not shown explicitly. It is only through work of the commandments that God's light is then shown in the world. All this is so because God desires *lehatzdik* to vindicate His creations. He therefore made room for this to be revealed through Israel's actions.[25]

It seems that creating with 'one hand' is synonymous with God's conceal-ment. 'The hands of heaven' in contrast indicates the revelation of divine immanence, which happens through human activism. This is made clear in the continuation of the passage:

וכמו שמצינו בעת שנגמר בנין בית המקדש היה כל האומות מכירים
התגלות השי״ת בעולם וזה נקרא בשתי ידים היינו בשלימות הגמור

As we found at the time when the building of the Temple was completed: all the nations then recognized the revelation of God in the world. This is what is called 'with two hands', meaning, in complete *sheleimut* perfection.

The symbol of acosmic humanism that is integrated into human con-sciousness is none other than the *mikdash*, the Temple in Jerusalem. Once again the Temple is an essential part of the cluster of concepts and terms that form Solomon's wisdom of acosmic humanism, which we will explore in detail in volume 2.

Another two-hands passage revolves around uniqueness and radical in-dividualism, a theme which we have already seen in these texts. The dif-ference between this and the previous passages is that here the hands are human hands rather than God's hands. The context is the *shelamim* (whole offering) sacrifice, which apparently hints to the human perfection that comes from fully accepting one's unique story:

קרבן שלמים מורה שהאדם יתפלל להש״י שיטעימו מטוב הצפון לו לעוה״ב,
והוא כי ירצה לראות את מקומו ממי שהוא גדול וחפץ בהתנשאות, בזה
נאמר יביא את קרבנו ידיו תביאנה, היינו למסור כל בקשתו ותפלתו
להש״י...ע״ז מורה מה שנאמר ידיו תביאנה היינו בשני ידים כי באם האדם
ירצה לטעום מטובו בעוה״ז ומבקש מהש״י שיראהו מקומו צריך להיות נקי
מצדו... וזהו ידיו תביאנה כי הוא בשתי ידים

[The one who brings a *shelamim* offering] prays to God to al-low him to taste the goodness stored up for him in the world-to-come, and wants to see his place and whom he is greater than, and he wants to be lifted up. Concerning this it says, 'He shall bring his offering, his hands will bring it'. This means that he should surrender all his supplication and prayer to God...Thus the instruction, 'his hands will bring it', that is,

175

with two hands. For if a person wants to taste His goodness in this world and asks God to show him his place, he must be clean from his side...which is what is meant by 'his hands will bring it', since it is with both hands.[26]

If a person wants to know their place, their purpose cannot be to satisfy their narrow ego agenda. Rather, their purpose must be to embrace in a clean and pure way their unique place and their unique expression of divinity, whatever these might be. According to Lainer, this is the meaning of offering prayer and sacrifice with two hands.[27]

Lastly, we bring a passage that indicates the intimacy of 'God's hands' and shows that we are talking about a kind of unity with God's will that is very far from the theocentric and deterministic perspective advocated by Weiss:

כל קדושיו בידיך הוא לשון נוכח היינו העושים מאהבה הם ביד הש"י
ולנגדם מפורש הנוכח

'All of his holy ones are in Your hands'. This is a language of
unmediated presence; that is to say, those who act from love
are in the hand of God, and God is present to them in an
explicit and unmediated fashion.[28]

'Acting from love' and 'unmediated presence' are virtual synonyms for the Judah archetype, in which human action, emerging from clarified human will, is affirmed as expressing the will of God.[29] The hands of heaven, once again, are the hands receiving those who act from love, while those who act are united with God's unmediated presence, which is synonymous with merging with the *Shekhinah*.

The goal of religious endeavor is to achieve the level of enlightenment in which consciousness expands to the unmediated realization that human action is animated by God. In fact, all human action—in its purified post-*berur* form—is divine action as well. This reading of Lainer transforms the meaning of 'All is in the hands of heaven' from radical theocentrism to an equally radical humanism. Finally, the entire idea of *berur*, clarification of the nature of both reality and one's inner motivation, assumes as its point of departure a radically activist posture. These points support the idea of human activism even within post-*berur* consciousness, as well as the idea that *berur* itself is an affirmation of human activism.

176

Called by the Name of God

When we examine *MHs* texts bearing directly on the issue of human activism, we will see that the major motif in these processes is to dramatically empower human activism rather than undermine it. However, before turning to these texts, we first need to present a major motif that limns Lainer's entire discussion of human activism. This is the topic of 'name'. Examining this topic will allow us to more fully understand Lainer's theology, with particular emphasis on its activist expression.

As we have noted in several places, Weiss and other scholars[30] have read Lainer as wholly rejecting the ontological efficacy of human activism. Let us look at a key passage Weiss uses to support his core thesis that Lainer's theology of divine will leads to a radical devaluing of human action.[31] Weiss cites a central mantra-like refrain appearing throughout *MHs*: human action is 'called by the name of God.'[32] Virtually all students of *MHs* [33] understand this to mean that the actions of the human being belong to God and have no connection to the human being; however, as a divine gift to the human, God allows actions to nonetheless be 'called by the name of man'. This gift is the human illusion that human activism is valuable and that therefore one's actions should be called by one's name; when indeed the ontological truth is that human activism is irrelevant. A closer reading of this very passage, however, suggests a very different interpretation. Especially in the context of many other passages dealing with names, which together form a coherent cluster, a very different picture emerges that dramatically supports acosmic humanism, rooting it in one of the most central kabbalistic doctrines: the secret of the name of God.[34]

Lainer, emerging from a long kabbalistic tradition and going one step further in his conclusions, actually teaches the paradoxical identity between the name of God and the human name. Human actions are correctly ascribed to human beings: 'called by the name of man'. And they are also ascribed to the name of God. This is the great paradox of acosmic humanism. Religious difficulty only arises when human actions are ascribed solely to the name of the human, that is to say, when the human being claims the ability to act independently of the divine name and will.[35] Thus in the part of this text not cited by Weiss, Lainer teaches that 'both names should be affixed in the human heart': both the name of *ADNY* that ascribes actions to independent human agency and the name *YHVH* that ascribes actions to God. In the future world, the illusion of difference between these two names will collapse and God's name will be one; that is, there will be a realization of the ontic identity between God and human.[36] It is not, as Weiss's reading of the passage implies, that the name *ADNY*, which suggests human will and autonomy, will disappear. Rather, it will be absorbed and integrated into *YHVH*.[37]

We will examine below the three distinct levels of consciousness that are operative in *MHs*. At the first level, there exists a necessary illusion that human effort independent of God is what creates change in the world. This corresponds to what Lainer refers to here as actions 'called by the name of man'. This illusion fails when one ascends to the second stage of consciousness, in which one realizes that all is called by the 'name of God'. However, a third level of consciousness exists at which, once again, one realizes that human action is indeed 'called by the name of man'. At this level of consciousness one realizes, however, that the name of the human and the name of God are ontically identical.[38]

The essence of redeemed consciousness, as we have already seen, derives from what Lainer refers to as *binah*. It is in 'Binah-consciousness', so to speak, that a person can incarnate and intend the will of God. It is this state which is referred to as 'being called by the name of God'. In other words, Lainer understands *Binah*-consciousness in terms of 'name'. In the following passage, Lainer is analyzing the commandment that on Purim a person should drink 'ad delo yada', meaning, 'until he does not know' the difference between Haman and Mordecai. Concerning *binah*, he states:

עד דלא ידע היינו בלי לדעת והכרה רק מהבינה שבלב ידע ארור המן וברוך
מרדכי, וזה המנהג שמחלפין בגדיהם הפורים מורה שאף בלי הכרה על
הלבוש יראו כל עמי הארץ כי שם ה' נקרא עלינו ויהי' ניכר נפש הישראל

[T]his means [he should know] *beli leda'at vehakarah* without any conscious knowledge or recognition—only from *ha-binah shebalev* the understanding in the heart—so will he know that Haman is cursed and Mordechai blessed. And this is [the meaning of] the custom to exchange clothes on Purim, which teaches that even without *hakarah* recognition of external appearance, the peoples of the world will see that the name of *Hashem* is called upon us, and the soul of Israel will be recognized.[39]

178

Here, what is accessed on Purim is not drunkenness but the redeemed consciousness of *binah* associated with visibly personifying the name of God. We will show that Lainer means here that the name of the human participates in the identity of the name of God, and <u>not</u> that it is effaced into nothingness by the divine name. This reading is made clear in a critical series of passages, each of which makes the point in a different way.

In the first passage, Lainer interprets the rabbinic saying: למה צדיקים דומין בפני השכינה כנר בפני אבוקה 'What is the relation between the *tzadik* and the *Shekhinah?* That of a candle before a torch':

שלא אמרו כנר בפני השמש, משום דשרגא בטיהרא מאי מהניא,...,
שמתבטל ומתכלל במקור האור שהוא השמש. אבל נר בפני אבוקה אינו
מתבטל, שהוא חלק ממנו וניכר בו אור בפני עצמה. וע״כ נמשלו צדיקים
בפני השכינה כנר בפני אבוקה, לומר שגם בעת שיתגלה הבהירות מאורו
של השי״ת ויתראה כי אין מציאות לבחירה ועבודה, בכל זאת יהיה השארה
למעשה הצדיקים שייגעו וסבלו בעולם הזה בעת ההסתר להיות נקרא
עבודתם על שמם

They did not say like a candle before the sun...for in that image, the light would be nullified and absorbed in the source of the light, which is the sun. But a candle before a torch is not *mitbateil* 'nullified'...it remains a light unto itself. It is in this sense that the relationship of the righteous to *Shekhinah* was held to be analogous to a candle's relation to a torch. That is, even at that time when the clarity of divine light will be revealed and it will be seen that choice and human activism have no independent *metzi'ut* (ontology), nonetheless, the work of the righteous, who toiled and endured in this world in the time of occlusion [of the *Shekhinah*], will have a *hash'arah* (something immortal that remains theirs),[40] through their *'avodah* work being called by their name.[41]

It is very clear in this passage that human activism (expressed by human actions being called by the 'name of man') has ontological value. The ontological efficacy of human action is clear as well from the following passage:

כי כן מנהג השי״ת שאדם מקבל טובה ואח״כ נעלם ממנו, ועל ידי זה מרעים
וצועק בכל לבו ומתפלל להשי״ת כמו שכתיב (תהילים קב) כי נשאתני
ותשלכני, ועל ידי זה הנעקה מחזור לו השי״ת כל מה שאבד בהוספת טובה

179

ובזה נקראו הטובות על שמו כי קנה אותם ע"י שסבל מהם וע"י זה נקבע
הקדושה בלבו יתד שלא תמוט לנצח

> So is it God's way that a person receives some divine good
> (i.e., blessing) and after that it is hidden from him...and he
> prays to God as it is written, 'You exalted me and you cast
> me out' (Psalms 102:11[42]), and by means of this crying out
> God returns to him what he has lost with added good. And
> through this, the good [he received] is called by his name, for
> he acquired it through his suffering. And through this [suffer-
> ing] holiness is established in his heart firmly, so that it will
> not be undermined *lanetzah* forever.[43]

The revelation of divine light in the future world, as Lainer explains above,
removes the illusion of independent human action but does not undermine the ontological value of human activism. Rather, as we have seen,
it is empowering, lending *tekufot*, power, audacity, and determination, to
the human being, who becomes conscious that he participates in divinity.
Ontology means, as in the previous passage, that the name of man and the
name of God are identical. A key phrase is *hash'arah* indicating that human action has effect in the world not only in a relative sense, but also in
an absolute ontological sense, as an expression of the true divine nature of
reality. A second key phrase in this passage is מעשה צדיקים *ma'aseh tzadikim*,
the work of the righteous. Lainer regularly uses this phrase to refer not to
the Hasidic *tzadik* but to any person who realizes their ontic identity with
the divine and thus intends the will of God.[44] The category of *tzadik* was
extended by Lainer to the entire Judah archetype, which, as we shall see below, is the archetype of one who has realized the identity between human
and divine will and therefore can *mekavein retzon Hashem* 'intend the will
of God'.[45] We have already seen, in our discussion of divine will, that the
category of one who can intend the will of God is not limited to any particular elite but includes in theory all of Israel מקטון ועד גדול *mikaton ve'ad
gadol* (this means both 'young to old' and 'small to great').[46] That deeds are
referred to by the name of man, נקרא על שמו *nikra 'al shemo*, means therefore not that the actions are merely human actions. Rather, this means that
human action, symbolized by the human name, participates in the name
of God.

The significance of נקרא על שמו *nikra 'al shemo*, namely, that actions are
ascribed to the human, is not an illusion. Only human action independent

of God is an illusion. The idea that whatever is *nikra 'al shemo* possesses real ontological status, i.e., the name of God, is expressed in many other *MHs* texts. In one example, Jacob, according to Lainer, wants God to inform him ואיזה ברכה וקדושת השם ישאר אחריו השארה קיימת להיות נקרא על שמו 'what blessing and sanctity of God (lit. 'the name') will remain after him [as] a lasting legacy to be called by his name?'[47] The phrase השארה קיימת *hash'arah kayemet* is of course a *terminus technicus* in *MHs* for ontologically real.[48] Jacob wants to know that his life—his unique individuality—has lasting ontological value; in Lainer's refrain throughout *MHs*, Jacob wants to know what will be *nikra 'al shemo*.[49]

In another critical passage, Lainer deals directly with the efficacy of human actions in the context of name and makes very clear what he means when he says human actions are 'called by the name of man':

> הכ"ח עתים...רומזים שלא יסמוך האדם על כללי ד"ת לבד רק יביט
> להשי"ת בכל פרט מעשה ולפי העת מה שהשי"ת חפץ, וזאת אין ביכולת
> האדם לכוון בלתי עזר השי"ת, וכיון שכן הוא אם כן מה יתרון לעושה, כיון
> שכל העבודות שהאדם עובד להשי"ת הכל הוא מרצון השי"ת שהשפיע
> לו, ולא נקראו על שמו אם כן מה יתרון לעושה, ע"ז אמר באשר הוא עמל
> שזה יתרונו מה שמגיע עצמו שרוצה מצדו לקיים רצון השי"ת זה נשאר לו
> לעולמי עד, ועל ידי זה יסכים השי"ת על כל מעשיו שיקראו על שם האדם
> העושה...רק צריך להזהר ולהבין לעשות ולכוון רצון השי"ת בכל עת וה'
> יגמור בעדו

[A] person should not rely on the general principles of Torah alone. He should only look to God in every specific action, according to the specific time, [to know] what God desires, but this is not within the ability of a person to intend without the help of God. And since this is true, 'What is the profit' (Eccl. 3:9) for the one who takes action, since all the acts of service a person does for God derive from the divine will which flows to him, and they will not be called by his name?...Regarding this, it says [in the continuation of the verse] 'in whatever he has toiled over', for this <u>is</u> his profit: however he exerts himself by wanting from his side to fulfill the will of God, this [exertion] remains for him *l'olmei 'ad* forever (i.e. it is ontologically real), and as a result, God *yaskim* agrees concerning all his actions that they will be called by the name of the person who acts...so one must take care and understand how to do

181

and intend the divine will at every moment, and God *yigmor
ba'ado* will complete [his actions] for his sake.[50]

The human being in this passage is charged with an activist spiritual posture. Instead of relying on the precedent of the law, he must seek anew in
every situation to discern the specific will of God. It is clear in this passage
that human activism has lasting significance. The phrases at the end of this
passage, 'God agrees', i.e., affirms human action,[51] and 'God completes' human action,[52] are often used by Lainer to express acosmism in a way that
affirms rather than effaces the human being.

The parallel phrase expressing acosmic humanism in *MHs* which underlies the ontic identity between the name of God and the name of man is
that 'God seals his name' upon human action. In one example, a text that
comes from the Wisdom of Solomon genre, Lainer states: ועל דוד המלך
ע"ה יחתום הש"י תיכף את שמו על כל מעשיו קודם שיצא להתפשתות 'God seals his
name instantly on all the actions of King David even before they are made
manifest'.[53] David represents one who has realized his identity with the
divine will and therefore can intend the divine will. Thus, just as a person's
name is sealed upon their actions through their effort, so too is God's name
sealed on their actions through their *tekufot*. Human action, in its most
perfect expression, is both symbolized or called by the name of the human,
and merged or sealed with God's name. There is no sense here of David
being effaced or overpowered by divinity. Quite the opposite, David personifies divine will and name rather than being overwhelmed by it.

That this conjoining of the human and divine names is at all possible is
because of the ontic identity between human and divine will. Contrary to
Weiss's understanding, name is not shown to be mere illusion, even in the
full light of the eschaton.

Called by the Name, Ontology, Uniqueness, and Unique Will

Lainer uses name to express uniqueness throughout *MHs*.[54] A particularly
important example of the identification between name and uniqueness appears in Lainer's discussion of the rabbinic adage that every person has
three names. This passage is important because it affirms the ontological
status of the unique name acquired by the human being as result of human
action.

ושם שקונה לעצמו היינו מה שמתקן ומרפא החסרון שלו...גדול מה שקונה
הוא לעצמו, כי מלת שם בכל מקום מורה על שורש החיים, שכל הנפש הוא
מדוגל בו

'The name that he acquires for himself' comes through fixing
and healing his [unique] *hisaron*[55] ...Great is what the person
acquires for himself, for the word 'name' always indicates the
root of life, through which every person is distinguished...[56]

'Root of life' refers to the divine. Lainer states here that the name acquired
by human action is not effaced at all; to the contrary, it participates in the
divine. The prism for that participation, as this passage makes clear, is the
healing embrace of one's unique individuality, expressed in one's unique
hisaron. This is a recurrent theme in *MHs*.

Lainer makes it clear that the human being's name is never independent;
rather, it is in and of itself the name of God. This is the realization of redeemed consciousness. This idea emerges in the following passage, where
Lainer explains a *midrash* about Aaron's son Eleazar fleeing the tribes, who
have 'risen up against him'.[57] Lainer applies the verse 'The name of God is a
tower of strength; the righteous man will run into it and be lifted to safety'
(Prov. 18:10) to Eleazar:

מי שחוסה ובא בשם ה' יש לו מגדל עז, אפילו שעושה מעשה שאינו מיופה
על הגוון שנדמה שעושה במרוצה, מכל מקום יש לו תקופות ומגדל עז כיון
שהוא שם ה', אף שבו ירוץ, מכל מקום מכוון לעומק רצון השי"ת, כיון
שאינו עושה רק מה שהוא רצון השי"ת, וזה ונשגב שהמעשה הזה הוא
למעלה מהשגת תפיסת האדם בעוה"ז

One who flees and comes in God's name has *migdal oz* 'a tower
of strength', even when he does something that is not right on
the surface...In any case, he has *tekufot* (sacred audacity) and
migdal oz, since he is *shem Hashem* the name of God [!] even
running into [the name] (i.e., merging with it); in any case,
he intends the depth of God's will...and this is the meaning
of *venisgav* 'and lifted to safety' (Prov. 18:10): this action is
[lifted] beyond the reach of a person's grasp in this world.[58]

We will analyze the portion of this passage referring to the Judah archetype below in our discussion of the same in Chapter Twelve; for now it

is sufficient to notice that the person who reaches the level of post-*berur* consciousness merges with the name of God. The person's audacity is the audacity of God, because the ontic identity between the individual's name and the name of God has been realized. The *tekufot* of the individual and the עוז *oz* of the name of God are one and the same. This is a classic expression of acosmic humanism: 'For he is the name of God'.

It is not at all surprising then to learn that Lainer identifies name not only with uniqueness but also with *ratzon*:

כי שמו מורה על רצון, כמו שנמצא בבני אדם שנקראים ע"ש מעשיהם
ואומנתם לפי שכל רצונם הוא בדבר שהם עוסקים בה, וגם שמו בגימ' רצון

> For His name expresses will. Just as we find with people that their deeds and crafts are are called the name, because all of their will is manifest in that which they are engaged by their actions, and 'His name' in *gematria* (numerology) is [equivalent to] *ratzon*…[59]

In this passage Lainer speaks about the unity of the divine name and the divine will. In the next passage, we will see that both the human and the divine name are but another face of will. The name of God and the name of the human participate in the same ontological identity.

In the beginning of this passage, Lainer takes the phrase *da'at kedoshim eida*, 'I will know knowledge of the holy', to indicate the clarified consciousness of the Judah archetype that is embodied by Solomon. This passage then interprets a question in Proverbs[60] which is raised in the verse immediately following the statement *da'at kedoshim eida*. The question is:

מה שמו, שהאדם ידע בכל עת מה הוא רצון השי"ת כי שמו מורה על רצון
כמבואר בחלק ראשון (בהרבה מקומות). ומה שם בנו, שירגיש האדם
הולדת רצון חדש שמזה הגבול מתחיל רצונות חדשים, וזה שסיים כי תדע,
שתדע כל אלו הדברים על ברור

> 'What is his name?' (Prov. 30:4). That means, a person should at all times know God's will. For 'name' indicates will…'And what is his son's name?' That is, a person should sense the birth of a new will, for new will begins from this *gevul* boundary (i.e., the point where *heshek* crosses the boundaries of

halakhah).[61] This is why the verse concludes with *ki teida'* 'you would know'—meaning you will know all these things through *berur* clarification.[62]

The post-*berur* unification of the human name with divine will is an essential dimension of Lainer's acosmic humanism. It is through *berur* that one understands the ontic identity of will and name, and the unity of human will and God's will. Here we see that this knowledge is identical with both name and will. The boundary—e.g. the general principle of the law that is superceded by *heshek*—provides the measure which allows a person to know that he is experiencing the birth of a new will, which has been clarified.

The Dialectical Dance of Acosmic Humanism

This blurring between the human name and the name of God expresses itself in a dialectical and paradoxical dance in which the human is called by the name of God, as we have seen in some of the aforementioned passages. In the next passage we learn that God also desires to be called by the human name. In a passage underscoring the ontology of human action and linking it with God's desire to be called by the name of man, Lainer states:

היינו שנתן השי״ת מקום לעבודת ישראל עד שרצון השי״ת לקבוע מקום
לעבודתם למעלה מכל תפיסת אדם וכמו שכתיב (ישעיה מט) ישראל אשר
בך אתפאר שהש״י רוצה שיקרא ע״ש ישראל

> God gave place to the work of Israel, so much so that it is
> God's will to establish a place for their service (i.e., human ac-
> tion) higher than the grasp of man…as it says, 'Israel through
> whom I will be made glorious' (Isa. 49:3), meaning that God
> desires to be called by the name of Israel.[63]

In the human divine dance, a person gives up any sense of ownership deriving from their action and in direct response God affirms the ontological dignity of human action. According to Lainer, this paradox[64] is precisely the meaning of human action being called by the name of man. Using the building of the tabernacle as his model, Lainer devotes a very long passage to explaining that a human being can claim no real participation in manifesting the effects which seem to result from his action. However, as is the case many times in *MHs*,[65] Lainer's true position is revealed only in the last several lines of the passage.

185

ואף שהאדם יראה לעינים שאין שום התנשאות, אכן סוד ה' ליריאיו אחר
שהכיר שמצד עצמו אין לו התפארות בשורש, הראה השי"ת שיש לו
התנשאות מזה שהוא יגע במלאכה, והשי"ת מצדו בירר זאת שכתיב וימלא
אותו רוח אלהים, ולכן כתיב אחר כן ויעש בצלאל את הארון שנקראת
המלאכה על שמו

Even though the person sees that he has no *hitnas'ut* (distinction) [as a result of his efforts], nonetheless...after he recognizes that he has no independent adornment in his root,
God shows him that he does have *hitnas'ut* as a result of his
effort at his work. And God himself clarified this [in regard
to Bezalel], as it says, '[God] filled him with the spirit of God'
(Exod. 35:31), and after that it says, 'Bezalel made the ark'
(Exod. 37:1), that is, the work was called by his name.[66]

According to Lainer, Bezalel's participation in the work of the tabernacle
is ultimately not an illusion to be dispelled but that which accords him
hitnas'ut, individual distinction, a clear indication of ontological status in
Lainer's lexicon.[67]

A similar notion appears in regard to Lainer's understanding of the relationship between human thought and action. One might have thought,
states Lainer, that action was in human hands and thought in God's hands.
However:

אכן אם האדם מכיר שבאמת גם המעשה היא ביד השי"ת ואומר לה' הארץ
ומלאה, ומבלעדו לא ירים איש את ידו ואת רגלו, אז משלם לו השי"ת
שכרו מדה במדה ותולה גם המחשבה בהאדם...וזהו מאמר המדרש מה
בעטרה שעטרה לו אמו כו' לא זה מחבבה עד שקראה אמי, היינו אחר
שאמר דהמ"עה כי מידך נתנו לך היינו שתלה כל המעשה בהש"י ולזאת
לא זה מחבבה עד שקראה אמי, אמי היינו המחשבה, והוא כי אף המחשבה
נקראת על שמך

When a person realizes that action is also in God's hands ...
and that without Him, no one raises a hand or a foot, then
God gives him his reward quid pro quo, and ascribes even
thought to man, that is to say, ...even thought is called by
your name (i.e., by the name of man).[68]

Calling action by the name of the human is not a meaningless divine reward (though one might hear that tenor in the above passage). Rather, in light of the passages we have adduced thus far, one is paradoxically freed and empowered to the extent that one's actions and thoughts are called by one's name. Lainer's intention here becomes clearer. By recognizing that there is no thought or action independent of God, the human in effect realizes the ontic identity between the human and God, so that one's name participates in the name of God. The final source we will quote both captures the paradoxical nature of acosmic humanism, and makes clear that *nikra 'al shemo* specifically indicates the ontological efficacy of human action which has effect *l'olmei 'ad*, i.e., even within the framework of post-*berur* consciousness.[69]

In this passage, Lainer interprets the verse (Eccl. 3:9) מה יתרון העושה באשר הוא עמל 'What is the profit for the one who acts in what he has toiled over?' The context is Lainer's assertion that the twenty-eight times the word עת *'et* 'time' is mentioned at the beginning of Ecclesiastes imply that each moment has its own commandment which cannot be captured by the general principles of law; rather, a person must 'only look to God in every specific action according to the specific time, to see what God desires'.

If so, asks Lainer, what is the point of human activism 'since all the acts [a person performs] derive from the divine will…and they will not be called by his name…'. To this Lainer responds:

מה שמייגע עצמו שרוצה מצדו לקיים רצון השי״ת זה נשאר לו לעולמי עד,
ועל ידי זה יסכים השי״ת על כל מעשיו שיקראו על שם האדם העושה

> Whatever [way] he exerted himself in order from his side
> to fulfill the will of God…remains for him forever, and as a
> result, God agrees concerning all his actions that they will be
> called by the name of the person who acts.

In the first stage, when Lainer thought human action might be an illusion, he referred to human action as not called by man's name. However, in the second part of the passage, where he affirms his notion of acosmic humanism, God agrees to all human action, when the ontology and dignity of human activism has been affirmed. At that point, Lainer writes that human action is called by man's name!

187

Some Concluding Remarks on the Identity of Names

At the conclusion of our discussion of name, two more points are in order. First, three characteristics from our list of unique features of Lainer's acosmic humanism, *hitpashtut*,[70] the unity of human and divine *lema'alah mida'ato*,[71] and no-boundary consciousness,[72] are all identified by Lainer as manifestations of the name of God in human consciousness. Second, for Lainer, acosmic humanism, expressed in the idea that human actions are called by the human name—which means, as we have seen, that there is an ontic identity between the name of God and the human's name—is the very intent and purpose of divine creation, that is to say, this unique paradox of acosmic humanism is precisely the mystery of צמצום *tzimtzum*.[73] We see this position expressed in Lainer's comment on the biblical verse הן האדם היה כאחד ממנו 'The human has become as one of us', (Gen. 3:22) which he reads as a biblical allusion to acosmic humanism, directly citing Lurianic sources:

שקודם החטא היה אחיזתו קטנה בזה העולם, ואחר החטא הוקבע בקביעות בזה העולם כרצון השי״ת כדי שהטובה יהיה נקרא על שם יגיע כפיו, ואם היה עוד אחר החטא בגן עדן היה יכול לעשות תשובה בשלימות ולברר עצמו לגמרי, ורצונו השי״ת היה שהחטא לא יתברר עד לעתיד, כדי שכל הדורות אחריו יסגלו מעשים טובים שיהיו נקראים על שמם, לכן נתגרש מגן עדן

> …after the sin, man's stake in this world was firmly established in order that the good be called by his name…God's will was that the sin should not be clarified until the future,[74] in order for all the generations to acquire good deeds that would be called by their name, therefore they were exiled from the Garden of Eden.[75]

The very existence of sin is, for Lainer, synonymous with the possibility of human activism and therefore dignity. Sin is an expression of the divine intent for creation to be called by the name of man.

The Paradox of Human Activism: Levels of Consciousness

A broader perusal of the relevant *MHs* texts reveals paradox as a central theme in Lainer's theology.[76] In outlining what we mean by this, we note the obvious: acosmic humanism is a highly paradoxical notion. If this understanding of *MHs* is correct, the need to embrace paradox should be at the center of Lainer's understanding.

Lainer speaks in terms of the essential ontological paradox of acosmic humanism, in which the seemingly mutually exclusive concepts of activism and the nullification of independent human action are maintained as one.

In the nonacosmic humanist reading espoused by Weiss and those who follow him, each position addresses a different reality. Specifically, one addresses the pre-*berur* reality and one addresses the post-*berur* reality. Pre-*berur* human activism is important, while post-*berur*, human activism is not.[77] The psychological paradox, however, remains central even without adopting an 'acosmic-humanist' understanding of *MHs*, for it is apparent that Lainer believes that both positions need to be maintained together because of the essential fluidity of human experience.

This means that when both pre-*berur* and post-*berur* perspectives appear in one passage, it would be inappropriate/insufficient to draw conclusions based just one half of the teaching. *MHs* passages that, when read out of context, seem to be nullifying human action, are changed completely when read in a more comprehensive manner. For example, in the Korah passage adduced by Weiss, it is evident, when one reads the entire passage, that Lainer maintains that God *hafetz* 'desires' the actions of man.[78]

Human activism is an expression of divine will according to Lainer, and not just divine indulgence. Moreover, this is true even if we assume Weiss's non-humanist reading, which does not acknowledge the post-*berur* consciousness of acosmic humanism.

However, even in the reading suggested by the non-humanist model, the complete rejection of human action in post-*berur* reality, may not hold. To understand why, and to understand the relation between these seemingly incongruous assertions, we need to distinguish the two core models of *berur* in *MHs*. The first we will term the 'linear model', and the second we will term the 'dynamic model'.

In the linear model, once *berur* has been achieved, it is a relatively stable state of consciousness. In this stage, the individual transcends the law and responds to the voice of unmediated divine revelation.

וזהו עתידה של תורה שתשתכח מישראל, היינו שיהיה רצון הש״י נעלם...
בלי שום דעת ועצה מד״ת שהם תרי״ג עיטין...שיכוונו ישראל לרצון
הש״י...ויתברר שהם דבקים בהש״י

> The statement 'Torah will be forgotten from Israel' means that
> God's will will be hidden...without any knowledge or advice
> from Torah, which are the '613 suggestions'...For Israel will
> intend God's will, and it will be clarified that they are totally
> attached to God...[79]

It is perfectly clear here that after complete *berur* there is no longer any
need for the law. This linear model, though not dominant in *MHs*, appears
in several other passages as well. Lainer makes clear that the linear model
outlines not only the *berur* that will take place in the eschaton, but also the
berur that can be accomplished by any person in Israel in the context of the
pre-eschaton reality. For example:

והבירורים הללו המה בדעת כל אדם בכל ענינים...ובאם הוא גם ברצון
הש״י אז יוכל לעשות מה שלבו חפץ

> These forms of *berur* are in the consciousness of every person
> and should be applied in all matters...[After the *berur* has
> been accomplished, however,] when the person intends the
> will of God, then he can do what his heart desires.[80]

Note that this passage precludes any attempt to limit the linear model to
passages concerning the eschaton. This is made clear in the following passage as well:

ובזה המעשה שעושה יחקור ויתבונן אם המעשה והרצון הזה הוא מבורר
שיהיה קיים כן לעולמי עד אפילו לעוה״ב...ובאמת כפי מה שהאדם מקרב
עצמו לה׳ כן זוכה להתגלות אור ה׳ מבלי לבושים שהם גדרים וסייגים, כי
באור הברור, שם לא נמצא שום סייג ואיסור

> In this action that he does he should search [in order to] un-
> derstand whether this act and will are clarified *mevorer* [in the
> present] such that it will exist forever *le'olmei 'ad*, even in *'olam
> ha-ba*[81]...for however much a person brings himself close to
> God, so does he merit the revelation of divine will without

'clothing', i.e., the fences and limitations; for in the *or ha-barur* clarified light there is neither limitation nor prohibition.[82]

These passages highlight the distinction between Lainer's concept of ontic identity with the divine as a stable state achieved post-*berur*, and the far more fragile and fleeting achievement of ontic identity with the divine in the *unio mystica* strain of sources both in Hasidism and in earlier Kabbalah.

There is, however, a second model in Lainer as well, which we term the dynamic model. It is this model that seems to be dominant in most of Weiss's prooftexts. In these passages, Lainer at once affirms and devalues human action. The underlying assertion in these texts is that once *berur* has been achieved, a person does not simply acquire a stable consciousness in which human action is irrelevant. Rather, one enters a dynamic state of consciousness in which both human and divine agency, as well as human and divine activism, are simultaneous realities existing in a relationship of paradoxical complementarity. In this model, Lainer is not rejecting human action, he is asserting that a person can be constantly moving between pre- and post-*berur* consciousness. Hence, both human action and its devaluation might be simultaneously true on both a metaphysical and psychological level.

Theoretically, in the non-humanist reading espoused by Weiss, if we deploy the linear model, then human activism would in fact become irrelevant post-*berur*; if we deploy the dynamic model, however, it would still remain relevant.

Nevertheless, quite independent of all this is the essential acosmic-humanist nature of Lainer's theology, which affirms that once a person has achieved full *berur*, human action does not become irrelevant. Rather, the notion of human action independent of God becomes absurd. The result, however, is not an effacing of human dignity and activism, but radical human empowerment. In this reading, post-*berur* human activism is radically affirmed in the realization of one's ontic identity with the divine. The individual's action and divine action are identical.

Up to now, in our acosmic-humanist reading of Lainer, we have affirmed the ontological dignity of human action in a reality of post-*berur* consciousness, that is, in a state of redeemed consciousness beyond the illusion of independence. Lainer, however, also makes clear in a number of passages that even in the not-yet-redeemed pre-*berur* consciousness, a sense of independent human action—although an illusion—is an expression of the divine will, because this is what initiates the human process of *ʿavodah*. It is God's will that initially 'it should appear to the person'[83] that there is independent *ʿavodah*. Therefore, היינו שהשי״ת ממדת טובו הציב שידמה 'God, in the attribute of his goodness, established that it should appear to the person that he merited through the toil of his hands'.

Once *ʿavodah* has been initiated, a person moves beyond it, to a place of 'choicelessness'.[84] The goal of what Lainer terms *ʿavodah*—a sense of human effort, responsibility and dignity—is not its transcendence as Weiss would have it, but simply the deep realization that there is no *ʿavodah* independent of God. Using the same language that he uses to affirm God's desire for independent human action, Lainer states:

וכל עוד שידמה האדם שיש לו איזה דמיון לומר כוחי ועוצם ידי, שיש לו הויה בפני עצמו, אפילו בעניני תפילות ועבודות, אז הוא עדיין בשעבוד הגלות ואינו בן חורין

> One to whom it appears that it is due to the strength and power of his hand that he has any existence on his own independent of God…then he [has not left Egypt and] is still in oppression and exile; he is not free.[85]

At a more developed level of consciousness, it is important to internalize the acosmic truth that all is God. This is not the *unio mystica* experience found in other strands of early Hasidism. Lainer insists on the human being retaining individual integrity and the ontological dignity of human activism even within the divine embrace, as we examined thoroughly above. The human being is like a candle before a torch and not like a candle before the sun.[86]

We have demonstrated up to this point that Lainer affirms human activism. To better understand what this means in the context of Lainer's acosmic humanism, it is helpful to map it in terms of three distinct levels of relationship to human activism in Lainer's thought:

At the first level, one experiences oneself as independent from God. This is a state desired by God because it initiates a person into effort and activism, which Lainer terms *ʿavodah*.

At the second level, which Lainer sometimes refers to as the level of *shabbat*, there is a realization that indeed there are no human actions whatsoever independent of God.

At the third level, totally free human activism is re-embraced, fully driven by clarified human desire. Here, the person realizes the ontic identity between God and human; this is the stage of acosmic humanism.

The sources Weiss cites describe the second level. By not realizing that these are second-level sources, he interprets them in a manner that leaves little room for hearing the nuance of paradox, particularly since Mordechai Lainer (and his compilers) had reason to conceal the radical goal of his system. In reality, the second level is the process of *berur*, the weaning away from the illusion of independent human action, which was initially necessary to initiate the process of *'avodah*. The first level might fairly be called the pseudo-independent stage, the second, the nullification level, and the third, the 'transparency' level.

The pseudo-independent level affirms human activism as a necessary illusion. The nullification level is the giving up of any notion of separateness or independence. At the third level, a person becomes transparent to the divine and the God force begins to flow within one and not around one. Viewed superficially, the first and third levels might seem similar. Both embrace human activism. However, the first-level illusion of independent action, is exposed by second-level consciousness. It is from this second level, where all human action is understood to be meaningless, that Weiss viewed Lainer as radically theocentric.[87] However, the third level is not a regression; rather, level three transcends and includes level two. At level three, the hands of the human and the hands of God become identical. The essence of the third level is transcending and unifying the dichotomy between levels one and two.

This notion of the three levels of consciousness is crystallized in one of the most central passages in *MHs*, which, as far as we have found, is not mentioned anywhere in Izbica scholarship. In this passage Lainer identifies the second and third levels, respectively, as שבת *shabbat-* and מקדש *mikdash-* consciousness.[88]

The ostensible issue at stake in the passage is the distinction between the *mikdash* or Temple, where the שופר *shofar* is blown on *shabbat*, and beyond the precincts (lit., גבולין *gevulin* 'boundaries') of the *mikdash*, where the *shofar* is not blown on *shabbat*. *Shofar* represents the highest level of human activism.

שהאדם מבטל כל פעולותיו שרואה מפורש שהכל הוא מהשי״ת לכן
פעולותיו אז בטילין ולכן בגבולין אסור תקיעת שופר בשבת, כי שבת הוא
כולל כל המצות, וכמו שכל הפעולות אפילו של מצוה אסורים בשבת מפני
ששבת גדול יותר מכל המצות...ואף תקיעת שופר שמחבר מצוה דלעילא
כיון שהוא ע״י פעולת אדם בהמצוה

...[Shabbat represents the time] when the person nullifies all of his actions, for he sees clearly that all is from God and therefore his actions are *beteilin* nullified. Therefore *shofar* is prohibited in the precincts outside the *mikdash* (Temple), for all human actions, including divine *mitzvot*, are forbidden on *shabbat*. For *shabbat* is beyond...even *shofar*, which is the ideal of human activism...*Because* it occurs through human action, [it is forbidden on *shabbat*].[89]

Until this point in the passage, it appears to be a dramatically theocentric passage. However, from this point it suggests a completely opposite conclusion.

Lainer moves to address why blowing the *shofar* is permitted in *mikdash* on *shabbat*. The essence of his answer is that since *mikdash* is the archetype of acosmic humanism, where the human being participates in divinity, just as divine action is permitted on *shabbat*, so is human action. In the *mikdash* on *shabbat*, moreover, it becomes clear that human action and activism are not nullified. Once the human being enters *mikdash*-consciousness, i.e., acosmic humanism, where one realizes that all human actions are animated by God—or, to express it even more sharply, are identical with divine action—human activism becomes fully desirable and in no way contradicts *shabbat*-consciousness. These points are made quite precisely in the second half of the passage:

אבל במקדש שם קרבנות דוחים שם שבת מפני ששם רואה האדם שכל מה
שהוא פועל השי״ת הוא הפועל, וכדאיתא במדרש (בראשית רבה יא ו)
ששאל טורנוסרופוס את רבי עקיבא למה הקב״ה מוריד גשמים ועושה
מלאכה בשבת והשיב לו כיון שהקב״ה אין רשות אחרת עמו, והיינו שאצל
השי״ת כל העולם ברשותו ולכן אין שום דבר אצלו מלאכה שהרי הכל בידו

ואין שום חילוק אצלו אף שישתנה מרשות לרשות וממצורה לצורה שהרי
הכל ברשותו ובידו, וכן בבית המקדש מתחבר מצוה דלתתא עם מצוה
דלעילא, כי שם רואה שכל פעולותיו, השי״ת פועל אותם, לכן קרבנות
דוחים שבת, וכן תקיעת שופר בשבת במקדש היו תוקעין כיון שזה עצמו
מורה ענין שופר שנתעורר הפנימיות האדם ונתחבר עם אור השי״ת

However, in the *mikdash* (Temple), we know that sacrifices
override the *shabbat*…For in the *mikdash*, a person sees that
everything he does is really done by God, as it says in the
Midrash[90] that Turnus Rufus asked Rabbi Akiva…Why is it
that God causes rain to fall and does work on *shabbat*? [R.
Akiva] responded that since there is no other being independent of God, and everything is included in God, therefore
nothing that God does is considered transformative work, for
everything is part of God. Thus it is impossible that something might move from one realm to another, for everything is
in the realm of God…So too in the *mikdash*…where one sees
that all of his actions are through the agency of God…thus
sacrifices override [the prohibition] of *shabbat*. And similarly,
blowing the *shofar* is permitted in the *mikdash*…for the essence of *shofar* is that it arouses the inner point of a person
and connects him with the light of God.

Lainer's dramatic point becomes clear in a careful reading. In the *mikdash*,
where one's divine nature is realized, the human's identity with God is revealed. Thus, the human is governed by the same rules as God. Just as God
can do work on *shabbat* because there is nothing independent of God, the
human, who is ontically identified with God, can offer sacrifices and blow
the *shofar* on *shabbat*. Essentially, Lainer maps out in this passage two of
our levels of consciousness. The level of *shabbat*, what we have termed level
two, is where a person moves beyond their narrow, human egocentricity
and realizes that all that they do is done by God.[91] This is the nullification
of any sense of independent human agency. At this stage of realization,
human action, even that of *mitzvah*, is forbidden on the Sabbath. However,
shabbat is not the *summa bonum* of spiritual consciousness. Beyond *shabbat*
exists *mikdash*-consciousness.

At this level, a human realizes that their action, far from being insignificant, is of ultimate value. Indeed, human actions participate in the divine,
and, thus, like divine action, transcend *shabbat*. The empowering nature

of acosmic humanism, the ultimate dignity and efficacy of human action, and *mikdash* as a symbol of acosmic humanism are all pointed to here. The preponderance of Izbica scholarship is fixated on the *'shabbat*-consciousness' level of *MHs*, where human actions are prohibited because one realizes that all is from God. However, *mikdash*-consciousness, the third level, allows us to recast in a profound way Lainer's theology. In *mikdash*-consciousness, the ontic identity between human and divine is realized; thus, just as God acts on *shabbat*, so may the human who is at that level.

As we have just demonstrated, the framework of levels of consciousness is a crucial hermeneutic key in unlocking Lainer's thought. At this point we will outline another important dimension of his theology which is best understood through the prism of levels of consciousness.[92]

A key notion in Lainer's metaphysics is the higher unity of הכרח *hekhrei'ah*, divine necessity, on the one hand, and *ratzon*, voluntaristic and free divine will, on the other. A basic feature of Lainer's thought is his assertion that on a higher level of consciousness, these seemingly disparate perspectives are actually part of a greater unity of experience and reality. Just as Lainer's views on human freedom appear to undermine the meaning of human action, a similarly strong element of metaphysical necessity on the divine level exists in *MHs* that prima facie might be seen as undermining the more classic expression of voluntaristic theism characterizing almost all of biblical and rabbinic literature. Such a tension is indeed present in *MHs*; this tension however is fully resolved once we realize that Lainer is referring to different levels of consciousness.

Commenting on the apparent redundancy of the phrase from the Passover *Haggadah* describing God as מלך במלוכה *'melekh bimelukhah'* (king of kingship), Lainer interprets the phrase to mean that God rules—that is to say, is absolutely free—with regard to kingship, which for Lainer is synonymous with the concept of divine necessity.[93] This is the classical Biblical and rabbinic view of divine voluntarism.[94] Similarly, in other passages, Lainer variously sets up Amalek,[95] the snake,[96] and the Tower of Babel[97] as symbols of the false argument that the world is ordered by divine necessity, as a result of which there is no need for *'avodah* (human activism). These texts as well seem to militate for the kind of voluntaristic theism typical of classic Jewish texts.

However, this position of Lainer's is contradicted by another set of passages. For example, in one text, he sets up a hierarchy consisting of three animals.

Lowest is the בהמה *beheimah*, an animal that turns in entreaty to people. Next is the חיה *hayah*, an animal that refuses to turn to people but looks only to God. Highest is the נחש *nahash* 'snake', whose sin is refusing to turn in entreaty to God, instead wanting to receive השפעה בהכרח *hashpa'ah behekhrei'ah* divine effluence by virtue of the natural divine necessity that is 'the way of the universe'.[98]

The *nahash*, whom Lainer compares later in the passage to Amalek, claims that there is no need for *'avodah*, and that locating oneself in the natural order of divine necessity represents a higher spiritual level than one who turns to God in entreaty. It is critical to note, however, that while in one sentence Lainer rejects these claims, later in the very same passage he clearly validates and identifies with these claims. In fact, Lainer writes in another passage that this theological position, which he identifies with *nahash* in the previous text, is the highest spiritual level.[99] The theological position of the *nahash* will be revealed in the *eschaton* as the true nature of reality, when, according to one Talmudic passage, *mitzvot*—which for Lainer represents human spiritual activism, experienced as independent of God—will be nullified.[100]

Lainer interprets in this light the *midrash* associating the sin of the Golden Calf with the commandment of *shabbat*. The Golden Calf, holding the theological position of the *nahash*, is identified with the future consciousness in which there will be no 'need for service'.[101] According to Lainer, Israel experienced that future moment and wanted to live it in the immediacy of their present. The result was the sin of the Golden Calf. The people were correct in principle, their intent being to demonstrate with the Golden Calf that human spiritual activism, experienced as separate from God, was no longer necessary. However, they erred in timing; the time was not yet ripe. They were, according to Lainer, like 'eaters of not yet ripe fruit'.

Lainer expands this line of argument in another passage, saying that the desire of the people in the episode of the Golden Calf was to 'move beyond the need for daily prayer...Rather, they wanted to be integrated into the divine order of the universe'.[102] Again, Lainer argues that the people were essentially correct, their sin being only in that they were ahead of their time. He makes the identical argument there to show that locating oneself in the natural divine order of necessity is spiritually superior to and ontologically higher than the entreaty of prayer.

Lainer argues that this higher level of enlightenment was the spiritual consciousness achieved in the Temple in Jerusalem. In the Temple, the people's prayers were answered as part of the natural divine order of things. The location of the people in this divine order of necessity is understood by Lainer as an expression of divine love, because in this state of consciousness the people realize that they are *devukim beHashem*, ontologically attached to God, in their natural state. This was the intention of the builders of the Tower of Babel as well. According to Lainer, their desire was to approximate the spiritual consciousness that was eventually realized in the Temple.[103]

We can now move towards resolution of these seemingly disparate elements in Lainer's thought. While one might be initially tempted to simply suggest that these are two exclusive strands of thought that exist side by side in *MHs* and need not be reconciled, this does not make sense in view of the fact that both positions are often expressed dialectically in the same passage. It is more logical to suggest that they are part of an integrated view.

In these texts, Lainer refers to a level of religious consciousness that, in its pure form, is the redeemed consciousness of the eschaton and *mikdash*. As we have seen, according to Lainer, this is the highest level of spiritual consciousness. It is fully accessible also in pre-eschaton reality.[104] Yet a slight misreading or misapplication of this same consciousness yields Amalek, the Tower of Babel, and the snake. Lainer here refers to different levels of consciousness in these texts in regard to human activism or voluntarism, as well as with regard to divine voluntarism versus divine necessity. He rejects Amalek, Tower of Babel, and the snake, because these positions dismiss the need for human activism. This need is endorsed by Lainer on two entirely different levels, which we have referred to above as level one and level three. We described above this process of evolution between the three levels. At level three, we which have called *mikdash*-consciousness, one realizes the ontic identity between the individual and the divine. Thus one realizes 'that everything one does is really done by God'.[105]

The danger in Amalek, as Lainer points out, is its ability to 'lead Israel astray'.[106] As is obvious upon close reading of these passages, the reason Amalek's religious consciousness might lead Israel astray is the great similarity between Amalek's theological understanding and that of *mikdash*-consciousness. According to Lainer, Amalek, the Tower of Babel, and the snake are false variations of level three. Level three is where one realizes that one is part of the order of divine necessity. According to Amalek's reading of this reality, (a) human activism is not necessary, and (b) the human being is part of an impersonal order compelled by divine necessity. Lainer's understanding of authentic *mikdash*-consciousness rejects both of these conclusions. According to Lainer, human activism is a necessary and natural expression of divine necessity, which is driven by a divine will that is warm and pulsing with divine love.[107] In fact, in one passage, Lainer interprets a classic Talmudic passage as expressing the metaphysical understanding that the gathering together of the community compels the presence of the will of God, using the same language (*behekhreiʾah*, 'by necessity') that he uses for the builders of the Tower of Babel, the only difference being that he introduces the motif of love, which does not play a role in Lainer's description of the Tower of Babel.[108]

Mikdash-consciousness naturally transcends this dualism. Lainer's distinction between the Temple and the Tower of Babel in another passage illustrates all of the points we have made. After writing that the intent of the builders of the Tower was ליקח את רצונו ית' ביד חזקה שיהיה שוכן אצלם למען יהיה להם קיום הויה בהכרח 'to force God's will with a strong hand so that God would dwell among them...by virtue of necessity',[109] Lainer contrasts this position with *mikdash*-consciousness:

הגם שאמת ויציב הדבר שבמקום שהברואים מתאחדים ביחד בלב אחד
שוכן ביניהם רצונו ית', אבל זאת האחדות והחיבור ביחד תלו נמי ברצונו
ית' במקום שחפץ השי"ת לשכון שם הוא מאחד אתהלבבות ושוכן ביניהם
אבל אין זאת ביד אדם לאחד את הלבבות מהברואים, כי ברצונו ית' אין
שום הכרח ח"ו, לכן האחדות שהם היו עושים נגד רצונו ית' ובהכרח היו
מתאספין ביחד, אחדות כזאת הוא באמת פירוד גמור, לכך נאמר ויפץ ה'
אותם משם על פני כל הארץ, היינו שהיה מראה להם בזה שהם בפירוד
גמור, אבל בנין בית המקדש היה כדכתיב אבן שלמה מסע נבנה, היינו שאף
הדומם היה מסייע לאותו הבנין כי היה רצון גמור

Even though it is true that in the place where people come
together as one, God's will dwells in their midst [by virtue of
necessity], this too, however, is dependent on divine will...
In the place where God desires to dwell, there he unites
hearts and dwells among them, but this is not in the hands of
man (i.e., independent of God), for in God's will there is no
necessity at all. Thus the union that [the builders of Tower

199

of Babel] did was against His will....[T]his form of union is complete separation...But in the Temple,...even the inanimate objects (the rocks) aided the building, for there was pure will.

In this complex passage, we see that Lainer rejects what he regards as a superficial dichotomy between divine necessity and free divine will. Both exist together in a higher unity. The human activism that is unnecessary in the redeemed consciousness of *mikdash* or in the eschaton is the kind in which the human will and human action are seen as somehow separate from divine necessity. However, once the ontic identity of will which demarcates *mikdash*-consciousness is realized, the false dualism between voluntarism and necessity, both divine and human, falls away.

At this juncture, it remains for us to further buttress three points that we have already made implicitly and for which we cited some supporting texts. We will accomplish this in the following three sections.

Activism Passages not Linked with Name

The first point that we wish to ground in further texts is Lainer's belief that human action has ontological efficacy and is not merely an illusion, to be dispelled when consciousness evolves or when the *eschaton* arrives. The texts we have seen until this point are passages in which human action that is *nikra 'al shemo*—called by man's name—has ontological efficacy.

At this point, we turn to activism passages that affirm the ontology of human action, which are not linked to the concept of name. In one long passage, Lainer at first indicates that there is no value in human activism:

אך מי שהקב"ה מאיר לו ומפקח עיניו יראה שכל מעשה בני האדם לא יפעלו לשנות מעומק רצון הש"י אף כחוט השערה

> However, whosoever is enlightened and whose eyes are
> opened by the Holy One, blessed be He, will see that no ac-
> tion of man can be efficacious in changing the deep [intention
> of] God's will even one iota.[110]

After stating this, Lainer wants to make sure that his teaching is not understood as undermining the ontological efficacy of human action (which was Weiss and Gellman's reading).[111] The context is the idea that all prop-

200

erty that is outside כפי מעלתו השייך לו בשורשו 'the boundary related to him according to his root' returns to the rightful owner in the Jubilee year.

זה יהי׳ נוסף על גבולו מאחר שבתחילה הרחיב גבולו לתוך של חבירו
והשתדל בעו״הז ישאר לו הגנה מועטת גם מחלק חבירו אף שיחזירה, וזהו
כל עסק השתדלות בעו״הז שהאדם משתדל, וישאר לו זאת ההכרה לעולמי
עד

But the boundary itself [which he acquired from his friend through his actions]...this shall remain for him...And so it is with all השתדלות hishtadlut striving of the human being: a recognition of it will remain for him forever.

Or, in another passage: כי כל מעשי האדם ישאר מהם השארה 'All actions of man leave something that remains (i.e., which is immortal) after them'.[112] A third passage states: ואחר כן מה שמשתדל וקונה ע״י פעולותיו זה נשאר לו לעוה״ב גם כן 'All that a person acquires through human effort, that which he acquires through his actions, this remains for him in the world-to-come'.[113] In a fourth passage, Lainer actually defines the nature of berur as a clarification about אם המעשה והרצון הזה הוא מבורר שיהי׳ קיים כן לעולמי עד אפילו לעוה״ב 'whether the action will have existence forever even in the world-to-come'.[114] The Hebrew term Lainer uses in most of these passages for 'forever' is לעולמי עד le'olmei 'ad, a term in MHs for ontological efficacy.[115]

Divine Animation of Human Action

The second point we need to ground further is the idea that divine will animates human action as an expression of the ontic identity between the human and God. What this entails is that virtually all of the passages stating that פעולת אדם pe'ulat adam 'human action' has no effect mean only that there is no such thing as a human action that is against or even independent of God. God animates all human action:

וכל עוד שידמה האדם שיש לו איזה דמיון לומר כוחי ועצם ידי, שיש לו
הויה בפני עצמו, אפילו בעניני תפילות ועבודות, אז הוא עדיין בשעבוד
הגלות ואינו בן חורין

As long as a person still imagines...that he has havayah bifnei 'atzmo (an existence independent of God)...he is still under the oppression of exile and is not a free man.[116]

201

Lainer's acosmism leads to an empowered and free religious persona. In the following passage, Lainer lays out his position clearly. His aim is to resolve an apparent contradiction in the biblical text. One text, את ה׳ אלהיך תירא ואתו תעבד ובשמו תשבע 'You shall fear God and worship Him, and swear by His name' (Deut. 6:13), uses the term of 'avodah for worship. 'Avodah is one of the words Lainer employs to describe human effort, so this verse can be read as an affirmation of human action. The second verse, ואמרת בלבבך כחי ועצם ידי עשה לי את החיל הזה 'Lest you say in your heart, my power and the strength of my hand has made me this might' (Deut. 8:17), is a rejection of human activism. Lainer explains that the first verse is necessary lest a person think that there is no need for service. This, of course, refers to the level before berur, the necessary illusion of independence, which we have termed the first level of consciousness. However, even after berur, Lainer states in regard to the second verse:

> כי לולא רצון השי״ת אין מעשה האדם כלום הוא הנותן לך כח היינו שכח
> העבודה והתפלה אינו רק מהש״י

...For without the will of God, the action of man is nothing... Remember that God gives you strength, for the strength of work and prayer comes only from God.[117]

Or, in another passage:

> אבל מדת הקב״ה אינו כן רק ישפיע טובה לכל העולם בטובת עין שיוכל
> לדמות לאדם שלוקח לו מעצמו ולא יחפוץ בהכרת טובה אך ישראל הם
> המכירים את בוראם ומכירים לו טובה על כל ובעוה״ז צריך להכיר ולברך
> להש״י על כל טובה לפי שיש או״ה האומרים על הכל כחי ועוצם ידי, אבל
> לעתיד שיראוהו כל המעשים...כי יכירו כל העולם שהכל של הש״י

The attribute of God is that in this world, He allows man to imagine that he takes from this world on his own...but [the people of] Israel recognize the good of the Creator...and give him credit for everything...not like the nations of the world, who say it is by 'my strength and the power of my hand'...for in the future when all actions will be seen...the entire world will recognize that all is from God.[118]

Ultimately, Lainer does not reject the claim that human action is kokhi ve'otzem yadi 'by the strength and power of my hand'. Rather, he rejects

202

this claim at the first level of consciousness while embracing it at the third. Rather, what Lainer drives home time and again is that there is no onto-logical basis for human action or agency independent of God, for God is בתוך כל מעשה *betokh kol ma'aseh*[119] (God animates every human action). Lainer's acosmic humanism also supplies a metaphysical basis to the ethi-cal imperative against hubris. However, Lainer does not reject human agency. Crucially, in this same passage, which Weiss cites as evidence for his general view that Lainer undermines human action,[120] Lainer states:

אך רואה את הנולד הוא בזה המעשה עצמה שהוא עושה חקור ויתבונן אם
המעשה והרצון הזה הוא מבורר שיהי' קיים כן לעולמי עד אפילו לעוה"ב

[A] person searches out and understands whether [his] act
and will be clarified so that they will have existence forever,
even in the world-to-come.

This is a clear affirmation that God's inherent presence animating human action in no way contradicts the ontological efficacy of human action.

One particularly important passage offers powerful support to this reading when read in context of the other passages. Commenting on the rabbinic epigram 'He who wants his property to remain in his possession should plant an Adar tree on it,'[121] Lainer explains:

אדר היינו לשון תקופות וחיזוק ועיקר החיזוק הוא לאדם כשיבין כי הש"י
הוא הנותן כח לעשות חיל ולא שיאמר כחי ועוצם ידי...אחר כל הטרדות
והיגיעות ידע האדם כי לה' הארץ ומלואה והוא הנותן כח לסגל לרכוש ובזה
יתקיימו קניני אדם באם יכיר את זאת

The Adar tree indicates *tekufot* and strength. And the essential
strength [and *tekufot*] for a person is when he understands
that God gave him the strength to act with power and that it
is not by the strength or power of his hand...For after all of
the effort...he should know that 'The earth and its fullness
are God's' (Psalms 24:1), and it is God who gives the person
strength to acquire his property....If he recognizes this, his
property will remain in his possession.[122]

The key word in the passage is *tekufot*, which Lainer identifies with a per-son's post-*berur* experience of the divine, when the person has realized the ontic identity between human and God. This experience is empowering, resting on the realization that all of one's actions inhere with the divine; it is precisely this realization that gives one strength. This is the intent of the verse האץ ומלואה 'לה 'The earth and its fullness are God's' (Psalms 24:1). This text is used by Lainer throughout *MHs* to indicate that the human has no independent authorship of events.[123] However, it is clear from the passage that, unlike what Weiss and Gellman suggest, Lainer does not interpret the verse as asserting that the human has no agency; rather, Lainer connects the verse to *tekufot*, thereby interpreting it to mean that the human has no independent agency.[124]

One of the most powerful expressions in *MHs* of God animating but not overwhelming the integrity of human action is contained in the passage we adduced above[125] to illustrate Lainer's third level of consciousness. The passage refers to the Temple in Jerusalem. Lainer writes that in the Temple, when כי שם רואה שכל פעולותיו, השי״ת פועל אותם...ונתחבר עם אור השי״ת 'one sees that everything he does is done by God...and he is connected with the light of God', one is allowed to blow the *shofar* because there is no longer any contradiction between human activism and the fullness of the divine presence. The natural corollary of this understanding, in Lainer's theology, is an acosmism that is empowering, as opposed to an acosmism that fosters a quietist religious persona of the kind found in early Hasidism as described amply by the religious anthropology of Weiss and Schatz-Uffenheimer.

Models of Activism: Pre- and Post-*Berur* Consciousness, Linear and Dynamic Models

The third point we need to explicate is the distinction we draw between two forms of human activism. The first form of human activism is in place before *berur* has been completed. We have also shown in our acosmic-humanist reading that human action has efficacy even post-*berur*, in a world of clarified consciousness, when one realized the ontic identity between human and divine will. Pre-*berur* activism is the process of *berur* itself, which includes *mitzvah*, *yir'ah*, and *'avodah*; *'avodah* is often referred to by Lainer as *yegi'a kapayim* (human effort). The second form of human activism takes place after *berur*, in the redeemed consciousness of *'olam ha-ba* when a person has *tekufot* and is fully in their *hayyim*.[126] This second form of human activism is the defining characteristic of the Judah archetype, which we will discuss below.

204

As we have noted, there are two models of relationship in *MHs* that distinguish between pre-*berur* and post-*berur* consciousness.[127] One model, which we termed the linear model, teaches that through *berur* one realizes one's identity with the divine. Lainer, by drawing on the classic Hasidic split between מצדו 'His (God's) side' and מצדנו 'our side', suggests that the human task is to move from 'our side', from fear, choice, boundaries, and contraction, to 'God's side', to love, choicelessness,[128] no-boundary consciousness, and expansion. Lainer states in a typical passage:

ור״ה מדבר באדם שנשלם בכל שלבו נמשך אחר רצון הש״י אז מותר לו
לעשות השתדלות ואח״כ יבקש מהש״י שיגמור בעדו...אבל בעוד שאין
האדם בשלימות אז צריך לקבל עליו עול מלכות שמים קודם כל מעשה

Rav Huna is speaking [in the Gemara] about a person who is perfected in everything (i.e., is post-*berur*), whose heart is drawn after the will of God, therefore he is permitted to make an effort and afterwards ask God to complete his action for him. However when a person is not *bisheleimut* perfected, he must first take upon himself the yoke of heaven, before every act.[129]

In another passage, Lainer states: כי מלך כל היוצא מפיו הם דברי אלקים...ואף שנראין לדברי חולין הם מהש״י 'Regarding a king, all the words that come out of his mouth are words of the living God...and even if they appear to be idle words, they are from God'.[130]

From the context of this passage, it is clear that Lainer refers not to a special principle about the laws of kings, but rather discusses the 'king' as a paradigm of the Judah archetype, namely, 'one whose heart is drawn after the will of God'.[131] These sources and many others seem to suggest that once one has reached post-*berur* consciousness, one is free to act in accordance with the will of God one naturally incarnates, having no more need for *yir'ah*, *'avodah*, *berur*, or at times even *mitzvah*. This is post-*berur* activism.

In the second model, which we termed the dynamic model, a person simultaneously maintains, in paradoxical tension, the very different experiences of consciousness, pre-*berur* and post-*berur*. In other words, both 'His side' and 'our side' exist. Seeking to make this very point, Lainer notes an anomaly in the biblical description of the Israelite journey in the desert.[132] Numbers 33:2 first states 'their departures to their journeys according to

God'. At the end of the verse, however, the order is inverted, and the verse states 'their journeys to their departures'. Lainer understands 'departures' (מוצאיהם *motsa'eihem*) to refer to a metaphysical source or point of origin. He thus reads the first phrase, 'according to God', as referring to the classical mystical category of מצדו *mitzido* (from His side) in which all human beings are utterly equal and human activism of the pre-*berur* type is unnecessary.[133] All *berur* of human actions, implies Lainer, takes place from God's side. The second phrase, however, where the order is inverted, is taken to refer to מצדנו *mitzideinu*, from our (humanity's) side. From this perspective, human action—that is to say, *berur*—is vital in acquiring perfection. A careful reading of the last several lines of the passage reveals that God's side and the human's side, מצד ה' *mitzad Hashem* and מצד האדם *mitzad ha-adam*, exist in dynamic paradoxical tension in the human experience. Lainer, in an exegetical flourish, views this tension as built into the literary structure of the biblical text. In this model, while there may be moments when we break through to God's side, for the most part, the two perspectives live in a dialectical relationship in which both are simultaneously true.

It must be emphasized that both models support reading Lainer as affirming human activism within the context of his acosmic humanism. In the linear model, the activism of the pre-*berur* and post-*berur* types take place consecutively, while in the dynamic model, the activism of the pre- and post-*berur* types may take place almost simultaneously. This is exactly how Lainer interprets the Korah story. Both sides, that of God and that of Korah, exist simultaneously in a paradoxical relationship.[134] Weiss, in analyzing this text, views the attribution of importance to human action there as an illusion, albeit according to Lainer a necessary illusion.[135] Actually, however, this may be more accurately seen as part of the dynamic paradox that exists throughout *MHs*.

In many passages, as we have seen, Lainer presents the paradox without any attempt to soften it. In other passages, in which the paradoxical model is implicitly acknowledged, he uses the element of time to distinguish between the approach from *yir'ah* and *'avodah* and the approach from love and choicelessness. Before the act has taken place, Lainer suggests that the act must be from *yir'ah*. However, after the act has taken place, one moves to a stance of *tekufot*, audacity, determination, and love, understanding that in fact whatever happened is what needed to happen and events could have been no other way than the way they were.[136]

206

Notes for Chapter Nine

1 Weiss, 'Determinism' 448.

2 See discussion of this point on p. 21 and p. 203; in addition to the texts in this section see also *MHs vol.* 2 Shelah s.v. *ahar* (Source 41 in volume 2).

3 For example, in many passages, one of which we saw above, he interprets the rabbinic phrase *tif'eret le'osehah* as 'beautiful in the eyes of the public' rather than the more literal 'beautiful for the one who does it', and he interprets *tif'eret lo min ha'adam* as 'beautiful to one's *tzurat ha'adam* (inner person)' as opposed to its natural reading of 'beautiful to people'.

4 Weiss, 'Determinism' 450.

5 We have discussed the levels of consciousness in the introduction and will expand on them below in the section 'The Paradox of Human Activism: Levels of Consciousness'.

6 See p. 176.

7 *MHs vol.* 2 Psalms s.v. *uvitevunot kapav.*

8 Tzadok refers to the Talmudic reading (*bAvod.* 19a) of the verse 'In the Torah of God is his desire and with his Torah he will engage day and night' (Psalms 1:2). In a radical reading, the rabbis suggest there that Torah belonged to God but was then acquired by and becomes the Torah of the human being. While in rabbinic literature this may be read homiletically, for *Tzadok* it is a description of ontology.

9 *Tzidkat Hatzadik* 229.

10 *MHs vol.* 2 Sukkah s.v. *umimai.*

11 This evolutionary impulse in Lainer's theology will emerge fully formulated in the thought of Abraham Yitzhak Hakohen Kook, who, as we shall explain, was heavily influenced by Lainer. See the section 'Lainer and Abraham Isaac Hakohen Kook'.

12 See longer discussion and analysis of these levels in the section 'The Paradox of Human Activism: Levels of Consciousness'.

13 Only by collecting all of these passages does it become apparent that this is an intentional genre in *MHs*. It is by reading all of the passages together that the implicit motif of acosmic humanism is made explicit.

14 *MHs vol.* 2 Psalms s.v. *yadekha 'asuni* (Source 16 in volume 2). Note that the actual verse uses the name '*Adonai*' rather than *YHVH* in the phrase 'sanctuary of God'.

15 See, e.g., *vol.* 2 Ki Tisa s.v. *elohei maseikhah* 1 (Source 4 in volume 2). For Temple sources, see p. 252ff and the sections 'Acosmism and *Mikdash* (The Jerusalem Temple)' and 'Model Five: The Wisdom of Solomon', and extensive discussion throughout volume 2.

16 For a similar distinction in Lainer's spiritual lineage, in the writings of the Seer of Lublin, see Elior, 'Temurot'.

17 See further discussion of this section in volume 2, Source 16. On the central role of *Shekhinah* conciousness in Lainer's acosmic humanism, see below in the

section 'Model Four: *Shekhinah*, The Eros of the Will of God', as well as the sources in Cluster 1 of volume 2. For a fuller discussion of the moon as a theme in *MHs*, see Cluster 4 in volume 2.

18 We will quote here only the brief snippets of this passage that focus on our theme, leaving out most of the complex Kabbalistic names and references. A fuller translation can be found in volume 2.

19 *MHs vol. 1* Likutim s.v. *Hashem YKVK* (Source 17 in volume 2). (Note that in the previous edition of *MHs*, this passage and the following, Likutim s.v. *ule'atid*, are listed under the heading of Uktzin Perek 3, under Likutei Hashas.)

20 *MHs vol. 1* Likutim s.v. *ule'atid*. This section appears under its own heading following the passage s.v. *Hashem YKVK* though it is a continuation of the same teaching.

21 See the section 'The Desire to Know One's Story'.

22 See section 'No-Boundary Consciousness' and the discussion there of *MHs vol. 2* Re'eh s.v. *ki yarhiv*.

23 See the section 'First Major Theme: Acosmism and Uniqueness' on the term *hitnas'ut* as it relates to uniqueness.

24 See section 'No-Boundary and Judah'.

25 *MHs vol. 2* Ketubot s.v. *darash Bar Kapra* (Source 18 in volume 2).

26 *MHs vol. 1* Tzav s.v. *hamakriv* (Source 19 in volume 2).

27 See also *MHs vol. 1* Megilah 7a s.v. *tani Rav Yosef* (Source 39 in volume2).

28 *MHs vol. 1* Vezot Haberakhah s.v. *kol*.

29 See Chapter Twelve.

30 E.g., Lever, *Principles* 139–143.

31 'Determinism' 451.

32 *MHs vol. 1* Pesahim s.v. *bayom*.

33 For example, Kabbalah scholar and teacher Miles Krassen related (personal communication, March 2003) that he assumed this reading to be correct, as did the other teachers of *MHs* that he knew.

34 See the section 'Model One: The Name' below in Part Four.

35 On the identity in *MHs* between name and will, see the following section.

36 *MHs vol. 1* Pesahim s.v. *bayom*. See also the parallel passage, *MHs vol. 2* Pesahim s.v. *bayom*, where Lainer states that this consciousness is available in this world as well through the vehicle of *mitzvah*, and in particular, the commandment of *sukkah*.

37 See Tzadok Hakohen, *Tzidkat Hatzadik* 174, for a similar understanding of the ontic identity of names; see also sources adduced by Lever (*Principles* 66, 139–142, 176–179, 287–291).

38 A related topic in Lainer is the נהמא דכסופא *nahama dekisufa* 'bread of shame'. A separate study on the relationship between Lainer's understanding of this term and Luzzatto's, would be invaluable. Lainer cites the 'bread of shame' numerous times in *MHs*, using this concept to explain the need for human effort and its ontological dignity. For example, in relation to human action being called by the

name of man, Lainer writes, 'All the actions of God in relation to Israel are intended to exalt the horn (i.e., power) of Israel, that is to say, that all their actions should be called by their name, should result from the effort of their hands, so they should not eat from the "bread of shame"' (MHs vol. 2 Ki Teitzei s.v. ki teitzei 1). For Lainer, the bread of shame refers to the shame of mortality when one eats only from bread, and not from the word of God, which for Lainer means the realization of the ontic identity of human and divine. On bread and the word of God in MHs, see above p. 156. On the acosmic implications of the bread of shame, see also vol. 2 Ki Teitzei s.v. lo ta'ashok.

39 MHs vol. 1 Megilah s.v. amar Rabah. See endnote 878 for commentary on Lainer's attribution of binah consciousness to non-Jews.

40 Hash'arah indicates an eternal, hence ontologically real, effect. As such it parallels other terms like binyan 'adei 'ad which indicate ontological adequacy.

41 MHs vol. 2 2 Pesahim s.v. lamah. We will return to this passage in our discussion of the Judah archetype.

42 Psalms 110:10 in the Christian ordering.

43 MHs vol. 2 Ki Tisa s.v. vayedaber Hashem el Mosheh leikh reid.

44 See e.g. vol. 2 Psalms s.v. yadekha 'asuni (Source 16 in volume 2).

45 MHs vol. 1 Matot s.v. nakom nikmat. See also below, endnote 893.

46 MHs vol. 1 Balak s.v. ka'eit.

47 MHs vol. 2 Vayehi s.v. vayehi.

48 See endnote 739 on השארה.

49 See also vol. 1 Vayeira s.v. vatekhaheish, where Abraham wants to be assured by God that Isaac will be nikra 'al shemo. This was the meaning of Abraham's laughter when he says: 'How will this be called by my name?' To be called by name, according to Lainer's reading, Abraham must be more than the mere channel for the miracle; he must also substantively participate in the creation of Isaac.

50 MHs vol. 2 Ecclesiastes s.v. mah yitron 2.

51 See also MHs vol. 1 'Ekev s.v. shegar; vol. 2 Bo s.v. vehayah; Pinhas s.v. vayar; Devarim s.v. havu (Source 6).

52 See also MHs vol. 1 Mikeitz s.v. vehineih; Vayehi s.v. vayikra.

53 MHs vol. 1 Likutim s.v. Hashem YKVK (Source 17 in volume 2).

54 See e.g. vol. 2 Pesahim, s.v. lamah, vol. 2 Vayehi s.v. vayehi.

55 On this concept, see section 'Hisaron and Uniqueness'.

56 MHs vol. 1 Vayeitzei s.v. shem ha-gedolah.

57 Tanhuma Pinhas 1. In the Midrash, Eleazar's marriage to a woman of Judah is seen unfavorably by everyone. This marriage, however, inspires him to act with the audacity normally ascribed to Judah. The beginning of the passage explains that God wanted Aaron to taste the portion of David, therefore Aaron married someone from the tribe of Judah, setting the precedent for Eleazar.

58 MHs vol. 2 Va'era s.v. vayikah (Source 15 in volume 2).

59 MHs vol. 1 Tazri'a s.v. ishah. On the relationship of name and ratzon see also MHs vol. 1 Beshalah s.v. Hashem ish milhamah; Shabbat s.v. 'atidah; vol. 2

Ecclesiastes s.v. *mah yitron* 2.

60 Prov. 30:4: 'Who has ascended to heaven?…What is his name, and what is his son's name, that you would know?'

61 See the relevant part of this passage which explains this point, p. 241.

62 *MHs vol. 2* Proverbs s.v. *ki va'ar* (Source 11 in volume 2)

63 *MHs vol. 2* Likutim Va'etchanan s.v. *ukeshartem*.

64 See Chapter Thirteen on paradox in *MHs*.

65 See, e.g., *MHs vol. 1* Noah s.v. *eileh*.

66 *MHs vol. 2* Vayak'hel s.v. *vayak'hel* 3.

67 On *hitnas'ut*, see also *MHs vol. 1* Bamidbar s.v. *se'u*.

68 *MHs vol. 1* Ruth s.v. *yeshalem*; *vol. 2* Yitro s.v. *vayishma'* 2. Lainer cross-references the commentary on Yitro to the one on Ruth. The quote is drawn from both passages.

69 *MHs vol. 2* Ecclesiastes s.v. *mah yitron* 2.

70 See, e.g., *MHs vol. 2* Re'eh s.v. *ki yarhiv*.

71 See, e.g., *MHs vol. 1* Behaalotekha s.v. *me'ayin*.

72 See, e.g., *MHs vol. 2* Re'eh s.v. *ki yarhiv*.

73 On the history of the idea of *tzimtzum* both in Kabbalah and in Kabbalah scholarship, see Idel, 'On the Concept'.

74 Although Lainer uses the word 'future', he is referring here, as throughout *MHs*, to the state of redeemed consciousness. See endnotes 206, 212 and the section 'Activism Passages not Linked with Name'.

75 *MHs vol. 2* Bereishit s.v. *ben ha-adam hayah*. On exile from the Garden of Eden as an intentional part of the divine plan in earlier Kabbalah, see Safran, 'Rabbi'. Lainer at the end of the passage explains that this is similar to Uziyahu, referring to *MHs vol. 1* Proverbs s.v. *semamit*.

76 Elior in 'Temurot' (409, 415) noted paradox as an implicit feature of his thought, without citing specific textual evidence. Elior is generally sensitive to the paradoxical nature of kabbalistic and Hasidic thought, particularly in the Habad school, which inevitably influenced Lainer. On paradox in kabbalistic thought, see Elior 'The Innovations' 41 nn. 16, 17, 18, and 42 n. 21; in Hasidic thought, see Elior 'Yesh'; in Habad in particular, see Elior, *Paradoxical*; 'The Innovations' 381–432. Nahman of Braslav, though not examined in the articles by Elior, is also an important model of paradox in Hasidism; see Weiss, *Mehkarim* 131.

77 See Weiss's analysis of the sources ('Determinism' 449); for further discussion; see the section 'Models of Activism: Pre- and Post-*Berur* Consciousness, Linear and Dynamic Models'.

78 *MHs* Korah *vol. 1* s.v. *vayikah*; Weiss, 'Determinism' 448. See further discussion below, p. 231.

79 *MHs vol. 1* Shabbat s.v. *vehineih* (Source 33 in volume 2). See also *MHs vol. 1* Lekh Lekha s.v. *vayiven*; Vayeira s.v. *vayeira eilav*, Vayeishev s.v. *vayehi Er*, Hukat s.v. *vayisa*; *vol. 2* Ki Tisa s.v. *shishah*; Vayak'hel s.v. *vayak'hel* 2; Psalms s.v. *Hashem menat helki* 1.

80 *MHs vol. 1* Kedoshim s.v. *ish 'imo.*

81 See discussion endnote 206.

82 *MHs vol. 1* Shemini s.v. *vayehi.*

83 *MHs vol. 2* Nitzavim s.v. *ki atem 2.*

84 See the section 'Lainer and Choicelessness'.

85 *MHs vol. 2* Yitro s.v. *anokhi.*

86 *MHs vol. 2* Likutim 2 Pesahim s.v. *lamah.*

87 Weiss, 'Determinism' 448–451.

88 For further sources reflecting level three *mikdash* consciousness, see the passages cited in the sections 'Three: Shadows of Union and Activism', 'Acosmism and *Mikdash* (The Jerusalem Temple)' and in Chapter Thirteen; see also our further discussion below in 'Model Five: The Wisdom of Solomon'.

89 *MHs vol. 2* Rosh Hashanah s.v. *yom tov.*

90 Bereishit Rabbah 11:6.

91 See also *MHs vol. 1* Kedoshim s.v. *ish* for a parallel understanding of *shabbat*-consciousness. 'On the Sabbath it is clearly recognized that nothing is accomplished through the action of man'.

92 The alternative to deploying the 'levels of consciousness' hermeneutic is to see multiple contradictions throughout the *MHs* text. However, the preponderance of *MHs* scholarship, with which we concur, has argued that *MHs* is a relatively unified and coherent theological treatise.

93 *MHs vol. 2* Proverbs s.v. *melekh bimelukhah.*

94 Urbach, *The Sages* 19–36, 66–79.

95 *MHs vol. 1* Beshalah s.v. *Hashem yilaheim.*

96 *MHs vol. 2* Bereishit s.v. *veha-nahash.*

97 *MHs vol. 2* Likutim Noah s.v. *vayomru.*

98 *MHs vol. 2* Bereishit s.v. *veha-nahash.*

99 *MHs vol. 2* Ki Tisa s.v. *vayomer 1.* See also, *vol. 1* Ki Tisa s.v. *vayomer 2.*

100 Cf. Gafni, 'Evolving Consciousness' which includes a general discussion of the messianic implications of snake imagery in Jewish and non-Jewish sources.

101 *MHs vol. 2* Bereishit s.v. *veha-nahash.*

102 *MHs vol. 1* Ki Tisa s.v. *vayomer 3*; in the Ki Tisa passage as well, he draws on the same conceptual association between the Golden Calf and the Sabbath.

103 *MHs vol. 2* Likutim Noah s.v. *vayomru havah.*

104 On *mikdash* consciousness, see also 'Acosmism and *Mikdash* (The Jerusalem Temple)' and texts cited p. 252ff.

105 *MHs vol. 2* Rosh Hashanah s.v. *tok'in.*

106 See *MHs vol. 2* 2 Samuel s.v. *vayeilekh,* where Lainer likens Amalek to the pig that shows its split hoof and claims therefore to be a kosher animal. See also *MHs vol. 2* Likutim Beshalah s.v. *vehayah ka'asher yarim.*

107 See 'Two: The Reality of Love in Lainer's Theology'.

108 *MHs vol. 1* Kedoshim s.v. *vayedaber.* Lainer asserts that the gathering together of the community, which compels the presence of the will of God, is the intent

of the Talmudic passage stating that the *Shekhinah* dwells wherever ten people gather. According to Lainer's reading, the indwelling of the *Shekhinah*, while a matter of necessity, is the function of a relationship between lovers.

109 *MHs vol. 2* Likutim Noah s.v. *vayomru havah*, from Gershon Henokh's *Sod Yesharim* Shaar Hashanah 60.

110 *MHs vol. 1* Behar s.v. *vesafarta*.

111 For Gellman, see, 'The Denial' 118–121.

112 *MHs vol. 1* Bekhorot s.v. *ayti*. See endnote 739 on השארה.

113 *MHs vol. 2* Baba Metzia s.v. *mai metzatiha*.

114 *MHs vol. 1* Shemini s.v. *vayehi*.

115 We also note that theurgy, the impact and interpenetration of human activity on the divine realm, is very much part of Lainer's theology. See above p. 42 along with endnote 162. Theurgy implicitly assumes the ontological reality of human action.

116 *MHs vol. 2* Yitro s.v. *anokhi*.

117 *MHs vol. 1* 'Ekev s.v. *hishamer*.

118 *MHs vol. 1* Berakhot s.v. *asur*.

119 *MHs vol. 1* Shemini s.v. *vayehi*.

120 See Weiss, 'Determinism' 451 n. 21.

121 *bBetz*. 15b. Note that Rashi *ad loc.*, interpreting the Adar tree as representing an assurance that the property will remain in the person's possession, twice states that the field should be *nikra 'al shemo*. This phrase probably moved Lainer to associate this passage with his theology of human activism.

122 *MHs vol. 1* Beitzah s.v. *ve'amar*.

123 See, e.g., *vol. 1* Vayeilekh s.v. *mikeitz*.

124 In this vein see also *MHs vol. 2* Isaiah s.v. *ha-'eiynayim*; *MHs vol. 1* Ha'azinu s.v. *ha-tzur*.

125 *MHs vol. 2* Rosh Hashanah s.v. *yom tov*. See our analysis of this passage in the section 'The Paradox of Human Activism: Levels of Consciousness'.

126 On the term *hayyim* as a description of post-*berur* consciousness, see discussion in endnotes 598 and 601.

127 See section 'Third Major Theme: Affirmation of Human Activism', p. 122.

128 See 'Lainer and Choicelessness'.

129 *MHs vol. 1* Mikeitz s.v. *vehineih*. In the Talmud passage cited (*bShab*. 69b), Rav Huna takes the position that a person who does not know what day *shabbat* falls on should count six days (relying on his own effort) and then rest on the seventh. See also vol. 2 Vayak'hel s.v. *vayak'hel* 2.

130 *MHs vol. 1* Shoftim s.v. *shoftim* 2 (Source 7 in volume 2).

131 For the equation between the king, Judah archetype, and one who is drawn after the will of God, see Chapter Twelve.

132 *MHs vol. 1* Mas'ei s.v. *eileh*.

133 This is one of two passages in *MHs* that seem to suggest a different understanding of activism than what we have outlined. See also *MHs vol. 1* 'Ekev s.v. *'al*

tomar above, endnote 160.

134 *MHs vol. 1* Korah s.v. *vayikah.*

135 Weiss, 'Determinism' 449.

136 See, e.g., *MHs vol. 2* Isaiah s.v. *ve'amar* 1 on the distinction between the name *Elohim*, which refers to להבא *leha-ba* (the future) and the name *YHVH*, which refers to לשעבר *leshe'avar* (the past).

Chapter Ten
The Nature of *Berur*

Our discussion of activism is based partially on the idea of *berur*, so we will conclude this discussion by briefly surveying the various models of *berur* in *MHs*.

While *MHs* contains a number of models, each is just a different manifestation of the same fundamental understanding of *berur*.[1] *Berur* means the clarification of some dimension of reality which, without the process of *berur*, would remain occluded.

The most essential form of *berur* discussed in *MHs* brings in its wake an expansion of consciousness. We will term this 'acosmic *berur*'; it is what allows a person to realize the unified divine nature of all of reality.[2] Acosmic *berur*, in Lainer's nomenclature, is what brings a person from *gavan*, a superficial understanding of reality, to *'omek*, a deep understanding of reality. Acosmic *berur* involves seeing through the *gavan* of duality to the *'omek* of nonduality.[3]

Berur also includes a clarification of one's own internal psychological reality. We shall term this 'psychological *berur*'. Psychological *berur* is essential because human intent and motivation are naturally shrouded in obscurity. Thus, in order for a person to act in authenticity, one requires *berur*.[4] The point of authenticity is the divine point in the human being. Even a prophet, writes Lainer, requires *berur* to clarify their divine core.[5] In this sense, psychological *berur*, like acosmic *berur*, is a clarification of the essential divine nature of one's own reality.[6] In a similar vein, Lainer describes *berur* as the expansion of consciousness, where one realizes that redemption is not imminent but rather is already present. One realizes during the process of *berur* that exile is but an illusion of constricted consciousness.[7]

The third kind of *berur* we will term 'antinomian *berur*'. This is a major motif throughout *MHs* and describes the process of clarification that allows one to transcend the general principles of the law and apprehend the unmediated will of God.[8] This form of *berur* engenders *tekufot*.[9] We have seen that in order to access the unmediated will of God, a person must be deeply connected to their own uniqueness. This leads us to the fourth model of *berur* appearing in *MHs*, namely, what we will term 'the *berur* of individuality'. Here again the *berur* involves a clarification of the inner divine nature of reality, one expression of which is, according to Lainer, the radical subjectivity of each human being.[10]

A fifth form of *berur* is the *berur* of idolatry.[11] Here again, *berur* clarifies the inner divine root of paganism.

We must make three other distinctions in models of *berur* to complete our discussion. The first is between nomian and anomian *berur*. In nomian *berur*, accomplishing any of the above clarifications occurs through the methodology of *mitzvah*.[12] In anomian *berur*, achieving the same goals occurs through any one of many internal introspective processes that are not specifically mandated by law.[13] The second distinction is between *berur* done in the present, which cleanses the doors of perception and reveals the divine nature of all of reality, and *berur* done in the eschaton, which retroactively reveals the divine nature of all that was. The *berur* of the eschaton is that affected by God. This brings us to the third distinction: *berur* initiated by the human as compared with *berur* affected by God.[14] Nevertheless, Lainer, moving towards a collapse of the distinction between human and God in the process of *berur*, writes that *berur* requires illumination and can never be done independently by the human.[15] Finally, Lainer discusses a sixth form of *berur, berur teshukah*—the clarification of desire. This will be the topic of Chapter Eleven.

Notes for Chapter Ten

1 On *berur* in *MHs*, see the brief discussion in Faierstein, *Hands* 58–61. *Berur* is also a major theme in Seeman, 'Martyrdom'. However, neither Seeman nor Faierstein distinguishes between the various models of *berur* in *MHs*.

2 On acosmic *berur*, see *MHs* vol. 1 Va'et'hanan s.v. *shema'*, where acosmic *berur* is listed as the first of five forms of *berur*; also see *vol. 1* Vayeira s.v. *adam*, Mishpatim s.v. *ve'eileh*; vol. 2 Shoftim s.v. *ki*; Mishpatim s.v. *reishit*; Nitzavim s.v. *ki atem*; Yitro s.v. *anokhi*.

3 On the *berur* of *gavan* to see the '*omek*, see *MHs* vol. 1 Lekh Lekha s.v. *lekh*.

4 On authenticity as the major goal in religious service according to Lainer and his student Tzadok, see Rosenberg (Shagar), 'Teshuvah'.

5 *MHs* vol. 1 Kedoshim s.v. *veilohei maseikhah*.

6 On psychological *berur*, see, e.g., *MHs* vol. 1 Vayeishev s.v. *vayehi*; Kedoshim s.v. *veilohei maseikhah*. On psychological *berur* as identifying the divine point from which the human must act, see *MHs* vol. 1 s.v. *harimoti*; vol. 2 Zevahim s.v. *kol ha-zevahim*.

7 See, e.g., *MHs* vol. 2 Toldot s.v. *vaya'al*.

8 On antinomian *berur*, see *MHs* vol. 1 Vayeishev s.v. *vayehi*; Lekh Lekha s.v. *vayiven*; Vayikra s.v. *vayehi*; Hukat s.v. *vayisa*; Ki Tisa s.v. *shishah*; vol. 2 Vayak'hel s.v. *vayak'hel 2*; Psalms s.v. *Hashem menat helki*.

9 See, e.g., *MHs* vol. 1 Vayeira s.v. *vayeira eilav*.

10 On the *berur* of individuality, see *MHs* vol. 1 Va'et'hanan s.v. *ve'ahavta*; Ki Teitzei s.v. *ki yikareh*; Lekh Lekha s.v. *vayiven*; vol. 2 Psalms s.v. *Hashem menat helki*.

11 See, e.g., *MHs* vol. 1 Vayehi s.v. *uvedam* (Source 35 in volume 2).

12 See, e.g., *MHs* vol. 2 Megilah s.v. *amar*.

13 We discuss the actual process of *berur* in contrast to the mystical techniques that engender *unio mystica* in the section 'Post-*Berur* Consciousness vs. *Unio Mystica*: The *Berur* and *Bitul* Models'.

14 On *berur* initiated by God, see *MHs* vol. 1 Toldot s.v. *ve'ahavta*; vol. 2 Shoftim s.v. *ki*; Pekudei s.v. *eileh*.

15 *MHs* vol. 2 Ki Tavo s.v. *ki tekhaleh*.

Chapter Eleven
The Way of *Teshukah*

The final characteristic of Lainer's acosmic humanism is the quality of *teshukah*. According to Lainer, *teshukah*, the primal life force of desire, identified also with *yetzer ha-ra'* in *MHs*,[1] is an essential characteristic of the ideal religious persona. Lainer's emphasis on the primacy of *teshukah* shifts our characterization of Lainer's religious archetype from a sober *berur*-oriented type to a more passionate religious type who is both connected to their own *teshukah* and understands that it participates in the divine *teshukah*. The *teshukah* element in Lainer's thought complements and deepens the erotic character of the *MHs* passages cited above in which Lainer explained being drawn after the will of God in terms of seduction.[2]

This affirmation of *teshukah* in *MHs* is a direct function of Lainer's acosmism.[3] Moreover, it is precisely the humanistic cast to Lainer's acosmism that leads him to affirm the ontological dignity of human *teshukah*. He views it not as an undesirable state to be overcome but as a primary quality of divinity as well as a pivotal agent of revelation, making Lainer's attitude to *teshukah* a key part of the humanist cast to Lainer's acosmism.

According to Lainer, *teshukah* is either the primary life force itself, or the most basic expression of that life force which is even more primary.[4] *Teshukah* is described as the *ikar* 'essence' of life and growth, both physically and spiritually:

ע״י אותה התשוקה...נתגדל אצלו החיים...זאת ההתפשטות יקרא דמות,
וכמו כן בנפש...התשוקה...לד״ת נקרא דמות...כי זה היה עיקר בריאות
האדם בכדי שישתוקק בכל פעם להתרבות ד״ת

By means of that very desire...life grows in him...This expansion [of *tzelem* 'image'] is called *demut* 'likeness', and so too in the soul, desire for Torah is called *demut*...for this was the essence of man's creation: that he should constantly desire to increase words of Torah...'[5]

219

In this passage, it is not the desire for Torah that is ontologically prior, but rather the desire itself. In another text, Lainer states, העיקר הוא התשוקה 'The essence is desire';[6] among other things, this means that a person is defined not by where they actually are but by the direction towards which their desire opens.

Here and throughout *MHs*, Lainer interprets the rabbinic statement 'Greater is שמושה *shimushah*, serving Torah, than לימודה *limudah*, learning her'[7] as an approbation of desire. The Hebrew word for service, which can have an erotic dimension,[8] is interpreted by Lainer as *teshukah*.[9] *Shimushah*, states Lainer in a parallel passage, has no limit or boundary, while *limudah* is limited and bounded.[10]

The centrality of *teshukah*, like that of *hisaron*, to which it is essentially related in Lainer's thought,[11] is best discerned through a phenomenological prism. What are the effects of *teshukah* in the religious anthropology of Lainer? Divine *teshukah* moves God to choose the patriarchs, initiating the election of Israel.[12] *Teshukah* allows the vast metaphysical gulf between Jew and non-Jew in Lainer's theology to be traversed;[13] it is the catalyst that effects what would otherwise be impossible: the conversion of a non-Jew to Judaism.[14] Divine *teshukah* is reflected back to God through the *teshukah* of Moses, which causes him to be the one 'chosen' to receive the Torah.[15] Similarly, divine *teshukah* is reflected back to God through the prism of the desire in the souls of the Jewish people, which initiates redemption.[16]

Lainer interprets another rabbinic dictum in his thought as an affirmation of the centrality of *teshukah*: 'A person only stands firm upon the words of Torah if he has first failed in them'.[17] According to Lainer, the very purpose of *kishalon* 'failure' is to engender *teshukah*, which in turn allows for *divrei Torah* 'to enter further into the heart'.[18] The term *divrei Torah* in this text and in many others implies not merely Talmudic debate or other formal study of sacred texts, but, in a more general sense, stands for the holy.[19] Crucially, according to Lainer, *teshukah* initiates both the revelation to Moses and also the personal revelation to the individual that is the core of Lainer's religious anthropology. Lainer states:

ועיקר הי׳ אצלו תשוקה לידע מי הוא בעל הבירה...ע״כ נראה אליו
הש״י...והוא ישב פתח האהל כחום היום היינו שהי׳ מתחמם ומתלהב בו
אהבת הש״י...וזה פי׳ פתח האהל היינו שהי׳ פתוח לפניו

The essence of Abraham was the *teshukah* to know who was the master of the castle...It was for this reason that God was revealed to him...'He would sit at the entrance to the tent at the heat of the day' (Gen. 18:1): this means that he would make himself hot and passionate in the love of God...and this is the meaning of 'at the entrance to the tent', that he was open before Him.[20]

In this typical passage on *teshukah* and revelation, we see clearly the almost erotic, ecstatic quality[21] introduced by Lainer as a dimension of revelation.[22] *Teshukah* is also the catalyst for revelation. In Lainer's nomenclature, revelation is referred to as הארה *he'arah*,[23] דברי תורה חדשים *divrei Torah hadashim*, התחדשות *hit'hadeshut*,[24] or related terms. Law plays a similar function in the *berur* of *teshukah* to its role in relation to *retzon Hashem*.[25] Paradoxically, the *kelalim* of Torah allow one to transcend those very *kelalim* and access unmediated *retzon Hashem*. Similarly, the *kelalim* of law, that is, the *taryag* (613) *mitzvot*, develop in one the ability to trust the unmediated revelation catalyzed by *teshukah*. It is mastery of the *mitzvot* that gives one the right to rely on the *teshukah*.[26]

However, even when a person is not perfected, Lainer insists on the ontological dignity of *teshukah*. It is here that his acosmic humanism finds one of its clearest expressions. This is shown in his interpretation of the biblical law of the beautiful captive woman (Deut. 21:10-15). He begins in his first comment on the narrative by interpreting the captive woman as *teshukah* which is in captivity in the nations of the world[27] and which needs to be redeemed by Israel. True *teshukah*, asserts Lainer, exists only within Israel, כי כח התשוקה אינו רק מהש"י וזה אין שייך להם רק לישראל 'for the power of *teshukah* is from God alone and therefore essentially connected...only to Israel'. Leaving aside the chauvinism of this statement,[28] in the context of Lainer's acosmism, this means that human *teshukah* is ontologically significant precisely because human *teshukah* participates in divine *teshukah*. Given this ontological grounding of *teshukah*, he continues his exegesis as follows: כי באמת כל מה שיעלה חן בעיני ישראל בטח נמצא בו דבר טוב, אך צריך לברר 'Anything that arouses favor in the eyes of Israel certainly has some good in it...yet it requires *berur*'.[29] Here *hen* 'favor' operates as a synonym for *teshukah*. Lainer makes a twofold assumption, highly characteristic of his thought. First, an authentic experience of *teshukah* is sacred and therefore must be affirmed, even if it seems to lead in the wrong direction. Second, *teshukah* must be clarified, i.e. interpreted, so that its true intent can be discerned. The hermeneutics of desire is thus a central concern of Lainer's thought.

This line of thought is the underlying assumption in another passage on the same set of laws. There Lainer asserts that the חשק *heshek* (a synonym for *teshukah*) that the man originally felt could not have been in vain, even though (in this case) the beautiful captive turned out to be not as she appeared, and bore a son who was a *ben sorer* (rebellious son) who was executed by the court. The entire passage is committed to proving this assumption. Lainer insists that רק הי' נמצא בו דבר טוב 'something good' is enfolded in the story, because: שאצל...ולא לחנם הי' חשק האב לקחת את אמו. '...the father's הש"י נמצא תיקון על כל הדברים...שלא ידח מהם נדח משום חשק *heshek* to take his mother was not for naught...and in God is the fixing for all things...and nothing from them will be rejected from any *heshek*.'[30]

Naturally, in this passage as well as in previous passages, *berur teshukah* 'the clarification of desire' is required. This is a recurrent theme in the *berur* passages throughout *MHs*.[31] Indeed, according to Lainer, original sin is at least in part bound up with Adam's failure to effect *berur teshukah*.[32] False desire is always nestled in the wings of true desire.[33] However, Lainer's relationship to *teshukah* remains uniquely affirming, to a degree rarely seen in classical kabbalistic or Hasidic sources.

The next passage gives an even stronger affirmation of *heshek/teshukah*. Here, Lainer is interpreting the verse, 'Who constrains water in a garment? Who has established all the ends of the earth?' (Prov. 30:4), as highlighting the erotic nature of Solomon's wisdom, in which *teshukah/heshek* is a central component:

> מים הוא חשק וזה מי צרר מים שיצרור ויגביל את החשק בגבולים ולעשות
> תחומין במעין שעד גבול זה מותר לחשוק, ומגבול זה ולהלאה אסור.
> מי הקים כל אפסי ארץ, שיהיה להאדם כח להחזיק ולקיים אלו הכוחות
> שיתקיימו אצלו לעולמי עד...שירגיש האדם הולדת רצון חדש שמזה הגבול
> מתחיל רצונות חדשים

> Water signifies *heshek* passion, and this is [what is meant by]
> 'Who constrains water?'—that he would constrain and bind
> passion within boundaries and make limits in the spring; that
> up to this boundary it is permissible to desire, and beyond
> this boundary it is forbidden.'...Who has established all the

222

ends of the earth?'—[this means] that a person will have the power to hold onto and sustain these powers that arise in him forever... for new will begins from this *gevul* boundary.[34]

Lainer's point is that water cannot be constrained, and that *teshukah* must go beyond the boundaries, e.g. beyond the boundaries of *halakhah*—it is only from the point at which one goes beyond the boundary that *teshukah* becomes real. This *teshukah* has within it a power which extends to eternity, that is, it is ontologically real.

Only Abraham Isaac Hakohen Kook—who was probably directly influenced by Lainer—accords *teshukah* such a central place in his metaphysics.[35] Musar writings from the same general historical era as Lainer emphasize the dangerous qualities of *teshukah*, as does much of the classic Hasidic literature.[36] It is left to Lainer, as a function of his acosmic humanism, to affirm the innate ontological dignity of all *teshukah* and to insist on *teshukah* as a vital guiding force in reaching for the unmediated will of God.

Notes for Chapter Eleven

1 *MHs vol. 1* Ki Teitzei s.v. *zakhor*. In this world, explains Lainer, *teshukah* is associated with *yetzer ha-ra*, that is, they derive from the same source. Even in the future world, *yetzer ha-ra'* will remain associated with *teshukah*, because the memory of *yetzer ha-ra'* will engender fresh *teshukah*, which will naturally be channeled to the intention of *retzon Hashem*.

2 See section 'The Second Quality of Will: Eros and the Will of God'. This ideal religious archetype includes not only desire but even a modicum of Dionysian ecstasy. See e.g. *vol. 1* Vayeira s.v. *vayeira eilav*.

3 See, e.g., *MHs vol. 1* Pesahim s.v. *R. Simlai*, where Lainer connects the ability to rely on *teshukah* with the metaphysical quality of the Jewish people. As we have seen, the metaphysical quality of the Jewish people is one of his codes for the ontic identity between the person and God.

4 See *MHs vol. 1* Bereishit s.v. *zeh sefer*. See also *vol. 1* Hayyei Sarah s.v. *veAvraham* and Gilyon Hayyei Sarah s.v. *veAvraham* where Lainer views as the subject of a Talmudic dispute the issue of whether *teshukah* itself is the primary life force or an expression of the more basic life force. In other passages, e.g., *MHs vol. 2* Ki Teitzei s.v. *ki teitzei 2* (Source 25 in volume 2), he states '*teshukah* is called life', which seems to indicate that *teshukah* itself is the primary life force. This issue, however, remains unclear.

5 *MHs vol. 1* Bereishit s.v. *zeh sefer*.

6 *MHs vol. 2* Yitro s.v. *vayishma' 5*.

7 *bBer*. 7b

8 The root of *shimushah* is also the root of the term *tashmish*, which is used in rabbinic literature as a euphemism for sexual relations (see e.g. *mNidah* 2:4).

9 *MHs vol. 1* Bereishit s.v. *zeh*. See also *MHs vol. 2* Ki Teitzei s.v. *ki teitzei 2* (Source 25 in volume 2).

10 *MHs vol. 1* Berakhot s.v. *ve'amar Rabi Yohanan…gedolah shimushah*.

11 On the interrelationship between *hisaron* and *teshukah* in Lainer's thought, see, e.g., *MHs vol. 1* Toldot s.v. *vayeishev* (Source 3 in volume 2): 'Through the realization of his *hisaron* he came to new desire'. See also *vol. 2* Ki Teitzei s.v. *ki teitzei 2*: 'One only has desire for what one is lacking'.

12 *MHs vol. 1* Ki Tisa s.v. *vayomer*.

13 *MHs vol. 2* Yitro s.v. *vayishma' 5*.

14 *MHs vol. 1* Vayikra s.v. *vayikra 1*.

15 *MHs vol. 1* Vayikra s.v. *vayikra 1*. See also *vol. 1* Vayikra s.v. *vayedaber* regarding the *teshukah* of Moses as the reason he and not Aaron received the commandments about sacrifices.

16 *MHs vol. 1* Hukat s.v. *umisham*.

17 *bGit*. 43a. See further discussion of this dictum in *MHs* at endnote 213 and p. 95.

18 *MHs vol. 1* Vayeitzei s.v. *veha-aretz*.

19 For this type of broad usage of the term *divrei Torah* in *MHs*, see *vol. 1* Vayeishev s.v. *vayeishev*; Vayehi s.v. *Gad*; *vol. 2* Yitro s.v. *vayishma'*; and many additional passages. For discusion of a parallel usage of the idea of *devar Torah* in Maimonides, see Twersky, 'Some'.

20 *MHs vol. 1* Vayeira s.v. *vayeira eilav*.

21 Note, however, Lainer's critique of ecstasy in *MHs vol. 2* Hosea s.v. *Ashur*, which he says is insufficient to establish the authenticity of a religious moment.

22 This dimension has not yet been explored in the scholarship on *MHs*. This is consistent with the more general tendency to overlook the key controlling mechanism in *MHs*, namely, the human incarnation of *Shekhinah*, and its roots in the matrix of the Wisdom of Solomon (see the section 'Model Five: The Wisdom of Solomon').

23 On *he'arah* and *teshukah* see the continuation of the *MHs* passage just quoted.

24 On *teshukah*, *hit'hadeshut*, and *devar Torah* see *MHs vol. 1* Beshalah s.v. *vayelkhu*. See also *MHs vol. 1* Toldot s.v. *vayeishev* (Source 3 in volume 2).

25 See section 'Freedom and Law'.

26 *MHs vol. 1* Pesahim s.v. *R. Simlai*.

27 *MHs vol. 1* Ki Teitzei s.v. *ki teitzei*. On *teshukah* and its place among the nations of the world, see also *MHs vol. 1* Hagigah s.v. *darash Raba*; *vol. 2* Vayishlah s.v. *vayishlah*, Va'era s.v. *vehifleiti*. See esp. *MHs vol. 2* Ki Teitzei s.v. *ki teitzei 2*, analyzed at length in volume 2, Source 25.

28 Lainer's radical chauvinism is rooted theologically in a substantive metaphysical abyss that separates the Jewish from the gentile soul. Yet in this passage, *teshukah*, which is an essential if not the essential life force, is in exile among the nations of the world. Lainer never explains how it is that the nations hold this primal life force, which, according to Lainer's theology, is related essentially only to Israel. A similar pattern prevails in Lainer's comment, cited at p. 193, that the nations of the world will access *binah* consciousness to recognize the true nature of Israel. A different fissure in Lainer's chauvinism is found in his assumption, drawn directly from his Lurianic sources, that a soul can transmigrate from a Jew to a non-Jew and back again. This would seem, both for Lainer and Luria, to significantly blur the distinction between Jew and non-Jew. See, e.g., *MHs vol. 1* Matot s.v. *vayiktzof*. However, Lainer, and to the best of our knowledge, Luria, do not develop the more liberal potential inherent in this doctrine of transmigration.

29 *MHs vol. 1* Ki Teitzei s.v. *vehashakta*. In Lainer's interpretation, the commandment that the captive woman take off שמלת שביה ('the raiment of her captivity') indicates the *berur* of stripping away what is superficially attractive (כל הגוונין) in order to discover the true nature of one's desire.

30 *MHs vol. 1* Ki Teitzei s.v. *ki yihyeh*.

31 See, e.g., *MHs vol. 1* Nitzavim s.v. *vehayah*.

32 *MHs vol. 1* Bereishit s.v. *vayomer*.

33 See, e.g., *MHs vol. 1* Va'et'hanan s.v. *shema'*; 1 Kings s.v. *ve'Adoniyahu*.

34 *MHs vol. 2* Proverbs s.v. *ki va'ar* (Source 11 in volume 2).

35 See below, 'Lainer and Abraham Isaac Hakohen Kook'.

36 *Teshukah* 'desire' was seen as that which needed to be overcome at all costs in order for a person to be an עבד ה' *eved Hashem* 'servant of God'. For a classic presentation of the Musar view of *teshukah*, reflecting the history of the Musar movement, see two essays in Shmuelevitz, *Sihot Musar*: Eved Hashem (Servant of God) sec. 1 Essay 11 and sec. 2 Essay 16. On the anti-existential stance of early Hasidism and its relevance to this issue, see Schatz-Uffenheimer, *Hahasidut* 31-40.

Chapter Twelve
The Judah Archetype

All of the fundamental characteristics of acosmic humanism we have discussed above are manifested by the Judah archetype.[1] Before discussing these characteristics, we note that for Lainer, living the way of the Judah archetype is not optional; for those who are called to this life it is an absolute obligation which, if ignored, calls down divine curse.[2] Judah represents the typology of one who has realized their ontic identity with the will of God. Lainer contrasts Judah with Joseph,[3] and sometimes with Levi.[4] While Joseph and Levi are characterized by *yir'ah*, fear or awe,[5] the Judah archetype is characterized by love.[6]

Judah consciously participates in divinity, realizing that his name and the name of God are one. His acosmic consciousness is accomplished through a process of *berur* in which he understands that there is no such thing as human action independent of God. Rather, he knows and experiences every action he takes as being fully animated by divine will. This acosmic realization is radically empowering for him. Judah manifests and is identified with the quality of *tekufot*: the personal power, sacred audacity, and determination that are direct results of realizing one's divine core. Therefore, in Lainer's language, he can naturally מכוון רצון ה' *mekaven retzon Hashem* 'intend the will of God'.[7] He feels himself called by his inner divine voice,[8] his own personal revelation, to expand beyond the boundaries foisted upon him by external structures (Lainer terms this *hitpashtut*). Judah affirms the dignity of his *teshukah*.[9] Moreover, he allows himself to be guided by his *teshukah* once it has undergone a process of *berur*.

No-Boundary and Judah

When Judah is born, Lainer describes יקרת נפש יהודה 'the special nature of the Judah soul' as being *beli shum gevul* 'without any boundary'.[10] Lainer repeatedly mentions that Judah is connected to the awareness of אין לו גבול *ein lo gevul*: 'He has no boundary'.[11] Judah is identified with *retzon Hashem* even *lema'alah mida'ato*,[12] beyond his conscious will. He has realized no-boundary consciousness. His prayer, repentance, Torah, and desire all derive from this consciousness, which moves him, even when he is misunderstood by his own community, to sometimes break the law in order to respond to an order of revelation more immediate and personal then the original revelation of Sinai.

Judah's path to no-boundary consciousness is unique. More than participating in the general divine will, he incarnates the unique divine will. Unmediated revelation addressed specifically to him, refracted through the prism of his unique soul, is expressed in his unique self and his unique *hisaron*. He has undergone a process of *berur*, which allows him to identify his unique *helek* and *shoresh*, i.e., his unique manifestation of the divine light, which is the root of his soul. He is particularly connected to his unique *mitzvah*, for which he must even be willing to give up his life. Because the very essence of his *hayyim* is his uniqueness, to live without his uniqueness would be deadly. In short, Judah is the personification of acosmic humanism.

Paradox, Activism, and Judah

Judah also symbolizes the paradox of human effort. Lainer applies the rabbinic dictum of 'I have not worked yet I have found, do not believe him'[13] to the birth of Judah. Leah invested great effort in the first three sons and none in Judah, who was a special gift from the side of God. Yet the effort invested for the first three sons yielded Judah as well. At the same time, it was metaphysically important for Judah to be a gift from God's side and not a direct result of human effort. Lainer suggests that built into the very moment of Judah's birth was the paradoxical consciousness that one must hold with regard to human effort. It is, on one hand, absolutely necessary, and yet at the same time all is really a gift from God.[14]

The Will of God, Judah and the Name

The blurring between the name of God and the name of the human is fully crystallized in Judah. Lainer states, 'כי באותיות יהודה נמצא שם הוי' 'In the letters of Judah the name *Havayah (YHVH)* is found'.[15] As we have seen, Lainer associates the *shem havayah* with a person incarnating the will of God.[16] While in the future world the *shem havayah* will express the realized ontic identity between every human and God,[17] in this world, Judah already overcomes that split to incarnate the divine. In describing the Judah archetype, who 'is the name of God', Lainer states:

228

כיון שאינו עושה רק מה שהוא רצון השי״ת, וזה ונשגב שהמעשה הזה...
הוא למעלה מהשגת תפיסת האדם בעוה״ז וזה שנאמר ותלד לו את פנחס,
שהשי״ת חתם עצמו על זה המעשה שהוא נשגב מאוד כמו שכתיב (במדבר
כה:יב), לכן אמור הנני נתן לו את בריתי שלום, שהשי״ת חתם עצמו עליו.
עליו.

[H]e intends the depth of God's will, since he does nothing
except what is God's will. And this is the meaning of *venisgav*
'and he is lifted up'—that this action is beyond the reach of
a person's grasp in this world. [Therefore] God sealed (or,
signed) Himself upon this deed, which is very exalted...
Therefore it is written, 'I have given him My covenant of
peace', for God has signed Himself upon him.[18]

God 'signs' onto whatever the Judah archetype wills as an expression of divine empowerment. Human will is identified with the will of God, but in a
way in which the human is affirmed and not effaced. This is not in any way
what Weiss termed מיעוט דמותה של עשייה אנושית *mi'ut demutah shel 'asiyah
enoshit*, a devaluation of human activism.

Regarding the king who, in *MHs*, is a manifestation of the Judah archetype, Lainer similarly states:ונקודת המלך ישראל הוא תקופות גדול עד שכל מה
שבלבבו יעשה, כי מה שעולה בלבבו הוא בטח רצון השי״י 'The essence of the king of
Israel is great *tekufot*, so much so that whatever is in his heart he does, for
anything that arises in his heart is certainly *retzon Hashem*.[19]

Judah personifies the preference for personal revelation over the law. The
immediacy of personal revelation in the present overrides all preceding revelations of yesterday. Judah represents עליה לרגל *'aliyah* laregel (ascending
on foot to Jerusalem), understood by Lainer to mean transcending (עליה
'aliyah) the routine (רגל *regel*) of the law.[20] Lainer states:

ושורש החיים של יהודה הוא להביט תמיד להש״י בכל דבר מעשה...ולא
להתנהג ע״פ מצות אנשים מלומדה אף שעשה אתמול מעשה כזו...רק
שהשי״י יאיר לו מחדש רצונו ית׳

The root of life of Judah is to always look to God in every
action...and not to be guided [by precedent], even though
he may have acted this way yesterday. Rather, he desires that
God grant him a new revelation of His will.[21]

As the paradigm of 'one who is drawn after the will of God', Judah is guided by *binat ha-lev*. According to Lainer, reaching this level is the inner intent of the covenant and the meaning of the declaration repeated by the Israelites at Sinai: נעשה ונשמע 'We will do and we will listen' (Exod. 24:7). 'We will do' represents receiving and following the law; 'We will listen' expresses reaching beyond the law to the specific will of God.[22] In this sense, Judah is for Lainer the paradigm for the stage that every Israelite must eventually reach, as we will touch on further below.[23]

Judah, Uniqueness, and Individuality

In our discussion of *ratzon*, we have seen two general categories. The first is *tif'eret le'osehah*, which represents the Joseph archetype, who is committed to general principles of law.[24] The second category, identified with Judah, is *tif'eret lo min ha-adam*. This category represents one who is committed to one's *tzurat ha-adam*, their inner human form, i.e., the divine being that is one's essence—even when it contradicts the rule of the *halakhah*. Lainer states:

פרץ הי' נשמת ער כי פרץ הוא לשון תקופות היינו תפארת לו מן האדם
היינו אף שהוא הפך מתפארת נגד בני אדם לא ישגיח על זה כי אף שנראה
שפרץ עושה נגד ההלכה

> Peretz was the soul of Er (Judah's son), for *peretz*, breaking forth, means *tekufot*, which is *tif'eret lo min ha-adam*. This means that even if it goes against what other people perceive as *tif'eret* (appropriate), he will not be concerned about this... even though it appears that Peretz acts against the law.[25]

Peretz, a Judah archetype, responds to the revelation addressed to his unique soul. Based on this revelation, he disregards the *kelalim*, the general principles of law, when they clash with the *peratim*, the specific revelation of God to him.[26] Lainer describes this as the characteristic of the eschaton, the era of redeemed *'olam ha-ba*–consciousness, which will be the time of נר *ner* 'candle':

כי נר הוא דבר פרטי, ואור הוא כללי...אכן מהנס שנעשה בהמנורה קבעו
נר פרטי לכל אחד ואחד להאיר האור הפרטי לבחירת כל נפש מישראל
בפרט...וזהו משתשקע החמה כי חמה רומז על כללי ד"ת ולעתיד לא יצרך
לכללים רק הש"י ישפיע לכל אדם בינה מפורשת בכל פרט מעשה

230

...for a candle is a unique individual thing, but אור *or* is general...Therefore from the miracle that occurred through the *menorah*, they established a unique candle for each individual, to illuminate the individual light of every unique person in Israel...and that is what it means [that candles should be lit] 'when the sun sets', for the sun symbolizes the general principles of Torah, and the in future there will be no need for the *kelalim*. Rather, God will cause the flow of explicit *binah* to every person in every individual act.[27]

Naturally, the manifestation of this consciousness in the Judah archetype in the pre-eschaton reality engenders tension between him and the rest of the community. This theme is developed throughout *MHs*, including in the aforementioned text. The essence of *tif'eret lo min ha-adam* is a willingness to clash with the norms of the community in order to be true to his inner divine self.[28]

Lainer makes two key points about Judah that render his thought both radical and compelling. First, it is clear that Judah is not just a possible religious archetype; rather, he is Lainer's religious ideal. Second, this religious ideal is accessible to everyone, at least in potential. It even seems that, according to Lainer, achieving this ideal is incumbent on all those for whom it is possible. The ideal is not limited to an elite: not to the ancient institution of kingship, nor to the Hasidic institution of the *tzadik*. Furthermore, as is made clear in Lainer's grandson's essay *Dor Yesharim*, Mordechai Joseph fully identified with the Judah persona.[29] While Faierstein, as we noted in Part One, rejects this characterization as a projection of Gershom Henokh's own messianism onto his grandfather,[30] the internal codes in *MHs* clearly reveal the messianic overtones of Lainer's activity in general and particularly of the Judah archetype.

Additionally, in the classic passage that sets up the typology of Judah, Lainer states in regard to the Joseph archetype: כי בנין עדי עד אינו שייך לחלקם רק לחלק יהודה 'for a *binyan 'adei 'ad*, eternal structure, is not connected to [Joseph's] portion, only to Judah's portion.'[31]

Lainer's second key point about Judah is that, as we pointed out above,[32] the Judah archetype is not limited to any particular group. The idea that the human being participates in ontic identity with the will of God is found in Hasidism in regard to the *tzadik*; what is unique in Lainer is that he expands this idea beyond that narrow realm.[33] In effect, Lainer makes every person a potential *tzadik*. The classic passage that we have already adduced above in our discussion of will is really a description of the Judah archetype:

היינו בכל רגע ורגע יודע כל נפש מישראל מקטון ועד גדול מה שהש״י חפץ עתה ויבינו ע״פי בינת לבבם שעתה רצון הש״י הוא כך, ולא על פי כללים

> At every instant, every soul in Israel *mikaton ve'ad gadol* from young to old knows what God desires now, and understands, based on the *binah* of their hearts, that this is the will of God, and not based on the general principles (law).[34]

Indeed, the overwhelming majority of the passages in *MHs* seem to be addressed to everyone.[35] No distinction is drawn between groups of people and there is no limitation on who can be a Judah persona. However, in a small number of other passages, Lainer indicates that Judah is a particular *helek* or *shoresh* that does not relate to everyone, and one who acts as Judah when it is not their root soul is regarded as having acted in bad faith.[36]

We might say that there are two strands of thought in *MHs* on this central topic, indicating an internal ambivalence on Lainer's part. However, this is not necessarily so: Lainer seems to indicate in one passage that the same person can be at different times both Judah and Joseph.[37] This would mean that the Judah archetype can be accessed by virtually everyone at some point in their lives. However, accessing it at the wrong time, ובאם לא יתנהג האדם במדה הראוי לו 'when a person does not act in the measure fitting to him'[38] renders these actions wrong, אסורים שלא במקומם הראוי להם 'forbidden because they are not in the place fitting for them.'[39]

Notes for Chapter Twelve

1 The division of the population into distinct religious typologies in which one enjoys a privileged intimacy with the divine has roots going back to the beginning of Hasidism. See e.g. Jacob Joseph of Polnoye's distinction between אנשי חומר *anshei homer* (people of physicality) and אנשי צורה *anshei tzurah* (people of form). On this distinction, see, e.g., Scholem, 'Tsaddik' 131; Rapaport-Albert, 'God and the Tzadik'.

2 *MHs vol. 2* Ki Tavo s.v. *arur makleh aviv ve'imo*.

3 The Judah-Joseph contrast has much older roots in classical Jewish sources. See Magid, *Hasidism* 337 n. 8. Lainer's interpretation, however, is highly original and unique in both its antinomian and democratic character.

4 See *MHs vol. 2* Ki Tavo s.v. *arur makleh aviv ve'imo*; Ki Tavo s.v. *arur ha-ish* (Source 43 in volume 2).

5 On Levi see, e.g., *MHs vol. 2* Ki Tavo s.v. *arur ha-ish*. On Joseph see, e.g., *MHs vol. 1* Vayeishev s.v. *vezeh* (Source 9 in volume 2).

6 For sources on David (an expression of the Judah archetype) and love, see 'Two: The Reality of Love in Lainer's Theology'.

7 See for example *vol. 1* Shabbat s.v. *amar Rav; vol. 2* Berakhot s.v. *kol ha-neviim*.

8 *MHs vol. 1* Nitzavim s.v. *vehayah*.

9 See, e.g., *MHs vol. 1* Pesahim s.v. R. *Simlai*.

10 *MHs vol. 1* Vayeitzei s.v. *vatomer*.

11 *MHs vol. 2* Behaalotekha s.v. *im yihyeh* (Source 5 in volume 2), Likutim Psalms s.v. *utevunot yadav*.

12 *MHs vol. 2* Psalms s.v. *temunot*.

13 *bMeg.* 6b

14 *MHs vol. 1* Vayeitzei s.v. *vatomer*.

15 *MHs vol. 1* Vayehi s.v. *vayikra*.

16 See, for example, *vol. 2* Va'era s.v. *vayedaber*.

17 *MHs vol. 1* Pesahim s.v. *bayom*, discussed above, p. 192.

18 *MHs vol. 2* Va'eira s.v. *vayikah* (Source 15 in volume 2). Here the Judah archetype is embodied by Aaron's son Elazar, as is discussed in the next volume.

19 *MHs vol. 2* Tetzaveh s.v. *ravu'a*. See also *vol. 1* Shoftim s.v. *ki tavo'u*. It is clear in this passage that the king is an archetype, and not limited to the formal king. On the right of the Judah archetype to act in accordance with his desire, see also *vol. 1* Shoftim s.v. *shoftim* 2 (Source 7 in volume 2) and *vol. 2* Shemini s.v. *yayin* 2 (Source 31 in volume2).

20 *MHs vol. 1* Hagigah s.v. *darash*.

21 *MHs vol. 1* Vayeishev s.v. *vezeh* (Source 9 in volume 2). See also *MHs vol. 1* Shabbat s.v. *amar Rav*.

22 *MHs vol. 2* Mishpatim s.v. *vayikah*.

23 In the section, 'Model Three: The *Tzadik* and the Democratization of Enlightenment'. See also above, 'The Democratization of Enlightenment', Chap. 8.

24 On the Joseph archetype see, e.g., *MHs vol. 1* Vayeishev s.v. *vezeh* (Source 9 in volume 2). On *tif'eret le'osehah,* see vol. 1 Vayeishev s.v. *vayehi,* Bereishit s.v. *vayitzmah.*

25 *MHs vol. 1* Vayeishev s.v. *vayeired.*

26 On the direct connection between Judah and the personal revelation of the divine will that countermands the general principles of law, see, among other passages, *MHs vol. 2* Behaalotekha s.v. *im yihyeh* (Source 5 in volume 2).

27 *MHs vol. 1* Shabbat s.v. *mai Hanukah.*

28 See also *MHs vol. 1* Vayeishev s.v. *vezeh* (Source 9 in volume 2); Vezot Haberakhah s.v. *ve'eilu.*

29 Hayyim Simhah Lainer, *Dor Yesharim* 9a–11a; also G. H. Lainer, *Beit Yaakov* Introduction 10b. See also Morgenstern, 'Tzipiyot'. Morgenstern provides the Kotzk background to Lainer's messianism. Note also Magid (*Hasidism* 337 n. 8), who critiques Tishby for ignoring the messianic arousal in Kotzk, Izbica, and other places.

30 Faierstein, *Hands* 104.

31 *MHs vol. 1* Vayeishev s.v. *vayeishev. Binyan 'adei 'ad* is an expression similar to others we have discussed that connotes ontological status. See endnote 222.

32 See *MHs vol. 1* Balak s.v. *ka'eit* and also *vol. 1* Shabbat s.v. *mai Hanukah,* cited in endnote 178.

33 In fact, the classical Hasidic concept of the *tzadik* plays virtually no role in *MHs.* See Faierstein, *Hands* 77, 81.

34 *MHs vol. 1* Balak s.v. *ka'eit.*

35 This reading of *MHs* is supported by Elior, 'Temurot' 48.

36 *MHs vol. 2* Ki Tisa s.v. *shishah.*

37 *MHs vol. 1* Balak s.v. *ki lo nahash.*

38 *MHs vol. 2* Ki Tisa s.v. *shishah.*

39 *MHs vol. 1* Balak s.v. *ki lo nahash.*

Chapter Thirteen
Paradox in *Mei Hashiloah*

The last issue we must explore, to which we have referred repeatedly, is the idea of paradox in *MHs*. We noted that the theme of paradox is prominent in a series of passages scattered throughout *MHs*, and that these passages in particular have been largely ignored by Izbica scholars.[1] These texts indicate that the embrace of paradox was a fundamental part of Lainer's theology as we have outlined it thus far. Not recognizing the central place of paradox in Lainer's system, scholars have for the most part interpreted him either as a radically theocentric determinist or as embracing radical human autonomy. Actually, as we have argued, neither is the case. Lainer embraces acosmic humanism, which asserts the radical presence of God as affirming and empowering the human, because the human substantively participates in God who lives and flows through people.

An important master's thesis was written in 1993 by Amira Lever about the place of paradox in the thought of Lainer's major student, Tzadok Hakohen. However, while Lever suggests that paradox is central to Tzadok, she does not consider it a substantive theme in *MHs*. She writes that in Lainer's thought, 'There is no emphasis on the paradoxical nature of things.'[2] While Lever recognizes that Tzadok embraces the dual perspectives of *mitzido* and *mitzideinu*, the divine and human perspectives respectively, she suggests that in *MHs* there is no such paradoxical embrace and that Lainer only affirms the ontic reality of *mitzido*.[3] Lever relies heavily on the textual snippets cited by Weiss, which indeed display a theocentric bias. A closer examination of the sources reveals paradox to be a central motif and that Lainer paradoxically embraces *mitzido* and *mitzideinu*, simultaneously. Indeed it would be strange for such a central theme to be so dominant in Tzadok and entirely absent in his teacher Mordechai Lainer.

We now turn to the texts of paradox in *MHs*. In the next several texts we will cite, which embrace the idea of radical paradox, the issue under discussion is *mikdash*, the Temple. Lainer understands the secret of the Temple to be no less than the paradox of acosmic humanism. Many passages indicate that the secret of acosmic humanism is the basis of the Wisdom of Solomon, and that Solomon intended the Temple to incarnate this wisdom.[4] In the first passage, the Talmudic text on which Lainer comments discusses why at certain times the *shofar* and the trumpets are blown in the Temple. Lainer reframes the issue in terms of why the *shofar* and the trumpets are both blown specifically in the Temple. Lainer states:

חצוצרות הוא אהבה וקול שופר הוא יראה והם הפכים, ולפני המלך ה' היינו במקום המקדש ששם הוא החיים האמיתים שם מתקשרים ומתאחדים יחד

> The trumpets represent *ahavah* 'love' and the...*shofar* is *yir'ah* 'fear', and they are *hafakhim* 'opposites'. And 'before the king, God' refers to the Temple, for there [in the Temple] is the place of true life, and there [the opposites] are bound up and integrated as one. [5]

In another passage referring to the priestly vestments in the Temple, specifically, the פעמון *pa'amon* 'bell' and רימון *rimon* (pomegranate ornament), Lainer comments: פעמון רומז על יראה...ורמון מורה על תקופות...שאף שיהיה להאדם תקופות עצום מ"מ יהיה בהתקופות יראה עצומה באמצע *pa'amon* alludes to *yir'ah*...and *rimon* teaches about *tekufot*...For even if a person has great *tekufot*, in the *tekufot* he should have great *yir'ah*.[6]

In a comment occasioned by one of the first verses about the tabernacle, Lainer states, commenting on a *midrash*:

בעניני העולם הזה אין בהם שני הפכים מתאחדים כאחד כי זהב הוא יראה וכסף הוא אהבה, לכן בשורשם המה שני הפכים ובשורשם אינם מתאחדים בעולם הזה, וכן שדה היא התפשטות וכרם הוא סדר כדאיתא בגמ' (ברכות סג:) כשנכנסו רבותינו לכרם ביבנה, אבל בד"ת נמצאים כל ההפכים ומתאחדים שם כאחד לעבוד בהם את השי"ת.

> In the matters of this world, two *hafakhim* 'opposites' do not merge as one, for gold refers to fear and silver refers to love. Similarly, *sadeh* 'field' refers to *hitpashtut* (expanded consciousness) and *kerem* refers to order, but in Torah we find that all opposites unite as one in the service of God.[7]

In all of these passages, the divine locus is capable of holding paradox. Love, *tekufot*, expanded consciousness, silver, and the field all represent one modality of service, which, as we have seen, is associated in *MHs* with the post-*berur* ability to access the will of God. In contrast, gold, limitation, and fear, all represent the way of the law, i.e., the general principles of Torah. These are the qualities of the pre-*berur* individual who lives with a sense of an empowered persona and who initially experiences the self as independent from the divine. Though these are profoundly contradictory religious modalities, paradoxically, both are necessary for service.

In general, paradox becomes whole in the divine place, be it Torah, Temple, or God's participation in the grace after meals. Lainer writes in this regard:

העניין בזה כדאיתא בגמ' (ברכות נח.) שאין דעתם דומה זה לזה ואין
פרצופיהן דומים זה לזה והנה כשיאכלו שלשה אז רואה השלישי שיש שני
דעות נפרדים והפכים, מזה מכיר שיש השי״ת שברא אלו ההפכים והשי״ת
הוא מאחדים

> The issue in the *Gemara* (*bBer.* 58a) is that 'people's perspective and faces are not similar to one another'…and so, when three people eat together, the third sees that there are two opposite and contradictory opinions, and from this recognizes that God creates these contradictions and God unites them.[8]

From the viewpoint of God, all paradox is resolved in the higher unity.

Lainer relates that *teshukah* allows a person 'to fulfill commandments that stand in stark opposition to each other, while the human intellect cannot grasp two opposites in one matter'.[9] The ability to maintain paradox, continues Lainer, allows a person 'to be drawn after the will of God…it is in this sense that the forefathers were called a chariot for the *Shekhinah*'. In this passage, we see that the ability to access the unmediated will of God (to be merged with a chariot for the *Shekhinah*) is bound up with the ability to hold paradox.[10]

In another passage, Lainer relates the Judah archetype to this same ability. Regarding the children of Leah and the children of Rachel, symbols in *MHs* for the Judah and Joseph archetypes respectively, Lainer states:

וכיון שהם מתנגדים אלו לאלו א״כ היאך יוכל להיות שכולם טובים…אכן
אהרן הכהן נשא אותם על כתיפיו…שכל אחד פועל במדתו גם למעלה
מדעתו ובעתו ובזמנו מכוין לרצון הש״י ואלו ואלו דברי אלהים חיים.

237

Since they contradict each other, how can it be that they are both good? Thus Aaron carried them both (the stones of remembrance, which according to Lainer represent Judah and Joseph) on his shoulders...For each one (i.e., both Joseph and Judah)...intends the will of God and these and these are the words of the living God.[11]

Finishing his passage with the classical Talmudic statement of pluralism, Lainer views the holding of paradox as that which allows us to affirm the religious ways of both Judah and Joseph. In a parallel passage, Lainer defines the ability to embrace both Solomon and Moses (who in this particular passage incarnate respectively, love, *tekufot*, and the Temple on one side, and the law, fear, and limitation on the other) as the essence of messianic consciousness.[12] Similarly, the quality of *hitnas'ut* (exalted uniqueness), which as we have seen is the expression of 'soul print' (the infinite uniqueness of every person), is in itself defined by Lainer as the ability to embrace paradox:

כי תשא שרומז על התנשאות למעלה להתכלל בשורשו, כי מזה הוא עיקר
ההתנשאות כשמאחד כל הנפרדים ונתכלל לשורשו

'When you shall raise' alludes to being raised up in order to be integrated in the source, for this is the essence of being raised up, when all things split apart are united and integrated in the source.[13]

According to Lainer, this is the essence of maintaining paradox. It means the ability to take two contradictory ideas, orientations, or concepts that are mutually exclusive, and to find their common root in the higher frame of reality that includes them both. In Lainer's phrase: ובאמת בהשקפה ראשונה נתראה כשני הפכים אבל באמת בשורשם אחד הם '...they look like two opposites but in truth in their root they are one'.[14] The higher frame of reality, according to Lainer, is God. The symbol that expresses this notion perhaps most often in *MHs* is the Temple incense, described in a Zoharic passage repeatedly adduced by Lainer as the 'incense of all'[15]; that is, the incense that integrates all of reality.[16] This is the holding of paradox, which, according to Lainer, forms the core of the *mikdash* and the acosmic humanism it symbolizes. This conception of paradox, explicitly embraced by Lainer, becomes the defining feature of his entire system.

Laughter and Paradox in *Mei Hashiloah:* An Excursus

One of the fascinating hidden structures containing the idea of paradox in Lainer's theology is laughter. Like paradox itself, this theme has until this point escaped the notice of Izbica scholars.

Lainer emerges from a long kabbalistic tradition that views laughter itself as both a faculty of perception and a very particular path of the spirit. This tradition dates back to *Sefer Yetzirah*,[17] which suggests that each of the twelve months of the Hebrew calendar corresponds to a particular faculty of perception. Of course, the author assumes that human beings possess not five but twelve major faculties of perception. The twelfth and highest month is the last month of the year, Adar, during which the rabbinic holiday of Purim falls. Not surprisingly, the faculty of perception for this month is laughter. Just as smell yields something that sight cannot, and so on, this implies that laughter allows us to grasp a dimension of reality that cannot be accessed through the other faculties.

The thesis I suggest is that according to the Kabbalists, laughter is the faculty of perception that enables us to hold paradox.[18] Most significantly, according to Lainer and his student Tzadok, the ability to maintain paradox is a mark of divinity and, perhaps, the most profound expression of redeemed consciousness. Peter Berger in part refers to this dimension of laughter when he suggests that laughter 'intends eternity'.[19]

Lainer refers to this sort of laughter[20] in four different passages. Three of these passages refer to his fundamental construct of the Judah archetype, who is able to intend the unmediated will of God that may even contradict the law, and the fourth passage refers to Isaac.[21] In the first three passages, Lainer explicitly relates laughter to a strange and humorous Talmudic passage in Tractate *Shabbat* and to an even stranger Zoharic text, which, interpreting the Talmudic passage, identifies King David as the בדחנא דמלכא *badhana demalka* 'Jester of the King'. To fully understand laughter in Lainer's theology, we will adduce and analyze these Talmudic and Zoharic passages, and then see how he uses these texts to explain the Judah archetype.

First, the Talmudic passage, which reads:

> R. Judah said in Rav's name: One should never [intentionally] put himself to the test, since David King of Israel did [so] and

failed. [David] said before [God], 'Master of the World! Why do we say [in prayer], "God of Abraham, God of Isaac, and God of Jacob," but not "God of David"?' He (God) replied: They were tried by Me, but you were not. [David] said: Master of the Universe, examine and try me, as it says, 'Examine me, O Lord, and try me' (Psalms 26:2). [God] answered: I will try you, and will grant you a special privilege; for I did not inform them [of the nature of their trial beforehand], but you I will tell. I will try you in a matter of adultery'. Straightaway [it says], 'And it came to pass that evening, David arose from off his bed', etc. R. Yohanan said: He changed his night bed to a day bed, but he forgot the rule: There is a small organ in man—if he satisfies it, it is hungry, while if he starves it, it is satisfied…Raba expounded: What is meant by the verse, 'Against You, You only, have I sinned, and done this evil in Your sight, so that You may be justified in Your words, and made right in Your judgment' (Psalms 51:6)? David said to the Holy One, blessed be He: You know full well that had I wished to suppress my desire, I could have done so. However, I said, 'Let people not say, "The servant triumphed over his Master"'. Raba expounded: What is meant by the verse, 'For I am ready to halt, and my sorrow is continually before me?' That Bathsheba, the daughter of Eliam, was predestined for David since the six days of Creation, but that she came to him with sorrow. And the school of R. Ishmael taught likewise: She was worthy (i.e., predestined) for David since the six days of Creation, but he enjoyed her before she was ripe.[22]

The Talmud tells an irreverent tale tinged with ironic humor. David is offended that in the daily prayers, the three patriarchs merit mention but he does not. God responds, 'They were tested by me and found worthy, and you were not'. David responds, 'Well then, test me, God'. God, apparently thinking that David will not pass the test, nonetheless assents, and even gives David an advantage by informing him that the test will involve his ability to withstand the temptation of adultery. David fails the test. However, apparently in response to God taking him to task, David offers a semi-comical defense of his actions. David says to God, 'You said I would fail the test and I said I would pass. It would be highly inappropriate had I been right and you been wrong. Therefore I had no choice but to fail the test in order to uphold your honor'.

The underlying issue behind this strange and somewhat comic exchange between David and God is actually one of weightiest issues in both Jewish and general thought: the relationship between free will and divine determinism or, in more classic medieval terms, between free will and divine foreknowledge. On one hand, the topic of the passage is a test of the kind that Abraham, Isaac, and Jacob underwent and passed, and for which they are rewarded, in part, by mention in the daily prayers. The very concept of a test that the human being can either pass or fail seems to assume free will. And yet God knows the result of the test before it occurs: David will fail. Moreover, David, in his seemingly irreverent dialogue with God, is pointing to the same paradox. In effect, David is saying that a person sometimes has no choice but to sin. As we have understood the passage, the logical paradox in such a statement is so glaring that the Talmudic writers can maintain its truth only through the container of laughter expressed through David's dialogue with God. This understanding of the passage is implicit in the *Zohar's* rereading of the dialogue between David and God:

> Come and see: Every artist, when he speaks, speaks through his art. David was the Jester of the King, and although he was in pain, since he was before the King he returned to his usual manner of jesting, so as to entertain the King. He said, 'Master of the world, I said "Examine me, O Lord, and test me", and You said that that I would not pass Your test. So I sinned, "so that You may be justified in Your words" (Psalms 51:6), and Your words be true. For if I had not sinned, my words would have been true and Your words would have been empty. Now that I have sinned, in order that Your words be true, I have created a place for Your words to be justified, and this is why I did it, "so that You may be justified in Your words, and made right in Your judgment"'. David returned to his art, and even in his suffering, spoke humorously to the King.

> We learned: David was not worthy of such a deed, for it was he who said, 'And my heart is empty within me' (Psalms 109:22), and that was in fact the case. But David said, 'The heart has two chambers. One has blood, the other breath. The one that fills with blood is the dwelling place of the evil inclination. But my heart is not like this, for it is empty, and I have given no place to the evil blood, so that the evil inclination could dwell there, and so my heart is truly empty, without

any evil dwelling there'. And since this is the case, David was not worthy of that sin that he sinned. It was only in order to provide a place for sinners to speak, as they will say, 'King David sinned, and returned, and the Holy One, blessed be He, forgave him—all the more so must this be the case with other people'. Concerning this it says, 'I will teach sinners Your ways, and sinners will return to You' (Psalms 51:15).[23]

The *Zohar* retells the Talmudic story. However, while the Talmud could be read in a more limited fashion, ignoring the humorous element we limned in our reading, the *Zohar* cannot. The *Zohar* explicitly suggests that the spiritual craft of David is to tell jokes before God; in fact, David is labeled by the *Zohar* 'the Jester of the King'. As in Shakespeare's King Lear, the Jester tells the truth to the king's face, the truth that everyone knows but no one voices. In the *Zohar* passage, David performs his divine service before the King by evoking the paradoxical truths that can perhaps only be held in the container of laughter. 'I could have controlled my inclination', says David, 'but I did not, "so that You may be justified in Your words"'; that is, in order not to make God a liar, since God had already declared that David would not pass the test. While in the Talmud the joke is implicit, in the *Zohar* it is made far clearer: 'I slept with her, for you, God, to fulfill God's will'.

This is, of course, the great paradox of sinning for the sake of God, which is a core theme in the writings of Tzadok and Lainer.[24] According to Lainer, God's will is fulfilled in its apparent violation; this is the paradox of acosmic humanism, which is, in some sense, a restatement by Lainer and Tzadok of the old paradox of divine foreknowledge and human free will.[25]

This passage describes a close relationship between laughter and paradox, which appears as a recurrent theme in several *Zoharic* passages.[26] The second part of the *Zohar* passage (beginning with the words 'We learned') introduces a new reading of the story which Lainer adapts for his idea of the Jester of the King. David says, 'My heart is empty'. 'Empty' here parallels the Buddhist conception of emptiness, expressed in Hasidic literature and in earlier Kabbalists as the experience of אין *ayin*.[27]

Now let us turn to *MHs* to examine two passages that utilize the motif of the Jester of the King. The context of the first is the *locus classicus* in *MHs* that contrasts the Judah and the Joseph archetypes, Judah being the highly paradoxical character who transcends the apparent law to fulfill the unmediated will of God. Joseph of course is the more linear character who adheres to the law in its classical forms.

Lainer states:

ויהודה הוא נגד שר המשקה כי דהע"ה נקרא בדחנא דמלכא ועל ניסך היין נשמעין שירי דוד, ובאמת ליהודה במעשה דתמר וכן בכל המעשים משבט יהודה הדומין לזה נתן בהם הש"י כח התאוה כ"כ עד שלא הי' באפשרותם להתגבר וכמו שמבואר שמלאך הממונה על התאוה הכריחו, ולכן לא לא עליו האשם במה שלא הי' יכול להתגבר על יצרו וזה פירוש בדחנא דמלכא היינו שמניח את עצמו להנצח מהש"י כמו שאמר דוד המלך ע"ה למען תצדק בדבריך למי נאה שיוצדק אני או אתה.

> Judah corresponds to the wine steward,[28] for King David is the Jester of the King…And this is so for Judah in the story of Tamar, and this is the case with all the deeds of the tribe of Judah that are similar to this: God gave them such strong desire that it was not in their capacity to overcome it…And this is the meaning of the Jester of the King…he allows himself to be defeated[29]…as King David said, 'so that You be justified in Your words'—for whom is it more appropriate to be right, me or You?[30]

Lainer, making use of the both the Talmud and the *Zohar*, suggests that fundamental to the Judah archetype is the idea of sin that is paradoxically the will of God. In Lainer's reading, David's heart is not only empty of all superficial human will experiencing itself as independent of God, but is also full of the divine will with which David consciously identifies. This finds particular expression in *MHs* in regard to actions for which one has no free will because the desire to sin is so overwhelming that it cannot be resisted. According to Lainer, this 'insuperable urge' (to use Joseph Weiss's wonderful phraseology of this Izbica motif)[31] is, paradoxically, itself the very indication that this act is really the will of God. This paradox, which lies at the core of Izbica, is identified with David, the classical Judah archetype figure. In effect, Lainer has taken the *Zohar's* reading of the dialogue between David and God after David's sin with Bathsheba and transformed it from an aggadic curiosity to one of the cornerstones of his highly paradoxical Judah archetype, who fulfills God's will not in overcoming his desire but rather by allowing himself to be overpowered by his desire, which he paradoxically understands to be the voice of God.[32]

243

Lainer's reading of the Jester of the King motif is consistent, and is expressed even more clearly in a second passage. The context is the distinction between the 'righteous' who, in this passage, are said to follow the general principles of law, and the 'straight of heart' whose 'hearts are drawn after the will of God'. Lainer states:

אף שעל הגוון נתראה שלפעמים יסור מדרך התורה גם זה הוא ברצון
השי״ת וכמו שאיתא בגמ' (שבת נ״ו.) כל האומר דוד חטא אינו אלא טועה
יען כי לבו היה נמשך אחר רצון השי״ת... וכמו שכתיב (תהלים נ״א, א')
למען תצדק בדברך...דלא לימרו עבדא זכי למריה .

> Even though on the surface it appears at times that he strays
> from the path of the Torah, this also is God's will, just as one
> finds in the Talmud, 'Whoever says David sinned is mistaken',
> because his heart was drawn after the will of God...As it is
> written, 'So that You may be justified in Your words' (Psalms
> 51:6)...'So that they should not say that the servant was more
> correct than his master' (bShab. 56a).[33]

In the conclusion of the passage, Lainer refers to all the texts we adduced above and again asserts that this is a description of the Judah archetype. Moreover, he explicitly relates these texts, with their notion of laughter embracing paradox, to his core distinction between one who is drawn after the will of God, and the general principles of the Torah. It is this energy of laughter that powers David's ability to give himself up to God and live in the great existential and logical paradox of acosmic humanism. It is this very laughter that powers the Judah archetype and allows it to directly access the will of God.

Finally, Lainer asserts in a third text[34] that each person in Israel must investigate oneself to know their true nature and to see whether one is like 'Judah, a jester of the King' or, implicitly, a Joseph persona who is bound by the normative law. In effect, Lainer is suggesting that there are two models of divine worship: the model of paradox held in the sacred container of laughter modeled by David who is the Jester of the King, and the model exemplified by Joseph who lives in yir'ah. According to Lainer, the higher mode of service is, as we have shown, the Judah model. For Lainer, a defining characteristic of redeemed consciousness, i.e., of acosmic humanism, is the ability to maintain paradox.

Notes for Chapter Thirteen

1 The exception is Elior, who, while not adducing most of these passages, is sensitive to the paradoxical nature of Lainer's thought. See above, endnote 775.

2 Lever, *Principles* 19, 45, 52.

3 Lever, *Principles* 69, 70.

4 See e.g. Source 18 in volume 2.

5 *MHs vol. 2* Rosh Hashanah s.v. *lifnei ha-melekh*.

6 *MHs vol. 2* Tetzaveh s.v. *pa'amon*.

7 *MHs vol. 2* Terumah, s.v. *vayik'hu* 2.

8 *MHs vol. 2* Berakhot s.v. *sheloshah she'akhlu*.

9 *MHs vol. 1* Behukotai s.v. *im* 3.

10 For an explanation of Jacob's spiritual development in terms of his ability to maintain paradox, see *MHs vol. 2* Vayishlah s.v. *vayifrotz*.

11 *MHs vol. 2* Tetzaveh s.v. *vesamta*.

12 *MHs vol. 1* Shoftim s.v. *shoftim* 2 (Source 7 in volume 2).

13 *MHs vol. 2* Ki Tisa s.v. *vayedaber*.

14 *MHs vol. 2* Bamidbar s.v. *tifkedu*.

15 See *Zohar* 3:224a.

16 See also *MHs vol. 1* Naso s.v. *yevarekhekha*.

17 *Sefer Yetzirah* Ch. 4.

18 Laughter seems to operate in much the same way as Arthur Koestler suggests. See *Insight* 37.

19 See Berger, *Redeeming*.

20 In addition to the three passages cited below, Lainer touches on this theme in *MHs vol. 2* Yitro s.v. *vayishma'* 3, where he refers to the more negative dimensions of laughter.

21 See *MHs vol. 1* Vayeira s.v. *vatekhaheish* for the passage on Isaac. The other three passages are adduced below. Weiss adduces this passage as well. See Weiss, 'Determinism' n. 13.

22 *bSanh.* 107a.

23 *Zohar* 2:107a.

24 See 'The *Menutzah* Sub-Cluster' of Cluster 6 in volume 2 for further discussion. Gellman (*The Fear* 45–71) suggests a distinction between Lainer and Tzadok in this regard.

25 Tzadok and Lainer's restatement of this old paradox in terms of *retzon Hashem* on one hand and human choice (which Lainer terms 'avodah) on the other, was also noticed by Lever (Paradoxical 139).

26 See also e.g. 3:47b, 1:103b.

27 On the concept of *ayin* in Hasidism, see the section on Hasidism in 'Ayin', Daniel Matt's excellent discussion of *ayin* in kabbalistic literature.

28 On the broader relationship of wine to the Judah archetype, see Cluster 6 in volume 2.

29 Being defeated by God is a basic idea in *MHs* which appears a number of times in what we term the '*Menutzah* Passages', which are analyzed as one 'sub-cluster' in volume 2, under Cluster 6.

30 *MHs vol. 1* Vayeishev s.v. *vayeishev* 1 (Source 44 in volume 2).

31 See Weiss, 'A Late Jewish Utopia' 228.

32 For a parallel reading of the Jester of the King motif in Lainer's student Tzadok, see *Tzidkat Hatzadik*. For a different reading of the Jester of the King in Nahman of Braslav, see Mark, 'Shigaon'. Also in Hasidic literature, see Sudilkov, *Degel Mahaneh Efrayim* Hayyei Sarah s.v. *o yomar* and Levi Isaac of Berdichev, *Kedushat Levi* Beshalah s.v. *Hashem yimlokh*.

33 *MHs vol. 2* Va'eira s.v. *vayikah* (Source 40 in volume 2).

34 *MHs vol. 2* Ki Tisa s.v. *shish*ah.

PART FOUR

Models for Acosmic Humanism
Within the Tradition of Kabbalah

Chapter Fourteen
Introduction

Part Four continues the general argument of this volume that Lainer is deeply rooted in sources that preceded him even as he extends them beyond their original intention, an argument to which we return in volume 3. We began in Part Two to analyze three strands in Jewish intellectual history that engendered Lainer's theory of individualism. In Part Three, we examined the theology of Lainer in relation to the primary texts and suggested a new term to characterize Lainer's thought, acosmic humanism. Now we turn to four models for Lainer's thought found in earlier texts, all four of which are rooted in personal revelation and the ability of the human to access unmediated divine will through the realization of his ontic identity with the divine. Just as the core humanistic principles that find expression in *MHs* are not unique to Lainer, the idea of substantive identity between God and human is not unique to Lainer.

Post-*Berur* Consciousness vs. *Unio Mystica:* The *Berur* and *Bitul* Models

Before we look at these models however, a number of differing constructs in Hebrew mysticism dealing with the ontic identity between human and God need to be examined. The primary one is *unio mystica,* which was a dominant tradition in many canonical Hasidic works forming the intellectual inheritance of all Hasidic masters in Lainer's generation.[1] Importantly for our purposes, Idel has gathered many texts demonstrating the strong embrace of *unio mystica* in mainstream Hasidism.[2] There was an important strand of Jewish sources prior to *MHs* in which the goal of religiosity was the realization of the original ontic identity between God and human. The shared ontology of the soul and God is what allows for *unio mystica,* or mystical attaching (*devekut*).

Lainer, who clearly affirms the ontic identity between human and God, shares much in common with these sources, but the differences are profound. We will term these different models for realizing the ontic identity of human and God the *berur* and the *bitul* models, representing, respectively, *MHs* and the *unio mystica* traditions.

A close examination of these models precludes collapsing *bitul* and *berur* into one general process. In the *unio mystica (bitul)* model, terms such as *devekut* 'attaching', *ayin* 'nothingness', and *bitul* 'nullification' are the reigning metaphors.[3] In the *berur* model these are glaringly absent. Beyond nomenclature, the *berur* and *bitul* models each comprise a very different *homo religiosus* and suggest diametrically opposed normative conclusions.

The *bitul* model is characterized by seven core characteristics, which we will outline using the terminology suggested by Idel and Matt. First, a 'transformation' of the person into a divine being occurs. The person must shed their corporeality in order to return to God.[4] Second, the process of transformation is typically some type of ecstatic process.[5] Third, ecstasy is intentionally aroused through some type of mystical technique.[6] Fourth, the result is attainment of *unio mystica* for what is usually a very short time.[7] Even though some teachers enjoin one to hold to this peak for as long as possible,[8] its character remains that of a peak experience and not a stable plateau. Fifth, essential to *bitul* is a process that has been referred to as annihilation or nullification.[9] In one early Hasidic source, it is expressed as follows: '...the branch arrives at its root, this [arrival] being a union with the root....as in the simile of a single drop which has fallen into the great sea...'[10] The sixth feature is that *unio mystica* is generally considered to be a highly impersonal process. Its 'radical impersonal stand',[11] in Idel's phrase, is not a detail but the essence of the experience, as we see in this quote from Schneur Zalman of Liadi:

> 'This is true attachment: [a person] becomes one substance
> with God into whom he was swallowed, without being sepa-
> rate from him to be a distinct entity at all. That is the meaning
> of the verse, "and you shall attach to him" (Deut. 13:5):
> [to attach] literally'.[12]

The seventh characteristic of *unio mystica* is that it is a fundamentally conservative doctrine.[13]

Berur differs from *bitul* in all seven of these salient characteristics. First, *berur*, as we have already noted, leads directly to antinomian conclusions. While Idel has already pointed out the essentially conservative character of *devekut* even in its extreme form of *unio mystica*, *berur* is highly radical and nonconservative in character. The essential achievement of *berur* is the ability to move beyond the *kelalei divrei Torah* and access the unmediated will of God, even if it contravenes the law.[14]

Second, nullification is not a major feature of *berur*. Both the content and language of *bitul* and *ayin* are virtually absent in *MHs*. Third, not only is self-nullification not part of *berur*, it actually is the opposite of the *berur* process, which is grounded in one's unique individuality.[15] A primary technique of *berur*, according to Lainer, is what we will term the intensification of uniqueness.[16] He states:

> הנה האדם צריך להביט ולהבין מימי עלומיו טרם יצרו גבר עליו בתקופות, צריך להבין לאיזה דבר גברה אז תאותו ומאיזה דבר רחק לבו ומזה ישכיל איזה דבר הכין לו הש״י לנסותו בה שיברר א״ע ובדבר הזה צריך להתגבר ולשמור, כי לכל אדם חלק הש״י דבר מיוחד למען יברר א״ע בה והאדם צריך לבוא על בירר איזה דבר השייך לו

> From the time of a person's youth, before his desire can overcome him with *tekufot*, he must examine and understand towards what his passion [uniquely] forces him and from what does his heart repel him. From this he will understand what God challenges him with, through which he needs to clarify himself…For God has given every person something unique through which he must clarify himself. So a person must come to clarify what is uniquely related to him…[17]

If the technique for achieving *unio mystica* is annihilating the unique self, the technique for achieving *berur* is identifying the unique self. This is the portal to the consciousness of ontic identity between human and God. Fourth, *berur* is not a fragile or ephemeral state achieved for a short duration, but rather a relatively stable stage of consciousness.[18] Whether one emphasizes the linear model present in some *MHs* passages where *berur* is achieved permanently, or the dynamic model where one might move back and forth between levels, the *berur* state is not dependent on annihilation or leaving corporeality behind. Therefore, it would make sense for it to be a far more stable state. According to one Lainer passage, true wisdom is distinguishing whether one is at present in a Judah or a Joseph state of consciousness. The implication would be that even if *berur*-consciousness does change, it nevertheless endures for some stable period of time.[19]

At the same time, similarities exist between *berur* and *bitul*. In both, a stage of enlightenment is achieved, whether through psychological introspection in the case of *berur* or mystical technique leading to annihilation in the case of *bitul*. In both, at some point that state recedes and one returns to normal consciousness.

Regarding the seventh distinction, namely, the pronounced absence of an ecstatic dimension in *berur*, an anti-ecstatic strand does run throughout much of *MHs*. For example:

> אכן באמת צריך האדם לראות שיהיה לו ישוב הדעת ומתינות בכל דבר,
> שזה נקרא תדיר כמבואר בחלק ראשון (פרשת משפטים ד"ה ראשית בכורי
> אדמתך ובליקוטי הושע ד"ה אשור) אכן לפעמים צריך האדם להשתמש
> במדה מהירות, שימסור נפשו ולא יהיה לו שום מתינות בזה ואז נקרא זאת
> מקודש כמבואר שם, והנה בדורות הראשונים היה חפץ השי"ת בעבודה
> במסירות נפש עצום, ולכן יכון שהשתמשו בזה המדה במקום שהשי"ת חפץ
> בה לכן אתרחיש להו ניסא היפך מדרך הטבע, אכן אחר כן חפץ השי"ת
> בעבודה בישוב הדעת ומתינות

A person must...employ *yishuv ha-da'at* mental stability (or, balance) and *metinut* judiciousness in every matter...In earlier generations, a person had to employ the quality of *mehirut* swiftness (i.e., an impulsive and ecstatic quality that is the opposite of *metinut*)...God wanted to be worshipped with intense *mesirut nefesh* (lit., 'giving over of the soul'; often implying ecstasy and rapture in Hasidic texts)...[Now, however,] God desires worship with *yishuv ha-da'at* and *metinut*...[20]

While the goals of both ecstatic *bitul* and *berur* may be the same, that is, the realized ontic identity between human and God, *berur* can be conceived of as both a safeguard against and an alternative to ecstasy. One of Lainer's key passages on the precise method of *berur*[21] is set in precisely such a context. When Jacob receives the news that his son Joseph is alive, he is, naturally, ecstatic. However, Lainer is mistrustful of overwhelming emotion and suggests four stages of *berur*. The four stages are: (1) The interruption of pleasure in order to internalize an awareness of its impermanent and transitory nature; (2) the study of sacred text, which provokes the awareness that the same pleasure that one is sacrificing can be found in the realm of the sacred; (3) the cultivation of the awareness that everyone is where they need to be, everyone has their own place, and there is no need to usurp the place of another; and (4) an actual visualizing of the day of one's death.

If, after *berur*, one still feels the strong emotion, in this case Jacob's ecstasy, one can be assured that is the will of God.

Berur (introspection) is focused on an individual's appreciation of their own state of being in the world and is more existential than metaphysical.

Besides the aforementioned text, two other *MHs* passages detailing the actual process of *berur* all reflect the same nonecstatic sensibility. In one passage, three types of *berur* are enjoined as a kind of litmus test to ascertain whether an act is *retzon Hashem*. One's action must not cause damage to self, community, or God. If the act meets these three standards, it is considered to be clarified as the will of God. Once one is sure that one is doing the will of God, post-*berur*, then, paradoxically, 'one may act in accordance with the desire of his heart'.[22]

In the last passage we will adduce on the methodology of *berur*, the nature of the process is broadened beyond the psychological to the metaphysical.[23] Here, Lainer suggests five distinct stages of *berur*. (1) clarifying that everything in the world is included in the unity of God, (2) clarifying that one is willing to abandon the pleasures of the world for the sake of loving God, (3) clarifying one's commitment to serve God with all of one's passion even if one does not feel any lack that needs to be filled, (4) committing to accept in trust, with no anxiety, all that God gives them, and (5) committing not to give honor to those who hate the divine. However, it is not clear in the passage how one goes about these clarifications. The process seems to involve some combination of intellect, affirmation, and perhaps also process of meditation and prayer.

All these passages, of course, deal with anomian *berur*. The second form of *berur* in *MHs* is accomplished through the classic system of study and commandments. Like its anomian counterpart, the performance of *mitzvot* 'commandments', often termed by Lainer *yegi'a* 'effort' and *'avodah* 'work', is not particularly ecstatic.

These seven characteristics, taken together, affirm acosmic humanism as central to understanding Lainer's theology. Ultimately *bitul* and *berur* create different religious types with *berur* being far more humanistic and anthropocentric in its sensibilities and *bitul* being far more theocentric. Thus, while related to the older traditions, *berur* can be seen as a distinct departure from them.

The Matrix of Apotheosis

With these caveats, we can examine *unio mystica* and traditional motifs of apotheosis as bases for related notions in Lainer. In fact, Lainer (and Abraham Kook, who was highly influenced by him)[24] may represent the latest stage in this great Jewish rabbinic and mystical tradition.

Unio mystica is, in Idel's phrase, a 'certain kind of apotheosis'[25] in which a person is in some sense 'transformed into God'.[26] This idea may be traced to the starting point of the apotheosis tradition in the ancient Hebrew myth of Hanokh-Metatron.[27] Scholem has already pointed out the affinity between the Hanokh tradition and the *yordei merkavah* (the formal term for ancient Hebrew *merkavah* mystics).[28] Hanokh, who first appears in the Bible, is demonized in rabbinic material and then reintroduced as a mystical hero in the Heikhalot literature.[29] Idel regards the Hanokh-Metatron tradition as a crucial antecedent to both the *unio mystica* tradition of Abulafia and the *unio erotica* (*zivug 'im ha-Shekhinah*) tradition of the *Zohar*.[30] This tradition, while not cited directly by Lainer, is cited by his student Tzadok Hakohen.[31] Tzadok cites the Hanokh tradition as an example of what we have termed acosmic humanism. He describes Hanokh both as the realization that all human action is animated by God, and as a model for the erotic merger with *Shekhinah*. Hanok was also central to the canonical Hasidic works which Lainer would have studied.[32]

All the models we will discuss below suggesting or implying ontic identity between man and God may be traced back to this myth.[33] By understanding something of the place of apotheosis in Jewish intellectual history, we can place Lainer's radical theology in the context of this larger current of thought.

Moshe Idel outlines two basic models in Hebrew myth.[34] The first model focuses on the human's response to the revelation of divine will. At the model's center are concepts of history and commandment. God descends to reveal Himself to the human and the world.

The second model focuses less on God's descent and more on the human being's ascent to the divine, or alternatively, the human being's immersion in the depths of the divine.[35] This strand is ultimately expressed by the human desire to become God or to unite with the divine realm manifesting by the human becoming an angel or similar being, through *unio mystica* or through the human identification with a divine *sefirah*.[36]

254

The Hanokh-Metatron tradition is important for our discussion because it affirms the possibility of the ontic identity between human and God.[37] It is particularly relevant to *MHs* because the subtext of the Hanokh story is the ability to, in Idel's phrase, gain 'unmediated access to God'.[38] While this tradition is not antinomian, it does, in many interpretations, take an ano-mian position, suggesting that the will of God can be best served through channels other than the 'four cubits' of the law.[39] Furthermore, Hasidism, rooted in older kabbalistic tradition, transforms the Hanokh-Metatron tradition of one who merges with God into the tradition of 'Hanokh the Mystical Cobbler', in which Hanokh, by stitching shoes, stitches together heaven and earth. Isaac of Acre notes that Hanokh the Cobbler is an ex-plicit interpretation of the old Hanokh-Metatron tradition.[40] Finally, in the earliest versions of this myth, what allows Hanokh to access unmedi-ated divinity is his great love of God.[41] Love as a vehicle for accessing un-mediated divinity is, as we have seen, a major motif in *MHs*. In this sense the mystical Hanokh the Cobbler tradition, which is a very central motif in pre-Lainer Hasidic texts,[42] can be viewed as a foreshadowing of Lainer's own position.[43]

The story begins with an ambiguous biblical verse: 'Hanokh walked with God and he is no more for God has taken him' (Gen. 5:25). In *Hanokh Hashelishi*, this is taken to mean that the human being Hanokh is tak-en to the heavenly realms and transformed into a semidivine or even di-vine being, Metatron.[44] In the *Hanokh Hashelishi* text, discussed in Dan, Hanokh/Metatron relates that '[God] called me *YHVH Ha-katan* "the small God" before all of His court on high, as it is written, "for my name is in him" (Exod. 23:21)'.[45]

The power and even seductive quality of this myth lies in its blurring of the lines between the human and divine and its affirmation of the virtually infinite potential of the human.[46] At this point we will examine several mo-tifs in this tradition that foreshadow important themes in *MHs's* theology of acosmic humanism.

Metatron, like God, sits on a divine throne, wears a crown, and has a light hovering above him.[47] Hanokh/Metatron unites the lower and higher worlds as well as the lower and higher wisdoms,[48] and all the secrets of creation are known to him.[49] Metatron, in much of kabbalistic literature, is also a symbol for *Shekhinah*.[50] In effect, Hanokh's merging with Metatron is a precursor of the Zoharic idea of the human being erotically merging with the *Shekhinah*.[51] (Solomon plays a similar role, as we will discuss in volume 2.[52]) As we have noted and will expand on below, merging with the *Shekhinah* is a core matrix for Lainer's thought. According to Lainer, the human ability to access the unmediated *retzon Hashem* is the same as the embrace of the *Shekhinah*.[53]

Another motif, found in the *Tikunei Zohar* literature, views Metatron as a kind of 'surrogate lover' for the *Shekhinah* during the exile, when her divine lover is separated from her. In a radical twist on the Talmudic passage that enjoins us not to 'replace' God with Metatron, *Tikunei Zohar* suggests that in exile, Metatron has in fact replaced God. Metatron stems from the Tree of Knowledge, is called the עבד *'eved* (servant), and is an expression of post-Eden duality. This implies a certain danger, expressed in a little-noticed *Tikunei Zohar* text, that Metatron may go over to the other side and become identified with Satan.[54] One of the theurgic tasks of the *tzadik* (synonymous with the *sefirah* of *Yesod*) is to 'replace the replacement'—that is, to replace Metatron as the divine lover of the *Shekhinah*.[55] This theme is particularly important because, as we shall show below, Lainer's concept of the Judah archetype is in part a democratization of the apotheosis of the *tzadik* in Hasidism. This apotheosis itself, as we have seen, is an unfolding of the earlier Hanokh-Metatron myth;[56] Hanokh is identified with the figure of the *tzadik*.[57] As we shall see below, the apotheosis of the *tzadik* in its democratized form is a fundamental matrix of acosmic humanism, expressed by Lainer in the Judah archetype. Whereas in earlier Hasidic literature, the erotic merger with the *Shekhinah* was the role of the *tzadik*, who was often identified with the *sefirah* of *yesod*, in Lainer's teachings that role is assumed by the Judah archetype, which is potentially in every person.

Metatron is also identified in kabbalistic sources with the *sefirah* of *Binah*.[58] In *MHs*, as we have seen, access to *binah*, i.e. to the *sefirah* of *binah*, is synonymous with *retzon Hashem*, that quality that allows the Judah archetype to transcend the law.[59]

Moreover, Hanokh is described as a kind of '*adam kelali*', an archetypal person who encompasses within him all other souls.[60] Precisely the same kind of description is used by Lainer in the previously cited passage regarding the Judah archetype.

Another feature of the apotheosis tradition that is important in our context is that in the conception of *Heikhalot* mysticism, mystics who reach the divine retain their individuality.[61] While this is a very different model than that suggested by Lainer, it is still worth noting that inclusion of the individual in the Godhead does not make the individual disappear.

The most dramatic feature of the apotheosis of Metatron that reappears in slightly different form in *MHs* is the human incarnation of the divine name, which we will explore in detail below.[62] For now it is sufficient to notice that the idea of the human being incarnating the divine name is clearly foreshadowed in the ancient tradition of the apotheosis of Hanokh to Metatron, who is said to incarnate the name of God (כי שמי בקרבו *ki shemi bekirbo*[63]). As we have seen, the ontological identity of the human and divine names is critical to the edifice of Lainer's acosmic humanism is built. We have cited above the most important appearance of this name motif, where Metatron is described as '*YHVH Ha-katan*'. In the unfolding of the Hanokh-Metatron tradition, the blurring of the human and divine names (the unification of names) remains an idea that recurs repeatedly in different forms.[64]

For example, commenting on the biblical verse 'And to Moses He said, Come up to God',[65] the Talmud asks why does it not say 'Come up to Me', answering that 'to God' refers to Metatron, who has the characteristic שמו כשם רבו *shemo keshem rabo* (his name and God's are the same).[66] The rabbis in the Talmud are not surprisingly concerned lest Metatron be confused with God. They interpret the biblical verse that speaks about the angel God sends to guide Israel in the desert (Exod. 23:21) as an allusion to Metatron. While the verse reads: אל תמר בו כי שמי בקרבו *al tamer bo ki shemi bekirbo* 'do not rebel against him, for My name is within him', in our context, the Talmud reads these words as אל תמרני בו *al temireini bo* 'do not exchange Me for him', for there was an immediate danger that the people would do just that.

At this point we turn to the four models of apotheosis that are explicitly adduced by Lainer as matrices for his acosmic humanism. As we shall see, virtually all of the major themes in the Metatron tradition of apotheosis are echoed in *MHs*. In fact, Lainer's theology can be viewed as one of the last expressions of the ancient Hebrew tradition of apotheosis.

Model One: The Name of God

The first model for acosmic humanism in *MHs*, for which we have adduced many sources above, is the name model. This model teaches that the
human being incarnates the divine name, or that the human name and divine name merge in ontic identity. This concept, as we have already seen in
regard to the apotheosis of Hanokh, is deeply rooted in classical Kabbalah.

In his pioneering study of the name of God in kabbalistic literature,
Gershom Scholem points out that the name of God is far more than a
mere human appellation of divinity. Rather, the name of God is the metaphysical origin of all language, which in turn is the origin of all reality. This
is so because, for the kabbalist, language is the DNA-like essence of the
universe.[67] Scholem reminds us that for the mystic, the human name is not
a mere divine appellation or description. Rather, 'a close and substantial
relation exists between the name and the name's bearer'.[68] The potency of
names lies not in their appellative character but rather, in Joseph Dan's
phrase, 'in their intimate meta-linguistic relationship to the mystical divine being'.[69] In Dan's analysis, name is not only associated with essence,
but also with the unique essence of that being named.[70] Here we see that
Lainer's identification of name and uniqueness, although more highly pronounced than in previous sources, is nonetheless rooted in old kabbalistic
traditions.

The name is God's incarnation in the world, and the place of the name is
the Temple in Jerusalem.[71] In the central ritual of the Yom Kippur liturgy,
the peak expression of *mikdash*-consciousness was the high priest calling
out the name.[72] Therefore, it is not surprising that, according to kabbalistic
tradition, a particularly pristine prism in which the name of God is revealed in the world is the human being, who incarnates the name of God
in the human name.[73] As we have noted, the Temple for Lainer is a primary
symbol for acosmic humanism. The Temple is where the human and divine
names blur into one.[74] This basic principle of acosmic humanism is the
core of Solomon's wisdom, according to Lainer.

The *Midrash* states that whenever Song of Songs refers to Solomon
(*Shelomoh*), it refers not to King Solomon but to מלך שהשלום שלו *melekh
sheha-shalom shelo* 'The King to whom peace belongs',[75] that is to say, God.
From the perspective of later Kabbalah, this means that Solomon's very
name incarnates divinity. In this sense, the names of God and the name

of man merge. In Idel's words, 'The names are intended to bring about the ontic identification between the human and the divine.'[76] In Solomon's Temple, according to some Zoharic texts,[77] the high priest on Yom Kippur would merge with the *Shekhinah* in sacred union. The expression of this union was the calling out of the Tetragrammaton, the explicit name of God. In the rabbinic tradition, after the destruction of the Temple, the name of God is 'completely withdrawn into the realm of the ineffable.'[78] However, for Lainer, who views himself as the inheritor of Solomon's wisdom, God's name is accessible in the world through the prism of the human name incarnating the name of God.[79] This is the essence of acosmic humanism. Attaching to the name is an essential part of early kabbalistic descriptions of *deveikut*. According to Nahmanides, through attaching to the name, the human unifies with divinity or with the higher spiritual world, and is thus able to perform miracles.[80] According to Elijah da Vidas, the *tzadik* who attaches to the Tetragrammaton 'even after death is considered alive' as a function of attaching to the divine name.[81] One can receive new revelation[82] or can even know the future, through recitation of the divine name. The implication, of course, is that attaching to the divine name involves the human being's accessing of divinity, which invests one with power beyond one's natural human potency.

The sources describing attachment also often describe what is referred to as 'unifying' the divine name, as in the following commentary from Meir Ibn Gabai:

> ...the worshiper ought to contemplate and intend during his worship to unify the great name and join it by its letters... and to unify them his thought....And thereby the person who unifies will attach to the great name.[83]

While these passages do not clearly discuss the identity of names between human and God, the first glimmerings of such a notion are already evident. Idel's reading of an Isaac the Blind text is instructive: 'By the act of contemplation...of the...divine name, human thought is filled with these contents and presumably becomes identical with them.'[84]

Idel's reading of these sources as what he calls 'an interiorization of the Divine'[85] foreshadows the direction in which Lainer will take this tradition. The mystical technique of unifying the name involves a process of integration within the human being, a process which in turn also takes place within God. While this could be explained in terms of structural affinity between the human and the divine,[86] and not in terms of identity, the line between the two is very thin. In the kabbalistic presentation of these sources,[87] unification of the name is a theocentric process often having theurgic implications, effecting a healing reorganization of the intradivine world.[88]

Abulafia, whose teachings were transmitted to many other kabbalistic readers as well as the Hasidic masters, through Cordovero's citation of his ideas in this regard,[89] understands the recitation of divine names as an essential part of the process of *unio mystica*.[90] Moreover, he understood the Kabbalah of divine names to be an integral part of the unfolding messianic process. In fact, such a relationship between messianic consciousness and divine names was read into the biblical verse that is recited at the end of the עלינו *Aleinu* prayer: 'God will become king over the entire world; On that day He will be one and His name will be one'.[91] Lainer's concept of the ontic identity of the human and divine names has clear messianic implications,[92] though this process was in no way reserved only for the eschaton. The unification of the name runs as a theme through much of Hebrew mysticism in both nomian and anomian forms.[93] Much of prayer, including classic prayers such as שמע shema'[94] and קדיש *kaddish*,[95] has been understood as intending to unify the human being with the divine name; even the entire spiritual project of the commandments could be seen this way.[96] In Idel's language, 'the way of names unifies human with divine thought'.[97]

We close this perusal of sources with a passage from Abulafia.[98] Abulafia points out that the union of divine love and human love—each symbolized by אחד *ehad* 'one', which has a numerical value of thirteen—in *unio mystica* yields twenty-six, which is the numerical value of the Tetragrammaton, the four-letter name of God. He implies that the union of God and human yields the divine name. Idel interprets this source as saying that 'the human existence is included in the divine name'.[99]

We turn now to several kabbalistic and Hasidic sources that have not been adduced heretofore by scholars in this regard, which suggest even more explicitly the ontic identity of the human and divine names.

Source One: *Zohar*

One critical source for Lainer, arguably quintessential in establishing the concept of ontic identity between the human and God names, is found in the Idra Raba section of the *Zohar*. Commenting on Psalm 118, the *Zohar* states the following:

ות"ח רזא דמלה דבכל אתר דאדכר אדם הכא לא אדכר אלא בשמא
קדישא. דהכי אתחזי משום דלא אקרי (הוה) אדם אלא במה דאתחזי ליה.
ומאי אתחזי ליה. שמא קדישא. דכתיב וייצר יי אלקים את האדם בשם מלא
דהוא יי אלקים כמה דאתחזי ליה...ומה דאמר מה יעשה לי אדם הכי הוא.
דתנא כל אינון כתרין קדישין דמלכא כד אתתקנן בתקונוי אתקרון אדם
דיוקנא דכליל כלא

Come and see: The secret of the matter [in the verses of this Psalm] is that whenever *adam* man is mentioned here, he is only mentioned [together] with the divine name. And this is fitting, for *adam* would only called by what is fitting... [which is] the holy name. As it is written, 'And *YHVH Elohim* formed man' (Gen. 2:7). This contains the complete name, as is fitting for him (man). ... And regarding the statement, 'What can *adam* do to me?' (Psalms 118:6) we learned: All these holy crowns of the King, when they are repaired with their *tikunim*, are called *adam*, the image that contains all.[100]

The name of humanity, *adam*, both contains and is God's full name. This can occur because the human image, which is the name, includes everything, that is, all names and all images. As the Idra itself says when speaking of Ezekiel's vision:

ועל דמות הכסא דמות כמראה אדם עליו מלמעלה. כמראה אדם דכליל כל
דיוקנין. כמראה אדם דכליל כל שמהן

[Concerning the verse] '...an image like the appearance of a human being *kemar adam* on [the throne] from above' (Ezek. 1:26)—like the appearance of a human being, which includes all images; like the appearance of a human being, which includes all names.[101]

Source Two: Avodat Hakodesh

We find a later source for the ontic identity of the human and the divine names in Meir Ibn Gabai's monumental work, *Avodat Hakodesh*. Here Israel, in her uniqueness, is seen as an ineradicable part, an expression, of the divine name:

לכן קבע במפתח ההוא שלשלת והוא שלשלת הייחוד סוד האצילות...
שנשתלשלו משם, והם חלקו מיוחדים לו, והוא השם הגדול המיוחד שהוא
משותף בהם ובו הם חיים...כי הם חלק יי ונחלתו...ולזה אמר והכריתו את
שמנו ומה תעשה לשמך הגדול כביכול שאין השם שלם אלא בהם, ולזה אי
איפשר בהם החלוף ולא הכליון, כי הם צורך גבוה והגבוה צרכם

He therefore secured with that key a chain, which is the
chain (or, process) of unification, the secret of emanation that
evolves from there, and they (Israel) are a part of it, unique to
it, and it is the great and unique name which participates in
them, and through it they live, 'For they are a part of God and
His inheritance'(Deut. 32:9). And because of this it says, 'And
[if] they cut off our name, what will be of Your great name?'
(Jos. 7:9), for it is as if the name cannot be complete except
through them. For this reason, it is impossible that [Israel]
will ever be exchanged or totally destroyed, for...the Most
High needs them.[102]

In the view of Meir Ibn Gabai, it is not only the human who is affected by
God's choosing to make Israel partner to His divine name. God Himself
would be vulnerable if Israel were to be destroyed, for He has made the
Jewish people part of His name. Ibn Gabai directly foreshadows in the text
the idea of a human being as a *helek*, part of God, which as we have seen is
so central to Lainer's acosmic humanism.[103]

Source Three: Degel Mahaneh Efrayim

I conclude with a citation from the work of the grandson of the Baal Shem
Tov, Efrayim of Sudilkov, who makes clear the ontic identity of the human
and the divine names.[104] He writes:

כי האדם הוא הקב"ה בחינת שם הוי"ה ב"ה במילוי מ"ה מספר אדם
ואורייתא היא ברמ"ח מצוות עשה ושס"ה מצוות לא תעשה ומשם נמשך
האדם דלתתא בבחינת רמ"ח אברים ושס"ה גידים וכשאדם עוסק בתורה
לשמה לשמור ולעשות אזי מקרב כל אבריו לשורשם מהיכן שנמשכו ונתהוו
היינו אל התורה ונעשה כל אבר שלו מרכבה למצוה פרטי המתייחס לאותו
אבר ונעשה הוא והתורה אחד ביחוד ואחדות גמור כמו יחוד איש ואשה

Man (or 'humanity') is the Holy One, an aspect of the name
YHVH in the full spelling [that adds up to] forty-five, which

262

is the numerical value of *Adam*. And the Torah is [composed of] 248 positive commandments and 365 interdictions, and man below develops from there, [so that he has] 248 limbs and 365 connective tendons. And therefore, when a person *adam* studies Torah for the sake of her name…he and the Torah become one in unification, in a complete union, like the unification of a man and woman.[105]

In this text there is a clear ontic identity between the name of man, *adam*, the name of God, and the text of the Torah. The mystical study of Torah is the realization of the 'trinity' of God's three names: God, Torah, and Israel.[106]

Earlier Kabbalistic Sources for the Phrase
Nikra 'Al Shemo

The term *nikra 'al shemo*, which, as we have seen, is a key phrase in Lainer's acosmic humanism, indicating the ontic identity between man and God, can also be traced to kabbalistic sources, where it expresses the idea that when either God or a person manifests the attribute of a specific *sefirah*, they may be called by the name of that *sefirah*.[107] In the context of *MHs*, we mention two sources, one from *Tikunei Zohar*, and the other a lesser-known passage from *Zohar Harakiya*, in which this concept is developed towards its usage in *MHs*. The *Tikunei Zohar* source reads:

אבל בזמן שצריך קודשא בריך הוא להצדיק לצדיק, ולעשות עמו צדקה
שהיא מלכות, עם התחתונים, נכללים בו כל הספירות, ונקראין צדיקים על
שמו, ה׳ נקרא על שמו צדיק

…[W]hen the Holy One, blessed be, needs *lehatzdik* to rectify the *tzadik* righteous one and to do for (or, through) him *tzedakah* charity, which is *Malkhut*, with the lower worlds (signifying the union of the feminine *tzedakah/Malkhut* with the masculine *tzadik/yesod*), then all the *sefirot* are contained within him, and they (i.e., the *sefirot*) are called by his name, *tzadikim* 'righteous', and *Hashem* is called *'al shemo* by his name *tzadik* (i.e., by the name of the *sefirah* of *yesod*, which is *tzadik*).[108]

In this passage we see how *nikra 'al shemo* is used as an expression of the ontic identity that occurs when divine and human agency merge.

Hayyim Vital takes this concept yet another step further, in *Zohar Harakiya*:

כי השפעת הנשמות מלמעלה הוא חסד אל לתקנם בעולם הזה כדי שנזכה
לעולם הבא לאכול מדילהון ולא במתנה כנודע כי זה הוא כוונת בריאות
העולם...עכ"ז כל המצווה שאדם עושה יהיה על שמו והקרן קיימת לעולם
הבא

> For the divine flux of souls from above is a kindness of God, in order to fix them in this world, so that they can merit the world-to-come, to eat of their own [work] and not as a gift … therefore, any *mitzvah* that a person does will be *'al shemo* in his name, and 'the principal [amount of his reward] remains for him in the world-to-come'.[109]

In a passage following this one, we see where this may lead:

ויהיה לו יצר טוב ויצר הרע להיות בעל בחירה ולהיות זכויותיו מעשה ידיו
ולא במתנה...ולסיבה זו גם הוכרח לתת הקב"ה כח גדול ביצר הרע שהם
הקליפות כדי שיפותתו ויסיתוהו...ולכן אין צדיק בארץ אשר יעשה טוב
ולא יחטא כי הוא מוכרח לחטוא כדי שיהא בעל בחירה

> [A person] has a good inclination and an evil inclination in order to be one who can choose, so that his merits will be the work of his hands, and not a gift from His blessed hand… For this reason, the Holy One, blessed be He, had to instill great power in the evil inclination…and therefore, 'There is no righteous man on earth who can do good and not sin' (Eccl. 7:20), for he is compelled to sin in order to have free choice.[110]

Hayyim Vital's notion of necessary sin, which he connects to the idea of a human being's work being *nikra 'al shemo*, closely parallels the logic of *MHs*.

A final source worth noting, also by Hayyim Vital,[111] suggests that by identifying and healing one's unique *hisaron*, one attains the level of *nikra 'al shemo*. Vital, writing in Luria's name, clearly suggests that one's divine nature is realized through taking one's natural place in the divine

264

anthropos. This text, besides being a vital source for Lainer's own concept of *hisaron*[112]—which, as we have seen, is connected with the human being attaining his true name[113]—affirms our interpretation of *nikra 'al shemo* as concerning the ontic identity of names between human and God. These sources make clear that Lainer's concept of ontic identity between human and divine name is both original *and* deeply rooted in previous kabbalistic traditions. Without careful reading, these sources might be easily understood to be relating to the divine name as a force outside the locus of the human being, a transcendent entity. However, Idel's and other scholars' close readings, as well as the new sources we have cited, show otherwise. We therefore conclude that identity of human and divine name emerges from this strand of tradition.

Gershom Henokh, Lainer's editor and grandson, goes to some effort to conceal this radical teaching and others in *MHs*. Only upon carefully gathering and reading the sources does the dramatic position of Lainer become fully clear. The ontic identity of the divine and human is part of the great 'secret of the name' in the mystical tradition. In Lainer's unique reading, it is the empowering secret of acosmic humanism. Lainer subtly subverts to his humanistic vision the tradition that both the human being and the Torah are, at their root, incarnations of the divine name.[114]

Model Two: God, Torah, and Israel are One

Gershom Scholem suggests that the 'last and most radical step in the development of this principle of the infinite meanings of the Torah was taken by the Palestinian School of Kabbalists who flourished in 16th-century Safed'.[115] Our discussion in this section, however, will make it clear that Lainer extended the principle of the infinite meanings of the Torah one crucial and radical step farther than even the most extreme formulation of the Safed School.

The classic interpretation of the identity of God and Torah is, as just noted, that the Torah is indeed the name of God. In Dan's phrase, God 'not only inspired the scriptures…but He himself (the divine name) exists in the scriptures'.[116] The connection between human and Torah was dramatically extended and deepened by the kabbalistic dictum that 'God, Torah, and Israel are one'. What emerges from this dictum is that both the human being and the Torah are ontologically equal; if the Torah is indeed the name of God, then so too is Israel.

Based on the inner logic of these ideas, God's will, as refracted through His name, should have the potential to become incarnate in a human being in a manner equal in value, and perhaps even prior to, the will of God incarnated in the sacred texts. One might even venture to base the priority of the former on its dynamic quality versus the seemingly static quality of the latter. The first thinker to actually draw this conclusion from the sources is Lainer. He accomplished this in part by breaking the dependency of the interpreter on the text. In Lainer's view, the interpreter can access their own 'letter in the Torah' through direct access to the divine will—without the mediating body of the text. This is precisely the radical step that Lainer takes in *MHs*.

The second model for acosmic humanism, which is explicit in at least two Lainer sources and implicit in many other sources, is this kabbalistic dictum assumed by Lainer to be Zoharic in origin: 'God, Torah, and Israel are one'.[117] Lainer cites this dictum 'God, Torah, and Israel are one'[118] as an explanation for the essential idea in his theology that Israel can transcend the *taryag mitzvot*, which are termed in the passage from the *Zohar* that he cites תרי"ג עיטין *taryag 'itin* 'the six hundred and thirteen suggestions'.[119] For the *Zohar*, the *mitzvot* are not only commandments, but are also *'itin*, directional guides to *devekut*.[120] In a similar vein, for Lainer, the primary purpose of *mitzvot* is to catalyze the process of *berur*, after which one can access the unmediated *retzon Hashem*.[121]

Lainer also cites this dictum to affirm the no-boundary nature of Israel (as contrasted with the nations), and to assert that this principle allows Israel to access revelation.[122] As we saw in our discussion of no-boundary consciousness, this dictum is used in *MHs* as one of a cluster of terms that indicate the Judah archetype's ability to access the unmediated will of God.

Thus it emerges that the old dictum 'God, Torah, and Israel are one' is a key source for Lainer's idea that one's personal perception of the unmediated will of God can override the national revelation of Sinai as expressed in the law; that is to say, it is a key source of his acosmic humanism. It remains for us to study other usages of this phrase in kabbalistic literature, in order to see whether Lainer's reading is completely radical or in fact deeply rooted in earlier readings even as he extends its meaning one step further. We will argue that the latter is the case.

This dictum, 'God, Torah, and Israel are one', is found extensively in kabbalistic sources as a principle of kabbalistic hermeneutics. To understand

266

how Lainer emerges from and extends the kabbalistic hermeneutics, we first need to understand the kabbalistic mystical hermeneutics within the larger frame of conventional Jewish hermeneutics.

The Jewish religion, as Idel reminds us,[123] did not begin with the radical emphasis on textual hermeneutics. It began as a nomad religiosity focused on the tabernacle, which was then transposed to a nation-state centered around Temple ritual, and only then emerged as a religion centered around a canonical body of writings and their hermeneutics. Elsewhere we have seen that this shift represents a re-orienting of erotic energy.[124] The original center of eros was the tabernacle and the Temple with their erotically intertwined cherubs, and the fullness of divine presence, expressed in part in ecstatic ritual.[125] However, the center of eros shifted to text, in a process that can be called the 'textualization of eros'.[126] With *MHs* we see a return to eros that bypasses the text and to some extent involves a return to Temple-consciousness, inviting a direct relationship with the divine unmediated by text.

Idel has already pointed out that, in rabbinic literature, 'it is through the canonized reification of …voice, in written documents that most of the rabbinic masters conceived of their encounter with the divine'.[127] Idel calls this the 'textualization of religious life'.

Since all texts were said to be possessed of secret divine meaning (the arcanization of text), hermeneutics became a categorical religious imperative. While, in the tabernacle and Temple periods, God was experienced as transcendent and speaking from beyond, in the textual epoch, God is experienced primarily as immanent within the text itself. The human meets God in the depths of the text. Idel notes that this move from exoteric religion to its more esoteric form implied one crucial axiom: The divine will was not obvious.[128] The בת קול *bat kol,* the divine voice that spoke from without, was largely excluded from the rabbinic study hall.[129] The divine spirit considered to be essential to the formation of the canon is excluded from its interpretation.[130]

While this characterization is true of the bulk of classical rabbinic literature, it does not hold true for Kabbalah. The Kabbalists reintroduced the divine voice into the study hall.[131] Not all of the Kabbalists, of course; Elijah of Vilna was well known for his opposition to utilizing the aid of a *magid* in study. The Baal Shem, in contrast, and many sources before and after him in the kabbalistic tradition had no such aversion; in fact, they viewed the *magid* as an expression of divine favor.[132]

In this sense, the kabbalistic move to reintroduce the divine voice into the study hall can be viewed as a desire to return to the prerabbinic world of *mikdash*. Lainer, who viewed a return to *mikdash*-consciousness as essential to his religious project, can be viewed as emerging from the matrix of this kabbalistic tradition.[133] However, while his predecessors viewed the divine voice as most essential to understanding the text, Lainer was prepared on occasion to abandon text altogether,[134] demanding on certain occasions that *kelalim* of the Torah be overridden in favor of the divine voice that spoke from the *binat ha-lev*,[135] as we have seen and will continue to see throughout this volume.

Lainer's idea, radical as it may seem at first, is actually deeply rooted in the classical kabbalistic sources. However, Lainer was the first to extract the latent antinomian conclusions implicit in the sources.

The underlying assumption of the adage 'God, Torah, and Israel are one' is a shared ontological matrix among God, Torah, and Israel. While, as Heschel has pointed out, rabbinic sources were virtually unanimous in rejecting a common ontology for all three, giving primacy to God over both Torah and Israel,[136] later kabbalistic sources were equally radical in insisting on a shared ontology of this central Jewish trinity. While in the *Zohar* these three were seen as deeply interrelated, it was only later kabbalistic sources that claimed that they were *ehad*, a unity.[137] In some of the sources, two of the three are paired up, e.g. the *Zohar*: 'God and Israel are fully one'.[138] The identity of God and Torah is very common in other early kabbalistic sources.[139]

Of course, once God was ontologized in the text of the Torah, the infinity of God naturally became the infinity of text.[140] The next natural step was that such an arcanized text required a strong interpreter.[141] The key element that sets the stage for Lainer's theology, however, is the third identity, between Israel and the Torah. This identity is highly accentuated in the Lurianic School and then even more sharply crystallized in Hasidism. The identity between Israel and Torah underlies the structural parallelism between the 600,000 letters of the Torah and the 600,000 souls of Israel. As we saw in Part Two, this parallel was a central building block for the Safed one-letter theorists.[142] They taught that, rather than the unique soul producing the unique hermeneutic, the unique hermeneutic is the meta-physical source of the unique soul.[143]

This identity between Israel and Torah is even more dramatically emphasized in Hasidic texts. Here are a few examples. Gedaliah of Lintz states, regarding the phrase זאת התורה אדם (Num. 19:14; read as 'this is the Torah: man…'): 'meaning that Israel and the Torah are one'.[144] Elimelekh of Lishensk explicates how this unity is the basis of the hermeneutic act:

> It is known that God and Torah are one. Therefore, the soul
> that attaches to its divine source through the holy letters
> raises speech upward and attaches to the divine unity. This is
> the union of *kudsha berikh hu* and *Shekhinah*; it is [also] the
> union of the holy Torah and his holy soul through the study
> of Torah.[145]

Efrayim of Sudilkov expresses a similar idea:

> …Israel comes from the *'atzmut* substantive essence of God…
> and זאת התורה אדם this is the Torah which is man,…for the
> Torah is literally of the same substance of man, and this is
> what 'God, Torah, and Israel are one' means.[146]

In another text from *Degel Mahaneh Efrayim*, the emphasis is on the complete trinity: 'God, Torah, and the soul of Israel are one'.[147] The essence of these and many other similar sources is the radical blurring, between the human being, God, and Torah, to the point of identity.[148] As Idel writes in reference to kabbalistic hermeneutics, 'in most forms of Kabbalah, man's separate identity or self is jeopardized'.[149]

For the kabbalist, all of this naturally yields a powerful interpreter. Hence, the nature of interpreter becomes critical.[150] The Safed one-letter theorists, speaking to the nature of the interpreter, added to the concept the ontology of the unique individual. In the sources that we analyzed in Part Two, we saw that according to the Lurianic theorists, every unique individual is invited and even obligated to reveal the unique interpretation that is the root of their soul.[151] This tradition is taken even one step farther in the Hasidic tradition of orality, where the Sabbath afternoon homilies of the great masters were virtually canonized on the spot as Torah. This phenomenon highlighted the ontological unity experienced in Hasidism between Israel, Torah, and God, all of which were manifested indivisibly in the persona of the *tzadik* saying Torah.[152] Idel's remark on the nature of kabbalistic hermeneutics rooted in the adage 'God, Torah, and Israel are one', is relevant here: 'To a certain extent the process of exegesis is a recirculation of divine power as embodied in man, when striving to return to its source'.[153]

Mordechai Lainer's theology emerges directly from these sources. What we have seen thus far is that thinkers before Lainer, both in his Hasidic milieu and considerably earlier, were highly focused on the Israel dimension in the trinity of God, Torah, and Israel. This focus yielded a powerful interpreter who shaped the text with enormous audacity.[154] The individual was seen not as inferior to the text, but as ontologically coextensive with the text. Lainer is shaped by this sensibility. He states:

כידוע שכל נפשות ישראל המה בשורש דבוקים כל או״א באותיות התורה,
והנה נשמת מרע״ה הי׳ נגד דבור אנכי ועסקו הי׳ בעוה״ז לברר בעולם
אחדותו ית׳ שמו בעולם

> As is known, all the souls of Israel, each and every one, are in their root attached to the letters of the Torah, and the soul of Moses was attached to the word *anokhi*. His mission in this world is to clarify His unity, may His name be blessed, in this world.[155]

This source, which is clearly an echo of the Safed one-letter theorists, also reminds us that the unity of a person with their letter in the Torah is ipso facto the unification of the divine name. In light of the sources on name that we have adduced above, this would mean that when one merges with one's own deep essence (i.e., with one's name, which is one's letter in the Torah), one merges with the divine name, thus unifying the name of God in the world.

All of this takes place, at least until Lainer, through the prism of text. Jabes captures the pre-Lainer kabbalistic sensibility beautifully and succinctly:

> The Jew lives on intimate terms with God, and God with the Jew, within the same words: A divine page. A human page.
> And in both cases the Author is God, in both cases the Author is man.[156]

Jabes sees human and God meeting on the page, that is, the text. Until Lainer, that was a correct description of kabbalistic hermeneutics. The crux of Lainer's innovation is that, while being nurtured and formed by this kabbalistic sensibility, he moves beyond the text. With all of their ontological audacity, none of the Hasidic thinkers before Lainer was willing to break the interdependence of this trinity. The individual always appears in relation to the text and never independently of it. No one is willing to leave the page behind. No one, that is, except Mordechai Lainer.

According to Lainer, hermeneutics, which is described by Idel as 'maneuvering between texts',[157] is only one way of ascertaining the will of God; the second and clearly preferred method is to, at least on occasion, leave the text behind. If, as Heschel pointed out, rabbinic sources virtually always asserted the primacy of God over Torah and Israel, and kabbalistic sources insisted on their necessary interdependence (as Scholem, Tishby, and Idel have shown), then Lainer can be said to assert the primacy of Israel over Torah. Heschel explains: for Lainer, 'the law serves Israel and Israel does not serve the law'.[158]

Lainer is even more radical than this formulation. For Lainer, at least at certain times, Israel becomes the law. This is the crux of the radical messianic character of Lainer's thought. Radical as it may seem, however, its possibility, as Scholem correctly sensed when he wrote the first scholarly analysis of kabbalistic hermeneutics, is already inherent in the classical sources.[159]

Lainer takes two subtle but crucial steps beyond previous Kabbalists. In the pre-Lainer sources we saw, because both the human being and the text participated in God, the human hermeneutic engagement with text was considered ontologically to be the word of God. The text, divine as it might be considered, always mediated between human and God. Lainer's first step is to remove the sacred text of revelation and law from between human and God. According to Lainer, a human being is a text of revelation. Lainer argues that the human Torah of the unmediated divine will is capable of overriding, and at times must override, the old revelation, which is, according to *MHs*, not God's will today but yesterday.[160] Lainer then takes a second key step that is rooted in the sources we adduced in Part One in our discussion of unique individuality and antinomianism, and to which we returned again in Part Two, in our discussion of the one-letter hermeneutic school of Safed. Lainer argues, both explicitly and implicitly, that the portal for revelation of the unmediated divine will that can override the law is none other than unique individual. It is in the depth of unique individuality rather than in its abandonment that one hears the voice of the infinite God contracted to the *lehishah*,[161] the whisper of personal revelation. According to Lainer, one can only access the revelation of the personal whisper to the unique individual through the identification and embrace of one's uniqueness. This 'soul print' is the prism of the personal revelation of the unmediated divine.

As we have noted already, the essence of Lainer's position is conveyed in his careful and consistent terminology. As we saw in Part One, throughout *MHs*, the word *perat* almost always signals a discussion of unique individuality. We also saw that personal revelation, which manifests itself through the realization that one incarnates the will of God and one can therefore intend the divine will, is also called peratim or *peratei divrei Torah*. Using this literary device repeatedly, Lainer makes his intent very clear. One accesses personal revelation, *peratei divrei Torah*, through the prism of one's own *perat* nature, that is to say, one's unique individuality. In fact, as we have seen, for Lainer, the *terminus technicus* פרטית השגחה *hashgahah peratit* means far more than the providential caring of a transcendent God. It is, rather, one's participation in divinity through the prism of their unique (*perat*) nature that ipso facto allows them to access the personal revelation and thus guidance of the divine.[162] The divine speaks through one's unique divine self.[163]

According to Lainer, every individual participates in another letter in the autobiography of God. The person who is the interpreter is the text. Just as the Baal Shem Tov and earlier Kabbalists taught 'the book of the *Zohar* has each and every day a different meaning',[164] so too does the 'unique human divine' of the individual's sacred autobiography have a new interpretation every day. The text of Sinaitic revelation and its rabbinic hermeneutic, is והעיקר הוא להבין בד״ת בכל זמן את רצון ה' אינו נוהג אלא לזמן only for the hour, מה רצונו בכל רגע לפי העת והזמן' but the essence is to understand in Torah the will of God at every time, what is God's will in every second in accordance with the peculiar nature of the moment'.[165] Implicit in this passage is that this can easily change every day for every person.

Before proceeding with the third acosmic framework in *MHs*, it is worth briefly noting the integral link between the first two frameworks. The trinity of God, Torah, and Israel is in essence a trinity of divine names. The

Torah is the divine name, and Israel is the Torah, so ipso facto, Israel—that is, the person—is the divine name. It is through accessing one's own unique name that one can reveal one's unique interpretation of the Torah, which is itself a divine name. It is in this sense that every person has a letter in the Torah: That letter itself is their name. In effect, the spiritual project of a lifetime according to the one-letter theorist is to identify one's name in the Torah. For Lainer, however, this is but the preamble; one's highest name is received in the unmediated revelation of God within the person.

In Lainer's highly existential development of kabbalistic hermeneutics, the unmediated *retzon Hashem* (which for Lainer is virtually synonymous with *peratei divrei Torah*) commands the individual, sometimes even in contradiction to the *kelalim* (general principles of law). Idel writes that the 'looseness of hermeneutic method' that characterizes kabbalistic interpretation was by definition open-ended and could produce highly 'heterogeneous results'. Nonetheless, according to Idel, this tendency never erupts into antinomianism because it is counterbalanced by conservative 'doctrinal inhibitions'.[166] It would seem, however, that *MHs*, in asserting the primacy of Israel (at least at key points), and in releasing Israel from the hermeneutic obligation to interpret text, overruns doctrinal inhibitions and fulfills the antinomian danger or possibility that Scholem originally senses in this strand of Kabbalah.

Nonetheless, as we have seen in light of Lainer's affinity with the earlier sources, Lainer's idea seems much less radical than we might have thought. Even if his radical formulation does not fully appear in earlier sources, the mystical conceptions and religious warrant for his radical move are deeply rooted in classical kabbalistic texts, particularly those of the Renaissance period, including but not limited to the Safed school.

Model Three: The *Tzadik* and the Democratization of Enlightenment

The third model for acosmic humanism is the institution of the *tzadik*.[167] The *tzadik* in Hasidism is one of the latest expressions of the Hebrew tradition of apotheosis.[168] Indeed, as we saw earlier, the *tzadik* was often explicitly related back to Hanokh (Enoch). Scholem, in his seminal essay on the *tzadik*, already notes representative sources that blur the distinction between the divine *sefirah* of *yesod*, which is also referred to as *tzadik*, and the earthly *tzadik*.[169] Idel has also referred to 'the divine or semidivine' status of the *tzadik* in the Hasidic movement.[170]

According to Weiss, two schools of thought are represented in the writings of the Magid of Mezerich and his students on the relation between the *tzadik* and God. One school speaks in terms of the 'correspondence or parallelism' that exists, as it were, between the *tzadik* and God.[171] The second, however, is far more radical, discussing 'the union of Man and God'.[172] Weiss speaks of the *tzadik's* 'intrinsic oneness with God…sometimes comprehended as an organic consubstantiality of body'. The *tzadik* and God, according to the Magid, are like the hand and foot that form one unity.[173] Indeed, Louis Jacobs referred to one master's understanding of the *tzadik* as 'bordering on the blasphemous', at least in comparison with more normative Judaism.[174] Habad Hasidism even went so far as to declare that the *tzadik* was עצמות אין סוף *'atzmut ein sof*, of the essence of the Infinite.[175]

Though Lainer rejected the classical idea of the *tzadik* as it appeared in other Hasidic courts, Lainer used this idea as a source for his own notion of apotheosis. In Lainer's theology, however, the *tzadik* is transposed into the Judah archetype.[176] The Judah persona, unlike the *tzadik*, is a possibility 'for every person…from young to old'.[177] As such, it represents the democratization of the idea of the *tzadik*.[178]

Lainer has a complex relationship to the notion of *tzadik*. More than just introducing the idea of every person realizing their divine status, the Judah archetype is also a rejection of the classical Hasidic notion that the *tzadik* is the only one with unmediated access to God.[179] Lainer's Judah archetype presumes that everyone (or at least every Jew) has the capacity or potential to approach to God,[180] without mediation of the *tzadik* or the law.[181]

The *tzadik* is often identified in *MHs* with Joseph[182] and *yir'ah* fear,[183] while Judah is identified with *ahavah* love.[184] The tension between and transition from the *tzadik* to the Judah model in Lainer's theology is often expressed in terms of this contrast between Judah and Levi or Joseph, who represent *yir'ah* and total commitment to *kelalei divrei Torah*, the general principles of the law. In the following passage Levi is the foil that stands for the traditional *tzadik*:

ולע״ע קודם שנגמר הבירור בישראל בחר מהם בשבט לוי ומתוכם הכהנים
ומהם הכהן גדול ונתן לו מצוה בפרט להדליק את המנורה, והנה בימי
חשמונאי שהאיר להם הקב״ה מההארה של עתיד שזכה הכ״ג למלכות כמו
שעתיד להתגלות ע״י משיח בן דוד שיגמור הבירור ואז יהי׳ הבחירה בשבט
יהודה

In the present, before the *berur* is complete in Israel, [God] chose Levi, and from amongst them, the priests, and from them, the High Priest, and He gave him the specific commandment *mitzvah biferat* to light the menorah. However, in the days of the Hasmoneans, who were directly enlightened by God from the future enlightenment, the High Priest merited kingship, as will be revealed *le'atid* in the future by the Messiah, son of David, who will complete the *berur*. At that time, the choice will be the tribe of Judah [and not Levi].[185]

The move from Levi and Joseph to Judah is the move from the restricted consciousness of *tzimtzum* to the expanded consciousness *hitpashtut* of love.[186]

For Lainer, the בעל תשובה *ba'al teshuvah*, one who is penitent or returns to the fold, becomes a foundation for democratizing the Judah archetype. Contrary to what one would expect in classical Jewish theology, Lainer's *ba'al teshuvah* does not signify one who acknowledges and repents for sinning, but rather one who always remains optimistic because they know that ultimately even their sin was the will of God.[187] Judah rises above fear and invites every person in Israel to live in enlightened consciousness, as we see in the following passage:

ועיקר זאת התקופות נמצא בשבט יהודה, ע״כ ויגש אליו יהודה אף שלא
נראה עתה חדשות בדבריו אך שמראה בדבריו גודל...כרב יהודה דאמר
כל העובר עבירה ושנה בה הותרה לו קמ״ל, היינו שבאמת נמצא איזה
מקום גם לזה כמבואר על פסו׳ ויד תהי׳ לך, וזה הי׳ תקופות יהודה אחרי
אשר אירע לו שאמר אנכי אערבנו, ועבר על מה שנאמר הרחק מן הערבות
ואעפ״כ הי׳ בטוח שיוצמח לו הישועה

The essence [of the *ba'al teshuvah's* nature] is the *tekufot* found in the tribe of Judah...just as Rav Yehudah taught (bSotah 22a): 'Anyone who violates a sin and repeats it, it becomes permissible'[188]—meaning that in truth there is even a place for this...and this was Judah's *tekufot*, [that] even though [he transgressed], he was certain that salvation would emerge for him.[189]

Lainer's extremely radical reading of *teshuvah* is grounded in the realization that every place in which one has been, one needed to be. Lainer continues in the passage to explore the *ba'al teshuvah* in relation to the *tzadik*:

אכן נפש הבעל תשובה נחצבה ממקום יותר עליון מנפש הצדיקים...ומכל
מקום דמה ניתן למטה מחוט הסיקרא...והיינו שאין נפשו מגיע למעלה כל
כך...ודמו נזרק למעלה, היינו שנפשו גדול מאוד

> The soul of the *ba'al teshuvah* is hewn from a higher place
> than the soul of the *tzadik*... for the blood [of *tzadik's* burnt
> offering] is thrown below the *hut ha-sikra* (a dividing line on
> the altar in the Temple that has legal import)...and it shows
> that his soul does not reach so high...[But regarding the *ba'al
> teshuvah* who brings a sin offering,] his blood is thrown above
> [the *hut ha-sikra*], showing that his soul is very great.[190]

It is a well-known dictum in Jewish thought that 'where the *ba'al teshuvah*
stands the *tzadik* cannot stand'.[191] However, Lainer assimilates the entirety
of the Judah archetype to this framework, implying again that the consciousness represented by Judah is accessible to all. Lainer writes in the
beginning of the passage, לא ישאר לעתיד שום חטא על נפש מישראל 'ultimately,
le'atid, no trace of sin will remain in any soul among Israel'. A person who
fully realizes this truth is called by Lainer a *ba'al teshuvah*. In essence, the
ba'al teshuvah, like Judah, embraces his unique sin as being animated by the
will of God.

Thus the basic quality of the *tzadik*—the *tzadik's* divine ontology—is not
rejected by Lainer, but rather is transposed to the Judah persona. Six additional features of the *tzadik* archetype are also transferred to the Judah
archetype. The first is that the *tzadik* is said to be כולל כל הנפשות *kolel kol
ha-nefashot*, 'to include all souls', meaning that included within the *tzadik's*
general soul are all the souls of Israel.[192] This precise quality is transferred
by Lainer to the Judah archetype as one of Judah's defining qualities.[193]

The second element is the emphasis on the sacred nature of שיחת חולין *sihat
hulin*, idle or everyday speech. In particular, the *tzadik* was said in Hasidic
teaching to possess the power of raising the *sihat hulin* of the common
person to a level of holiness. 'The leader of the generation is able to ennoble
all of the speech and idle talk of his contemporaries, to unify the material
and the spiritual'.[194] This idea was transposed by Lainer, after undergoing a
transformation, to the Judah archetype of the king. According to Lainer, it
is not that the king raises the idle speech of everyone else; rather, his words
are considered the 'words of the living God...Even though they appear to
be *divrei hulin*, they are from God'.[195] It is in this regard that the comment

276

of the Magid of Mezerich about the *tzadik* is equally apt in describing the Judah archetype: 'The *tzadikim* make God, if one may phrase it thus, their unconscious.'[196]

The third quality of the *tzadik* transposed by Lainer to the Judah archetype is his engagement with sin, understood as the descent of the *tzadik* into the *kelipot* (husks) in order to redeem the sparks trapped there. In Scholem's words, 'By its very nature the *tzadik's* path is fraught with peril and skirts abysses. These dangers cannot be pushed aside or avoided by some clever maneuver, but are a substantive part of his task and must be confronted head on'. It is, writes Scholem, 'the demand to live dangerously that provides the most salient characteristic of the figure of the *tzadik* in Hasidism'.[197] We have already noted that according to Lainer, the Judah figure 'sins for the sake of God' (to use common but imprecise nomenclature). The Judah figure lives dangerously. He must leave the easy certainties of the law behind in order to intend the unmediated will of God, even when it violates the normative law. In the theology of Izbica, he embodies the Talmudic dictum, 'A person only stands firm upon the words of Torah if he has first failed in them'.[198]

The fourth characteristic of the *tzadik* model which Lainer transfers to the Judah archetype is radical uniqueness and originality. Here again, we cite Scholem's description of the Hasidic *tzadik*:

> [T]he *tzadik* is the constantly changing one, whose essence is flowing and original...Hasidism places the image of the truly original man in the center...Every *tzadik* finds his own way or path...one must remember that emulation is not as authentic as the original thing...everything [the *tzadik*] does becomes infinitely significant, like the revelation itself.[199]

Scholem's understanding in regard to the *tzadik* is virtually the best description one could imagine for the Judah archetype. Indeed, as we have seen in the previous chapters, all of these features are intensified in the Judah archetype far beyond their expression in mainstream Hasidism.

The fifth quality of the *tzadik* figure that is likewise transferred to the Judah archetype is the *tzadik's* association with the *Shekhinah*,[200] along with the role of the *tzadik* in merging with the *Shekhinah*,[201] which are staples of both Hasidism and older Kabbalah. We will explore this motif as one of the major models upon which Lainer's thought is based in the following section.

The sixth quality of the *tzadik* that is transferred to the Judah figure is his identification with *teshukah*, desire. The *tzadik* in the *Zohar* is also the manifestation of *teshukah*.[202] According to Lainer, *teshukah* that cannot be controlled can be a divine quality whose very inexorability informs us that it is the will of God.[203]

Model Four: *Shekhinah,* The Eros of the Will of God

In the fourth and most central model upon which Lainer draws, his full erotic intent becomes clear. The expression of Lainer's conception of acosmic humanism—almost always implicitly but sometimes explicitly—is built on the kabbalistic tradition of *zivug 'im ha-Shekhinah* (the erotic merging of the human being with the *Shekhinah*). The centrality of *Shekhinah* to Lainer's theology cannot be overstated, and yet, to the best of our knowledge, the material and themes related to *Shekhinah* have not been discussed in previous scholarship. This idea, its very unique appearance in Lainer's theology, and the classical sources upon which he draws, will engage us for the remainder of this chapter.

The first place that *Shekhinah*-consciousness is hidden in Lainer's thought is in his most essential language. Throughout *MHs*, Lainer uses the language *retzon Hashem*, which is accessed by the individual, unmediated by *kelalei divrei Torah*. One of the basic ideas that many scholars missed when reading *MHs* is that for Lainer *ratzon* generally means *Shekhinah*. Or, in a slightly different reading, to access unmediated *retzon Hashem* is simply to embrace the *'ratzon of Hashem'. Hashem*, literally 'the name', often means *Shekhinah* in Zoharic sources; thus, the *ratzon* of *Hashem* is an appellation for an aspect of the *Shekhinah*. More precisely, according to Lainer, this phrase can mean *Shekhinah* without her *levushim*.[204]

Alternatively, *retzon Hashem* might mean the *Shekhinah* of God, the name *YHVH* itself, which is *kudsha berikh hu*, the masculine pole of the Godhead. In this reading, *retzon Hashem* means for Lainer the same as it does in classic Zoharic nomenclature: the *ratzon* of *Hashem*, that is to say the *Shekhinah* (the *sefirah* of *Malkhut*[205]) of *Hashem* (the *sefirah* of *Tif'eret*). In classical Kabbalah, *Keter* is *ratzon*, but as Arthur Green[206] reminds us, *Keter* is simply the highest expression of *Malkhut*, while *Shekhinah*, the tenth *sefirah*, is the lower *Malkhut*. In kabbalistic literature, *Keter* and *Malkhut* enfold in each other, which is part of what allowed Lainer to identify *Shekhinah*, the lower *Malkhut* as *ratzon*.

Yehudah Hayyat writes about the interpenetration of *Keter* and *Malkhut*, which came to be referred to in kabbalistic shorthand as *Keter-Malkhut*: '...the lion points to this, curling his tail onto his head....for this reason *Malkhut* is called *'atarah*, because she curls up to be a crown on the king's head'.[207] *Malkhut* (*Shekhinah*) is also called *'atarah*, meaning crown, because in her rising to the highest level of the *sefirot* (*Keter*, the head of the divine anthropos) she becomes one with *Keter*.[208]

We also find such usage in 'Hashmatot' (Addenda) to the *Zohar*:

אשרי אדם מצא חכמה דא אדם עלאה דאשרי עלוי טיבו דעתיקא אימתי כד
מטא חכמה כד"א מצא אשה מצא טוב ויפק רצון מיי׳. דא רעוא דעתיקא
ומאי איהו האי זעירא דהיא רברבא באתחברותא לעילא

'Happy is the man who finds wisdom' (Prov. 3:14). This refers to supernal man, upon whom rests (*ashrei* 'happy' can be interpreted as meaning 'rests') the goodness of *'atika*. When is this? When he reaches wisdom, as it says, 'He who finds a woman, finds goodness, and obtains *ratzon* favor from God' (Prov. 18:22). This refers to the *ra'ava* (Aramaic for *ratzon*) of *'atika* (the Ancient One). And what is it? It is that *ze'ira* small one (one of the *Zohar's* names for *Shekhinah*), who becomes great when she is connected above.[209]

Whether this is to be interpreted as meaning that *hokhmah ze'ira* is called *ratzon*, or whether it means that she is the object of *'atika's ratzon*, the link between *Shekhinah* and *ratzon* is evident.

In *MHs*, this idea is echoed by Lainer's direct association between *ratzon* and *Shekhinah*. In the three sets of sources we will present, it will become clear that according to Lainer, to intend the unmediated will of God is to incarnate or merge with the *Shekhinah*. This will be apparent in the sources we adduce in the remainder of this chapter, which show several forms of linkage in *MHs* between *Shekhinah* and the unmediated *retzon Hashem*.[210]

To cite at the outset one example from *MHs* of the linkage between *ratzon* and *Shekhinah*, Lainer reads the biblical narrative about Vashti as an attempt to access the unmediated will of God, or, in other words, to 'embrace the *Shekhinah* without her *levushim*'. The king's demand that Vashti appear and dance naked before him is an expression of the archetypal mystical core of the story: the desire to embrace *Shekhinah* in her nakedness, unmediated by *levush* (the clothing of the law).[211]

Human access to the unmediated will of God is Lainer's reworking of the old mystical notion of the *Shekhinah* without her garments. What is unique in *MHs* is that in the merger with *Shekhinah*, the human being is not lost, absorbed, or swallowed as in the more classical forms of *unio mystica* prevalent in early Hasidism.[212] Rather, for Lainer, the merging with the *Shekhinah* involves not getting lost but becoming found. In the embrace of one's fullest sense of humanity—one's *tzurat ha-adam*, the inner form of one's humanness—one realizes that one's will is identical with the will of God.[213] This realization engenders an empowerment whose *summa bonum* for Lainer is the freedom experienced when one's 'heart is drawn after the will of God' and one can trust that all of one's intuitions, desires and actions follow God's will. One can then very literally go with the flow,[214] and follow one's clarified desire.[215] Lainer is suggesting a humanistic *unio mystica* where the merging takes place not through ecstatic process, prayer, or even meditation, but primarily through the realization of the core ontological identity between the human and divine beings, which is expressed most powerfully in the identity of wills. This is accomplished, according to Lainer, by the process of *berur* in all of its manifold forms.[216]

We now turn to some of the texts of *MHs* that lead us towards an understanding Lainer's thought in terms of a reworked notion of *zivug*. This merging will express itself both in terms of *Binah*,[217] the higher *Shekhinah*, and in terms of *Malkhut*, the lower *Shekhinah*. The following passages in *MHs* explicitly reference what we will term the '*Shekhinah* matrix' of Lainer's thought.

Our discussion assumes Lainer's position that every individual in Israel is דבוקים בה׳ *devukim beHashem*[218] (ontologically merged with or attached to God), and we have shown how this position is the basis of Lainer's humanism, in all of its many manifestations. Lainer explains Israel's identity with the divine will in the following manner: אבל בישראל אינו כן כי ישראל הם מרכבה לשכינה וכפי רצונו ית׳ כן יתנהגו 'With Israel it is not like [Pharaoh], for they are a מרכבה *merkavah* chariot for the *Shekhinah* and they act according to God's will'.[219]

280

Here Lainer, characteristically, takes the concept of *zivug 'im ha-Shekhinah*, which the Kabbalists applied to the *tzadik*,[220] and extends it to all of Israel.[221] In the next source, Lainer makes even clearer his identification between accessing the unmediated divine will and the notion of *zivug 'im ha-Shekhinah*. Interpreting Psalms 32:2, he teaches:

זה הפסוק נאמר על נפש יקר שהוא מרכבה לשכינה שאין ברצונו שום
נגיעה לשום דבר רק מרצון השי״ת שמשפיע לו

> This verse refers to the precious soul who is a *merkavah*
> 'chariot' for the *Shekhinah*, who has no inclination (personal
> agenda) in any direction independent of the will of God.
> [He] only has [inclination toward] the divine will which flows
> through him.[222]

It is in light of this understanding that Lainer explains Abraham's question that (according to the *Midrash*) led him to God: 'Who is the owner of the castle?'[223] In Lainer's reading, God's response to Abraham is: 'Look within yourself', that is to say, you are an incarnation of the God-voice and in your question itself, God speaks through you.

In this formulation we hear the echo of a master with whom Lainer must have been familiar, Levi Isaac of Berdichev. Indeed, Lainer's idea that acosmism might engender some form of humanism, while unique in the Hasidic universe, nevertheless finds an important source in the writings of Levi Isaac of Berdichev. Moshe Idel has already remarked on the 'extreme statements and expressions' of what might be termed the passionate, even ecstatic theocentric axis that marked Levi Isaac's acosmism.[224] At the same time, the traditions about Levi Isaac challenging God and even putting God on trial for alleged crimes against the Jewish people are well known.[225] According to both Levi Isaac and Lainer, the human being, rather than being silenced by the overwhelming totality of divinity, finds voice in the divinity of his own being. This truth means that, for Levi Isaac, the human is able, as it were, to challenge God. Indeed, challenging the divine, which Lainer generally refers to as תרעומת *tir'omet* (a complaint or objection to God), is also an important motif throughout *MHs*.[226]

The third expression of Lainer's *Shekhinah* matrix, is the idea of 'his heart is drawn after the will of God', which as we have seen, is central to *MHs*. According to Lainer, this refers to some form of merged state with the

Shekhinah.[227] As Yehuda Liebes has noted, the essential religious activity of the *Idra Raba*, the 'Great Assembly' convened by R. Shimon bar Yohai in the *Zohar*, was *zivug* with the *Shekhinah*.[228] It is thus significant to notice Lainer's statement about this episode:

וזה שאמר השי״ת אם יש לך זכות בחקתי תלכו תכוון לעומק רצוני ולשורש החיים, וזה היה האדרא של רבי שמעון בן יוחאי שכוון לזה העומק

[T]his is what God says: if you have merit, 'you will walk in my statutes'—you will intend the depth of my will and the root of life,[229] and this was [the purpose of] the Idra of R. Shimon Bar Yohai, who intended this depth.[230]

The language used in the passage, including *'omek* 'depth', 'intending the will of God', and 'root of life', is the classic nomenclature of the Judah archetype used throughout *MHs*. Given the understanding of the Idra as a mystical gathering whose purpose in part was *zivug* with the *Shekhinah*, it is fair to suggest that Lainer understood his radical project as a continuation of the energy and goals of the Idra Raba. R. Shimon bar Yohai is described by Lainer as being the שושבינא דמלכא *shushvina demalka*, another image for *zivug* with the *Shekhinah*. The archetype whose energy Bar Yohai continues in the *Zohar* is Moses;[231] Moses is also described by Lainer as being the *shushvina demalka*.[232] Lainer teaches that it is this reality that enables Moses to be fully attuned to *retzon Hashem* not only for himself but for every person in Israel.

The connection between *retzon Hashem* and *Shekhinah* exists as a subtext throughout all of *MHs*. In reference to the positioning of the candles of the *menorah* 'towards the *Shekhinah*', as the Sages interpreted the biblical verse in Numbers, Lainer makes the following comment:

כי אף במקום שכוונת האדם לש״ש צריך להבין ולהשכיל איך יעשה ואיך הוא רצון הש״י, וז״ש שבעת הנרות כי נר השביעי הוא נגד כוונה לש״ש וגם זאת צריך להטה כלפי שכינה היינו שיבין עומק רצון הש״י להיכן הוא נוטה

Even when a person's intent is for the sake of heaven, he must understand and perceive how he should act and how it is God's will, and this is what it means when it says 'the seven candles': The seventh candle corresponds to having intention for the sake of heaven, and even this [intention] must incline towards the *Shekhinah*, which means he should come to understand the depth of God's will to [know] toward what it inclines.[233]

Here again, ascertaining the unmediated will of God beyond the law is bound up with *Shekhinah*.

Lainer states in a number of texts that the goal one reaches after the stage of *yir'ah* (fear), which is almost always associated in *MHs* with *berur*, is some form of receiving or manifesting *Shekhinah*.[234]

One crucial phrase which Lainer uses to characterize his acosmic humanism is *tokho ratzuf ahavah* 'its inside is lined with love' (Cant. 3:10).[235] This verse, as we noted in the section 'Two: The Reality of Love in Lainer's Theology', is a reference to Solomon's *apiryon* 'palanquin', which is a symbol for the *sefirah* of *Malkhut* or *Shekhinah*.[236]

An entirely different strand of *Shekhinah* sources, some of which we have already adduced above in this model, forms a major motif in *MHs*. This strand is the association of *retzon Hashem* with *binah*. The *sefirah* of *Binah*, of course, is classically referred to in kabbalistic sources as *Shekhinah ila'ah*, the higher *Shekhinah*. In numerous *MHs* passages, the accessing of *retzon Hashem* is equated with *binah* or *binat ha-lev*, and occasionally with *hayyim, shoresh ha-hayyim*, or *'olam ha-ba*, all of which are kabbalistic symbols for *binah*.[237] This reference to binah is especially prevalent in the sources that contrast ratzon with *kelalim*, the general principles of law. It is in this context of accessing *retzon Hashem*, the will of God unmediated by the *kelalim*, that Lainer equates the will of God with *binah, binat ha-lev*, or בינה מפורשת *binah meforeshet*.[238]

In one set of passages, Lainer links all of the symbols by implicitly relating *binah* and *retzon Hashem* to *Shekhinah*. Interpreting the verse in Balak, 'Now it will be said to Jacob and Israel what God has done' (Num. 23:23), Lainer states: יודע כל נפש מישראל מקטון ועד גדול מה שהש״י חפץ עתה ויבינו ע״פי בינת לבבם שעתה רצון הש״י הוא כך, ולא על פי כללים 'Every soul of Israel…knows what God wants now, and they will understand according to the *binah* of their hearts that now God's will is thus, and is not according to general principles of law'.[239] Lainer understands *binah* in this passage to refer to a level of consciousness where human knowing participates in divine action, מה פעל אל *mah pa'al El* 'what God has done'. This is the level of Holy Spirit, *ruah kodesh*, as Lainer terms it.

In explaining the same biblical text in the second volume of *MHs*, Lainer interprets it in terms of the Talmudic description of the righteous 'sitting and deriving pleasure from the radiance of the *Shekhinah*'.[240] This passage is, of course, classically understood in kabbalistic sources as referring to *zivug 'im ha-Shekhinah*.[241]

Finally, the centrality of *teshukah* in the Judah archetype is directly related by Lainer to *Shekhinah*. In the laws about the beautiful captive woman, analyzed above in 'The Way of *Teshukah*', the captive woman, representing *teshukah*, is understood as the *Shekhinah* in exile who is redeemed by Israel. Clarified *teshukah* itself is viewed by Lainer as either identical with or a manifestation of *Shekhinah*. It is in this vein that Lainer writes about Jacob that 'all his desires are like "the smell of the field which *YHVH* has blessed" (Gen. 27:27)—this is the חקל תפוחין קדישין *hakal tapuhin kadishin* field of holy apples'[242]—meaning the *Shekhinah*.

Before we introduce Lainer's unique matrix for *Shekhinah* theology below, we should first note that Lainer emerges out of a long tradition of kabbalistic and Hasidic discourse on *Shekhinah*, and its relation to name, eros, hermeneutics, and *unio mystica*, which most certainly nourished his own theology.

We will briefly examine some salient points in the kabbalistic and Hasidic general tradition that provide important context for Lainer. In sources ranging from early Kabbalah to Hasidism, we have reports of seeing the *Shekhinah*[243] and suffering with the *Shekhinah*.[244] Many of these sources, particularly those describing a visual experience of the *Shekhinah*, seem to externalize the *Shekhinah*; they describe an experience that is considerably less than a *unio mystica* experience and certainly does not affirm Lainer's idea of the ontic identity between the human being (particularly the Judah archetype) and the *Shekhinah*. The element of suffering with the *Shekhinah* assumes a higher level of empathy between the human being and the *Shekhinah*. While this experience may in certain sources be conflated with *unio mystica* or the realization of ontic identity with the *Shekhinah*, in and of itself it falls short of the higher-level mystical experiences and realizations.

However, a strong tradition in both Kabbalah and Hasidism does speak in terms of union and experiencing the *Shekhinah* as talking through the human being;[245] some sources even seem to hint at an ontic identity between the person and the *Shekhinah*. These sources are important antecedents to *MHs*. There is a strong tradition foreshadowed in the midrashic litera-ture,[246] amplified by the Kabbalists, and embraced by the Hasidic writers, of the person being a *merkavah* 'chariot' for the *Shekhinah*.[247] As we have seen, this tradition echoes in Lainer.

Jacob Joseph of Polnoye writes, in his highly influential Hasidic classic, *Toldot Yaakov Yosef*, 'tzadikim are the chariot of the *Shekhinah*'.[248] In an im-age often conflated with *merkavah*, but which seems to move even closer to ontic identity, another strand of sources conceives of the human being as no less than the limbs of the *Shekhinah*.[249] Still another set of texts talks of the *Shekhinah* being enclothed by the person.[250] Borrowing Idel's phrase, in many of the Hasidic sources, 'the distance between man and the *Shekhinah* is obliterated'.[251]

Often these sources express a strong erotic motif, describing the human merging with God as a kind of mythic sexual/erotic intercourse with the *Shekhinah*. The most oft-cited text in this regard is the Zoharic reading of Moses as אלהים איש *ish Elohim*, the husband of the *Shekhinah*.[252] However, while in many sources the *tzadik* in the place of Moses is the masculine partner of the *Shekhinah*, in other texts the *tzadik* incarnates the feminine pole.[253] In *MHs*, the Judah archetype who intends the will of God, replac-ing the *tzadik*, incarnates the *Shekhinah* herself.[254]

The theme of erotic union with the *Shekhinah*, already strong in earlier Kabbalah,[255] also played a strong role in Hasidism.[256] It was an important expression of a substantial erotic motif that appears—less graphically than in the *Zohar* or Luria perhaps, but unmistakably—throughout Hasidic literature.[257] The erotic motif, as we have seen, is a major underlying motif, both in terms of *teshukah* and in terms of the unmediated embrace of the *Shekhinah*; it colors all of Lainer's theology. Finally, it is highly relevant to *MHs* that this erotic motif expressed itself prominently in kabbalistic and Hasidic hermeneutics. The act of study and interpretation was understood by a large body of Kabbalists as an essential erotic act of merging with the *Shekhinah*.[258] It was precisely the erotic merger and ontic identity with the text that allowed the mystic to recover its meaning. However, Lainer once again moves a step beyond this tradition. Rather than the act of study being understood as erotic merger, the process of *berur* reveals the hu-man being, either as *Shekhinah* incarnate or as erotically merged with the *Shekhinah*. Lainer removes the mediation of text, just as he did in his expansion of the idea that God, Torah, and Israel are one.

The Face-to-Face Encounter

The Lurianic trope of coming 'face-to-face' with the *Shekhinah* recurs as a theme in a number of *MHs* passages, most of which have as their subject accessing the unmediated will of God.[259] In Luria, 'face-to-face' refers to the *zivug* that will be achieved between *nukva* and *Ze'ir Anpin*[260] when they become equal, after *tikun ha-nukva*.[261] In the following passages we will look at this theme as it appears in Lainer.

שש שנים יעבד ובשביעית יצא לחפשי חנם. זה רומז על ענין שמיטה שאף
שעבד הנמכר בגניבתו הוא מחמת שלא יוכל לקבל מהש״י פנים בפנים
בלתי דרך אמצעי׳...ובעת שימצא בו עבודה וציפוי להש״י, שזה נקרא שנת
השמיטה שרומז על עבודה, אז אין שום רשות יכול לשלוט עליו

'He shall work for six years, and in the seventh year, he goes out free' (Exod. 21:2). This [verse] alludes to the matter of *shemitah* (the Sabbatical or seventh year), because even [in the case of] a slave who was sold for having stolen, it was because he could not receive from God face-to-face without a means of mediation...But whenever work and expectation for God are found within him—this is called the *shemitah* year, which alludes to work—then no other authority can rule over him.[262]

The topic of the passage is *shemitah* or Sabbatical year which is usually identified in kabbalistic literature with *Malkhut/Shekhinah*, the seventh *sefirah*.[263] A person is sold into slavery because they are unable to receive from God face-to-face and require an intermediary, in this case the master. The redemptive *Shekhinah* moment of *shemitah* is when the slave goes free and regains the face-to-face relationship.

The second part of the passage discusses *Yovel* or Jubilee, which is often associated in Kabbalistic literature with 'the higher *Shekhinah*', meaning the *sefirah* of *binah*.

ושנת היובל שאז שולט רצון הפשוט ואז יתעורר בלב כל נפש מישראל רצון
הפשוט, לכן אין שום שיעבוד על שום נפש מישראל

And the Jubilee year is when the simple desire *ratzon ha-pashut* rules, and when simple desire will be awakened in the hearts of each soul of Israel. Therefore there can be no subjugation over any soul in Israel.

286

The *sefirah* of *binah* is when every person in Israel is able to access their *ratzon ha-pashut;* the deep and purifed will of the human being is identical with the unmediated will of God. This is of course a quintessential expression of acosmic humanism, wonderfully conflated with the motif of 'face-to-face'.

In the next passage, Lainer asserts that the goal of prayer is to move from 'behind the *Shekhinah*' to a state of being 'face-to-face' with the *Shekhinah.*

והענין הוא שבכל התפלה נחשב המתפלל כאילו עומד אחורי השכינה וכו׳
וכשמגיע האדם לברכת שים שלום אזי צריך האדם ליתן שלום ברישא לצד
צפון שהוא שמאל דידיה, משום שהוא ימינו דקב״ה, כי כביכול ית׳ עומד
אז נוכח פניו של המתפלל וכו׳, הרי שעיקר הזווג פנים בפנים נעשה דווקא
בברכת שים שלום שהוא אחר הפירוד שמקודם שהיה בבחינת וראית את
אחורי

> [D]uring the entire prayer service, a person praying is considered as if he is standing in back of the *Shekhinah* during the entire prayer. And when a person reaches the *Sim Shalom* blessing, the person should give greeting *shalom* to the north, which is his left side, but is the right side of God, for it is as if God is standing directly in front of the person praying. The essential face-to-face *zivug* is made specifically in the *Sim Shalom* blessing, which comes after the previous separation, which was the aspect of 'And you will see my back' (Exod. 33:2).[264]

Before the end of the prayer, one sees *ahorei ha-Shekhinah,* the back of the divine. However, when a person gets to the last blessing of the silent prayer, *Sim Shalom,* he turns to be in *zivug,* in erotic embrace with God, face-to-face.

Characteristically, the cosmic rectification of the relationship between masculine and feminine as envisioned by Luria is replaced by (and achieved through) the realization of the individual's relationship with *Shekhinah.* Thus, the intra-divine process becomes a human-divine process—an essential feature of acosmic humanism—and the messianic realization of this process enters into the present tense.[265]

Yihud Ha-sheimot (Unification of the Names)

Shekhinah as a divine name is also relevant in another framework that may have had significant influence on the formation of Lainer's theology of acosmic humanism. This is the idea of *yihud*, unification, which has a long history in kabbalistic literature.[266] Usually, *yihud* refers to an intradivine unification of different divine principles, primarily *sefirot* (divine names), and, in particular, the feminine and masculine poles of divinity. The idea of *yihud* plays an important role in the Zoharic conception of the Wisdom of Solomon, which underlies much of Lainer's theology.[267]

While kabbalistic writings on *yihud*, especially Luria's, have a decidedly theocentric cast, the discussion of *yihud* in Hasidism takes on a far more anthropocentric character, in which the *yihud* that takes place within the interiority of the human being effecting and participating in the *yihud* of divinity.[268] Though the history of the idea of *yihud* is beyond the parameters of this work, the idea of יחודא עלאה *yihuda 'ila'ah* and יחודא תתאה *yihuda teta'ah*, lower and higher union, a subset of the theme of erotic merger with the *Shekhinah*, deserves our attention. This idea, which has sources in the Zohar[269] and is particularly prominent within Habad theology,[270] may have been a substantive influence on Lainer's acosmic humanism.[271]

We discussed above an essential passage from *MHs* on Tractate *Pesahim*.[272] For Lainer, the *yihud* between the names *ADNY* and *YHVH* alluded to in this Talmudic passage affirms the ontic identity of names between human and God. This paradoxical identity of human and divine names is also the identity of human and divine action. It has deep roots in the older kabbalistic and Hasidic sources on *yihud* mentioned above, particularly in connection with ייחוד השמות *yihud ha-sheimot* (the unification of names).

According to Lainer's interpretation of the Talmudic passage in question, in the future world, the divine name of אדנות *adnut* (indicating Lordship and implying an affirmation of the ontological dignity of all of reality and particularly human activism) and the Tetragrammaton (expressing radical divinity) will be united. Lainer calls this reality ייחוד בשלמות *yihud bisheleimut* (complete unification of the names). In this reality, as we saw above, actions will be called both by the name of God and by the human name. This is the essence of Lainer's paradoxical acosmic humanism.

In Habad literature, a very similar idea of *yihud* appears in two central chapters of Schneur Zalman of Liadi's classic work, *Shaar Hayihud Vehaemunah (The Gate of Unification and Faith)*. In chapter six of his work, Schneur Zalman discusses one of the better-known dimensions of Habad metaphysics: total self-annihilation in the face of the absolute. The term used to express this idea is *bitul*, nullification of reality in order to attain the supreme realization that all is God (אלץ איז גאט *altz iz Got*[273]). This is called the upper unity, *yihuda 'ila'ah*.

The higher *yihud* is the realization that while the infinite sets boundaries to our perception out of love, in order to allow the world to exist in our perception, in truth, there is no world. This type of contemplation leads to the awareness that there is no world: 'the dimension of time and place are nullified absolutely' in relation to the ultimate divine ontology.[274] However, as Loewenthal points out in his analysis of these chapters, this is neither the final nor the highest stage of contemplation. After higher unity comes lower unity. Loewenthal, in his close reading of Schneur Zalman, observes that lower unification is not a 'coming down after a mystical pinnacle, a return to reality', that is to say, to the illusion of reality after experiencing the higher truth of higher unification. Rather, lower unification is 'a more advanced stage of contemplation'. In this later stage, the worshipper re-embraces the ontological reality of the world, realizing that 'nonetheless [God] is also to be found below in time and space...that is, His being and essence, called the blessed *ein sof* Infinite, actually fills the entire universe within time and space'.[275]

It is here that Schneur Zalman affirms the objective reality of material universe,[276] according it full ontology and therefore dignity.[277] According to Isaac Homil, an important Habad theologian who was a student of Schneur Zalman and then of his son Dov Ber, the lower unification, which affirms the ontological dignity of this world, is the merging of *Ze'ir Anpin* with *nukva*, that is to say, *zivug 'im ha-Shekhinah*.[278] In fact, in his teaching, this unification is the essential experience of the עמידה *'amidah*, the eighteen silent benedictions that thrice daily climax the Hebrew prayer service. This unity of the lower and higher unifications is, according to Schneur Zalman, the goal of messianic consciousness and the achievement of the fully purified *tzadik*.[279]

The similarity to Lainer is striking. Like Lainer, Homil affirms the paradoxical nature of reality as expressed through the unification of names which reveals that all is God, seemingly exhibiting a radical theocentricity, and yet, at the same time, affirming that the world and the human are also fully real and dignified, as part of God. Both express this paradoxical nature of reality through the same two prisms, the unification of names and the erotic merging with the *Shekhinah*. In Habad, this unification is accomplished by the *tzadik* but it is also the intention of every worshipper in the daily *amidah* prayer. In *MHs*, this merging with the *Shekhinah* is the role of the Judah archetype and is, at least in potential, the province of every person.

Although Lainer explains the *Pesahim* text using the term *yihud bisheleimut*, he does not use the Habad terms higher and lower *yihud*. However, Tzadok Hakohen, Lainer's most important student, does use these terms.[280] According to Tzadok, lower unification expresses the idea of 'there is no king without a people'. For Tzadok, the sense of separate existence is represented by the name *Adonai* and the *sefirah* of *Malkhut*, that is to say, *Shekhinah*. Lower unification, according to Tzadok, is about the realization in consciousness that the names *havayah* and *adnut* are one, and that what appears to be separate existence is indeed part of God, even as it is not illusion but completely real and possessed of full ontological dignity.[281]

Model Five: The Wisdom of Solomon

Another, entirely different, strand of sources in *MHs* makes it fully evident that incarnating *retzon Hashem* is Lainer's recasting of the old idea of *zivug 'im ha-Shekhinah* in terms of his acosmic humanism. These are the Wisdom of Solomon sources, mentioned above, which we will examine cursorily here and return to in volumes 2 and 3. In this hidden vein of thought, the identification between the *Shekhinah* and *ratzon* is made explicit and given context and depth.

A first indication of Lainer's intentions will conclude our discussion of *Shekhinah*. Lainer creatively re-interprets the rabbinic dictum 'After the destruction of the Temple, God has in this world only the four cubits of law'.[282] For Lainer, this is not a positive statement in praise of the law but a lament. The law in his reading is referred to as *kelalim*, the general principles. In contrast to the *kelalim* is the *retzon Hashem*, the will of God referred to also as *binah*, which addresses the *peratim*, the individual, and the myriad realities of life in which the will of God is not accessible from the law itself. *Binah*, as we have already seen, is for Lainer virtually synonymous with *Shekhinah*. The *mikdash* is the place of *Shekhinah*.[283] This set of associations allows us an initial glimpse at another dimension of Lainer's theology. With the destruction of the *mikdash*, the *Shekhinah* dimension of religious experience, characterized by unmediated experience, ecstasy, and religious intuition, is lost. God has left in this world only the four cubits of law. Lainer's project involves a return to some facet of the *Shekhinah*-consciousness that characterized *mikdash*; it is in the place of *Shekhinah* that one can move past law and access the unmediated *retzon Hashem*. The implicit nexus between *Shekhinah* and *ratzon* is very tight in this passage.

A plethora of passages from *MHs* indicates that the Temple, so strongly identified with Solomon, is in Lainer's reading the archetypal symbol of a theology of acosmic humanism. Lainer views himself as the inheritor of the Wisdom of Solomon, which is, in his understanding, no less than acosmic humanism. Acosmic humanism is rooted in the human incarnation of *Shekhinah* energy. Thus, Lainer moves to reclaim the fundamental *Shekhinah* energy of *mikdash*.

Summary

As evidenced, *MHs* goes a number of important steps further than all of these earlier *Shekhinah* traditions. First, the Zoharic motif of *Shekhinah* as name is understood by Lainer to imply the ontic identity of the human and divine names. While we adduced Zoharic sources in which this idea was implicit, in Lainer it becomes far a central theme. In effect, what this means is that the human being incarnates the *Shekhinah*.

Second, in this light, we understand that according to Lainer, the idea of the *Shekhinah* speaking through the human differs somewhat from the conceptions cited above. The 'Shekhinah speaking through the throat of Moses' appears in *MHs*, in Lainer's idea that the *divrei hulin*, the casual unconscious words of the Judah archetype are 'the words of the living God'.[284] In most of the earlier sources that engage this concept, the kabbalist is a channel for the divine. The persona of the kabbalist is effaced and God speaks through him. *MHs*'s understanding of *divrei hulin* is different. Lainer asserts that in regard to the purified person (the Judah archetype incarnating the *Shekhinah*), we may assume that even—or perhaps especially—their unconscious is divine.[285] However, the human unconscious remains very much one's own. The human being is not effaced and does not become a mere channel for a divine voice that has nothing to do with oneself.

Third, the human unconscious remaining one's own implies—in contrast with most of the sources adduced above, where one employs a mystical technique to achieve some form of *unio mystica*—that one's true divine persona (i.e., the *Shekhinah* that is one's essence) speaks naturally from within. For Lainer, as we have noted, the mystic is not effaced. Rather, through *berur*, he becomes so conscious as to become transparent to his divine self.

Fourth, Lainer extends the erotic motif beyond hermeneutics and applies it to reading the 'text' of the person's 'soul print', which allows them to recover the personal revelation of divine will which addresses them. Erotic merger with the *Shekhinah* yields not the hermeneutics of sacred text but the hermeneutics of sacred autobiography.

Fifth, in Lainer's theology, the unmediated embrace of the *Shekhinah* becomes antinomian in a way in that is clearly different than in any of the previous sources. Lainer's incarnational *Shekhinah* theology is both empowering and limned with humanistic undertones.

Notes for Chapter Fourteen

1 On the use of the word 'canonical' to describe these works, see Idel, Absorbing *Perfections* 471–481.

2 See *Perspectives* 59–73, as well as the sources cited in Idel, 'Universalization'. Moshe Idel has shown that *unio mystica* was a central element of kabbalistic thought in both the theosophical and ecstatic traditions. See also Matt, 'Ayin', where Matt adduces and analyzes many of the texts that Idel cites in *Perspectives* and elsewhere.

3 On *devekut*, see Idel, *Perspectives* 35–73 and 'Universalization'. On *ayin*, see Matt, 'Ayin'. On *bitul*, see Elior, 'Iyunim' 157–166; *Torat HaElohut* 178–243; 'HaBaD' 181–198; Jacobson, 'Torat'.

4 Idel, 'Universalization' 28, 29.

5 Idel, *Perspectives* 59–73; 'Universalization'; Matt, 'Ayin', particularly the Hasidism section. For a discussion of ecstasy in Hasidism particularly relevant to this discussion, see also Idel, *Hasidism* 53–65.

6 Idel, *Perspectives* 73 (the concluding paragraph of the *unio mystica* chapter) and 74–111 on specific mystical techniques.

7 As Cordovero writes, '*devekut* on a higher level is possible only in an intermittent manner' (*Shiur Komah* fol. 10d, cited in Idel, 'Universalization' 200 n. 39). Idel also states, 'with rare exceptions, extreme unitive experiences are short events' ('Universalization' 56).

8 Abulafia suggests that one must stay as long as possible in the unitive state. (Moshe Idel, personal communication, 2004).

9 See Matt, 'Ayin' 144; Idel, *Perspectives* 66; 'Universalization' 41ff.

10 R. Yehiel Mikhael of Zloczow, *Mayim Rabim* fol. 15a, cited in Idel, *Perspectives* 68 n. 84.

11 Idel, *Perspectives* 69.

12 *Seder Hatefilah* 1 26a, quoted in Idel, *Perspectives* 71.

13 Idel, 'Universalization' 53–55. See Scholem, 'Redemption', and Liebes, 'Shabbtai' for certain Sabbatean teachings which are exceptions to this rule.

14 See our discussion in the section 'Freedom and Law'.

15 See our discussion in the section '*Berur* (Clarification) and Uniqueness'. Also on *berur* and uniqueness, see *MHs vol. 1* Va'et'hanan, s.v. *ve'ahavta*; Ki Teitzei s.v. *ki yikareh*; Toldot s.v. *ahi*; *vol. 2* Bereishit s.v. *ben ha-adam*; Psalms s.v. *Hashem menat helki*.

16 The term 'intensification' to describe the process of *berur* in contradistinction to the *bitul* of *unio mystica* was suggested by Moshe Idel (personal communication, February 2004). Idel suggested the term הגברה *hagbarah* (intensification), not in the context of uniqueness but rather as a generally useful term to describe the phenomenology of *berur* in *MHs*.

17 *MHs vol. 1* Psalms s.v. *Elokim*.

18 On the term 'fragile' to describe the stage achieved in *unio mystica*, see Matt,

'Ayin' 142. *MHs* texts viewing post-*berur* as a stable state of consciousness include: *MHs vol. 1* Lekh Lekha s.v. *vayiven*; Vayeira s.v. *vayeira eilav*; Vayeishev s.v. *vayehi Er*; Hukat s.v. *vayisa*; Ki Tisa s.v. *shishah*; *vol. 2* Vayak'hel s.v. *vayak'hel 2*; Psalms s.v. *Hashem menat helki*. On the linear vs. the dynamic model of *berur* in *MHs*, see the section 'Models of Activism: Pre- and Post-*Berur* Consciousness, Linear and Dynamic Models'. However, even in what we have termed the dynamic model, one does not sense the transitory and fragile nature of consciousness that one senses in *unio mystica*.

19 For this implication, see, e.g., *MHs vol. 1* Balak s.v. *ki lo nahash*.

20 *MHs vol. 2* Berakhot s.v. *kol ha-nevi'im*.

21 *MHs vol. 1* Vayigash s.v. *vayomer Yisrael*.

22 *MHs vol. 1* Kedoshim s.v. *ish*.

23 *MHs vol. 1* Va'etchanan s.v. *shema*.

24 See below, 'Lainer and Abraham Isaac Hakohen Kook'.

25 Idel, 'Universalization' 35.

26 Idel, 'Universalization' 29, 30.

27 See Idel, *Perspectives* 60. We will see below that a unique interpretation of the *unio erotica* tradition lies at the core of Lainer's thought.

28 Scholem, Jewish Gnosticism 60.

29 Idel, 'Hanokh is Metatron' 157.

30 Idel makes this claim explicitly; see 'Hanokh is Metatron' 158–159 and related endnotes. See also Idel, *Perspectives* 60; Idel, 'Metatron: He'arot' 33.

31 See Hakohen, *Divrei Sofrim* s.v. *vehu*, adduced in Idel, 'Hanokh Tofer Minalim Hayah' 284.

32 Idel, 'Hanokh Tofer Minalim Hayah' 276–283.

33 See Scholem, *Major Trends* 365 n. 101; *Pirkei* 125–126. See also Dan, 'Metatron'. For a detailed discussion, see several articles by Idel: 'Enoch is Metatron'; 'Hanokh Tofer Minalim Hayah'; 'Adam'; 'Metatron: He'arot'.

34 Idel, 'Metatron: He'arot' 29–30. Idel echoes Lovejoy's distinction between ascending and descending models in Plato, Plotinus and all subsequent European thought. (See below, p. 328.) For another important discussion of Hebrew myth, particularly in its mystical context, see Liebes, *Studies* 1–64.

35 Reflecting the ancient terminology of the *merkavah* mystics who 'go down to the chariot'.

36 Idel points out that, broadly, the theosophical Kabbalah might be viewed as manifesting the first myth, while the prophetic Kabbalah of Abulafia often typifies the second. Of course, both schools have texts that reflect the other model as well.

37 See Abrams, 'The Boundaries'.

38 Idel, 'Hanokh Tofer Minalim Hayah' 265.

39 Idel, 'Hanokh Tofer Minalim Hayah' 280, 281.

40 Acre, *Meirat Einayim* 398, 399; cf. Idel, 'Hanokh Tofer Minalim Hayah' 266. For a complete bibliography of scholarly analysis of the mystical cobbler motif in Jewish literature, see Idel, 'Hanokh Tofer Minalim Hayah' 266 n. 4.

41 For sources see Idel, 'Hanokh Tofer Minalim Hayah' 268.

42 Idel, 'Hanokh Tofer Minalim Hayah' 277 esp. n. 50.

43 On love as a central mechanism in determining the unmediated will of God in *MHs*, see the section 'Two: The Reality of Love in Lainer's Theology'.

44 Dan, 'Metatron' 85–86 (Hebr.), 112–114 (Eng.).

45 'Metatron' 86 (Hebr.), 117 (Engl.) . Similarly in the Talmud, Metatron has the characteristic שמו כשם רבו *shemo keshem rabo* 'his name is like his master's name' (*bSanh.* 38b).

46 See also Molho, *Sefer Hamefo'ar*, cited in Idel, 'Enoch is Metatron' 154 n. 26.

47 See Dan, 'Metatron' 84, 86 (Hebr.), 114, 117 (Eng.); see also Idel, 'Metatron: He'arot' n. 40.

48 See Idel, 'Hanokh Tofer Minalim Hayah' 269–270.

49 Dan, 'Metatron' 86.

50 Or, as in Cordovero (*Pardes Rimonim Shaar* 22 Ch. 4), a chariot for the *Shekhinah*. See Idel, 'Hanokh Tofer Minalim Hayah' 267, 270 (also 272, 275, 281ff).

51 For a discussion of *zivug 'im ha-Shekhinah* in the *Zohar*, see Liebes, 'Hamashiah' 185, 205–207; see also Wolfson, *Through* 386–388.

52 There are significant parallels between Hanokh and the image of Solomon in rabbinic and Zoharic literature. Like Hanokh, Solomon is described as sitting on the throne of God in some of the aggadic and Zoharic sources which we analyze in volume 3. Solomon's place on the divine throne also indicates that he unites the lower and higher worlds. See *Shemot Rabbah* 15:26 (Source 4 in volume 3). These sources on both Hanokh and Solomon provide the matrix for the Wisdom of Solomon genre of *MHs* which we explore in the remaining volumes of this work.

53 See 'Model Four: *Shekhinah*, The Eros of the Will of God'.

54 See Tikunei Zohar 15a.

55 This theme is recurrent in *Tikunei Zohar* literature. See, e.g., *Tikunei Zohar* 2b, 15a, 79a, 98b. It is mentioned by Idel in his preface to E. Gottlieb's *Haketavim Haivriyim*.

56 On the relationship between Hanokh-Metatron and the Hasidic *tzadik*, see Idel, 'Hanokh Tofer Minalim Hayah' n. 19.

57 See Scholem, *Reishit* 253, cited by Idel, 'Hanokh Tofer Minalim Hayah' n. 19.

58 See Idel, 'Enoch is Metatron' 158 n. 57.

59 *MHs vol.* 2 Behaalotekha s.v. *im yihyeh* (Source 5 in volume 2).

60 Idel, 'Enoch is Metatron' 165 n. 20.

61 See Idel, 'Metatron: He'arot' 34. This is different than the later development of this idea in the *unio mystica* of Abulafia.

62 See next section.

63 *Hanokh Hashelishi* (*Heikhalot*) in Dan, 'Metatron', esp. 86–87 (Hebr.), 117–118 (Eng.).

64 On Metatron and the name, see also Idel, 'Enoch is Metatron' nn. 27, 62; Idel, 'Adam' 199. The unification of names remains a major theme in the later Hanokh material as well. See, e.g., Idel, 'Hanokh Tofer Minalim Hayah' 277, 285. These

last sources may be fruitfully compared to *MHs vol. 1* and 2 Pesahim s.v. *bayom*.

65 Exod. 24:12.

66 *bSanh.* 38b.

67 Scholem, 'The Name' 63; see also Dan, 'The Name' 228–230.

68 Scholem, 'The Name' 65.

69 Dan, 'The Name' 232.

70 Dan, 'The Name' 234.

71 On the name as a central motif of the Temple and tabernacle, see Scholem, 'The Name' 66, 71.

72 See *bYoma* 66a.

73 It is interesting to compare the theology of the pseudo-Dionysian treatise, *The Divine Names* quoted by Dan ('The Name' 228) and Lainer's understanding of the divine name 'Dionisiam'. Lainer understands this name as expressing the human incarnation of divinity expressed through the prism of the divine name, which inheres in the human being who has realized Judah-consciousness. See *MHs vol. 1* Likutim s.v. *ule'atid*. Hallamish (personal communication, 2003) concurred with my intuition of a probable relation between the two. However, a full analysis of this relationship would be needed to confirm this.

74 Haviva Pedaya's *Hashem* (34–69) adduces many texts that support this general reading, and provides much of the intellectual background from early Kabbalah to Lainer's understanding of name and its linkage to the Temple.

75 Bemidbar Rabbah 11:3.

76 Idel, 'Defining' 110.

77 See e.g. *Zohar* 3:296a–b.

78 Scholem, 'The Name' 67.

79 On the relation between the name of God and the human name, see Wolfson, 'The Mystical Significance'. See also Landy, 'The Name'.

80 See Nahmanides, 'Commentary on Job' 1:108 and Idel, *Perspectives* 46. On miracles and the divine name, see also Idel, *Perspectives* 204 n. 202; see also *Perspectives* 51 for Idel's discussion of Isaac of Acre's understanding of *devekut* and attaching to the name.

81 See *Reishit Hokhmah* Shaar Ha'ahavah Ch. 10.

82 See, e.g., Eleazar of Worms, *Sefer Hahokhmah* 55b adduced in Idel, *Perspectives* 98–99.

83 *Avodat Hakodesh* vol. 2 6 (29a), as adduced by Idel in *Perspectives* 54–55.

84 Idel, *Perspectives* 55.

85 *Perspectives* 54

86 On the primary sources for such structural affinities, see Idel, *Perspectives* 114–119.

87 See Ibn Gabai, *Avodat Hakodesh* vol. 2, 1:2 (125d); adduced in Idel, *Perspectives* 189.

88 Idel, *Perspectives* 51, 54, 55.

89 Cordovero, *Pardes Rimonim* 97a and b; see Idel, *Perspectives* 101 nn. 190, 191.

On Cordovero's influence on Hasidism, see, e.g., Sack, *Beshaarei* Introduction.

90 See Wolfson, 'Circumcision and the Divine Name'; 'The Mystical Significance'.

91 Zekhariah 14:9.

92 See Idel, *Perspectives* 100 n. 186, 101. On vocalization and visualization of the divine names as mystical techniques of *devekut*, see *Perspectives* 106, 108, 110.

93 Idel, *Perspectives* 111.

94 See Mopsik, 'Union'. For further discussion, see also Idel, 'Sefirot' 278–280.

95 See, e.g., *Midrash Konen* 254; see Idel, *Perspectives* 192 n. 144.

96 Idel, *Perspectives* 169.

97 Idel, *Perspectives* 147 n. 310.

98 Abulafia, *Or Hasekhel* 115a; see Idel, *Perakim* 81.

99 Idel, *Perspectives* 303 n. 28.

100 *Zohar* 3:139a.

101 *Zohar* 3:135a. See also the Lurianic interpretation of this section, in Vital, *Eitz Hayyim* Shaar 25 Perek 1.

102 Avodat Hakodesh vol. 1 18.

103 See p. 129ff, and sections 'The Individual's Unique *Helek* (Portion) of Torah' and 'The Metaphysics of Individuality'.

104 On this source see also Tishby, 'Kudsha' 483 n. 21.

105 *Degel Mahaneh Efrayim* 65d Aharei Mot s.v. 'od.

106 In a related passage, Mordechai of Chernobyl asserts: 'If a man makes holy each of his limbs and attaches to Torah, an attachment of spirit to spirit…he himself becomes a complete Torah….[This is the mystical meaning of the verse] 'this is the Torah of man' (based on Num. 19:14)…since the man himself becomes Torah and 'The Torah of God is perfect'…It causes the human soul to return to her source and her source is restored to the supernal place' (*Likutei Torah* 14d–15a). Here again the identity between Israel and Torah is clear. See Idel, *Perspectives* 245. This translation and that of the *Degel* text are taken from Idel, with slight alterations.

107 See, e.g., Gikatilla, *Shaarei Orah* Shaar 1 Sefirah 10; Shaar 5 Sefirah 6; Shaar 10 Sefirah 1.

108 *Tikunei Zohar* 40b.

109 Tzemah, *Zohar Harakiya* 69b–c.

110 Tzemah, *Zohar Harakiya* 79d, 80b. This teaching is probably a pre-Sabbatean expression of the idea of עבירה לשמה *'aveirah lishmah*. A brief history of this idea may also be found in Brill, *Thinking* 134-146. See also Gafni *Safek*.

111 *Shaar Hagilgulim* Introduction 3.

112 See our discussion of this correlation in Chapter Three. See also related discussion in the section 'Hisaron, Tikun, and Kabbalistic Theories of Evil'.

113 *MHs vol. 1* Vayeitzei s.v. *shem ha-gedolah*. See our discussion of this source in Chapter Three, particularly in the sections 'Hisaron Meyuhad' and 'Hisaron and Uniqueness'.

114 For more sources and analysis of this fundamental kabbalistic idea, see

Scholem, 'The Names' 78–80 and nn. 31–34. See also Dan, 'The Name' 237, and Wolfson, The Mystical Significance', esp. sections 1 and 2.

115 Scholem, 'The Meaning' 65.

116 Dan, 'The Name' 237.

117 On this trinity, see Tishby, 'Kudsha'; Heschel, 'God, Torah'; *Beshaarei* 103–109. On Cordovero's use of the adage, see also Idel, *Absorbing Perfections* 497 n. 49. The understanding of this adage is a leitmotif in the first three chapters of *Absorbing Perfections,* esp. 95–100.

118 Lainer assumed this dictum to be Zoharic in origin. On the much later provenance of this dictum in the writing of Luzzatto, see Tishby, 'Kudsha'. However, Tishby notwithstanding, the Zoharic source for this dictum is quite clear. In *Zohar* 3:73a, we read:

ת״ח זכאין אינון ישראל דחולקא עלאה קדישא דא נטע בהו קב״ה דכתיב כי לקח
טוב נתתי לכם. לכם ולא לעמין עכו״ם. ובגין דאיהי גניזא עלאה יקירא שמיה ממש
אורייתא כלא סתים וגליא ברזא דשמיה. וע״ד ישראל בתרין דרגין דרגין אינון סתים וגליא
דתנינן ג׳ דרגין אינון מתקשרן דא בדא קב״ה אורייתא וישראל. וכל חד דרגא על
דרגא סתים וגליא

Come and see: Israel is fortunate that the Holy One, blessed be He, planted this high and holy portion [the Torah] within them…As we learned, these three levels are tied to each other: the Holy One, blessed be He, the Torah, and Israel. And each one has level upon level, hidden and revealed.

119 *MHs vol. 1* Shabbat s.v. *vehineih* (Source 33 in volume 2), citing *Zohar* 2:82b.

120 On the instrumental relationship of *mitzvot* to *devekut* in Kabbalah, see Hallamish, *Mevo* 81–86.

121 *MHs vol. 1* Shabbat s.v. *vehineih*. See our discussion of law in the section 'Freedom and Law' as well as our discussion of *berur* in the section 'Models of Activism: Pre- and Post-*Berur* Consciousness, Linear and Dynamic Models'.

122 *MHs vol. 1* Hulin s.v. *amar*.

123 See Idel, *Absorbing Perfections* 3, 4.

124 I use the term 'erotic' not in the sexual but in the more platonic sense of the word, similar to its usage by Liebes in his classic article 'Zohar Ve'Eros'. See my discussion of eros in Gafni, *Mystery* 3–77.

125 On the eros that underlies Temple-consciousness, see Gafni, *Mystery* 3–10. See also *Mystery* 361–363 for a bibliography on this issue.

126 See Gafni, *Mystery* 67. For a more extensive treatment, see Gafni, *On Eros*. On the textualization of eros, see also Elon *Alma Di* 56–75, and Liebes, 'Zohar Ve'Eros' 67–73.

127 Idel, *Absorbing Perfections* 4–5.

128 Idel, *Absorbing Perfections* 7.

129 Largely, but not entirely. However, in the case of the *bat kol,* the exception proves the rule. See *bBaba Metzia* 59b. On this classic passage regarding the divine

voice in the study hall, see I. England, 'Majority'.

130 Idel, *Absorbing Perfections* 27. See also Urbach, 'Matai'; 'Halakhah'. See also Glatzer, 'A Study'.

131 See Idel, *Perspectives* 234–249; 'The Concept' 35–37; *Absorbing Perfections* 164–201. On the *tzadik* as a prophet in the Hasidic movement, see also Green, 'Typologies', esp. 146–149, and nn. 38–45 for a bibliography of prophetic voices that continued to echo even in the rabbinic and post-rabbinic periods.

132 See Idel *Hasidism* 50–54, 273 n. 31–38; see also Etkes, 'HaBesht', esp. 35–36.

133 On the kabbalistic understanding of itself as a continuation of the Temple tradition, see Pedaya, *Hashem* 34–69.

134 In none of the texts dealing with accessing unmediated *retzon Hashem* is there ever a suggestion that this is anything other than an internal process taking place in the depths of the human soul and psyche.

135 On *binat ha-lev* as a central construct in Lainer's antinomian thought, see the section 'Model Four: *Shekhinah*, The Eros of the Will of God'.

136 Heschel, 'God, Torah' 194–199.

137 Tishby, 'Kudsha' 480 and n. 1 *ad loc.*

138 *Zohar* 3:78–79, cited in Tishby, 'Kudsha' n. 16.

139 See, e.g., *Zohar* 2:60b and 90b, cited in Tishby, 'Kudsha' n. 4. Idel (*Absorbing Perfections*) points out that this identity is already found in the *Heikhalot* literature. See also Idel, 'The Concept'.

140 On textual and interpretive infinities, see Idel, *Absorbing Perfections* 80–110.

141 The concept of the strong interpreter in Jewish hermeneutics is approached from a variety of different perspectives in Idel, *Absorbing Perfections* 27–136.

142 See Tishby, 'Kudsha' nn. 20, 23, 29, 58. For a more nuanced discussion of these sources, see Idel, *Absorbing Perfections* 80–110.

143 See our discussion in the sections 'Strand Two: The Hermeneutic One-Letter Tradition' and 'Strand Three: Soul Sparks and *Tikun* (Repair)'.

144 Lintz, *Teshuot Hen Tazria* 21b. See Tishby, 'Kudsha' 480.

145 *Noam Elimelekh* Metzora 59b. For a more extended treatment of Elimelekh's understanding of *talmud Torah*, see Nigal, 'Hasidic' 174–181, 239–242.

146 Cf. Tishby, 'Kudsha' n. 43.

147 *Degel Mahaneh Efrayim* Bereishit 1a; Tishby, 'Kudsha' n. 17

148 On the blurring between God, human, and Torah implicit in kabbalistic hermeneutics, see Idel, *Absorbing Perfections* 82, 83; *Perspectives* 243.

149 *Absorbing Perfections* 107.

150 *Absorbing Perfections* 81, 82.

151 See the section 'Strand Two: The Hermeneutic One-Letter Tradition' and the section 'Strand Three: Soul Sparks and *Tikun* (Repair)'.

152 See Idel, *Absorbing Perfections* 470–481.

153 *Absorbing Perfections* 20.

154 See Idel, *Absorbing Perfections* 107.

155 *MHs vol. 1* Bo s.v. zot hukat.

156 Jabes, 'Key' 357, cited in Idel, *Absorbing Perfections* 497 n. 49.

157 Idel, *Absorbing Perfections* 22.

158 Heschel, 'God, Torah' 203–205.

159 On Scholem's awareness of the antinomian possibility latent in kabbalistic hermeneutics, see Scholem, 'The Meaning' 65–77.

160 See, e.g., *MHs vol. 1* Vayeishev s.v. *vayeishev* and, more importantly, *MHs vol. 1* Vayehi s.v. *vayomer*.

161 On whisper as an image of personal revelation, see *MHs vol. 1* Emor s.v. *emor*.

162 See Lainer's use of the term פרטית השגחה *hashgahah peratit* in *MHs vol. 2* Baba Metzia s.v. *kevan denafal*; *MHs vol. 1* Shabbat s.v. *mai Hanukah*; *MHs vol. 1* Bamidbar s.v. *vayedaber*.

163 See the section 'The Metaphysics of Individuality' and sections following it.

164 Sudilkov, *Degel Mahaneh Efrayim* 98; see also Safrin, *Zohar Hai* Introduction 3a. See Idel, *Perspectives* 248 nn. 247–249.

165 *MHs vol. 1* Mas'ei s.v. *kein mateh* 2.

166 Idel, *Absorbing Perfections* 107.

167 For an intellectual history of the term and institution of *tzadik*, see Scholem, 'Tsaddik'. Arthur Green, citing Rudolf Mach's work, critiques and corrects Scholem's incomplete view of the rabbinic *tzadik* (Green, 'Zaddiq').

168 *Absorbing Perfections* 471.

169 See Scholem 'Tsaddik' 125. See also Scholem's citation of Ibn Gabai in this regard (113). See also 105. For references on the blurring of the *tzadik* with *sefirat yesod*, see also Green, 'Zaddiq' 333, 338; Elior, *Harut* 173–175, 185, 188 and 'Bein' 204.

170 Idel, *Absorbing Perfections* 471. See also Green, 'Zaddiq' 331; Rapoport-Albert, 'God and the Tzadik', esp. 321–325; Elior, 'Bein' 202, 203.

171 Weiss, 'The Saddik', esp. 189.

172 Weiss, 'The Saddik' 190.

173 Mezerich, *Magid Devarav LeYaakov* 42, 43; cited in Weiss, 'The Saddik' n. 16.

174 Jacobs, *Hasidic Prayer* 131.

175 See Elior, *Harut* 173, 174.

176 See Elior ('Temurot' 48), who notes this transposition of the *tzadik*. See also Weiss, 'A Late Jewish Utopia' 215–216, who notes that in *MHs* the elect are not identical to the *tzadikim*. Faierstein was also aware that Lainer rejected the classical concept of the *tzadik* (*Hands* 81–84). However, Faierstein did not notice how Lainer adopted the concept in radically different garb.

177 *MHs vol. 1* Balak s.v. *ka'eit*.

178 For initial movements in the history of Hasidism towards the democratization of the idea of the *tzadik*, see Menachem Nahum of Chenobyl, who teaches in *Meor Einayim* (110) that the souls of all Israel make up the *tzadik*. See the discussion of this passage in Idel, *Messianic* 222; see also Green, 'Zaddiq' 339, who adduces Hasidic sources on the expansion of the notion of 'Moses is in every generation' to 'Moses is every Jew in every generation'. Note that Scholem initially

raised the notion of democratization in Hasidic theology in terms of his reading of *devekut* ('Devekut' 208). Rapoport-Albert critiques Scholem and Weiss in this regard ('God and the Tzadik' 306).

179 See Rapoport-Albert, 'God and the Tzadik' 313; Elior, 'Bein' 211 n. 105 (also nn. 180, 203, 305, 306); and Tishby and Dan, 'Hasidut' 801. See also Elior, *Harut* 170, 171, 173, 176, 190. See, however, Idel's critique of Rapaport-Albert's position in *Hasidism* (321 n. 153), where he argues that the *tzadik* also enabled the direct experience of God on the part of the Hasid.

180 On Lainer's rejection of the mediation of the *tzadik*, see, e.g., *MHs vol. 2* Vayeishev s.v. *vayehi*. See Faierstein, *Hands* 81.

181 On the preference of the Judah archetype over the *tzadik*, see also *MHs vol. 2* Tzav s.v. *vayedaber; MHs vol. 2* Berakhot s.v. *kol ha-nevi'im; MHs vol. 2* Sukkah s.v. *le'atid*.

182 On the *tzadik* as Joseph who is unsure of the will of God (which is known to the tribe of Judah), see *MHs* Beshalah s.v. *vayehi*. On the identification of Joseph and *tsadik* throughout kabbalistic literature, see, e.g., Scholem, 'Tsaddik' 91. This identification, of course, does not carry with it the negative valence which Lainer gives to the *tzadik* in *MHs*.

183 On the identification of the *tzadik* and *yir'ah*, see also *MHs vol. 1* Beshalah s.v. *vayehi*.

184 On occasion, however, Lainer identifies the *tzadik* as one who does intend the will of God. In these cases, he is using the term *tzadik* as a synonym for an enlightened person, that is, a Judah persona, rather than as reference to the formal Hasidic institution of the *tzadik*. See, e.g., *MHs vol. 2* Behaalotekha s.v. *'al pi*. In some of these passages, Lainer refers not to the *tzadik* but rather to what he calls a נפש יקר *nefesh yakar* (precious soul). See, e.g., *MHs vol. 2* Psalms s.v. *ashrei adam*.

185 *MHs vol. 1* Shabbat s.v. *mai Hanukah*.

186 See, e.g., *MHs vol. 2* Terumah s.v. *ve'asu*, where the *tzadik* is identified with *tzimtzum*. In *MHs*, *tzimtzum* is a synonym for *yir'ah* and is contrasted with *hitpashtut*. On these clusters of terms in *MHs* and in the Seer of Lublin, see Elior, 'Temurot'.

187 *MHs vol. 1* Vayigash s.v. *vayigash 1, vayigash 2*; see also *vol. 2* Berakhot s.v. *kol*.

188 In its context, this dictum is understood by Rashi *(ad loc.)* to refer (perjoratively) to someone 'who commits a sin and then teaches [that] it was permitted to him'. Note that 'teach' and 'repeat' have the same root, ש.נ.ה.

189 *MHs vol. 1* Vayigash s.v. *vayigash 1*.

190 *MHs vol. 2* Berakhot s.v. *kol ha-nevi'im*. See also *MHs vol. 1* Bereishit s.v. *vayitzmah*.

191 *bBerakhot* 34b.

192 On this quality in the *tzadik*, see Horowitz, *Zot Zikaron* 11, 12; cf. Elior, *Harut* 179. See Lishensk, *Noam Elimelekh* 27a; cf. Elior, *Harut* 181. See also Green's discussion of the soul of Moses and Adam, and the primary and secondary sources adduced there ('Zaddiq' 336, 337). See also Elior, 'Bein' 181.

193 See *MHs vol. 2* Behaalotekha s.v. *im yihyeh* (Source 5 in volume 2), where Lainer compares Moses and Solomon—both expressions of the Judah archetype in this passage who included in their souls all the souls of Israel.

194 Polnoye, *Ben Porat Yosef* 11a, cited in Scholem, 'Tsaddik' 129.

195 *MHs vol. 1* Shoftim s.v. *shoftim* 2 (Source 7 in volume 2). Note that Lainer has shifted the terminology from *sihat hulin* to *divrei hulin*.

196 Mezerich, *Or Torah* 135; cf. Scholem, 'Tsaddik' 139.

197 Scholem, 'Tsaddik' 126. While a detailed study of the Hasidic theology of *tzadik* in this regard is clearly beyond the purview of this work, Kabbalah scholarship has noticed the strong nexus between the *tzadik* and sin. Scholem notes that the antinomian sting which this idea had at its point of origin (which for Scholem is Sabbateanism) has been removed from the Hasidic texts.

198 *bGit.* 41a; see Lainer's use of this term in *MHs vol. 1* Vayeitzei s.v. *ha-aretz*; Yitro s.v. *zakhor*; Devarim s.v. *ahad 'asar*.

199 Scholem, 'Tsaddik' 137. See, e.g., Mezerich, *Likutei Amarim* 36a.

200 See Weiss, 'The Saddik' 189, 190.

201 The *tzadik* incarnates *sefirat yesod* (see p. 298), whose primary action is the erotic merger with *Shekhinah* in order to effect the flow of effluence to the world. See Tishby, 'Kudsha' 482 n. 11; Elior, *Harut* 183.

202 Scholem, 'Tsaddik' 108 n. 45.

203 *MHs vol. 2* Va'eira s.v. *vayikah* (Source 40 in volume 2). The term for this in *MHs* is מנוצח *menutzah*, being overpowered by God and by desire.

204 Alternatively, but in the same general vein, *Hashem* can mean קודשא בריך הוא *kudsha berikh hu* 'the Holy One', the masculine pole of the Godhead; thus, *retzon Hashem* would then mean the *Shekhinah* of *kudsha berikh hu*.

205 For a scholarly discussion of the identity of *malkhut* and *Shekhinah*, see, e.g., Scholem, 'Shekhinah' 175.

206 Green, *Keter* 151–158.

207 Yehuda Hayyat, *Commentary to Maarekhet HaElohut*, adduced in Green, *Keter* 155.

208 Green, *Keter* 151.

209 *vol. 3* 262a.

210 In addition, this is greatly amplified in the Wisdom of Solomon sources in Lainer and in earlier precedents in Kabbalah and Hasidism. See Chapter Eight, esp. section 'The Second Quality of Will: Eros and the Will of God'.

211 See *MHs vol. 1* Megilah s.v. *veha-karov* and *vol. 2* Megilah s.v. *bise'udato* (Source 29 in volume 2).

212 See our discussion of the difference between the *berur* and *bitul* models in the section 'Post-*Berur* Consciousness vs. *Unio Mystica*: The *Berur* and *Bitul* Models'.

213 See above p. 162ff

214 On the image of 'flow' to represent the post-*berur* consciousness in *MHs*, see, e.g., *MHs vol. 2* Ki Tisa s.v. *vayifen*; *MHs vol. 2* Psalms s.v. *ashrei*.

215 See *vol. 1* Behukotai s.v. *im* 2 cited above.

216 See section 'Berur (Clarification) and Uniqueness' and in Chapter Ten.

217 For a scholarly discussion of *binah* as the higher *Shekhinah*, see Scholem, *On the Mystical Shape 174–176*.

218 E.g., *MHs vol. 1* Vayeira s.v. *ki 'atzor* (Source 1 in volume 2); see further discussion in the section 'No-Boundary Consciousness'.

219 *MHs vol. 1* Mikeitz s.v. *vehineih*.

220 On the *tzadik* as a *merkavah* for the *Shekhinah*, see Scholem, 'Shekhinah' 178; On the *tzadik* as a *merkavah* in *MHs*, see *MHs vol. 1* Shoftim s.v. *ki teitzei; vol. 2* Likutim Vayigash s.v. *vayigash*.

221 On the human incarnation of *retzon Hashem* as *merkavah laShekhinah*, see *vol. 2* Vayeira s.v. *vayikra* (Source 28 in volume 2). See also below, 'Empowering Acosmism and *Tekufot*'. On the human being as a chariot for the *Shekhinah* in Hasidism, see Idel, *Hasidism* 187, 203.

222 *MHs vol. 2* Psalms s.v. *ashrei*.

223 *MHs vol. 1* Lekh Lekha s.v. *vayomer*.

224 See Idel *Perspectives* 69, 70, 72. See also Idel, *Hasidism* 128; 316 n. 103; 317 n. 107.

225 See Laytner, *Arguing*.

226 For example, according to Lainer, *tir'omet* catalyzes the choosing of Abraham (see e.g. *vol. 1* Lekh Lekha s.v. *vayomer*). In other sources, Lainer distinguishes between *tir'omet*, which he rejects, and a טענה *ta'anah* 'claim' against God or a בקשה *bakashah* 'entreaty' to God that he explain suffering, which he affirms (see e.g. *vol. 1* Vayeishev s.v. *vayeishev*).

227 See, e.g., *MHs vol. 2* Vayigash s.v. *vayigash*, where Lainer links being drawn after the will of God with *Shekhinah*.

228 See Liebes, 'Hamashiah' 185, 205–207.

229 In *MHs*, the Hebrew phrase שורש החיים *shoresh ha-hayyim* consistently refers to *binah*, which is virtually synonymous with *retzon Hashem*. On the term *hayyim* in *MHs* see, e.g., endnotes 598 and 601.

230 *MHs vol. 2* Behukotai s.v. *im 1*.

231 The link between Moses and Bar Yohai is commonplace in kabbalistic material. See, e.g., Liebes, 'Hamashiah'. For other sources on Moses viewing him in terms that could make him a source for Lainer's acosmic humanism, see also Meeks, 'Moses' 354–371.

232 *MHs vol. 1* Bamidbar s.v. *ve'etkhem*. Lainer is, of course, merely echoing the old Zoharic theme of Moshe the *ish Elohim*, the erotic partner of the *Shekhinah*. For a scholarly discussion of these sources, see Idel, *Perspectives* 209, 227–228.

233 *MHs vol. 1* Behaalotekha s.v. *vayedaber*.

234 See, e.g., *MHs vol. 1* Shelah s.v. *beha-sidrah* (in the last paragraph of a very long passage), and Lekh Lekha s.v. *vayomer*. For Lainer's emphasis on the manifestation of *Shekhinah* as a primary religious goal, see also *vol. 1* Vayeira s.v. *vayeira vehineih*: 'When Isaac was born the *Shekhinah* descended into the world'; and see *vol. 1* Shemot s.v. *vayomer; vol. 2* Sukkah s.v. *veshe'einah; s.v. vetanya*.

303

235 See citations at endnote 546 above.

236 See endnote 549.

237 See Tishby, *Mishnat Hazohar* vol. 1 151–157. See also Green, *A Guide* 28–59.

238 See, e.g., *MHs vol. 1* Hukat s.v. *vayis'u*; Ki Tavo s.v. *ki yikareh*.

239 *MHs vol. 1* Balak s.v. *ka'eit*.

240 *bTan.* 31a, cited in *MHs vol. 2* Balak s.v. *ka'eit*.

241 For a provocative discussion of this passage, see Wolfson, *Through* 42, 43.

242 *MHs vol. 2* Toldot s.v. *vayigash*.

243 See, e.g., Benayahu, *Sefer Toldot HaAri* 231–232; Vital, *Sefer Hezyono*t 42. For an analysis of these sources see Idel, *Perspectives* 80–87.

244 See, e.g., Lishensk, *Noam Elimelekh* 29b; Idel, *Perspectives* 83, 84, 88.

245 E.g., Joseph Karo's experience, described in Werblowsky, *Joseph* 109–111.

246 E.g., Bereishit Rabbah 69:3.

247 On the human being as a chariot for the *Shekhinah* in Hasidism, see the discussion in Idel, *Hasidism* 187, 203.

248 Polnoye, *Toldot Yaakov Yosef* 66c; see Idel, *Hasidism* 373 n. 106, where he remarks that this image is common in Hasidic literature.

249 On the person as the limbs of the *Shekhinah*, see Idel, *Perspectives* 169 nn. 101–106, esp. n. 105; see also 308 n. 87.

250 See the Hasidic work by Zekhariah Mendel of Jaroslav, *Darkhei Tzedek* 4a–b; cf. Idel, *Hasidism* 325 n. 210.

251 The Magid of Mezerich writes (*Or Haemet* 39c): 'He should think that his soul is a limb of the *Shekhinah* as if he is a drop of the sea. Israel makes the words of their mouths into vessels in order to clothe the *Shekhinah* in them'. See Idel, *Hasidism* 168.

252 For sources on this theme and scholarly discussion of this motif, see Idel, *Perspectives* 209, 210.

253 Idel, *Perspectives* 209, 210. See also Idel, *Hasidism* 136; Tishby, *Mishnat Hazoha*r 1: 298–299; Wolfson, 'Circumcision, Vision of God'; Liebes, 'Hamashiah' 205–207.

254 On the Judah type as the incarnation of *Shekhinah* in *MHs*, see esp. *vol. 2* Proverbs s.v. *ki va'ar* (Source 11 in volume 2); see also *vol. 1* Emor s.v. *vahaveitem* (Source 24 in volume 2); *vol. 2* Ki Teitzei s.v. *ki teitzei*. For the same in Zoharic and post-Zoharic sources, see for example *Zohar* 2:248a.

255 On erotic motifs in Jewish mysticism, see Idel, *The Mystical* 179–205; Wolfson, 'Female' vol. 2 302–305; 'Walking'.

256 See Idel's discussion of erotic motifs (*Hasidism* 133–140).

257 One indication of the eros-laden *Shekhinah* consciousness of Hasidism is the substantial influence on Hasidic sources of Elijah da Vidas's parable of the beautiful woman cited in the name of R. Isaac of Acre, *Reishit* Shaar Ha'ahavah Ch. 4, adduced in Idel, *Hasidism* 61–63. A second indication is the erotic interpretation of prayer that seems to have originated with the Baal Shem Tov. See Jacobs,

Hasidic Prayer 60–61. See also Biale, *Eros* 121148 and Liebes, 'Hibur' 177–178.

258 This theme has been treated extensively in scholarship. See Liebes, 'Hamashiah' 135–145, 198–203; Idel, *Perspectives* 227–228; Wolfson, 'Circumcision, Vision of God' 207–213; 'The Hermeneutics' 323–324; 'Female' 295–298, 302–305.

259 In addition to the sources adduced in this section, see *MHs* vol. 1 Kedoshim s.v. *kedoshim* 1 (Source 22 in volume 2); Ki Tavo s.v. *ve'anita; vol.* 2 Korah s.v. *vayikah* (Source 20 in volume 2); Isaiah s.v. *ya'azov rash'a;* Psalms s.v. *ahat she'alti.* See also Sources 49 and 53 from Tzadok Hakohen, found at the end of volume 3.

260 Note that *Ze'ir Anpin* is more like a proper name, is not used with a definite article, and hence capitalized, while *nukva* is a more generic term, 'the feminine', and hence not capitalized.

261 This theme, and its relation to Lainer, are analyzed further in the section 'Tikun Ha-nukva' in volume 3.

262 *MHs vol.* 2 Mishpatim s.v. *sheish shanim.*

263 *See MHs vol.* 2 Likutim Behar s.v. *vehi tomru* where Lainer explicitly identifies *Shemitah* as *malkhut/Shekhinah.*

264 *MHs vol.*2 Likutim Pinhas s.v. *bayom ha-shemini.* This passage is collected in *MHs* from Gershon Henokh's *Sod Yesharim* Shemini Atzeret 18 s.v. *uvei'ur.* See volume 3, Source 49, where this passage is discussed in light of Tzadok Hakohen's writings about Shemini Atzeret. A greater part of this passage, along with further analysis, can be found in volume 2, Source 21.

265 Further discussion of this transformation is found both in volume 2 and volume 3.

266 For a discussion of *yihud* in Lurianic Kabbalah, see Fine, 'The Contemplative', esp. 70. On the shift from Luria to Hasidism in the usage of kabbalistic categories, see Elior, 'Hazika'. See Magid on this issue specifically in the Izbica lineage, *Hasidism* 74.

267 See 'Model Five' below and volume 2.

268 See Idel, *Messianic* 232–239.

269 E.g., *Zohar* 1:18a.

270 See e.g. *Shaar Hayihud* Ch. 7, discussed below.

271 Regarding possible Habad influence on Lainer, see Faierstein, *Hands* 109. Faierstein is not sure whether Habad influence is present in *MHs,* and concludes by saying that the 'question desires further study'. Lainer's relation to Habad has not heretofore been studied in scholarship. Habad influence on Lainer's student Tzadok Hakohen is however discussed in Lever, *Principles* 33, 63.

272 See above p. 192 on *MHs vol.* 1 Pesahim s.v. *bayom;* other related passages can be found in Chapter Eight.

273 On this phrase, see Loewenthal, 'Reason' 112–114.

274 Liadi, *Shaar Hayihud* Ch. 7, adduced in Loewenthal 'Reason' 114 n. 14.

275 Loewenthal 'Reason' 114 n. 14. Loewenthal's translation is used.

276 Hallamish and Jacobson support this view, against Elior's more theocentric perspective. Jacobson emphasizes the ontology of תחתונים *tahtonim* (the world of

time and space) as central to Habad, and discusses lower and higher unification. See Jacobson, 'Torat' 350, 354, 358. Cf. Loewenthal, 'Reason' 114 n. 16.

277 On the relationship between ontology and dignity, see Soloveitchik, *Lonely Man of Faith* 14–27. Soloveitchik explicitly reframes these chapters in Habad theology in more existential language in his opus 'Uvikashtem', beginning on 29.

278 See the discussion of Isaac Homil in Loewenthal, 'Reason'.

279 See Loewenthal, 'Reason' 119.

280 See Resisei Laylah 40.

281 See also Tzadok Hakohen's other discussions of higher and lower *yihud*, which support our reading of Lainer *(Sefer Hazikhronot* 58–59; *Dover Tzedek* 4–5; cf. Lever, *Principles* 121–126).

282 *MHs vol. 1* Hukat s.v. *vayis'u*.

283 The association of *Shekhinah* and Temple is very old; it is foreshadowed in biblical sources, explicit in Talmudic sources, and highly developed in kabbalistic writings. For a kabbalistic statement of this association, see Gikatilla, *Shaarei Orah* 9a–b (cf. Scholem, 'Shekhinah' 177–178). For the *Zohar's* treatment of the Temple cult, see Tishby, *Mishnat Hazohar* 2:183–246; see also Idel, 'Hermeticism' 61, 62.

284 *MHs vol. 1* Shoftim s.v. *shoftim* 2 (Source 7 in volume 2). See also p. 302.

285 This same understanding drives Lainer's understanding of *lema'alah mida'ato*; see the section 'Sixth Major Theme: *Lema'alah Mida'ato* (The Suprarational)'.

PART FIVE

Choicelessness, Continuing Revelation and Theology
in the Context of Lainer's Zeitgeist

Chapter Fifteen
Introduction

As we noted at the outset, Joseph Weiss views Lainer as a thinker who dis-
allows 'any free human action', teaching that 'the divine will overpowers human choice'. Weiss views this as complete departure from *masoret Yisrael*,
the Jewish tradition, which, states Weiss, is 'based on בחירה חפשית מוחלטת
behirah hofshit muhletet absolute free will'.[1] However, Weiss's assertion only
stands if we ignore acosmism and its potential corollaries; scholars have
already pointed out that these are dominant assumptions in much of post-
Lurianic Orthodox Jewish thought.[2]

The problem is that the very notion of free choice, at least on its face,
indicates that human existence has an independent ontology, which contradicts the acosmic axiom. Each acosmic thinker was forced to somehow
grapple with this issue.[3]

Naturally, the general trend was to seek to retain both the principle of acosmism and the reality of human free will at the same time. This was the direction charted by Habad Hasidism,[4] Nahman of Braslav,[5] Levi Isaac of
Berdichev,[6] and others. However, a strong parallel to Lainer's own treatment
of free will and acosmism developed in almost the same years as the Lainer
dynasty: the Musar movement. The Musar movement, as analyzed by Tamar
Ross,[7] contains several elements whose goal was to internalize acosmic consciousness to such a degree that one realizes that free will, in the conventional
sense, is only an illusion. Here, we briefly examine the example of Lainer.

Lainer and Choicelessness

Weiss's characterization of Lainer's theology as just described, which interprets Lainer as a narrow determinist who stands against free human
action, is a significant misreading. As we have seen above, the acosmic humanism that lies at the core of Lainer's thought affirms the radical ontology of the human action and the free human being as its religious telos
and *raison d'être*. Freedom and activism are defining characteristics of the
Judah archetype.

The kind of action described by Lainer as characteristic of post-*berur* consciousness, which has ontological gravitas, does not emerge from human choice in the classical philosophical sense of the term. Rather, it flows from what we will refer to, borrowing a term from Krishnamurti, as 'choicelessness'.[8]

According to Krishnamurti, choicelessness emerges from a consciousness that is 'beyond limitation', a nondual, mystical consciousness. In Lainer's terms, the post-*berur* state is characterized by a similar state of consciousness that is 'beyond boundaries'. This is specifically expressed by Lainer using the terms אין גבול *ein gevul* 'no-boundary', התפשטות *hitpashtut* 'expansiveness', and למעלה מדעתו *lema'alah mida'ato* 'suprarational consciousness'.

Krishnamurti indicates that the realization of this type of consciousness engenders a 'singularity that results from seeing something clearly as well as a singularity of action which is in accord with such seeing'.[9] He continues:

> If you become fully aware of the whole significance of this…
> you will experience…liberation from choice. Only when
> choice ceases is there liberation, richness of action which is
> life itself. Where there is choice and a capacity to choose there
> is only limitation.

This description is equally apt for Lainer.

Before proceeding, it is worth noting that one of the most profound readers of Izbica texts in our generation and the person credited by the Lainer dynasty with returning the study of these texts to the larger community, Shlomo Carlebach,[10] understood Lainer's concept of human action and free choice in a similar way. According to Carlebach, what we refer to here as the Judah archetype is 'so totally free' as to be 'beyond choice'.[11]

Carlebach's idea of 'beyond choice' is highly similar to the concept of choicelessness as we describe it here. Admiel Kosman, scholar and poet, has remarked generally on the broad similarity between Lainer and Krishnamurti in this matter.[12] Of course, there are real distinctions between the positions, largely in terms of the fact that because he is a Hasidic master, Lainer's vision of a personal God is combined with his more abstract ideas about the divine, and he understands the whole universe to be an expression of the divine intentionality. Choicelessness for Lainer is not a 'cold' concept in the way it is for Krishnamurti. Nor could

Lainer subscribe to the *dei natura* divine substance of Spinoza.[13] In fact, because Lainer emerges out of the kabbalistic tradition, choicelessness for him is suffused by intentional divine love that animates all and is the source of creation.[14]

Of course, kabbalistic acosmism and Eastern versions of nonduality are far from identical. A full comparison between the two is beyond the scope of this book. However, it is worth mentioning, as Arthur Green has noted, that in Hasidic texts, Buddhist-like metaphysics often appear side by side—in the same paragraph or even the same sentence—with a more personal and intimate experience, or a description of a loving God.[15] Daniel Matt has remarked on the similarity between the kabbalistic and later Hasidic idea of *ayin*, and the Buddhist notion of *sunyata*, emptiness.[16] Such nondual understandings and their implicit notions of choicelessness are, of course, common in the Buddhist tradition.[17] We add to Matt by pointing out the similarity between Lainer's and Krishnamurti's concepts of choicelessness.[18]

Lainer and the Idealists

However, this type of teaching on choicelessness is not limited to Eastern traditions, which one can assume did not influence Lainer, even in the indirect form of a 'Zeitgeist'. However, a strikingly similar understanding of the relations between human action, the divine, and choice appears in Western thought and was one of the dominant forces in the intellectual Zeitgeist of Europe during Lainer's period of work. This is the well-known school of Idealism, and particularly its major voices, Fichte, Schelling, and Hegel. The roots of their concept of choicelessness go back at least as far as Plotinus, probably as far as Plato, and are rooted in one of the great dilemmas of thought in the both the Eastern and Western traditions.

To fully understand the dramatic insight of the Idealists and its relevance to Lainer's thought, a brief digression is order. The following several paragraphs on the genealogy of Idealism starting from Plato are based on four major scholars: Arthur Lovejoy in his acclaimed work, *The Great Chain of Being*, Raymond Inge in his work on Plotinus, Charles Taylor in his classic work *Hegel*, and, finally, philosopher Ken Wilber in his magnum opus, *Sex, Ecology and Spirituality*. The goal here is not to offer an original analysis of Idealism. Rather, we will simply paint in broad strokes the backdrop in intellectual history for the following observation: the 'empowered choicelessness' that in Lainer's view was the position of a post-*berur* human being is not a conception unique to Lainer. The concept of empowered choiceless-ness is a corollary of a great philosophical tradition that was dominant in Lainer's own Zeitgeist. Lainer may have been profoundly influenced by the broader intellectual milieu in which he lived. Weiss did not consider this tradition in his interpretation of Lainer. We will lay out the intellectual backdrop necessary to make this observation in the next few paragraphs.

In a passage that scholars generally agree refers to mystical knowledge of the One, Plato writes in his seventh epistle:

> It is not something that can be put into words like other branches of learning; only after long partnership in a common life [contemplative community] devoted to this very thing does truth flash upon the soul, like a flame kindled by a single spark. No treatise by me concerning it exists or will ever exist.[19]

For Plato, this knowledge is the essence of all knowledge. There are two basic movements in Plato's thought, which have been outlined in great de-tail by Arthur Lovejoy.[20] The first is the path from the many to the One, an ascending path of eros and wisdom. The second is the descending path of agape and compassion; this is the flowing of the One into the many. The more well-known trajectory in Plato is the ascending journey of the soul from the material realm, to the mental realm of higher forms, to a 'spiritual immersion in the eternal and unspoken One'.[21]

As Lovejoy, Wilber and others point out however, this is only half of what Plato taught. Lovejoy goes on to remind us that no sooner does Plato reach his climax in the otherworldly direction, then 'he forthwith finds in this transcendent and absolute being the necessitating ground of this world; he does not stop short of the assertion of the necessity and worth of the ex-istence of all conceivable kinds of finite temporal imperfect and corporeal beings'.[22] This is what Lovejoy calls the descending path, which affirms the divinity of all expressions of the manifest world.

Lovejoy traces these two trends though the course of Western intellectual thought as two diverse and ultimately irreconcilable trajectories. Wilber and Inge, however, assert that it is the ground of nonduality that allows Plato and his spiritual and intellectual descendant Plotinus to hold the paradox of the ascending and descending paths.[23] Nonduality does not affirm, as is often mistakenly assumed, that the real world is an illusion; quite the contrary, the point of nondualism is that both the manifest and formless are expressions of the One. The paradoxical truth of both assertions is held in the affirmation of the nondual ground of being. This conception lies at the center of Plotinus's thought. Indeed, as Inge points out, Plotinus clearly and unequivocally affirms the reality of direct and unmediated experience of the nondual spirit.[24] For Plotinus, 'Spirit not only engenders all things—it is all things'.[25]

We will now skip forward in history to Lainer's Europe, to a controversy understood by scholars to be a direct conceptual derivation of the ascending-descending tension in Plato and Plotinus: Fichte vs. Spinoza. Charles Taylor refers to this controversy as the agony of modernity.[26]

In effect, Fichte the Idealist understands the human as infinite subject and pure ego, an expression of the ascending trajectory of thought. This is an expression of what Wilber calls '[t]he pure ascending subject, driven at its best by Eros'.[27] For Fichte, nature is not a limiting factor and radical freedom is the order of the day. Fichte represented for his—and Lainer's—age and Zeitgeist what Taylor calls the 'absolute subject'. Spinoza, on the other hand, represented what Taylor calls the 'absolute object'. Spinoza is the determinist for whom the old classical concept of the free subject has no meaning; all is pure substance, pure, and therefore determined, object.[28] Spinoza is the expression of the descending path. According to Spinoza, a person only finds their place in the matrix of divine determinism. Taylor goes on to say that the great question of the era was whether subjective freedom could be united with objective union.[29]

The great answer of the Idealists was a return to a nondual conception of being, which was the hallmark of Plotinus and Plato and which allowed them to hold to both the ascending and descending trajectories. In the matrix of nonduality, a human can be radically free as a subject and at the same time be in complete union with the One, and therefore enter a state beyond choice, which we termed above 'choicelessness'. Taylor's exposition of this 'choicelessness' comes very close to the structure of what we have seen in Lainer:

> If the aspirations to radical freedom and to internal expressive unity with nature are to be totally fulfilled together; if man is to be at one with nature in himself and in the cosmos

313

while also being most fully a self determining subject; then…it is necessary that this whole order within and without…tend to realize a form in which it can unite with subjective freedom. If I am to remain a spiritual being and not be opposed to nature in my interchange with it, then the interchange must be a communion in which I enter into relation with some spiritual being or force. But this is to say that spirituality, tending to realize spiritual goals, is of the essence of nature. Underlying spiritual reality is a spiritual principle striving to realize itself.[30]

Clearly, this is not identical to Lainer's thought, most notably in the substitution of 'Nature' for God. Nevertheless, for Lainer, the human is fully identified with the divine ground of being, which, paralleling Nature in the Idealist position, is the ultimate nature of reality. According to Lainer, in the realization of this ontic identity, a person achieves both their freedom and their choicelessness. This is the great paradox of acosmic humanism. When the infinitely subjective human meets the objective ground of the divine nature of being and realizes that they are one, complete freedom is achieved. Again, Taylor's summary will help us discern the parallels:

[W]hile Nature tends to realize spirit; that is self conscious-ness, men and women as conscious beings tend towards a grasp of nature in which they will see it as spirit and one with their own spirit. In this process men and women come to new understanding of self: they see themselves not just as individual fragments of the universe, but rather as vehicles of spirit…[This] provides the basis of a union between finite and cosmic spirit which meets the requirements that men and women be united to the whole and yet not sacrifice their own self consciousness and autonomous will.[31]

In effect, the great Idealist realization that formed a part of Lainer's Zeitgeist was the nondual understanding that both subject and object incarnate spirit. Thus, the unmediated human intuition discerned in freedom freely expresses the will of the human, which is the will of spirit. It is, of course, this highly paradoxical teaching that resonates in Lainer and forms the crux of his acosmic humanism.

Lainer and the Romantics

A final feature of Lainer's thought is the remarkable affinity between the fundamental intuitions of *MHs* and those of the Romantic movement, which was the dominant Zeitgeist of Lainer's period along with European Idealism.[32] The term Romanticism itself, as Arthur Lovejoy points out in his seminal essay, includes too many strands of thought and admits too many definitions to be helpful without some form of elucidation. Therefore, for the sake of clarity, we have chosen one scholar, Charles Taylor, upon whose authoritative, classic description of Romanticism we will draw, in order to make the case for the strong affinity between the fundamental matrices of Romantic thinking and those of Lainer.[33]

What is immediately apparent is that one need not exert much effort in stating the case. At least eight major parallels between the two are so clear and compelling that it becomes virtually impossible not to label Lainer a religious Romantic. All of this, however, should not efface the very real differences that separate Lainer's religious Romanticism from that of a Hegel, Fichte, or Schelling. In this regard we need only note that he emerges out of and remains committed to a theistic tradition.

Taylor himself notes that Romanticism's possible influence on various religious revival groups, including Hasidism, needs to be considered. In the case of one of these groups, Wesleyan Methodism, he even suggests that Romanticism was a 'crucial moulding influence'.[34] While Taylor is correct that the general emphasis on feeling and sensibility in the cultural Zeitgeist in which Hasidism was born needs to be noted, not less noteworthy are some of the other features of Romanticism that find an echo in Hasidism,[35] and are particularly sharply expressed in Lainer's theology.

The first feature of any description of Romanticism is almost always its radical emphasis on interiority. The cult of sensibility that is termed Romanticism is guided by what Laurence Sterne refers to as the 'divinity which stirs within'.[36] This is also Lainer's fundamental intent when he uses the term *binat ha-lev* (understanding of the heart). Second, Taylor notes that this emphasis on heart and interiority did not remain abstract, but had very real normative implications.[37] Not only did the Romantics, for the most part, view nature as a divine moral source, but they also viewed a person's evolution as connected to their ability to participate in the cosmic

315

spirit running through all of nature.[38] This divine yet accessible nature was seen by the Romantics as a guide to normative human action.

Third, because of all this, Romanticism often had a distinctly antinomian sensibility. Romanticism taught that one need stand against normative frameworks and follow one's sense of inner conviction, what came to be known as one's 'inner voice'.[39] Thus, Romanticism, according to Taylor, is invested with an almost inexorable impulse to slide away from Orthodox theology, to depart from traditional ethical codes, and to dissolve the distinction between the ethical and the aesthetic.[40] One's new and fresh understanding of the good virtually always triumphs over the old and stale understanding of the good. Precedent ceases to wield decisive authority. In Taylor's recapitulation of the Romantic position, 'Each of us must follow what is within and this may be without precedent'.[41]

It is in this sense that all the great writers on Romanticism have framed it in terms of a rejection of neoclassicism. Whatever previous type of classicism existed—whether philosophical, hierarchical, or, in the case of Lainer, legal—it is overridden by the sensibility of the moment which reveals a higher law. This parallels closely Lainer's emphasis on *binat ha-lev*. The normative implications of this tendency manifest as antinomian sentiments.[42]

Fourth, the Romantic tends to assert the primacy of will over intellect. The goal for the Romantic is the transformation of the human will. In Taylor's summation of the Romantic invitation: 'Our will needs to be transformed…by the recovery of contact with the impulse of nature within us'.[43] For Lainer, the transformation is accomplished by the realization of the ontic identity of wills between the human and the divine. In a parallel manner, the Romantics identify not only with the natural within us, but seek to become united with 'the larger current of life or being'.[44]

The fifth parallel concerns the radical uniqueness of the individual. While the dignity of the individual was already a dominant theme in the Renaissance, it was Romanticism that highlighted the idea of originality. Taylor writes:

> This is the idea…that each individual is different and original and that this originality determines how he or she ought to live…Just the notion of individual difference is of course not new. Nothing is more evident or more banal. What is different

is what really makes a difference to how we are called to live…
[which] lay[s] the obligation on each of us to live up to our
originality.[45]

What replaced the interlocking or hierarchical order of a classical worldview was the Romantic notion of a 'purpose or life coursing though
nature'[46] that addresses each individual uniquely.[47] Similarly, Lainer's radical emphasis on individuality and originality is the source of the personal
revelation that guides a person's life, even when it flies in the face of Mosaic
law itself.

Sixth, Taylor points out that the defining characteristic of the Romantic
personality is freedom. Romanticism, with its law of divine nature that
is beyond reason, becomes 'the basis for a new and fuller individuation'.[48]
We have already shown that freedom is a basic defining characteristic of
Lainer's religious ideal.[49]

The seventh parallel between Lainer's thought and Romanticism is the
affirmation of the ontological dignity of desire. When stripped of its dross
and reduced to its unvarnished essence, desire is the great guide towards
interiority and heart.[50] The affirmation of the ontological and normative
status of redeemed desire is a core feature of Lainer's theology.[51]

The eighth area in which Romantic concepts are reflected in Lainer's
thought is in his understanding of the idea of ongoing revelation. Silman
suggests three core models for revelation in Jewish thought, basing himself
explicitly on Lovejoy's well-known categories of the Romantic and the classical.[52] He identifies the first two models as classical and the third model
as Romantic.[53]

Silman calls the first model the 'total' model. This model assumes that the
totality of revelation was received on Sinai and given to Moses.[54] The second model, which he terms the 'revelatory' model, assumes, like the first
model, that the entire Torah was given on Sinai. However, this revelation
was not actual as the first model assumes; much of it was only in potential.
Thus, the first two models share the belief that the process of revelation
was completed, and that our purpose as receptors of this revelation is re-
storative: the remembering or reclaiming of all the wisdom that was either
explicit or implicit in the original voice of Sinai.[55] Silman calls these the
classical models.

The third model is far more empowering than the first two. It assumes that the first revelation was incomplete, both actually and in potential. In this model, revelation is not only technically ongoing, but also ontologically necessarily so. Time reveals not only what was implicit in the original voice, but also what was totally unknown to the original voice.[56] Lainer, as we have seen, presents a particularly radical formulation of this third model.[57]

These eight areas present striking parallels between Lainer's theology and the worldviews of Romanticism. One key difference between Lainer and the Romantic school is that Lainer does not fall into what Wilber has called the Romantic 'pre/trans fallacy'.[58] The Romantics, according to Wilber, failed to distinguish between the primal, prerational human experience and the far more subtle, moral, and evolved transrational human experience. Lainer's process of *berur* is his safeguard against this fallacy. His concept of *lema'alah mida'ato* is very much a post-*berur* transrational notion and not at all a prerational idea.

Even in areas of close resonance between Lainer and the Romantics, it would be incorrect to suggest that Lainer was simply influenced by Romanticism. As we have argued throughout, many elements of his thought emerge directly from the Jewish and particularly kabbalistic tradition.[59] However, it is possible to assert that Lainer's work is a unique Jewish mystical expression of some of the fundamental elements of the spiritual and intellectual Zeitgeist of his time.

Notes for Chapter Fifteen

1 Weiss, 'Determinism' 448.

2 Ross, 'Shenei' 155–162.

3 A substantive discussion of the implications of acosmism for בחירה חפשית *behirah hofshit* and a close examination of how each acosmic thinker dealt with this challenge is a monumental topic unto itself.

4 On free will in Habad see Jacobson, 'Torat'.

5 See Braslav, *Likutei Moharan* sec. 64; for an analysis, see Green, *Tormented* Excursus One 285–336.

6 The service of God through human free will is described throughout Levi Isaac's magnum opus, *Kedushat Levi*. See collected pieces in Blumenthal, *God*. At the same time, Levi Isaac appears throughout *Kedushat Levi* as a radical acosmist. On Levi Isaac, see Idel, *Perspectives* 69–70. The nature of Levi Issac's resolution of these two opposing poles is worthy of a separate study.

7 Tamar Ross, 'Hamahshavah'; see particularly 183–207.

8 Krishnamurti taught: 'When choice is involved there is always conflict. That is, when you have two ways of action, that choice merely produces more conflict. But if you saw very clearly within yourself, as a human being belonging to the whole world, not just to one petty, little country in some little geographical division, if you saw this issue clearly, then there would be no choice. Therefore an action which is without choice does not breed conflict' (*Action* 36).

9 Quoted in Forbes, Lecture.

10 Edwards, *The Living Waters* Translator's Introduction 10.

11 Cited in Edwards, *The Living Waters* 330 n. 60.

12 Personal communication, November 2002.

13 On Spinoza, see Yovel, *Spinoza* 282.

14 See the section 'Two: The Reality of Love in Lainer's Theology'.

15 See Green, 'Rethinking' 10–11.

16 Matt, 'Ayin' 121 n. 1. Matt notes, based on Katz, 'Language' 51–54, that while various mystics' descriptions of nothingness are similar, they cannot be considered to have had identical experiences, because each mystic is shaped by their own unique discourse. However, see Wilber's important critique of Katz. Wilber maintains that a core commonality of experience is shared by mystics from completely different cultural discourses (*Sex, Ecology* 627–632).

17 For a detailed discussion of nonduality in Buddhist sources and its implications for choice and freedom, see, e.g., Suzuki, *Studies*; *Essays*. On the Buddhist doctrine of 'no self', see also Wilber, *Sex, Ecology* 719–734.

18 On the relationship between choice and necessity in *MHs*, see the section 'Acosmic Humanism and Idolatry'.

19 See Wilber, *Sex, Ecology* 329–354.

20 Lovejoy, *The Great* 24–66.

21 Wilber, *Sex, Ecology* 329–354.

22 Lovejoy, *The Great* 45.

23 Plotinus scholar W. R. Inge traces Plotinus's nondualism to Plato (*The Philosophy of Plotinus*). See also Wilber, *Sex, Ecology* 329–354.

24 See Inge, *The Philosophy of Plotinus* 11.xi. See also Wilber, *Sex, Ecology* 346.

25 See Inge, *The Philosophy of Plotinus* 11.139.

26 See Taylor, *Hegel* 36; see also Taylor, *Sources of the Self* 382–383.

27 Wilber, *Sex, Ecology* 509.

28 See Taylor, *Hegel* 36; *Sources of the Self* 383–384.

29 Wilber's contemporary framing of this question may also be illuminating. He writes (*Sex, Ecology* 508–510):

> How do you unite a path of radical freedom and detachment heading in the direction of the ascending One, versus a path dedicated to descending Union and communion with the diverse Many?…

30 Taylor, *Hegel* 39.

31 Taylor, *Hegel* 44.

32 See 'Determinism' 441, where Weiss mentions the affinity between the Romantic spirit and Lainer, though he does not expand on it. Our remarks here may be regarded as an expansion of Weiss's observation. Our remarks on Romanticism in this chapter should also be viewed as an explication of our remarks in the Introduction, and in the sections 'Strand Two: The Hermeneutic One-Letter Tradition' and 'Strand Three: Soul Sparks and *Tikun* (Repair) 'suggesting that differing conceptions of the individual in Luria and Lainer reflected their Renaissance and Romantic sensibilities respectively.

33 Taylor, *Sources of the Self* 368–390.

34 *Sources of the Self* 302.

35 We note as well that the Musar school of Israel Salanter and his students may have also been influenced by the Romantic Zeitgeist. See Ross, 'Hamahshavah' 60–64, 217–218. While the Musar school affirmed the suprarational element already inherent in Kant's distinction between noumena and phenomena and reflected in Lainer's *lema'alah mida'ato*, it retained normative and rational safeguards to ensure the ethical nature of the suprarational will.

36 Sterne, *Sentimental Journey* 125, adduced in Taylor, *Sources of the Self* 302; see also 390.

37 *Sources of the Self* 370.

38 *Sources of the Self* 314.

39 *Sources of the Self* 370.

40 *Sources of the Self* 371, 373.

41 *Sources of the Self* 376.

42 On Lainer and antinomianism, see esp. the section 'Freedom and Law' above.

43 *Sources of the Self* 372.

44 *Sources of the Self* 377.

45 *Sources of the Self* 375, 377.

46 *Sources of the Self* 380.

47 On the very 'particular voice' that is the revelation of God/nature through the individual, see Taylor, *Sources of the Self* 369, 374, 375.

48 *Sources of the Self* 375.

49 See the section 'Freedom and Law'.

50 *Sources of the Self* 372, 411, 412, 417.

51 See the section 'Fifth Major Theme: The Ontological Dignity of Desire'.

52 Silman, *Kol*, citing Lovejoy, *The Great*. The most significant previous discussion of continuing revelation in Jewish thought is that of Shalom Rosenberg ('Hitgalut') who distinguished among three essential models which can be termed textual, historical, and intellectual. Silman incorporates Rosenberg's first and third models in a more sophisticated overall scheme.

53 Silman, *Kol* 11 n. 1.

54 Silman, *Kol* 21–88.

55 See *Kol* 89–118.

56 *Kol* 119–149. Silman unknowingly cites Lainer in his third model when he presents a Tzadok Hakohen text which Tzadok prefaces with *shama'ti* 'I have heard'. The phrase *shama'ti* in Tzadok's work, according to an old tradition, always indicates an idea that he heard from his teacher, Mordechai Lainer. This tradition is cited in a work entitled *Mei Tzedek*, collected by the descendants of Mordechai Lainer. See Gellman, 'The Denial' n. 10.

57 See 'Seventh Major Theme: The Human Being as a Source of Revelation'.

58 See Wilber, *The Marriage*, particularly the chapter on Romanticism, 90–102. See also the discussion of *berur* in 'Models of Activism: Pre- and Post-*Berur* Consciousness, Linear and Dynamic Models' above.

59 Most fundamentally, his acosmism emerges out of a significant post-Lurianic tradition. See Ross, 'Shenei'.

PART SIX

Echoes of Izbica in Modern
Jewish Thought

Chapter Sixteen
Introduction

In this final part of volume One, we briefly outline some of the significant spheres of influence of Lainer's theology on subsequent Jewish thought. Our purpose in doing so is to show that Lainer's influence on evolving Jewish thought is substantive and may well become more significant as time goes on. Lainer's work is already in the process of being reclaimed from relative obscurity to a place of special prominence in the contemporary neo-Hasidic attempt to forge a new Jewish theology at least partly from Hasidic sources.[1]

Here we will make some very general remarks about Lainer's influence on Abraham Isaac Hakohen Kook, Abraham Joshua Heschel, and, most recently, on what has been called 'neo-Hasidism'. We hope that scholarship will in due time flesh out a more complete picture.

Lainer and Abraham Isaac Hakohen Kook

Ish-Shalom seeks to locate Abraham Isaac Hakohen Kook's thought in the European Zeitgeist in which he writes.[2] Ross takes implicit issue with this approach and seeks to locate Kook within the kabbalistic tradition, arguing persuasively for a dominant influence of Habad on Kook's thought,[3] cross-fertilized with Lithuanian Kabbalah. Both Ross and Ish-Shalom make valid, important points. However, neither examines the thinker whose thought bears the most striking resemblance to that of Kook: Mordechai Lainer.

Hadari, in a general article, cites historical anecdote and testimonies as well as some very general conceptual frameworks linking Kook to Lainer's student, Tzadok Hakohen.[4] He also cites links between Kook and the lineage that preceded Izbica, namely the courts of Kotzk, Przysucha, and Lublin. However, as Hadari himself points out, it is difficult to discuss direct influence of Tzadok Hakohen on Kook since virtually all of Tzadok's books were published after Kook's death.[5]

We suggest that the primary source Kook drew from for these ideas was not Tzadok Hakohen but rather Mordechai Lainer of Izbica. In fact, we have more direct testimony that Kook studied *MHs* than Hadari has regarding Kook and Tzadok. Moshe Zvi Neriah, a close student of Kook's and a close associate of his son Zvi Yehudah Kook, reported to this writer that Kook studied *MHs* on a regular basis.[6] Neriah's testimony is substantiated by a second source, a small pamphlet by Shlomo Carlebach published as *Orot Shelomoh* that contains Carlebach's ruminations on Kook's *Orot Hateshuvah*. In the introduction, Carlebach writes that he once met Tzvi Yehudah Kook, who told him that his father's two greatest influences were Nahman of Braslav and the Torah of Izbica. Further substantiation is offered by the close connection between Rav Kook and the Hasidic dynasty of Radzyn, whose masters were the inheritors and direct descendants of Mordechai Lainer of Izbica.

Bezalel Naor, in the introduction to his translation of Kook's classic work *Orot*, describes the complex relationship that evolved between Kook and the Rebbe of Gur. While the latter had tried to mediate the conflict between Kook and the elders of Jerusalem, he also had substantive theological misgiving in reference to *Orot* and moved Kook to recant part of it. Naor notes by way of contrast that Kook's philosophy was highly valued and 'much appreciated within another Polish Hasidic tradition, Izbica-Radzyn-Lublin'.[7] Naor's scholarly conjecture is that the Radzyner Rebbe, Mordechai Joseph Eleazar Leiner, 'heard an echo of the "radical" theology of his Grandfather, Mordechai Joseph Leiner (sic) of Izbica' in the thought of Rav Kook.[8]

There are several virtually identical core structures in the theologies of Kook and Lainer that substantiate these historical testimonies. Though a full discussion of these issues would require another volume, our observations here may at least point the way for future scholarship.

The key parallel from which all the others flow is acosmic humanism itself. Rather than viewing Kook's acosmism as primarily influenced by Habad, as Ross suggests, a close reading reveals striking parallels with Lainer. For both, their acosmism yields highly humanistic corollaries, lending their writing an optimistic Romantic flavor that affirms the full dignity of the human being.

(1) One clear example of Lainer and Kook's shared thought involves Lainer's empowering acosmic corollary, his concept of *tzurat ha-adam* (the essential

divine form of the inner human).[9] Lainer's *tzurat ha-adam* is both infinitely unique and subjective. Paradoxically, it is also the divine center of the human persona. Kook expresses a virtually identical acosmic corollary in his concept of the אני עצמי *ani 'atzmi*,[10] the essential I. Both of these concepts affirm that the human being incarnates divinity and that divinity appears in the unique self of the radically subjective human.[11] Both of these ideas are fundamentally acosmic and yield conclusions that are not emasculating but rather highly empowering of the human being.

(2) Both hold will as the central category in their system and both affirm the ontic identity between the will of God and human will.[12]

(3) Both affirm the centrality and ontological dignity of *teshukah* as lodestones of their theologies.

(4) Both view revelation as an ongoing process.[13]

(5) Both understand that there are groups of *tzadikim* who act beyond the normative understanding of the law.[14] In this context we refer briefly to the major passage in Kook's published work that deals with the two types of *tzadikim*, because the passage itself contains a number of key ideational structures that seem to be rooted in Lainer's thought:

> There are two aspirations of being: that of *berur berurim* and the uplifting of worlds. The first is the work of every man and the second is the work of the righteous in every generation… those in whom the light of 'the breath of our nostrils, the messiah of God' (Lam. 4:20) flows in them.[15]

Like Lainer, Kook views the first type of *tzadik*, who represents the potential achievement of every person, as being involved in *berur*. In this model, according to Kook, the *homo religiosus* seeks to achieve purity of intent and action in every sphere of life.[16] This is a direct parallel to Lainer's Joseph archetype.

Kook's second model of *tzadik* is on a higher level, that of *'olam ha-ba*.[17] This is, of course, parallel to Lainer's Judah archetype, who is similarly identified by Lainer as a manifestation of the spiritual level of *'olam ha-ba*. However, an important distinction is that Kook, at least in this passage, seems to limit his second category of *tzadik* to the elite, while Lainer, whose goal is the democratization of enlightenment, suggests that this category is a genuine possibility for everyone.[18] In the continuation of the passage, Kook links his second category of *tzadik* to King David, to *teshukah*, to being subject to הכרח *hekhrei'ah* (higher divine necessity; i.e., what we have referred to as choicelessness), to messianic consciousness, and, particularly, to the messianic quality of מורח ודאין *morei'ah vada'in*. Literally, this means the certainty of smell; it refers to the divine intuition that defines the judgment of messianic consciousness.[19]

(6) Two other characteristics of this model of *tzadik* are implied in the passage. Kook's second type of *tzadik* establishes a more integrative relationship with evil and pathology, and is beyond the tension of human effort. All of these linkages are major motifs in Lainer's explication of his Judah archetype.[20]

(7) While in the passage quoted above, Kook limits his second *tzadik* model to the elite, in other passages, Kook, like Lainer, affirms the potential not only of the *tzadik* but also of the common person to reach this level.[21]

(8) Both explicitly distinguish between the Judah and Joseph archetypes.[22]

(9) Both affirm the nature of the divine to be that which holds paradox (or, that which holds opposites), and both view paradox as essential to their theology.[23]

(10) Both have an ambivalent relationship with paganism, each seeking in his own way to identify and redeem the sacred sparks of idolatry.[24]

(11) The idea that both the human being and God have some type of lack (*hisaron*) is central to both their ideologies.[25]

(12) Human freedom is central to both of their systems, and both root their concepts of human freedom in their acosmic metaphysics.[26]

(13) Kook follows Lainer in a very precise understanding of the higher unity of necessity and freedom. Thus, the final area where we will argue that a key concept in Kook's acosmic theology can be located in Lainer's metaphysics is the higher unity of הכרח *hekhrei'ah*, divine necessity on one hand, and voluntaristic and free *ratzon* divine will on the other.[27] Kook argues consistently that redeemed consciousness is expressed by the full

merger between *ratzon* and *hekhrei'ah*. *Ratzon* represents the voluntaristic and free element of reality, while *hekhrei'ah* (the same term used consistently by Lainer) represents the highest order of divine necessity. In redeemed consciousness, rather than these being viewed as opposites, they are experienced as a higher unity. This is, of course, the underpinning of the concept of choicelessness, as we have described it, in Lainer's theology.

Lainer and Abraham Joshua Heschel

A second figure greatly influenced by *MHs* was Abraham Joshua Heschel. Although an examination of Heschel's philosophy of law is clearly beyond the scope of this work, some very brief framing remarks are required in order to understand his relationship to *MHs*.

Yaffa Aranoff, responding to critiques of Heschel's philosophy of law, suggests that, rather than understanding Heschel in terms of subjectivism,[28] he must be understood in the context of Hasidic sources in general and particularly *MHs*.[29] Heschel expands the meaning of *mitzvah* beyond the parameters of the heteronomous act, explaining that all acts can establish a link between man and God, and as such can become *mitzvah*.[30] This is of course a classic Hasidic theme that emphasized the verse 'In all your ways know him'.[31] In Hasidic theology, as exemplified by the Habad system, the domain of neutral acts is effaced. Every act strengthens either the domain of the holy or that of the סיטרא אחרא *sitra ahra* 'the other side'.[32] At the same time, Heschel, similarly to Lainer, sees the law as that which keeps the human engaged in spirit.[33] 'The soul would remain silent were it not for the summons of the law and reminder of the law'.[34] Law guides and shapes the human's inner voice. Individual insight is necessary, but does not develop without the guidance of law.[35] However, according to Heschel, it is clear both that law serves the human ability to gain unmediated insight and that it does not by itself necessarily represent the will of God.

Throughout his writings, Heschel clearly distinguishes between *halakhah* and *aggadah*.[36] Heschel makes it clear that *aggadah* takes precedence over and is the source of authority for *halakhah*.[37] Crucially, according to Heschel, the basis of the obligation to observe commandments is not tradition, but rather revelation as a living, ongoing event, available not only to the elite but to all of the engaged.[38] At Sinai we received 'both the word and the spirit to understand the word'. For Heschel, 'everyone has within himself the power to legislate based on the fact that at Sinai we received both the word and the power to interpret the word.'[39] Aranoff concludes her analysis of Heschel's notion of revelation with the bold claim that for Heschel 'the individual has in some sense displaced the Rabbis'.

Although Aranoff does not link these basic structures in Heschel directly to Lainer, all of them support her conclusion that *MHs* teachings 'greatly influenced Heschel's thought not only in places where he cites *MHs*, but also in places where there is a mere allusion'.[40] We assert even more specifically that all of the defining characteristics of Heschel's *homo religiosus* are found in Lainer's Judah archetype. These include the affirmation of the law as that which leads one beyond the law; the affirmation of the human ability to access the unmediated will of God, and the democratization of enlightenment.

Heschel himself paraphrases at length what may be the most well-known Judah archetype text in *MHs*, to which we have referred above.[41] The passage compares Judah and Efrayim, the latter being the paragon of obedience to the law and the former representing the ability to transcend the law and access the unmediated will of God:

> …Judah has been appointed to concentrate on God and to be attached to him in all his ways. Therefore Judah is not satisfied to know the mere law but looks to God to reveal to him the depths of truth beyond the law itself…Judah refuses to be content with routine observance or perfunctory faith. Not content to do today what he did yesterday, he desires to find new light in his commandments every day. This insistence on fresh light sometimes drives Judah into doing actions for the sake of God which are against the strict law.[42]

Significantly, Heschel takes Lainer's democratization of enlightenment one step further than did Lainer himself. He writes immediately prior to his citation of *MHs*:

> There are situations when the relationship between law and inwardness becomes…gravely imbalanced…[T]he rabbis established a level of observance which in modern society is beyond the grasp of ordinary men. Must halacha [sic] continue to ignore the voice of aggada [sic]?

330

Here Heschel even ignores the requirement of *berur*, provocatively equating the Judah archetype and 'ordinary men'.

Lainer and the Neo-Hasidic and Jewish Renewal Movements

Much more recently, *MHs* has become perhaps the single most influential book in two modern Jewish movements. The first is the Orthodox neo-Hasidic movement, with Shlomo Carlebach at its center. The second is the Jewish renewal movement, which might be characterized as a non-Orthodox version of neo-Hasidism.[43] The acknowledged elder of Jewish Renewal is Zalman Schachter-Shalomi.[44] The Lainer dynasty itself credits Shlomo Carlebach with fostering the popular interest in *MHs*. Significantly, Shlomo Carlebach introduced *MHs* to Zalman Schachter-Shalomi, whose only doctoral student, Morris Faierstein, wrote his thesis on *MHs*;[45] in this volume, we have had ample opportunity to refer to Faierstein's work.

Bezalel Edwards accurately describes Carlebach's contribution in the introduction to his English translation of *MHs*. He sums up clearly the dramatic influence of Carlebach as well as the importance of *MHs* in certain neo-Hasidic centers of contemporary Orthodoxy.

> I once met with Reb Yaakov Lainer in Borough Park, Brooklyn. The son of the late Radzyner Rebbe and a direct descendant of the *Mei Hashiloah*, he is the current publisher of Isbitza [sic] books in the United States. He told me that thirty years ago, his father, of blessed memory, would sell some twenty copies of the *Mei Hashiloah* each year. It was like a dinosaur. He told me that at that time it was only really studied by Jews who came from certain towns in Poland. Then in the late 1960s, Reb Shlomo Carlebach, may his memory be blessed, began his work of traveling seven continents to light Jewish hearts with the fire of Hasidism. In his suitcase there was always a copy of the *Mei Hashiloah*. You could say that wherever he went, he took with him the light and profundity of the Isbitzer Rebbe, giving it to thirsty souls. I once heard him say, 'you cannot understand the Chumash without the *Mei Hashiloah*'...In the six years I spent with Shlomo, not a learning [session], not a Shabbos, went by without some light from the Isbitzer. Today it is found in every

331

Hebrew bookstore, and is taught in every yeshiva of new young spirit seekers desiring inspiration from the Hasidic masters. (Here Edwards describes encounters with three important Orthodox teachers who spoke with him about *MHs:* Reb Yitschak Asher Twersky of Boston (the Talner Rebbe), Rabbi Shlomo Riskin, and Rabbi Chaim Brovender, both in Efrat. He continues:) I mention these examples just to show how widespread the prevalence of the *Mei Hashiloah* has become for those receptive to the teachings of Hasidism, whereas fifty years ago the name *Mei Hashiloah* would have gone unnoticed.[46]

While the affinity between Jewish Renewal and Izbica has not been elaborated on by scholars, Shaul Magid makes passing reference to it in the conclusion of his book on Izbica: 'It is therefore no surprise that contemporary Jewish Renewal, a movement that in effect combines liberal religious critique, neo-Sabbatean religious reform, and Hasidic pietism, views itself as the spiritual inheritor of these texts.'[47] Without getting involved in an analysis of Magid's understanding of Renewal, the essential link between Renewal and Izbica is certainly correct.

On the Danger of High States and Stages

A brief aside feels necessary as part of these closing paragraphs. There is great danger, as evidenced in the example of many renewal contexts, in the appropriation of post conventional teachings of the radical Izbica nature without understanding the larger requirements of *berur* explicit in Lainer's teaching. This danger comes to the fore both in the New Age idolization of state experiences and the excessive premium that much of the Integral community places on complex levels of cognition. Higher levels of cognitive complexity do not make a better human being. Rarely are there posts in New Age or Integral blogs of higher development about kindness. Kindness is a value that all too often is relegated to the lower levels of amber or blue consciousness in the Integral and spiral dynamics color model. Worse still, it is given lip service even as it is ignored in practice when the real gods of cognition and power are worshiped. In New Age contexts, love is the buzzword, while the more practical and actionable quality of kindness gets very little play. Fairness and justice within the organization of movements gets even less attention. Justice is only raised as an issue when it comes to political or gender issues. It remains true, however, that the most powerful mechanism to assure kindness is fairness, and fairness is a conventional value rooted in law and integrity.

While both Integral and New Age spiritual contexts revel in being post conventional, all too often there is a failure to appreciate the requirement for what my rebbe Mordechai Lainer called berur, the clarification that comes from the due process of law, which includes impartial parties hearing all sides, clarifying ulterior motives and getting the facts straight. Many New Age spiritual contexts place a high premium on wonderful state experiences of ecstasy brought about through chant and prayer or through high structure stages of cognitive complexity, while all too often bypassing essential issues of ethics and integrity. One cannot move beyond the conventional without first honoring the great wisdom of the conventional. In the Radical Kabbalah of Mordechai Lainer, it is precisely in this transcending and including of the conventional in post conventional contexts that the Eros of the goddess, what he would call the *Shekhinah*, is incarnate. The entirety of Eros, for Lainer, is poured into assuring the correct verdict in what appears to be a petty case in small claims court. It is in the precision and caring for justice—in the details of justice—that the Eros of the goddess lives. Certainly when issues of great import are at hand which have implications for the lives of individuals and entire communities, the genuine Eros of *Shekhinah* demands careful fact checking, deliberation and direct communication, examination of the complex motivations at play, and fairness, decency and healing. Minimally a fair "court" must be established that truly seeks justice and healing and is willing to think past self-interest and communal pressure. The failure to put such mechanisms of fairness and integrity in play is tragic and is exactly the kind of violation of the goddess that post conventional contexts—whether of the Integral or New Age variety—must passionately and rigorously avoid at all costs.

Notes for Part 6

1 On neo-Hasidism and new theology, see Green, 'Hasidism: Discovery'.

2 See Ish-Shalom, *Haguto* 17–26. See also Goldman, 'Zikato'.

3 See Ross, 'Musag'.

4 Hadari, 'Shenei Kohanim', esp. 87–89 and notes *ad loc.*

5 Hadari, 'Shenei Kohanim' 88.

6 Personal communication, 1979.

7 Kook, *Orot* series 28 n. 60.

8 Naor, Introduction to Kook, *Orot* series 28–29.

9 For a discussion of this concept in Lainer's thought, see the section 'Freedom and Law'.

10 See Kook, *Orot Hakodesh vol. 3* 140; see also Lipshitz, Roeh 35–38.

11 On Kook and uniqueness see, e.g., *Orot Hakodesh vol. 3* 119, 140.

12 For an analysis of will in the thought of Kook, see, e.g., *Orot Hakodesh vol. 3* 108, 109; see also Ish-Shalom, *Haguto* 98–113.

13 On Kook's idea of ongoing revelation, see Ish-Shalom, *Haguto* 98–105; see also Rosenberg, 'Hitgalut' 131–132.

14 On this idea in Lainer, see Chapter Twelve.

15 Arpelei Tohar 20.

16 Arpelei Tohar 20–22.

17 For Lainer *on 'olam ha-ba*, see vol. 2 Psalms s.v. *Hashem menat helki*; see also above, p. 51ff.

18 Kook in this sense is similar to the Seer of Lublin's two models of religious service. The Seer is a major influence on Mordechai Lainer; he was the teacher of his teacher, Simcha Bunim of Przysucha. See the discussion and footnotes in Elior, 'Temurot'.

19 On *teshukah*, see Chapter Eleven. On King David, messianic consciousness and *morah vada'in*, see *MHs* vol. 2 Behaalotekha s.v. *im yihyeh* (Source 5 in volume 2). On *hekhrei'ah*, see 'Acosmic Humanism and Idolatry'. On the relationship to evil and pathology, see discussions in the section 'Uniqueness and Sin' and Chapter Three.

20 On the *tzadik* of this second variety and the quality of being beyond the tension of human effort, see p. 139ff.

21 In *Orot Hakodesh* 3:140, Kook applies the same verse from the previous passage to every person. There he writes that a person claiming their *ani ha-'atzmi* (essential I–ness) is an expression of messianic consciousness and a healing of the fall in Eden. He explicitly refers to this level of messianic consciousness as the achievement of every individual and not only the goal of the elite. On the spiritual power of the common person in Kook, see also *Orot Hakodesh* 2:364, 365; and the discussion of this passage in Ish-Shalom, *Haguto*.

22 See, in Kook's writings, 'Musar Hakodesh' 156, and *Orot Hateshuvah* 12 sec. 6.

23 On the centrality of paradox in Kook's system, see Ish-Shalom, *Haguto* 60–64.

24 On Lainer's relation to paganism, see brief comments above, p. 234. See also Cluster 5 of *volume 2*. On Kook's positive inclination towards a dimension of paganism, see, e.g., sources cited by Ross, *Perakim BeTorat* Ch. 5 and Ch. 10. See also Gellman, *The Fear* 99–114, esp. the section on Abraham and idolatry.

25 On *hisaron* in Kook, see, e.g., *Orot Hakodesh* 2:728–730, 748. See also Ben Shlomo, 'Sheleimut'. On *hisaron* in Lainer, see Chapter Three.

26 On freedom in Kook, see Ish-Shalom, 'Dat'.

27 See extended discussion of this issue in Lainer above, p. 217ff.

28 For a critique of Heschel in terms of subjectivism, see, e.g., Hyman, 'Meaningfulness'; Kaplan, 'Metaphor' 18.

29 Aranoff, 'Abraham', esp. 1 and 10–18.

30 See general discussion in Heschel, *God in Search* 174–336.

31 Prov. 3:7. On the centrality of this verse, see any classic study of Hasidism. See, e.g., Elior, *Harut* 99–114.

32 See Hallamish, 'Mishnato'.

33 For this theme in Lainer, see our discussion in the section 'Freedom and Law'. On Heschel and the law, see Eisen, 'Re-reading'.

34 Heschel, *God in Search* 343.

35 Aranoff, 'Abraham' 11.

36 Heschel, *God in Search* 336, as well as the entire work of *Torah Min Hashamayim*.

37 Heschel, *God in Search* 338: 'The Event at Sinai…[t]he Mystery of Revelation, belongs to the sphere of *aggada* [sic]…thus while the content of *halacha* [sic] is subject to its own reasoning, its authority derives from *aggada* [sic]'.

38 Aranoff, 'Abraham' 14–15, nn. 57–61.

39 Heschel, *God in Search* 174.

40 Aranoff, 'Abraham' 17. The specific examples of such influence cited by Aranoff seem tangential; the aforementioned principles of Heschel's thought are far more deeply rooted in Lainer's mode of thought than Aranoff's conjectures indicate.

41 *MHs* vol. 1 Vayeishev s.v. *vayeishev*. See endnote 955.

42 See Heschel, *God in Search* 342, cf. Aranoff, 'Abraham' 16–18.

43 A brief survey of the range of people studying and teaching *MHs* today would confirm the strong connection between *MHs* and both Carlebach *Hasidut* and Jewish Renewal.

44 Note that while 'Reb Shlomo', as he is called by followers, is generally characterized as 'rebbe' in the traditional Hasidic sense, 'Reb Zalman' eschewed the title.

45 Schachter-Shalomi, personal communication, Winter 2003.

46 Edwards, *The Living Waters* Introduction.

47 Magid, *Hasidism* 253.

INDEX–Selected Topics

AFTERWORD

"If you will desire her like you desire silver, and seek her out like you would seek out treasures, only then will you understand Awe of God, and only then will you discover Knowledge of Elohim" (Proverbs of Solomon 2:4-5).

A great and luminous work has come before my eyes, a vast and deep sea of illuminating wisdom embodied in clear and accessible writ. It is obvious from my reading of this fascinating work that its author, Rabbi Dr. Marc Gafni, has indeed sought her out as he would treasures, and has desired her far more than the desire for gold—let alone silver—she being *hokhmah*, the elusive matron of our people's rich and ancient wisdom, keeper of the mystery teachings of our ancestors, God's very first creation from whose womb all of creation emanated, as is written: "Through *hokhmah* did God establish the earth" (Prov. 3:19). For in this wondrous and masterful work, Rabbi Gafni takes us on an enchanting journey across the vast plains of Hebrew Scriptures, the sensuous hills of erotic kabbalah, the impressive mountains of Talmud and Midrash, to candle-lit corners of revered mystics like Rabbis Moshe Cordovero, Yitzhak Luria, and the more recent Mordechai Yosef Lainer, who in their inspired wisdom skillfully distilled the soul-deep, underlying intentions and lessons of our people's 4,000 year mystery schooling. But alas! Who amongst us has the time or even the capability to explore—let alone understand—the teachings of these great masters and to drink from their goblets? Who amongst us has the capacity to wade through all of the enormous libraries housing their writings, or to climb the towering shelves that carry the weight of their volumes? And who amongst us can thoroughly study their works and also find time to contemplate, translate, and interpret the meanings and implications of these writings, ultimately rendering them accessible to the rest of us?

I have only found one such blessed individual, a man who on his own volition, and out of his soul-deep passion for the wisdom of Torah, took it upon himself to endeavor where no one else rose to the occasion, and to expend his time and energy, even amid great personal suffering and against

343

overwhelming obstacles, to gift us with a massive compendium of long-neglected wisdom destined to lift our eyes above the stagnating ways in which we have been seeing for far too long, so that we might see anew, and our hearts become thereby opened wider to enable the removal of the many layers of ignorance and oblivion that have obscured our vision in the fog of our lengthy exile.

Where there is no one doing what needs to be done," Hillel the Elder demanded over two thousand years ago, "then YOU be the one to do it!" And thus did Rabbi Marc Gafni step daringly into the void created by the dearth of enlivening and invigorating teachings of our tradition, and blessed us with this important work whose teachings encourage and urge us to restore our passions once more as in days of old, to embrace the erotic in the sacred ways in which our ancestors did, and to acknowledge and honor the feminine attributes of the divine; to sip from the delicate, overflowing goblet of sweet wisdom, particularly the divine wisdom channeled by our revered tribal chieftain of 3,000 years ago, Solomon, whom God called "My son" and "beloved of God" (2 Sam. 12:24-25; 1 Chron. 17:13 and 22:10).

This work is a true masterpiece of the sort our people have not witnessed for many centuries, shaking us out of our stupor toward reclaiming life again, reclaiming our goddess heritage and teachings, and the bond with the ancient spark of eros of our so-called pagan ways of many of our aboriginal sisters and brothers, a bond we had begun to forge under Solomon and are destined to forge once again in the time to come. But Rabbi Gafni in his fine and original reading of Mordechai Lainer purifies the spark of its pre-personal ethical taint. In a Lurianic act of exalted scholarship and love he raises the spark of paganism and sets it in a new evolved ethical context so that the passion for the goddess expresses itself not in irresponsible abandon but in the infinitely sacred details of judicial procedure and fairness.

The erotic goddess is channeled into justice and small claims court becomes the arena of the goddess's revelation. This is in Gafni's reading the major wonder of Izbica and it is also the major goal Gafni's own life and work. It is Gafni's particular sensitivity and evolving passion for the ethical that reveals these strains in Izbica.

344

Much of this sacred work will raise brows, even more of it will challenge the way in which we have grown accustomed to think, and all of it, I pray, will finally restore us to our primal mindset, our original way of perceiving and encountering the divine in both its immanent and transcendent dances, so that the thousand songs and dances of the Pharaoh's daughter will no longer be for us the antithesis we had presumed it was, and instead become the sacred rite of divine connection it was intended to be.

For those who will approach this challenging and daring work with trepidation or with skepticism, or worse with criticism, be forewarned that Rabbi Gafni's work is fully supported by an enormous legion of ancient and medieval classical text sources from the earlier writings of teachers who are revered by the most traditional amongst us. He is not attempting in this book to introduce anything new to our eyes, but rather to introduce our eyes to what has been there all along, veiled from our sight by our own blindness. His work is a gift, a blessing, and most importantly a rare opportunity for all of us to reclaim the authenticity of our true selves, and to breathe the breath of Life back into our souls.

At the same time Rabbi Gafni introduces us to the great lineage from which he drinks and which inspired him to bring the great teaching of Unique Self into the world of world spirituality. We see the lineage of Unique Self rooted grandly in the hidden teachings of Mordechai Lainer which Mordechai Gafni reveals and shares and which his own Integral teaching broadens, deepens and evolves.

~ Rabbi Gershon Winkler

Rabbi Gershon Winkler is the erudite author of ten books of Jewish teaching and scholarship, a master of original Jewish texts and a highly beloved and respected teacher of Jewish sources and practice.

EXCURSUS TO VOLUME 1

On Scholarship and Methodology

In this excursus, I will give a more detailed account and critique of the prevalent view of the religious philosophy of Mordechai Lainer of Izbica held by scholars, which we touched on in the very beginning.

Previous scholarship on Mordechai Lainer can be divided into two basic approaches. The dominant approach championed by most of Izbica scholarship was first suggested by Joseph Weiss in two seminal articles on Mordechai Lainer.[1] Weiss characterizes the theology of *MHs*, Lainer's only extant work, as a highly theocentric system in which human activism is rendered not only irrelevant but ontologically meaningless. Weiss posits his understanding of Lainer on what he terms 'the removal of all human autonomy'.[2]

Morris Faierstein, author of the only scholarly work dedicated solely to *MHs*, consistently adopts Weiss's theocentric view.[3] The natural corollary of this position for Weiss—a corollary articulated by Faierstein as well—is that human activism is rendered, at least from the divine perspective, utterly meaningless. In this view, the denial of what Weiss refers to as human autonomy becomes an essential linchpin in Lainer's theology. Variations on this view are echoed by virtually all other Izbica scholars, including Miriam Feigelson,[4] Don Seeman,[5] Jerome Gellman,[6] Yehuda Ben Dor,[7] and Amira Lever.[8]

On the other hand, the second approach, suggested by Rivka Schatz-Uffenheimer[9] and sometimes adopted by Rachel Elior, reads Lainer as affirming radical human autonomy. Elior's summation of Schatz-Uffenheimer's position is that '[Rivka Schatz] claims that the theology of Mordechai Lainer of Izbica sees in human autonomy the only possible legitimate understanding of the term Divine will'.[10] Both sides of this debate make use of the term 'autonomy', a problem we will address in this excursus.

What we have established in Book 1, however, is an approach radically different, based on close readings of a large body of material not analyzed in previous scholarship. That reading assigns these different approaches to different levels of consciousness. This has allowed us to incorporate the key intuitions of both sets of scholars, even in the process of developing a more integral model.[11]

Our Methodology for Reading *Mei Hashiloah*

This approach corresponds well to the normative format of rabbinic exegetical works of most eras. Most classical Jewish texts, including both rabbinic and kabbalistic works, were not written as formally organized discourses. Typically, their form is 'local-exegetical', seeking to interpret a particular passage in the sacred canon. As a result, when one wants to discern an author's opinion on a given topic, one must gather a great number of texts from different places. This is especially true of Hasidic works, with *MHs* being a prime example. In the context of our work, this point is particularly important, because, as we have suggested, the mistakes in reading Lainer's thought are often a function of too narrow a selection of texts.

As mentioned in the introduction to this volume, the method we have adopted for demonstrating this is to identify heretofore unnoticed 'textual clusters'. Each of these clusters is formed from a large group of passages, drawn from all over *MHs*, which give shape to one common understanding. For example, one such textual cluster is what we termed the 'name cluster'. Central to Lainer's acosmic humanism is his notion that human action is 'called by the name of man'. This has been read by other scholars[12] as a kind of divine sop to man in which God allows human action to be 'called by the name of man' even though there is no ontological efficacy to human action. In contrast, we performed a much broader and closer reading of this notion in Lainer's thought, incorporating many texts unexamined by earlier scholarship. Applying this approach, we found that these texts suggest that at the highest level of religious consciousness, the names of man and God are ontologically identical. His is precisely the notion of מקדש *mikdash*-consciousness.

On Acosmic Humanism vs. Autonomy

Above and in the introduction we discussed the concept of 'autonomy', which divides the two main schools of scholarship on *MHs*. As we

348

discussed, the term 'autonomy' does not correspond well to the actual categories of Lainer's thought and has not been generally employed in this work. Instead, I coined the new term 'acosmic humanism' to describe Lainer's theology of the merging of the human with the divine will.

There are other methodological reasons which also militate against using the concept of 'autonomy' to explain Lainer's acosmic humanism. In the study of religious phenomena, we must always bear in mind the sound directive of Mircea Eliade: 'The surest method in the history of religions... is still that of studying a phenomenon in its own frame of reference, with freedom afterwards to integrate the results of this procedure in a wider perspective'.[13] In Hasidic scholar Jerome Gellman's presentation of Eliade, this means that one needs to understand the Hasidic text, to the extent possible, from the point of view of the 'natives', in this case the Hasidim or the Hasidic masters themselves.[14]

Eliade of course does not mean that the scholar must share the worldview of the natives.[15] However, the scholar cannot legitimately impose an external category that carries with it an entirely different felt experience, particularly one that is almost certainly alien to the internal experience of the Hasidic master.

This methodological concern relates strongly to several scholars' interpretations of the internal experience of erotic merger with divinity that is central to Lainer's theology.[16] When Schatz-Uffenheimer and Elior explain this experience as an instance of the Western understanding of autonomy, they impose the kind of external categories that Eliade, according to Gellman, warned against.[17] At the same time, Gellman's critique of Elior is not what we intend here. Gellman suggests that Elior misses the complete nullification of human agency, which, in his reading, is central to both the Seer and Lainer. In light of this nullification and the radical assertion of exclusive divine agency, Gellman cannot understand how either one's theology could be described in terms of human autonomy.[18] Gellman seems to assume that agency is an either/or proposition, whereas Lainer actually believes that these two perspectives, the divine and the human, merge once one has achieved what he calls הארה he'arah (enlightenment).[19] So, while Elior may be mistaken in using the terminology of autonomy, she is not wrong for the reasons Gellman suggests.[20]

When Elior writes, 'the person needs to make...an autonomous decision',[21] she describes the choice a person must make, according to Lainer, between following the law as expressed in the old static revelation of Sinai and acting in accordance with a new imperative. However, this new imperative emerges from the dynamic divine will, revealed in the eternal yet ever-changing present.

Classic Western notions of autonomy, on the other hand, have little to do with responding to a dynamic divine will. Autonomy is understood in the Western philosophical tradition as a flight from authority—particularly a flight from any sort of divine center of authority.[22] Derrida,[23] as expanded by Idel,[24] has already discussed the paradoxical affinity between the God-intoxicated Hasidic reader and the post modern atheistic reader. In Lainer's acosmic humanism, as in Western notions of autonomy, human action and decision-making are centered in the self. Both the experience of autonomy, and the mystical experience of merger with the divine, yield a sense of human freedom, power and audacity. However, these two experiences are fundamentally different.

For Lainer, there is no flight from the divine center but rather a reality in which the divine is both the epicenter as well as the basic monad of all reality. Acosmic humanism involves a sense of closeness, intimacy, and even identification with God, while Western autonomy emerges from a sense of distance, alienation, and even rejection of the Godhead's existence.[25] In Western autonomy, the self may well be only some version of the ego, while for Lainer, the realized self is ultimately no less than God.

A key feature of Lainer's acosmic humanism, as we have seen, is his emphasis on the religious centrality of the unique individual. For Lainer, an ultimate achievement of the ideal religious type is precisely the realization of the original and unique self. However, this notion also needs to be sharply distinguished from the kind of individuality spoken about by Thomas Hobbes and John Locke, upon which Western notions of individuality are built. For Hobbes and Locke, the individual is a discrete entity; the more individuality is heightened, the more separate and discrete the individual becomes. Indeed, this process drives the secularization that undermined much of classical religion.[26] For Lainer, individuality has precisely the opposite meaning: it is in the place of the individual's radical subjectivity that the boundary between the divine and human collapses and the great liberating realization of the ontic identity of wills is achieved.

Notes for Excursus

1 'Determinism'; 'A Late Jewish Utopia'.

2 'A Late Jewish Utopia' 244. Note that while Weiss's general characterization of Lainer's theology is highly theocentric, he does note passages throughout *MHs* which deviate from this truly theocentric strain and which are characterized by freedom and ontic identity of the human being with the divine. Weiss however views these passages as divergences from the major theocentric focus of the work, while we view these passages as forming the esssential crux of Lainer's theology, with the theocentric representing not divergences but rather expressions of a lower (but nonetheless high) level consciousness which precedes the realization of what we call 'acosmic humanism'.

3 *Hands* 29–30.

4 *The Theory of Mitzvot*.

5 'Martyrdom'. Seeman does correctly sense an activist strain in *MHs*. However, he attributes it to Lainer's ritual theories, as opposed to what he terms as Lainer's 'doctrine'. Apropos to this point, Seeman, basing himself in part on Geertz, critiques Weiss and Kabbalah scholarship in general for privileging doctrine over ritual. While on this point I think Seeman is correct, on the essential understanding of Izbica doctrine he implicitly adopts Weiss's reading. This is most apparent in Seeman's discussion of anger and ישוב הדעת *yishuv ha-da'at* in Lainer's theology, where, like Weiss, he assumes that human action is necessary and even approved of by God only in pre-*berur* consciousness. In contrast, we will emphasize the efficacy of human action in post-*berur* consciousness.

6 'The Denial' 114, 118.

7 *Normative* 18.

8 *Principles* 141 n. 89. Lever's thesis on Lainer's most important student, Tzadok Hakohen, which was written under the direction of Jerome Gellman, is mostly excellent. However, the sections comparing Tzadok to Lainer are weak because they follow Weiss's selection and readings of sources. See discussion in Chapter Thirteen, p. 251ff.

9 'Autonomiah' 556.

10 'Temurot' 415 n. 58. On the tension in Elior between the two approaches, see endnote 1370.

11 Naftali Loewenthal ('Reason') uses a similar method in pointing out the spiritualist and anti-spiritualist interpretations of R. Schneur Zalman of Liadi. Loewenthal ultimately rejects these separate interpretations as incomplete. He then offers a model that transcends and includes integrates elements of both.

12 E.g., Seeman, 'Martyrdom' 253; Ben Dor, *Normative* 26–27, esp. n. 55. Both Ben Dor and Seeman, although they do not cite Weiss directly in this regard, are based on Weiss's reading of name in *MHs*. See Weiss, 'Determinism' 451.

13 *Cosmos* 13.

14 Gellman, 'Hasidic' 393–397.

15 See Idel's discussion (*Perspectives* Introduction) of the relationship of Kabbalah scholars to their material in light of their general lack of mystical belief, let alone experience. Although Idel's discussion is developed along different lines, it is relevant to our discussion as well as to Gellman's discussion cited above.

16 This dimension is examined in Part Three and Part Four of this volume. For more general discussion of erotic merger with the divine in the genres of Kabbalah and Hasidic writing, see Liebes on the *Zohar* ('Hamashiah' 185, 205–207), and Idel on the Hasidic *homo religiosus* (*Hasidism* 133–141).

17 Gellman, 'Hasidic' 393–395. See also Seeman's critique of Schatz-Uffenheimer on this issue, 'Martyrdom' 259. Note that Scholem critiques Buber for similar reasons ('Martin Buber'; 'Reflections'). See however Idel's important analysis of the Buber-Scholem controversy (Idel, 'Martin Buber').

18 'Hasidic' 396. In an attempt to explain Elior, Gellman makes a number of rather weak conjectures as to what Elior might have been meant by the term autonomy.

19 See the section, 'Seventh Major Theme: The Human Being as a Source of Revelation'.

20 Elior is unique in Izbica scholarship in that she adopts both Weiss's position that Lainer's thought undercuts human activism, as well as Schatz-Uffenheimer's position, which affirms human autonomy as central to Lainer's project. While she is aware of the tension between these two positions in Lainer's thought, nowhere does she suggest a framework to integrate them.

21 'The Innovations' 421.

22 See MacIntyre 'After Virtue' 179 and 'A Short History' 215–269; see also Sokol 'Autonomy' 180–201. Sokol expands and applies MacIyntre's categories to rabbinic thought.

23 *Dissemination* 245, 344–345. Derrida writes that passages in the writings of Levi Isaac of Berdichev paradoxically evince 'a kind of atheism'.

24 *Absorbing Perfections* 77 n. 161 and related discussions in 'Radical' and 'The Book'.

25 For a modern sociological reading of loneliness as a natural corollary of Western autonomy, see Putnam, *Bowling Alone*. Loneliness engendered by autonomy does appear in some Jewish religious writings. For instance, it is an important dimension in the description of Adam I in Joseph Soloveitchik's classic *Lonely Man of Faith* 12–34.

26 See, e.g., Beckford, 'Religion Modernity and Postmodernity' 11–27. See also MacIntyre, *After Virtue* 23–79.

www.ingramcontent.com/pod-product-compliance
Ingram Content Group UK Ltd.
Pitfield, Milton Keynes, MK11 3LW, UK
UKHW041335150425
5491UKWH00024B/221